Digital Image Fundamentals

in MATLAB

Mohammad Nuruzzaman

Electrical Engineering Department
King Fahd University of Petroleum & Minerals
Dhahran, Saudi Arabia

author**HOUSE**™

1663 LIBERTY DRIVE, SUITE 200
BLOOMINGTON, INDIANA 47403
(800) 839-8640
WWW.AUTHORHOUSE.COM

First published by AuthorHouse 08/23/05

ISBN: 1-4208-6965-5 (sc)

Printed in the United States of America
Bloomington, Indiana

This book is printed on acid-free paper.

To my parents

iv

>>>>>>> **Preface** <<<<<<<

It goes without stating that the digital image manipulative equipment and appliance surround our everyday life in todayís hi-tech world. Colossal growth has taken place in the field of image processing especially in the Digital Image Processing in last several decades. Digital Image Processing underlies whatever image related activities nowadays we exercise, enjoy, or experience around us. Ranging from the household appliance to the satellite exploration never have we been so close to the digital imagery, as we do today. A prime part of the Digital Image Processing is to structure the machine especially the computer or robot to mimic the human vision. Anyhow let us see some end-use of the digital image technology which are sampled from the diverse imaging applications:

- ❖ ❖ Industrial applications such as automated inspection in car or electronic industry
- ❖ ❖ Preparing digital educational guide
- ❖ ❖ Computer animated movie making
- ❖ ❖ Image data bank for the archival
- ❖ ❖ High definition television (HDTV)
- ❖ ❖ Broadcasting in the public domain
- ❖ ❖ Monitoring with CCTV camera
- ❖ ❖ Weather forecasting via satellite monitoring
- ❖ ❖ Internet based videoconferencing
- ❖ ❖ Medical image capturing, storing, and processing
- ❖ ❖ Facsimile or fax transmission
- ❖ ❖ Forensic applications such as fingerprint and face identifications
- ❖ ❖ Seismic analysis for earthquake prediction

Yet the end-use of the imaging applications is being monotonically increased throughout the whole world. Since a picture self explains thousand words and as a proven technology, the Digital Image Processing is opening new horizon nearly to every aspect of our life.

In the past image processing was confined to the research community affiliated with the military applications. Also imperativeness on the multidimensional computation for the Digital Image Processing kept the field secluded. As soon as the faster speed computer processor becomes emergent, the impetus for the Digital Image Processing research in the public domain has been redirected and proliferated. Internet spreading of the imagery also contributed growing interest in the Digital Image Processing. Microsoft Windows Operating System and user-friendly package MATLAB have made the image processing facile to individual. Having gone through the basics of the Digital Image Processing, one can easily develop and market the business-oriented products through the wing of MATLAB.

The image we visualize on a monitor or TV screen is two dimensional (2D) but the actuality is worldly object possesses three dimensions (3D) sometimes even four dimensions (a moving 3D object). Nevertheless mapping a 3D or 4D object-oriented problem onto 2D monitor screen is no facile task. This is on whose account the Digital Image Processing problems often practice the mathematical intricacies of 2D or 3D. There is a need for the comprehensive digital image theory and its alongside implementation with the rapid expansion of the imaging marketplace. Analytical close form formula or expression has very little to do until it is materialized for the practical images. The word MATLAB has the elaboration matrix laboratory. As a worldly standard, this package has been very effective and appreciative in computing and visualizing the scientific and engineering problems. MATLABís familiarity and feasibility have continued to increase ever since its advent. Traditional programming, compiling, and debugging as happens in C or FORTRAN in many ways can be bypassed due to the numerous built-in functions available in MATLAB workspace. Furthermore, *Image Processing Toolbox* added one more convenience in its applicability. One appreciative feature of the Digital Image Processing in conjunction with MATLAB is that the image processing designer or programmer can view the end-result. Asking a computer to solve or simulate a Digital Image Processing problem means giving the understandable MATLAB code to the context of the Digital Image Processing problem – that is what the text is about.

Chapters 1 and 2 present a brief introduction to MATLAB and digital image fundamentals respectively. Digital image manipulation in the spatial domain has been emphasized in chapter 3. Many image analyses use transform terminologies which are covered in chapter 4. In the chapter 5 we highlight the digital image filtering. A digital image possesses a lot of quantitative and qualitative properties, which are covered in chapter 6. Digital image degradation and its remedy or restoration is addressed in chapter 7. Chapter 8 highlights common manipulations of the morphological image processing. As an introductory as well as supplemental text we did not cover all topics of the Digital Image Processing yet miscellaneous digital image problems are chosen in chapter 9 to increase the extent of the text. Finally, MATLAB programming features that can be relevant and effective to the context of the Digital Image Processing are outlined in chapter 10.

ì Writing and learning come togetherî is my experience while devising about the text. Honestly speaking, it is principally a delicate balance while considering theoretical and implementational subjectivenesses concurrently. Due to the vast extent of the field, each of which needs to be covered differently. We have tried to introduce most relevant undergraduate and graduate class-discussed Digital Image Processing topics along with further clues in a simplistic fashion since they are the main audience.

My words of acknowledgement are due to the King Fahd University of Petroleum and Minerals (KFUPM). I am especially appreciative of the printing and library facilities that I received from King Fahd University. Chapter table mentioned topics have been given MATLAB codes or explained on the point of the know-how in conjuction with the image processing toolbox functions. All illustrative image processing problems addressed in the text are implemented by a Pentium personal computer on Microsoft Windows operated system.

Mohammad Nuruzzaman

>>> Table of Contents <<<

Chapter 5 Digital Image Filtering

Chapter 6 Digital Image Properties and Edges

Chapter 7 Image Degradation and Restoration

Chapter 8 Morphological Image Processing

Chapter 9 Miscellaneous Image Processing

Chapter 10 Programming Issues

Appendix A

x

Appendix B

References

Subject Index

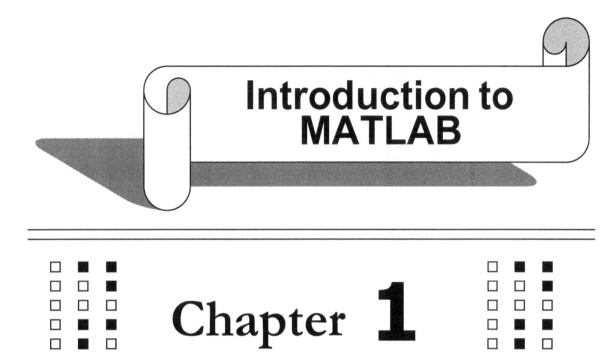

Introduction to MATLAB

Chapter 1

MATLAB is a computational software, which is the quickest and easiest way to compute the scientific and technical problems and visualize the solutions. As worldly standard for simulation and analysis, engineers, scientists, and researchers are becoming more and more affiliated with MATLAB. The general questionnaires before one gets started with the digital image processing using the platform of MATLAB are the contents of this chapter. We explain some features of the package when one starts navigating MATLAB. Our highlight covers the following:

❖ ❖ MATLAB and its features found in the MATLAB command window
❖ ❖ The easiest and quickest way to get started in MATLAB beginning from scratch
❖ ❖ Frequently encountered questions when one starts working in MATLAB environment
❖ ❖ Different forms of assistance about MATLAB and image processing toolbox functions

1.1 What is MATLAB?

MATLAB is mainly a scientific and technical computing software whose elaboration is the matrix laboratory. The command prompt of MATLAB ($>>$) provides an interactive system. In the workspace of MATLAB, most data element is dealt as a matrix without dimensioning. Since the digital image processing involves numerous matrix-oriented computations, the package is very advantageous for the digital image processing. MATLAB's easy to use platform enables us to compute the matrix manipulations, perform numerical analysis, and visualize different variety of one/two/three dimensional graphics in a matter of second or seconds without conventional programming in FORTRAN, PASCAL, or C.

1.2 MATLABís opening window features

If you do not have MATLAB installed in your personal computer, contact MathWorks (owner and developer) for the installation CD. If you know how to get in MATLAB and its basics, you can skip the chapter. Assuming the package is installed in your system, run MATLAB from the Start of the Microsoft Windows. Let us get familiarized with MATLABís opening window features. Figure 1.1(a) shows a typical firstly opened MATLAB window. Depending on the desktop setting or MATLAB version, your MATLAB window may not look like the figure 1.1(a) but the descriptions of the features are appropriate regardless of the latter versions and desktop setting.

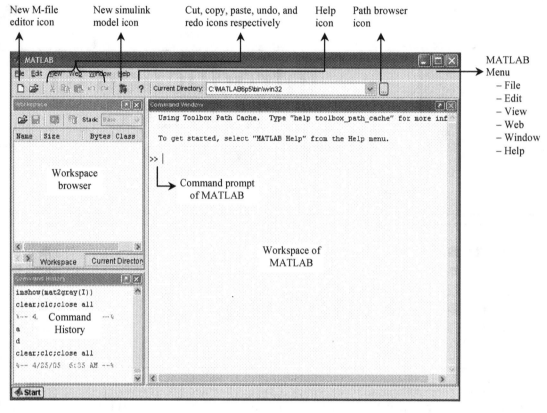

Figure 1.1(a) *Typical features of MATLABís firstly opened window*

✦ ✦ Command prompt of MATLAB

Command prompt means that you tell MATLAB to do something from here. As an interactive system, MATLAB responds to user through this prompt. MATLAB cursor will be blinking after >> prompt that says MATLAB is ready to take your commands. To enter any command, type executable MATLAB statements from keyboard and to execute that, press the Enter key (the symbol ⏎ for ëHit the Enter Keyí operation).

✦ ✦ MATLAB Menu

MATLAB is accompanied with six submenus namely File, Edit, View, Web, Window, and Help. Each submenu has its own features. Use the mouse to click different submenus and their brief descriptions are as follows:

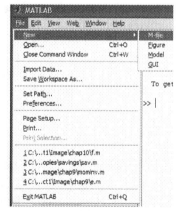

Figure 1.1(b) *Submenu File*

Submenu File: It (figure 1.1(b)) opens a new M-file, figure, model, or Graphical User Interface (GUI) layout maker, opens a file which was saved before, loads a saved workspace, imports data from a file, saves the workspace variables, sets the required path to execute a file, prints the workspace, and gives the provision for changing the command window property.

Submenu Edit: The second submenu Edit (figure 1.1(c)) includes cutting, copying, pasting, undoing, and clearing operations. These operations are useful when you frequently work at the command prompt.

Submenu View: The submenu View (figure 1.1(d)) is accompanied with various window viewing functions such as displaying the workspace variables information, current directory information, command historyÖ etc.

Submenu Web: The fourth submenu Web (figure 1.1(e)) provides the easiness to get connected with the MathWorks who is the owner of the software or other related WebPages assuming that your system is connected with the Internet.

Submenu Window: You may open some graphics window from MATLAB command prompt or running some M-files. From the fifth submenu Window, one can see how many graphics window under MATLAB are open and can switch from one window to another clicking the mouse to the required window.

Submenu Help: MATLAB is affluent in help facilities. The last submenu is the Help (figure 1.1(f)). Latter in this chapter, we mention how one can get help in different ways.

♦ ♦ Icons

Available icons are shown in the icon bar (down the menu bar) of the figure 1.1(a). Frequently used operations such as opening a new file, opening an existing file, getting help,Ö etc are found in the icon bar so that the user does not have to go through the menu bar over and over.

♦ ♦ MATLAB workspace

Figure 1.1(c) *Submenu Edit*

Workspace (figure 1.1(a)) is the platform of MATLAB where one executes MATLAB commands. During execution of commands, one may have to deal with some input and output variables. These variables can be one-dimensional

Figure 1.1(d) *Submenu View*

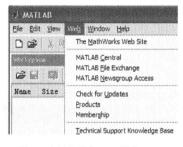

Figure 1.1(e) *Submenu Web*

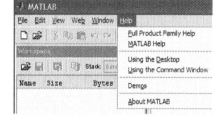

Figure 1.1(f) *Submenu Help*

array, multi-dimensional array, characters, symbolic objectsÖ etc. Again, to deal with graphics window, we have texts, graphics, or object handles. Workspace holds all those variables or handles for you. As a subwindow of the figure 1.1(a), its browser exhibits the type or properties of those variables or handles. If the browser is not open during the opening of MATLAB, click the Workspace from the figure 1.1(d) under View. Like Microsoft Excel, all workspace information can be saved to a file once some interaction with MATLAB is conducted.

♦ ♦ MATLAB command history

There is a subwindow in the figure 1.1(a) called Command History which holds all previously used commands at the command prompt. Depending on the desktop setting, it may or may not appear during the opening of MATLAB. If it is not, click Command History from the figure 1.1(d) under the View.

1.3 How to get started

New MATLAB users face a common question how one can get started. This tutorial is for the beginners in MATLAB. Here we address the following.

♦ ♦ How one can enter a vector/matrix

The first step is the user has to be in the command window of MATLAB. Look for the command prompt >> in the command window. One can type anything from the keyboard at the command prompt. Row or column matrices are termed as vectors. We intend to enter the row matrix R=[2   3   4   –2   0] into the workspace of MATLAB. Type the following at the command prompt from the keyboard:

>>R=[2 3 4 -2 0]   ← **Arial font set is used for the executable commands in the whole text**

There is one space gap between two elements of the matrix R but no space gap at the edge elements. All elements are placed under [ ]. Press Enter key from the keyboard after the third brace] and we see

R =

        2   3   4   -2   0

>>   ← command prompt is ready again

It means we assigned the row matrix to the workspace variable R. Whenever we call R, MATLAB understands the whole row matrix. Matrix R is having five elements. Even if R had 100 elements, it would understand the whole matrix that is one of many appreciative features of MATLAB. Next we enter the column matrix $C=\begin{bmatrix} 7 \\ 8 \\ 10 \\ -11 \end{bmatrix}$. Again

type the following on the blinking cursor from the keyboard:

>>C=[7;8;10;-11] ↵   you will see (↵ means ëPress the Enter Keyí),

C =
        7
        8
       10
      −11

>>   ← command prompt is ready again

This time we also assigned the column matrix to the workspace variable C. For the column matrix, there is one semicolon ; between two consecutive elements of the matrix C but no space gap is necessary. As another option, the matrix C could have been entered by writing C=[7 8 10 -11]'. The ' is the matrix transposition operator in MATLAB. As if you entered a row matrix but at the end just the transpose operator ' is attached. After that the

rectangular matrix $A=\begin{bmatrix} 20 & 6 & 7 \\ 5 & 12 & -3 \\ 1 & -1 & 0 \\ 19 & 3 & 2 \end{bmatrix}$ is to be entered:

>>A=[20 6 7;5 12 -3;1 -1 0;19 3 2] ↵   you will see,

A =
      20   6   7
       5   12   -3
       1   -1   0
      19   3   2

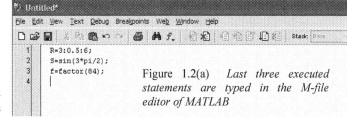

Figure 1.2(a) *Last three executed statements are typed in the M-file editor of MATLAB*

Two consecutive rows of A are separated by semicolon ; and consecutive elements in a row are separated by one space gap. Instead of typing all elements in a row, one can type the first row, press Enter key, the cursor blinks in the next line, type the second row, and so on.

♦ ♦ How one can use the colon and semicolon operators

The operators semicolon ; and colon : have special significance in MATLAB. Most MATLAB statements and M-file programming use these two operators almost in every line. Generation of vectors can easily be performed by the colon operator no matter how many elements we need. Let us carry out the following at the command prompt:

>>A=1:4 ↵   you will see,

A =
        1   2   3   4   ← We created a vector A or row matrix where A=[1   2   3   4]

Let us interact with MATLAB by the following commands:

>>R=1:3:10 ↵   you will see,

R =
        1   4   7   10   ← We created a vector R or row matrix whose elements form an
                                 arithmetic progression with first element 1, last element 10,
                                 and common difference 3

Vector with decrement can also be generated:

>>C=[0:−2: −10]' ↵   you will see,

C =
        0
       −2   We created a vector C or column matrix whose
       −4   ←   consecutive elements have the decrement 2 with the first
       −6   element 0 and the last element −10

$$-8$$
$$-10$$

MATLAB is also capable of producing vectors whose elements are decimal number. Let us form a row matrix R whose first element is 3, last element is 6, and increment is 0.5. That is accomplished as follows:

>>R=3:0.5:6 ↵   you will see,

R =
   3.0000   3.5000   4.0000   4.5000   5.0000   5.5000   6.0000

The reader is referred to chapter 10 for more about the colon operator. Then, what is the use of the semicolon operator? Append a semicolon in the last command and execute that:

>>R=3:0.5:6; ↵   you will see,

>>   ← Assignment is not shown

Type R at the command prompt and press Enter:

>>R ↵

R =
   3.0000   3.5000   4.0000   4.5000   5.0000   5.5000   6.0000

It indicates that the semicolon operator prevents MATLAB from displaying the contents of the workspace variable R.

♦♦ How one can call a built-in MATLAB function

In MATLAB, thousands of M-files or built-in function files are functioning. Knowing the descriptions of the function, the numbers of input and output arguments, and the nature of the arguments is mandatory in order to execute a built-in function file from the command prompt. Let us start with a simplest example. We intend to find $\sin x$ for $x = \frac{3\pi}{2}$, which is -1. The MATLAB counterpart (section 10.2) of $\sin x$ is sin(x), where x can be any real or complex number and can be a matrix too. The angle $\frac{3\pi}{2}$ is written as 3*pi/2 (π is coded by pi) and let us perform it as follows:

>>sin(3*pi/2) ↵

ans =
       −1

As another example, let us factorize the integer 84 ($84=2\times2\times3\times7$). The MATLAB built-in function factor finds the factors of an integer and the implementation is as follows:

>>factor(84) ↵

ans =
   2   2   3   7

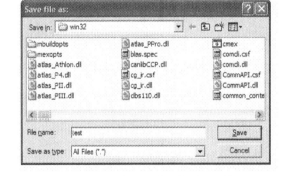

Figure 1.2(b) *Save dialog window for the M-file name*

The output of the factor is a row matrix. Thus you can call any other built-in function from the command prompt.

♦♦ How one can open and execute an M-file

This is the most important start up for the beginners. An M-file can be regarded as a text or script file. A collection of executable MATLAB statements are the content of an M-file. Ongoing discussion made you familiarize with the matrix entering, computing a sine value, and factorizing an integer. These executions took place at the command prompt. They can be executed from an M-file as well. This necessitates opening the M-file editor. Referring to the figure 1.1(b), you find the link for the M-file editor as **File → New → M-file** and click it to see the new untitled M-file editor. Another option is click the New M-file editor icon of the figure 1.1(a). However after opening the new M-file editor, we type the last three executable statements in the untitled file as shown in the figure 1.2(a). We made slight change in the statements. The sin(3*pi/2) and factor(84) are assigned to the variables S and f respectively and the displayings are suppressed by including the operator ; at the end. The next step is to save the untitled file by clicking the Save icon or from the Menu File of the M-file editor window. Figure 1.2(b) presents the File Save dialog window. We type the file name as the test (can be any name of your choice) in the slot of the File name in the window. The M-file has the file extension as .m but we do not type .m only the file name is enough. After saving the file, let us move on to the MATLAB command prompt and conduct the following:

>>test ↵

>>   ← command prompt is ready again

It indicates that MATLAB executed the M-file by the name **test** and is ready for the next command. We can check by calling the assignees whether the previously performed executions occurred exactly as follows:

>>R ↵

R =
        3.0000   3.5000   4.0000   4.5000   5.0000   5.5000   6.0000
>>S ↵   >>f ↵

S =   f =
        -1   2   2   3   7

Edit plot   Text Insert   Zoom In and
Icon   Icon   Out Icons

This is what we found before. Thus one can run any executable statements in the M-file. The reader might ask in which folder or path the file **test** was saved. Figure 1.1(a) shows one slot for the Current Directory in the upper right corner of the window. That is the location of your file. If you want to save the M-file file in other folder or directory, change your path by clicking the path browser icon before saving the file. When you call the **test** from the command prompt of MATLAB, the command prompt must be in the same directory where the file is in or its path must be defined to MATLAB.

✦ ✦ How one can plot a graph

MATLAB is very convenient for plotting different sorts of graphs. The graphs are plotted either from the mathematical expression or from the data. Let us plot the function $y = -2\sin 2x$. The MATLAB function **ezplot** plots y versus x type graph taking the expression as its input argument. The MATLAB code (section 10.2) of the function $-2\sin 2x$ is **-2*sin(2*x)**. The functional code is input argumented using the single inverted comma hence we conduct the following at the command prompt:

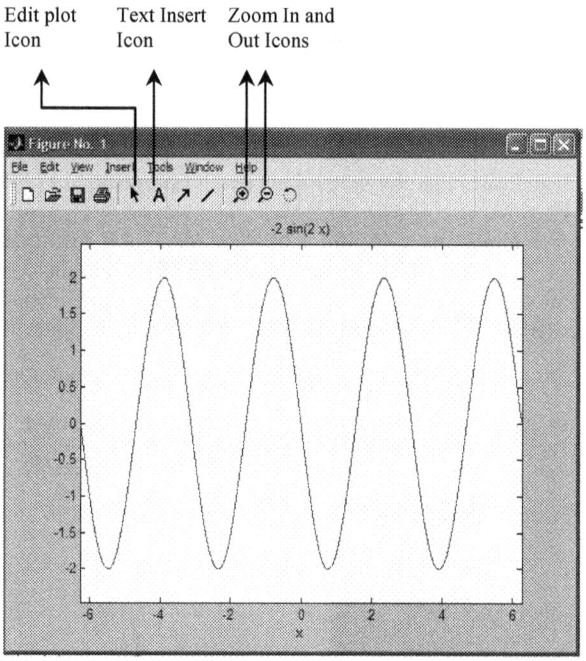

>>ezplot('-2*sin(2*x)') ↵

Figure 1.2(c) *Graph of $-2\sin 2x$ versus x*

Figure 1.2(c) presents the outcome from above execution. The window in which the graph is plotted is called MATLAB figure window. Any graphics is plotted in the figure window, which has its own menu (such as File, Edit, etc) as shown in the figure 1.2(c). The fourth submenu in the last figure is the Insert. Clicking the Insert, one can add title, x label, and y label of the graph. The graphical property (such as the line color of the graph) can be changed first by clicking the Edit plot icon of the figure and then rightclicking the mouse pointer on the line. If you want to write some text on the plot area, click the Text Insert Icon of the figure 1.2(c), bring the mouse pointer at the required point, and click to insert the text.

We hope the reader has had some introductory idea about MATLAB by now and that is our objective.

1.4 Some queries about MATLAB environment

Users need to know the answers to some questions when they start working in MATLAB. Some MATLAB environment related queries are presented as follows:

⌑ *How can I change the numeric format?*

When you perform the computation at the command prompt, the output is returned up to four decimal accuracy. This is due to the use of the short numeric format, which is the default one. There are other numeric formats also. To reach the numeric format dialog box, the clicking operation sequence is MATLAB command window ⇒ File ⇒ Preferences ⇒ Command Window. Under the Command Window, you find different data format options in a popup menu.

⌑ *How can I change the font or background color settings?*

One might be interested to change the background color or font color while working in the command window. The clicking sequence is MATLAB command window ⇒ File ⇒ Preferences ⇒ Command Window ⇒

Doubleclick to bring the Font & Colors Window. From the displayed 'Text Color' and 'Background Color', choose the desired color and click OK.

⧉ *How can I delete some/all variables from the workspace?*

In order to delete all variables present in the workspace, the clicking sequence is MATLAB command window ⇒ Edit ⇒ Clear Workspace. If you want to delete a particular workspace variable, select the concern variable in the workspace browser (assuming it is open) using the mouse pointer and then rightclick ⇒ delete.

⧉ *How can I clear workspace but not the variables?*

Once you conduct some sessions at the command prompt, monitor screen keeps all interactive sessions. You can clear the screen contents without removing the variables present in the workspace by the command clc or performing the clicking operation MATLAB command window ⇒ Edit ⇒ Clear Command Window.

⧉ *How can I know the current path?*

In the upper right position of figure 1.1(a), the current directory bar is located which indicates in which path the command prompt is in or execute cd (abbreviation of the current directory) at the command prompt.

⧉ *How can I see different variables in the workspace?*

There are two ways of viewing this – either use the command who or follow the clicking sequence MATLAB command window ⇒ View ⇒ Workspace. The workspace browser exhibits information about workspace variables. One can view, change, or edit the content of a variable by doubleclicking the concern variable situated in the workspace browser.

⧉ *How can I enter a long command line?*

MATLAB statements can be too long to fit in one line. Giving a break in the middle of a statement can be accomplished by the ellipsis …. We show that considering the entering of the vector x=[1:3:10]; as follows:

```
>>x=[1:3: … ↵
        10] ↵
x =
        1   4   7   10
```

Typing takes place in two lines and there is one space gap before the ellipsis.

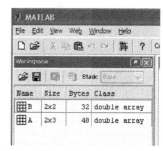

Figure 1.2(d) *Workspace browser displays the variables information*

⧉ *Editing at the command prompt*

This is advantageous specially for them who work frequently in the command window without opening an M-file. Keyboard has different arrow keys marked by ← ↑ → ↓. One may type a misspelled command at the command prompt causing error message to appear. Instead of retyping the entire line, press uparrow (for previous line) or downarrow (for next line) to edit the MATLAB statement. Or you can even reuse any past statement this way. For example, we generate a row vector 1 to 10 with increment 2 and assign the vector to x. The necessary command is x=1:2:10. Mistakenly you typed x+1:2:10. The response is as follows:

```
>>x+1:2:10 ↵
??? Undefined function or variable 'x'.
```

You discovered the mistake and want to correct that. Press ↑ key to see,

```
>>x+1:2:10
```

Edit the command going to the + sign using the left arrow key or mouse pointer. At the prompt, if you type x and press ↑ again and again, you see the used commands that start with x.

⧉ *Saving and loading data*

User can save workspace variables or data in a binary file having the extension .mat. Suppose you have the matrix A=$\begin{bmatrix} 3 & 4 & 8 \\ 0 & 2 & 1 \end{bmatrix}$ and wish to save A in a file by the name data.mat. Let us carry out the following:

```
>>A=[3 4 8;0 2 1]; ↵ ← Assigning the A to A
```

Now move on to the workspace browser of the figure 1.1(a) and you see the variable A including its information located in the subwindow as shown in the figure 1.2(d). Bring the mouse pointer on the A, rightclick the mouse, and click the Save Selection As. The Save dialog window appears and type data only (not the data.mat) in the slot of File name. If it is necessary, you can save all workspace variables using the same action but clicking Save Workspace As. One can retrieve the data file by clicking the menu **File** ⇒ **Import Data**.

⧉ *How can I delete a file from the command prompt?*

Let us delete just mentioned data.mat by executing the command delete data.mat at the command prompt.

⧉ *How can I know the data class and matrix size information of a workspace variable?*

Figure 1.2(d) presents the matrix size and data class information for aforementioned matrix A.

1.5 How to get help?

Help facilities of MATLAB are plentiful. One can access to information about a function file in a variety of ways. Command help can find the help of a particular function file. You are familiar with the function sin(x) and can have the online help regarding sin(x) as follows:

>>help sin ↵

SIN   Sine.
  SIN(X) is the sine of the elements of X.
Overloaded methods
  help sym/sin.m

One disadvantage of this method is that user has to know the exact file name of a function. For a novice, this facility may not be appreciative. Casually we know a partial name of a function or try to check whether a function exists by that name. Suppose we intend to see whether any function by name eye exists. We execute the following by the intermediacy of the command lookfor (no space gap between look and for) to see all possible functions bearing the file name eye or having the file name eye partially:

>>lookfor eye ↵
EYE Identity matrix.
SPEYE Sparse identity matrix.
XPHIDE   MATLAB's version of Human Eye Sensitivity towards moving objects.
⋮

The return is having all possible matches of functions containing the word eye. Now the command help can be conducted to go through a particular one for example the first one is EYE and we execute help EYE at the command prompt.

In order to have Window form help, click different windows of the pulldown menu of the figure 1.1(f). Make sure you have the full Help CD installed in your system. Any help item preceded by a bullet can be clicked to go inside the item. This help form is better when one navigates MATLAB's capability not looking for a particular function.

MATLAB has its own **Start** (located at the lower left corner of the command window) like the Microsoft Windows. To reach to the Image Processing Toolbox help, the clicking sequence is **Start ⇒ Toolboxes ⇒ Image Processing ⇒ Help**.

If you seek for the help of the image processing toolbox functions from the command prompt, carry out the following:

>>help images ↵

Image Processing Toolbox.
  Version 3.2 (R13) 28-Jun-2002

Release information.
  images/Readme - Display information about current and previous versions.

Image display.
  colorbar   - Display colorbar (MATLAB Toolbox).
  getimage   - Get image data from axes.
  image   - Create and display image object (MATLAB Toolbox).
  imagesc   - Scale data and displ
  ⋮

MATLAB exhibits a long list of functions, which are relevant mostly to the digital image processing. From the displayed list, let us choose the function colorbar and see the help about it as follows:

>>help colorbar ↵

COLORBAR Display color bar (color scale).
  COLORBAR('vert') appends a vertical color scale to the current
  ⋮

Thus you can view the descriptions of any other image processing function from the list.

Digital Image Fundamentals

Chapter 2

The subject matter in this chapter is to address the very basics of the digital image to the context of MATLAB. Our illustrations always start with a prototype image, which is understood by an average reader. A digital image assumes the structure of a two or three dimensional array depending on the data storage. However the know-how details of the chapter highlight the following:

❖ ❖ The concept of a digital image as well as its mathematical model for the gray and color images
❖ ❖ Different ways for obtaining the test images either from MATLAB or outside MATLAB
❖ ❖ Image types depending on the gray or color levels as planted in MATLAB
❖ ❖ A brief description of the image storing data classes including their conversions
❖ ❖ Image display options and reading the contents of an image in accordance with the theory discussed functions
❖ ❖ Digital image color space maneuvering alongside the simplistic colorbar generation

2.1 What is a digital image?

Nowadays our everyday life is very much encased by the digital images. Suppose we are watching a video CD. Have you ever thought what the types of these scenes are? Maybe, you are downloading some images from the Internet. What are these images? Talking to someone using Web Camera is commonly taking place. These all instances play with the digital images and a digital image is nothing but a rectangular matrix. A large size image means a large rectangular matrix. If you reduce the size of the image to half, so does the size of the rectangular matrix. Digital images can be still or moving with respect to time. The digital image for some circumstance captured at different times and placed in sequence form a tiny piece of movie. Computer animated movie such as Terminator 2 is composed of such thousands of pieces. A moving image means a moving rectangular matrix ñ the explanation of a digital image is as simple as that.

10

2.2 Mathematical representation of a digital image

In order to understand the mathematical model of a digital image, we first need to understand the concepts of the pixel or pel and gray level. Referring to the figure 2.1(a), we take some bold dots in the vertical and horizontal directions of the picture area for the digitization of the image. These dots are termed as the pixel. There

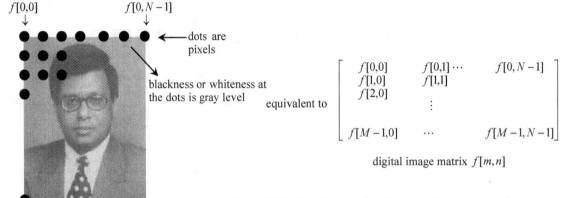

Figure 2.1(a) *Illustration of a digital image and its matrix equivalent*

are seven dots or pixels in the horizontal direction of the image ñ this is just for the sake of illustration. In a practical image literally there are hundreds of pixels, for example 128, 256, 512 Ö etc as the power of 2. How these pixel numbers are decided depends on how much space or area the image occupies and how much resolution is needed. If you use a scanner to scan a image, the scanner is manufactured providing some specific pixel numbers per inch. Again if

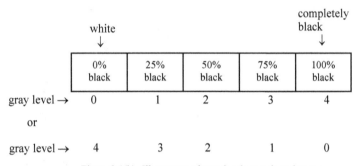

Figure 2.1(b) *Illustration of gray levels in a digital image*

you have a digital camera, the camera also takes the snapshots on some specific pixel numbers per inch. The pixel number per inch defines the resolution of an image system. Let us assume that the image area of the figure 2.1(a) has $M \times N$ pixels. These pixels necessarily represent a matrix of order $M \times N$. Figure 2.1(a) also shows the equivalence of the image with the digital image matrix $f[m,n]$. Throughout the text invariably we mean the digital image matrix by the term $f[m,n]$. There is some notational difference between the image processing textbooks and MATLAB which are $\begin{Bmatrix} m \text{ varies from 0 to } M-1 \\ n \text{ varies from 0 to } N-1 \end{Bmatrix}$ and $\begin{Bmatrix} m \text{ varies from 1 to } M \\ n \text{ varies from 1 to } N \end{Bmatrix}$ respectively. Whichever notation is

adopted does not change the image information at all only do the image related expressions become translated by 1 in each variable. Figure 2.1(a) shows the textbookís notation in which $f[1,2]$ means gray or color level value at the pixel position index $m=1$ and $n=2$. It is important to mention that a digital image is digitized both in the position and in the color or gray level. It necessitates that the m and n are the positive integers. We call them as the pixel variable or spatial coordinates of the digital image. The four corner points of the image in the figure 2.1(a) are arrow indicated by $f[0,0]$, $f[0,N-1]$, $f[M-1,0]$, and $f[M-1,N-1]$ for the upper left, upper right, lower left, and lower right respectively. Since the gray or color levels are also discrete, they have specific values. If we say there are two gray levels, then they can be numbered as 0 and 1. Again if we say there are 4 gray levels, they can be numbered as 0, 1, 2, and 3. Figure 2.1(b) shows the illustration of 5 gray levels for the black and white image with the uniform scale. Referring to the figure, we split the shade of 100% white and 100% black in five levels. The whiteness or blackness defines the gray level value or in other words the matrix element of $f[m,n]$. Numbering the gray levels is a relative matter. One can say 0 as the white or black. If you say 0 as the white, then the maximum gray level represents the black and vice versa. Both choices are also presented in the same figure. The number of the gray levels depends on the image system how so we save or scan the image softcopy file. By the way, the largest value of the gray level corresponds to the white in MATLAB.

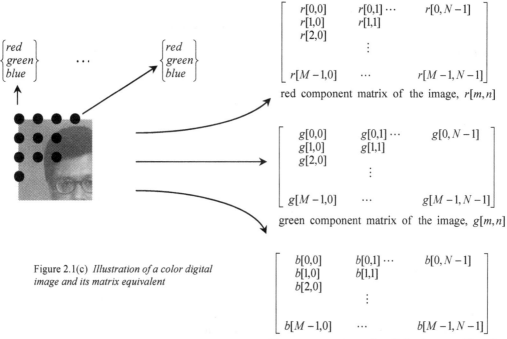

$$\begin{bmatrix} r[0,0] & r[0,1]\cdots & r[0,N-1] \\ r[1,0] & r[1,1] \\ r[2,0] \\ & & \vdots \\ r[M-1,0] & \cdots & r[M-1,N-1] \end{bmatrix}$$

red component matrix of the image, $r[m,n]$

$$\begin{bmatrix} g[0,0] & g[0,1]\cdots & g[0,N-1] \\ g[1,0] & g[1,1] \\ g[2,0] \\ & & \vdots \\ g[M-1,0] & \cdots & g[M-1,N-1] \end{bmatrix}$$

green component matrix of the image, $g[m,n]$

Figure 2.1(c) *Illustration of a color digital image and its matrix equivalent*

$$\begin{bmatrix} b[0,0] & b[0,1]\cdots & b[0,N-1] \\ b[1,0] & b[1,1] \\ b[2,0] \\ & & \vdots \\ b[M-1,0] & \cdots & b[M-1,N-1] \end{bmatrix}$$

blue component matrix of the image, $b[m,n]$

The image system we discussed is to the context of the gray scale image. A color image follows similar spatial and matrix notation but involves three color components – red, green, and blue. Figure 2.1(c) shows the schematic representation for a color digital image. Every pixel in the image has three color components – red, green, and blue thereby possessing three different color component matrices $r[m,n]$, $g[m,n]$, and $b[m,n]$ respectively. The variables m and n have their usual meanings. Each of the three matrices has the order $M \times N$ according to the pixels of the image. Like the gray level, now we have the color levels for example 0 to 100% red, green, or blue.

♦ ♦ Summary statements

⇨ Any digital black and white, intensity, or gray image is equivalent to a matrix $f[m,n]$, where m and n are the pixel coordinates, which become the position indexes of the matrix elements, and which are the integers decided by the pixels stored in the softcopy of the image

⇨ Any digital color image is equivalent to the matrix triplet $$\begin{Bmatrix} r[m,n] \\ g[m,n] \\ b[m,n] \end{Bmatrix}$$

♦ ♦ The meaning of the resolution

The resolution of any imaging system plays an important role in the image quality. This becomes a deciding factor when we purchase some digital camera or any other imaging system. One might ask how the resolution is related with the mathematical model of a digital image. Better resolution means the matrix size of $f[m,n]$ is larger and the matrix elements have wider range of variations or more levels.

2.3 How to get the images and written files mentioned in the text?

Figure 2.2(a) *A color image object is drawn with the help of the mouse and brush in Paint package*

Digital image analysis always requires that the reader must have an image to start with. In various chapters we implement the digital image fundamentals taking several practical images. The softcopy file size of these images is not so huge hence they can be transferred through email. Despite MATLAB is equipped with full fledged Image Processing Toolbox functions for the advanced users, preliminary Image Processing supportive M-files and/or functions sometimes need to be written by the reader in order to gain hand-on experience about the basic Digital Image Proccessing. The reader can get promptly the softcopy of any digital image or author-written M-file presented in the text by contacting at **nzaman@kfupm.edu.sa**. However, we demonstrate different ways of obtaining a digital image in the following so that the reader can have his own way of obtaining an image.

✦✦ Option 1

One can assume that a black and white digital image is nothing but a large rectangular matrix. Having found a large rectangular matrix in some way, it serves the purpose of the digital image matrix $f[m,n]$. There is a function called randint in MATLAB. One can quickly generate a large size digital image matrix $f[m,n]$ with the help of the function. Let us carry out the following:

MATLAB Command

    >>f=randint(128,256,32); ↵

The variable f contains the digital image matrix $f[m,n]$. The randint has three input arguments, the first and second of which are the image pixel height and width respectively for example here our image is of the size 128 pixels × 256 pixels. The third input argument of the function is the indicative of the gray levels in the image which is here 32. It means that every element in the matrix f has an integer value between 0 and 31. If the third input argument were 64, there would be 64 gray levels in the image indicated by any positive integer between 0 and 63.

✦✦ Option 2

Option 1 may not satisfy the reader because it is trivial. This option tells you the easiest way of getting a digital test image even if you do not have a digital camera or scanner. In Microsoft Windows, you can find the Start menu. From there you can easily reach to the Paint package via *Program → Accessories.* Open the Paint package, draw any image object in the untitled file with the help of the mouse, click the file menu of the Paint, and click the Save as option. At this point you see the prompt window for saving. In the dialog window there are two slots –

$$\begin{Bmatrix} \text{File name} \\ \text{Save as type} \end{Bmatrix}. \text{ Different image formats are found in the slot Save as type such as } \begin{Bmatrix} 24-\text{bit Bitmap} \\ 16\ \text{Color Bitmap} \\ 256\ \text{Color Bitmap} \\ \text{JPEG} \\ \text{GIF} \\ \text{TIFF} \end{Bmatrix}. \text{ From there}$$

one can choose any suitable image format he is interested in. Also name the image file in the dialog window, remember the image file name, and make sure that you are saving the image file in your working path of MATLAB. For example we have drawn the color image of the figure 2.2(a) in the Paint package and saved the file by the name test. If any bitmap option is chosen, the file extension will automatically be .bmp. While preparing the test image in the Paint package, the image size needs to be kept smaller otherwise the reader may face difficulty or warning in opening the file in MATLAB.

✦✦ Option 3

MATLABís inventory also grants users to have a large number of test images. We picked up some names from the inventory but all of these images are stored as tif format (section 2.6). Whenever you open MATLAB, you can call any of the following images either from the default-working path of MATLAB or from yours:

circles.tif	trees.tif	text.tif	kids.tif
enamel.tif	saturn.tif	mri.tif	pout.tif
tire.tif	shadow.tif	moon.tif	flowers.tif
rice.tif	spine.tif	logo.tif	lily.tif Ö . and many more.

✦✦ Option 4

Click the Start Menu of the Windows System you are operating. You find the Find or Search File options there and click the Pull Down/Up menu to see the prompt window. In the prompt window one can type partial or full name of any file existing in the computer. For example, you can search for all JPEG picture file that has the extension .jpg by writing the command *.jpg. Once the searching is finished, check the JPEG file location in the Search prompt window and bring the JPEG file in your MATLAB working directory or path through the copy-paste facility of the windows explorer.

✦✦ Option 5

Following example images are exercised all over the text for the implementations of the fundamental digital image processing theory. We wish to cite how these images are obtained:

    dip.bmp   A text ëDigital Image Processingí is written by free hand on a white piece of paper, scanned by Plustek USB Scanner at 400 pixels/inch, and saved as the 8-bit bmp format

man.jpg	A personís color photograph is scanned by Plustek USB Scanner at 1200 pixels/inch and saved as 24-bit True Color Scale in JPEG format at a compression ratio of 9
digital.jpg	A text ßDigitalí is hand written by a color pencil on a white piece of paper, scanned by the Plustek USB Scanner at 300 pixels/inch, and saved as the 24-bit True Color Scale in the JPEG format at a compression ratio of 9
test.bmp	We had drawn the image of the figure 2.2(a) using the option 2
text.jpg	The JPEG file contains a text image whose content is ìMATLAB is a nice softwareî
map.bmp	A scanned map object stored in bmp format
ABC.jpg	The file contains an image of the three letters A, B, and C placed side by side in JPEG format
A.jpg	The file contains an image of the letter A in JPEG format

2.4 Image types based on the gray or color storage formats

Our everyday life is very much surrounded by the digital images. Let us provide some examples: the images in the Internet, pictures taken by a digital camera, computer screen saver, any image displayed in computer monitor, pictures of videoconference, and pictures of computer animated movies. In a broad sense the digital images are divided into two categories, gray (also called monocrome) and color forms. Most image analysis considers the gray image as the test one because it paves the way for understanding the color images. A binary image is a special type of the gray image. Whatever be the image type, gray or color, we always concentrate on the digital image matrix $f[m,n]$ for the gray and the matrix triplet $\begin{Bmatrix} r[m,n] \\ g[m,n] \\ b[m,n] \end{Bmatrix}$ for the color in the image processing problems. In some way we have to acquire the image matrices before any image analysis. We know that the matrix elements of the digital image matrix or the triplet are the gray or color level values but these values have different storage formats for different images. However we address the commonly seen four types of digital images namely binary, gray, indexed, and RGB in the following.

✦ ✦ Binary image

A binary image is also called the bi-level image and has only two gray levels ñ 0 and 1. If the 0 means the complete black, then 1 does the complete white or vice versa. Since there are only two levels, the image matrix elements can be a logical one as well. For example, the matrix $f[m,n] = \begin{bmatrix} 1 & 0 & 0 & 0 \\ 0 & 1 & 1 & 1 \\ 1 & 1 & 0 & 0 \\ 0 & 0 & 0 & 0 \end{bmatrix}$ represents a prototype binary digital image in which we have the pixel dimension 4×4.

✦ ✦ Intensity, gray, black and white, or monochrome image

The intensity image has more than two gray level numbers. Figure 2.1(b) presents five equal levels between black and white therefore any element in the digital image matrix $f[m,n]$ must be from 0 to 4 there is no value inbetween any two gray levels. As an example, the matrix $f[m,n] = \begin{bmatrix} 1 & 4 & 0 & 0 \\ 0 & 2 & 3 & 4 \\ 1 & 2 & 0 & 0 \end{bmatrix}$ is an intensity digital image in which the pixel dimension is 3×4. We number the gray levels using the positive integers (often written as [0,4]). If the 0 means complete black, then the 4 means complete white or vice versa. In most standard image types we have the number of gray levels as the power of 2 for example $2^6=64$. Another representation of the intensity image is the decimal form in which the image matrix elements lie between 0 and 1. In order to obtain the decimal form, we divide every element in the matrix by the maximum level (which is here 4) for instance $f[m,n] = \begin{bmatrix} 0.25 & 1 & 0 & 0 \\ 0 & 0.5 & 0.75 & 1 \\ 1 & 0.5 & 0 & 0 \end{bmatrix}$ for the ongoing 5 level example. Now the decimal number instead of the positive integer represents a gray level.

✦ ✦ Indexed image for the color picture

The binary and the intensity images have only one matrix for the digital image representation and are suitable for the monochrome or gray image. On the contrary an indexed image is devised for the color pictures and requires two matrices for the image representation. The names of the two matrices are the intensity image matrix (which has the same size as the digital image pixel does) and the colormap matrix. The intensity image matrix elements are formed from specific levels using positive integers for example 0 to 127 (written as [0,127]). In general the digital image processing system numbers the levels from 0 to $N-1$ for N levels. Each level has some prearranged or pixel-dependent three component (red, green, and blue) color values indicated by a three element row matrix respectively. Therefore the numbers of the three element row matrices must be equal to the number of the levels in the intensity image matrix. If there are N levels in the intensity image matrix, then the colormap matrix must be of the order $N \times 3$. Each of the three color components in the three element row matrix is in between 0 and 1 and decimal (often written as [0,1]). As a prototype example, let us consider a five level image of the pixel dimension 3×4 whose intensity image matrix is $f[m,n] = \begin{bmatrix} 1 & 4 & 0 & 0 \\ 0 & 2 & 3 & 1 \\ 1 & 2 & 0 & 0 \end{bmatrix}$ and whose colormap is

$\begin{Bmatrix} level & R & G & B \\ 0 & 0 & 0 & 0 \\ 1 & 0.2555 & 0.7899 & 0.1111 \\ 2 & 0.5432 & 0.6789 & 0.6541 \\ 3 & 0.7921 & 0.7892 & 0.8543 \\ 4 & 1 & 1 & 1 \end{Bmatrix}$. The intensity image matrix pixel size and the level numbers in the matrix are

completely independent of each other. There are 5 levels in $f[m,n]$ that is why the colormap matrix dimension is 5×3. The level 3 has the red, green, and blue components as [0.7921   0.7892   0.8543] and each of the component is in between 0 to 1. The first component of any color is set as 0 that means 0% red, 0% green, or 0% blue. Again the last component is set as 1 that means 100% red, 100% green, or 100% blue. One can number the level from 1 to 5 instead of 0 to 4. That does not change the image information at all. If we exclude the colormap matrix from the indexed image and concentrate only on the image matrix $f[m,n]$, we own the gray counterpart or the black and white version of the color image but some image information is lost due to the exclusion.

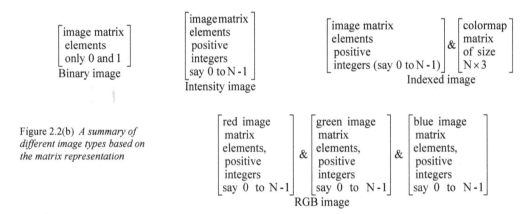

Figure 2.2(b) *A summary of different image types based on the matrix representation*

♦ ♦ RGB image for the color picture

The natural images are continuous as regards to the pixel position and gray or color level. To represent a natural image, truly speaking we need infinite number of pixels and infinite number of gray or color levels. Within the visual acceptance, we take finite number pixels as well as color levels to represent a digital image. We know that the red, green, or blue color level is discretized according to the number of levels present in the intensity image matrix of an indexed image. On the other hand, an RGB (short for red-green-blue) image stores the exact color at every pixel thereby involving three matrices of identical sizes ñ one for red, one for green, and one for blue. That is why the RGB image is also called the true color digital image. As an example, if we say each of the three basic colors has 5 levels, we may have a prototype RGB triplet $\begin{Bmatrix} r[m,n] \\ g[m,n] \\ b[m,n] \end{Bmatrix}$ representation of the pixel size 3×4 like

$r[m,n] = \begin{bmatrix} 1 & 4 & 0 & 0 \\ 0 & 2 & 3 & 1 \\ 1 & 2 & 0 & 0 \end{bmatrix}$ for red, $g[m,n] = \begin{bmatrix} 2 & 3 & 0 & 0 \\ 0 & 2 & 3 & 1 \\ 1 & 1 & 2 & 2 \end{bmatrix}$ for green, and $b[m,n] = \begin{bmatrix} 4 & 4 & 1 & 3 \\ 0 & 2 & 3 & 1 \\ 2 & 3 & 2 & 1 \end{bmatrix}$ for blue specifying

each of the color levels in [0,4]. The color level values can also be decimal in [0,1]. These three basic color matrices or the triplet are stored as a three dimensional array (chapter 10 for the three dimensional array).

Figure 2.2(b) presents the comprehensive matrix structures possessed by various image types.

Whiteness of the
image coincides with
the white paper

Figure 2.2(c) *A binary image*

Figure 2.2(d) *An intensity or gray image*

2.5 How to display a digital image?

The first step of displaying a digital image is to obtain the softcopy of the digital image (section 2.3) and place the image file in your working path of MATLAB with the help of the Windows Explorer. Another option is invoke any supplied digital sample image of MATLAB. Several digital image names are also mentioned in the section 2.3. Obtain the image man.jpg of the section 2.3, place it in your working directory, and execute the following command:

MATLAB Command

>>imshow('man.jpg') ↵

The reader should see the photographic image of the figure 6.1(a). MATLAB function imshow (abbreviation of the image show) can display many of the available image formats. The name of the softcopy digital image with its actual file extension must be placed under the single inverted comma as the input argument of the function. To cite another example, one can execute imshow('kids.tif') to see the picture of two kids together where kids.tif is a supplied image in MATLAB. The function is suited to multifaceted image displaying situations. Referring to the binary image matrix $f[m,n] = \begin{bmatrix} 1 & 0 & 0 & 0 \\ 0 & 1 & 1 & 1 \\ 1 & 1 & 0 & 0 \\ 0 & 0 & 0 & 0 \end{bmatrix}$ of the section 2.4, let us enter the image matrix and execute the following:

>>f=[1 0 0 0;0 1 1 1;1 1 0 0;0 0 0 0]; ↵

>>imshow(f) ↵

Obviously the first line of above command is to enter the binary image matrix $f[m,n]$ and assign that to the workspace variable f and the second line is the image display command. At the point, the input argument of the imshow is the image matrix name without the single inverted comma. Figure 2.2(c) presents enlargedly the output of the execution. You can maximize the window you are working in otherwise you find a small image object in the middle of the window. There are only two levels ñ 0 for black and 1 for white in the image. The whiteness of 1 in the binary image coincides with the white paper.

As the situation of displaying the second image type, let us see the intensity image matrix $f[m,n] = \begin{bmatrix} 1 & 4 & 0 & 0 \\ 0 & 2 & 3 & 1 \\ 1 & 2 & 0 & 0 \end{bmatrix}$ in [0,4], enter the intensity image matrix, and carry out the following:

>>f=[1 4 0 0;0 2 3 1;1 2 0 0]; ↵   ← $f[m,n]$ is assigned to f

>>imshow(f,[ ]) ↵

Figure 2.2(d) shows the displayed gray or intensity image (at the maximized window as well as enlarged) due to above execution. Now the imshow has two input arguments f and [ ] obviously the first of which is the intensity image matrix name. The second argument [ ] tells the function to display the image by mapping the minimum (which is 0 in $f[m,n]$) and the maximum (which is 4 in $f[m,n]$) gray levels to 0 and 1 respectively because the image matrix elements must be in [0,1] for the double class data (section 2.7). As the image displays, depending on the level we find different shades of gray levels in the image ñ five gray shades for the five levels.

Our third type digital image is the indexed image, which is applicable for the color images. Let us choose the intensity image matrix $f[m,n] = \begin{bmatrix} 1 & 4 & 0 & 0 \\ 0 & 2 & 3 & 1 \\ 1 & 2 & 0 & 0 \end{bmatrix}$ and the colormap matrix $\begin{bmatrix} level & R & G & B \\ 0 & 0 & 0 & 0 \\ 1 & 0.2555 & 0.7899 & 0.1111 \\ 2 & 0.5432 & 0.6789 & 0.6541 \\ 3 & 0.7921 & 0.7892 & 0.8543 \\ 4 & 1 & 1 & 1 \end{bmatrix}$ for the illustration (section 2.4). We assign the intensity image matrix and the colormap matrix to the workspace variables f and M respectively in the following two lines:

```
>>f=[1 4 0 0;0 2 3 1;1 2 0 0]; ↵
>>M=[0 0 0;0.2555 0.7899 0.1111;0.5432 0.6789 0.6541;0.7921 0.7892 0.8543;1 1 1]; ↵
>>imshow(f,M) ↵
```

Execution of the third line shows the indexed image, which is a color one. Since the text is written in black and white form, we can not present the color image but the image looks visually like the one in the figure 2.2(d) in which you find a green portion in the middle of the image as displayed in the MATLAB figure window (maximize the figure window). However the function imshow now holds two input matrix arguments ñ the intensity image matrix and its colormap respectively. Syntactically the command imshow(f,M) is correct but it is incorrect from the data class (section 2.7) viewpoint. For indexed image display, the data class of the intensity image matrix stored in f must be unsignd 8-bit integer or other where the colormap matrix data is double class and in [0,1]. Therefore the colormap matrix stored in M is okay but the f data class is not okay. You can solve the problem by going through section 2.7 but remembering the fact that the number of levels must be equal to the number rows of the colormap matrix.

Table 2.A   List of softcopy digital image file types that can be opened in MATLAB

Image Type	File Extension	Description
Graphics Interchange Format	.gif	Any 1-bit to 8-bit images
Hierarchical Data Format	.hdf	1. 8-bit raster image datasets with or without the colormap 2. 24-bit raster image datasets
Icons and Cursors	.ico or .cur	1-bit, 4-bit, and 8-bit uncompressed images
Joint Photographic Experts Group	.jpg or .jpeg	Any jpeg baseline image
Portable Network Graphics	.png	1. 1-bit, 2-bit, 4-bit, 8-bit, and 16-bit grayscale images 2. 8-bit and 16-bit indexed images 3. 24-bit and 48-bit true color (RGB) images
Portable Pixel or Gray Map Images	.pbm, .pgm, or .ppm	1. any 1-bit PBM image ñ raw (binary) or ASCII (plain) encoded 2. any standard PGM image ñ ASCII (plain) encoded with arbitrary color depth and raw (binary) encoded with up to 16 bits per gray value 3. any standard PPM image ñ ASCII (plain) encoded with arbitrary color depth and raw (binary) encoded with up to 16 bits per color component
Raster Images	.ras	1. 1-bit bitmap and 8-bit indexed images 2. 24-bit true color and 32-bit true color with alpha
Tagged Image File Format	.tiff or .tif	1. 1-bit, 8-bit, and 24-bit uncompressed images 2. 1-bit, 8-bit, and 24-bit images with packbit compressions 3. 1-bit images with CCITT compression 4. 16-bit grayscale and 16-bit indexed images 5. 48-bit true color (RGB) images
Windows Bitmap Format	.bmp	1. 1-bit, 4-bit, 8-bit, 16-bit, 24-bit, and 32-bit uncompressed images 2. 4-bit and 8-bit run length encoded (RLE) images
X Window Dump	.xwd	1. 1-bit and 8-bit ZPixmaps 2. XY Bitmaps 3. 1-bit XY Pixmaps
Zsoft Paintbrush Images	.pcx	Any 1-bit, 8-bit, and 24-bit images

The last image type of the last section is the RGB image whose modular triplet example can be

$$r[m,n]=\begin{bmatrix}1 & 4 & 0 & 0\\0 & 2 & 3 & 1\\1 & 2 & 0 & 0\end{bmatrix} \text{ for red, } g[m,n]=\begin{bmatrix}2 & 3 & 0 & 0\\0 & 2 & 3 & 1\\1 & 1 & 2 & 2\end{bmatrix} \text{ for green, and } b[m,n]=\begin{bmatrix}4 & 4 & 1 & 3\\0 & 2 & 3 & 1\\2 & 3 & 2 & 1\end{bmatrix} \text{ for blue. These}$$

three color level matrices are entered as the three dimensional array in which the first, second, and third pages correspond to the red, green, and blue components respectively (chapter 10 for the three dimensional array). But the noteworthy point is that the function imshow is written for the level values of the color components to be from 0 to 1 if the data class is double. For this reason we need to divide every element in each component matrix by 4 so that the data becomes in [0,1]. Anyhow the complete command set is as follows:

>>f(:,:,1)=[1 4 0 0;0 2 3 1;1 2 0 0]/4; ↵ ← Entering $r[m,n]$ to the first page of 3D image array f

>>f(:,:,2)=[2 3 0 0;0 2 3 1;1 1 2 2]/4; ↵ ← Entering $g[m,n]$ to the second page of 3D image array f

>>f(:,:,3)=[4 4 1 3;0 2 3 1;2 3 2 1]/4; ↵ ← Entering $b[m,n]$ to the third page of 3D image array f

>>imshow(f) ↵   ← Displaying the 3D image array whose all page elements are from 0 to 1

The command f(:,:,1) provides the control on the first page of the three dimensional array and so do the others. You can say the theory discussed triplet $\left\{\begin{matrix} r[m,n] \\ g[m,n] \\ b[m,n] \end{matrix}\right\}$ is stored in f as a compound one. Following the execution, the reader should see a small rectangular color image object in the figure window of MATLAB (at the maximized window) which is formed from differently colored square dots. As displayed, the input argument of the function imshow can be rectangular (for the gray image) or three dimensional array (for the RGB color image). Anyhow we addressed the image displaying options ranging from the digital image matrix to the softcopy file. One can see more help on the image displaying from the following execution:

>>help imshow ↵

2.6 Soft image file types supported in MATLAB

Transmission, retrieval, storing, or processing of a digital image requires that the image matrix data and other relevant information must be retained in a single softcopy file. Nowadays there are over a hundred image file formats available around the world. Out of them MATLAB supports a number of frequently encountered formats for the digital image manipulation. We present a brief description of available image file formats in the table 2.A, which can be opened in MATLAB.

Table 2.B   List of data class employed for the digital image data manipulation in MATLAB

Class Type	MATLAB Function Name	Description of the Class
Binary number	logical	Can hold the values 0 or 1 and require 1 byte per number
Characters	char	Can hold ASCII characters and requires 2 bytes per character
Single precision number	single	Can hold floating point or decimal numbers ranging from $ñ10^{38}$ to 10^{38} and requires 4 bytes per decimal number
Double precision number	double	Can hold floating point or decimal numbers ranging from $ñ10^{308}$ to 10^{308} and requires 8 bytes per floating point number
Unsigned 8 bit integer number	uint8	Can hold integer numbers ranging from 0 to 255 (256 numbers from $2^8=256$) and requires 1 byte per integer number
Unsigned 16 bit integer number	uint16	Can hold integer numbers ranging from 0 to 65535 (65536 numbers from $2^{16}=65536$) and requires 2 bytes per integer number
Unsigned 32 bit integer number	uint32	Can hold integer numbers ranging from 0 to 4294967295 (4294967296 numbers from $2^{32}=4294967296$) and requires 4 bytes per integer number
Signed 8 bit integer number	int8	Can hold signed integer numbers ranging from $ñ128$ to 127 (256 numbers from $2^8=256$) and requires 1 byte per integer number
Signed 16 bit integer number	int16	Can hold signed integer numbers ranging from $ñ32768$ to 32767 (65536 numbers from $2^{16}=65536$) and requires 2 bytes per signed integer number
Signed 32 bit integer number	int32	Can hold signed integer numbers ranging from $ñ2147483648$ to 2147483647 (4294967296 numbers from $2^{32}=4294967296$) and requires 4 bytes per signed integer number

2.7 Image data class and reading a digital image

From ongoing discussion it goes without saying that the digital image matrix elements are just numbers sometimes integer, decimal, or logical. Since a computer has specific data storage format, it is important to quote how the gray or color level values are stored as far as the finite memory of the computer is concern. When we call some image matrices in MATLAB, we want them to have in decimal form because arithmetic operation most frequently happens in double precision case. Storage data in the digital image softcopy is not in decimal always rather it occurs in the class like the unsigned 8-bit integer, which has the MATLAB code uint8. One can ask why it is 8-bit integer. From previous discourse we know that the gray or color levels are finite and discrete in number in the digital image matrix. A binary digit 1 or 0 can represent one gray or color level. So with the 8 bit, one can store up to $2^8=256$ gray or color levels. Furthermore $2^{10}=1024$ bits constitute one byte. If the three basic colors (R, G, and B) each with 256 levels require 3 bytes to hold one pixel information in a digital image and if the image has the pixel size 64×64, one needs 64×64×3=12288 bytes or 12.288 Kbytes for the representation of the digital color image. Not only the image data is stored in a file but also the file header or type information is stored in the softcopy that might also take few more bytes additionally 12.288 Kbytes. This is the file size we often find in the Windows Explorer as a softcopy file.

At the point we intend to explain some terms used in section 2.3 under the option 2. Recall that we mentioned the file saving options as $\begin{Bmatrix} 24-\text{bit Bitmap} \\ 16 \text{ Color Bitmap} \\ 256 \text{ Color Bitmap} \\ \text{JPEG} \\ \text{GIF} \\ \text{TIFF} \end{Bmatrix}$. Let us understand the meaning of the file types. The 24-bit Bitmap means that the three colors take 24 bits then each color shares 8 bits or 256 levels. The 16 Color Bitmap means that each basic color (R, G, or B) has 16 levels. However the unsigned 8-bit integer numbers are not the ones found as the data class in MATLAB. There are several data classes and their brief descriptions are presented in the table 2.B.

Having the image data available, the conversion from one data class to another can easily be performed with specifically provided functions in MATLAB. Let us say we have the digital image matrix $f[m,n] = \begin{bmatrix} 1.25 & 2.5 & 30.03 \\ 0.75 & 2.2 & 67.99 \end{bmatrix}$ employing the decimal or double class form. We wish to express the elements of $f[m,n]$ in the unsigned 8-bit integer form. The table 2.B says that the unsigned 8-bit integer ranges from 0 to 255. During the conversion the fractional part of the decimal number is discarded for example 1.25 or 67.99 turns to 1 or 67 thereby providing the converted matrix as $\begin{bmatrix} 1 & 2 & 30. \\ 0 & 2 & 67 \end{bmatrix}$. Let us implement the conversion as follows:

Conversion of $f[m,n]$ to 8-bit unsigned number:

```
>>f=[1.25 2.5 30.03;0.75 2.2 67.99]; ↵
>>n=uint8(f) ↵
```

```
n =
      1    2   30
      0    2   67
```

Conversion of $g[m,n]$ to 8-bit signed number:

```
>>g=[-1.25 -129 30.03;0.75 2.2 267.99]; ↵
>>m=int8(g) ↵
```

```
m =
     -1  -128   30
      0     2  127
```

The first line of the command is to assign $f[m,n]$ to the workspace variable f. In the second line the converted matrix is assigned to n. What if one intends to form the signed 8-bit integer number from the elements of $g[m,n] = \begin{bmatrix} -1.25 & -129 & 30.03 \\ 0.75 & 2.2 & 267.99 \end{bmatrix}$. Again the table 2.B mentions that the signed 8-bit integer number varies from ñ128 to 127. Any number more than 127 is clipped to 127 and the fractional part of any number is discarded like the unsigned counterpart. Also any number less than ñ128 is clipped to ñ128. In doing so we should end up the $g[m,n]$ matrix as $\begin{bmatrix} -1 & -128 & 30 \\ 0 & 2 & 127 \end{bmatrix}$. The implementation is also presented in the upper right portion above in which the converted matrix is assigned to the workspace variable m.

Occasionally we find digital image data computed in decimal form such as $g[m,n] = \begin{bmatrix} -1.25 & -129 & 30.03 \\ 0.75 & 2.2 & 267.99 \end{bmatrix}$ which is in double class. For displaying the data as an intensity image, we need to map them between 0 and 1 which is in double class as well. The function mat2gray (abbreviation of matrix data to (2) gray image level) can be helpful in this regard (example D of section 4.2 for the mapping formula of mat2gray).

For the reason of storing, one needs to convert the decimal form data of $g[m,n]$ to the fixed number of gray levels (let us say 256). Hence the minimum and maximum numbers of $g[m,n]$, which are ñ129 and 267.99, are mapped to 0 and 255 respectively. The MATLAB function im2uint8 (abbreviation of the image data to the unsigned 8-bit integer) finds the required conversion but considering the input numbers within 0 and 1. So first we map the minimum and maximum of $g[m,n]$ to 0 and 1 with the help of the function **mat2gray** respectively and then apply the function **im2uint8** as follows:

>>g=[-1.25 -129 30.03;0.75 2.2 267.99]; ↵   ← $g[m,n]$ is assigned to the workspace variable g

>>n=mat2gray(g) ↵   ← mat2gray turns the elements of $g[m,n]$ between 0 and 1

n =   ← n holds the number between 0 and 1 (ñ129⇔0 and 267.99⇔1)
    0.3218   0   0.4006
    0.3268   0.3305   1.0000

>>L=im2uint8(n) ↵   ← im2uint8 turns the elements of n to 256 levels in [0,255] and
                                          assigns those to the workspace variable L

L =
    82   0   102
    83   84   255   ← The gray level mapping happens as ñ129⇔0 and 267.99⇔255

However other kinds of built-in data conversion functions are also seen in MATLAB. Table 2.C presents several data class conversion functions available in MATLAB. Now very briefly we introduce the reading of a softcopy image file in the following.

Table 2.C   MATLAB functions available for the image data class conversion (elaboration in table 2.B)

MATLAB function Name	Possible elements of the input digital image matrix	Converts the elements of the image matrix to
im2uint8	logical, uint8, uint16, and double	uint8
im2uint16	logical, uint8, uint16, and double	uint16
im2bw	uint8, uint16, and double	logical
im2double	logical, uint8, uint16, and double	double
mat2gray	double	Double precision number in the range [0,1]

✦ ✦ Reading a digital image

We paved the way for reading a softcopy image in MATLAB by citing the data class and softcopy image file types. The function **imshow** of section 2.5 just displays a digital image without providing any control on the digital image matrix or the triplet. If the reader says I intend to have my digital image matrix, the necessity of an image reader function is obvious and which is given in MATLAB by the name **imread** (abbreviation of the <u>im</u>age <u>read</u>). Let us consider the image man.jpg of section 2.3. The image must be in your working path of MATLAB and let us execute the following:

>>f=imread('man.jpg'); ↵

The input argument of the **imread** is the softcopy image file name with exact file extension but argumented as a string under the single inverted comma. The suppression command ; is important, not using the command displays the image matrix elements. That is the reader would see the gray or color levels as rows or columns on the monitor screen without the operator. The whole image is assigned to the workspace variable f regardless of the image type. The image file format or the data class is completely hidden in the variable f. Depending on the image type (section 2.4), the f can be a two or three dimensional array. In order to know the details about the contents of f, the command **whos** (one space gap between **whos** and f) can be exercised as follows:

>>whos f ↵

Name	Size	Bytes	Class
f	361x253x3	273999	uint8 array

Grand total is 273999 elements using 273999 bytes

Our objective is to obtain the theory discussed digital image matrix or matrices. In order to know the image matrix nature, let us look at the size displayed by **whos**. The size of f is 361×253×3 indicating a three dimensional array and giving the hint that the image is a true color or RGB one as mentioned in section 2.4. Our immediate concern is to have the theory mentioned matrices $r[m,n]$, $g[m,n]$, and $b[m,n]$ for the red, green, and blue components of the triplet stored in the workspace f. To pick them up from the f, we exercise the following:

>>r=f(:,:,1); ↵   ← The first page of the 3D array is assigned to r which has $r[m,n]$

>>g=f(:,:,2); ↵   ← The second page of the 3D array is assigned to **g** which has $g[m,n]$

>>b=f(:,:,3); ↵   ← The third page of the 3D array is assigned to **b** which has $b[m,n]$

The **whos** execution also says that the matrix elements of $r[m,n]$, $g[m,n]$, or $b[m,n]$ are stored as the unsigned 8-bit integer numbers. To cite another example, let us obtain the image dip.bmp of the section 2.3, place the softcopy image file in your working path, and apply the **imread** and **whos** again on the dip.bmp as follows:

>>f=imread('dip.bmp'); ↵

>>whos f ↵

Name	Size	Bytes	Class
f	218x256	55808	uint8 array

Grand total is 55808 elements using 55808 bytes

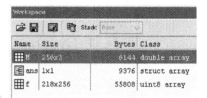

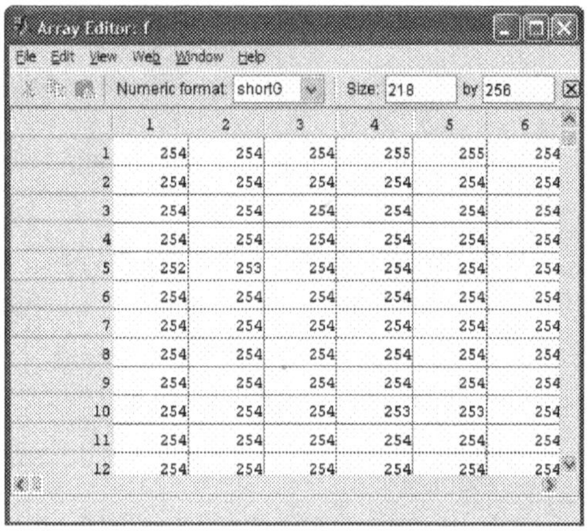

Figure 2.3(a) *Workspace browser contents*

Figure 2.3(b) *Array editor holding the image matrix* **f**

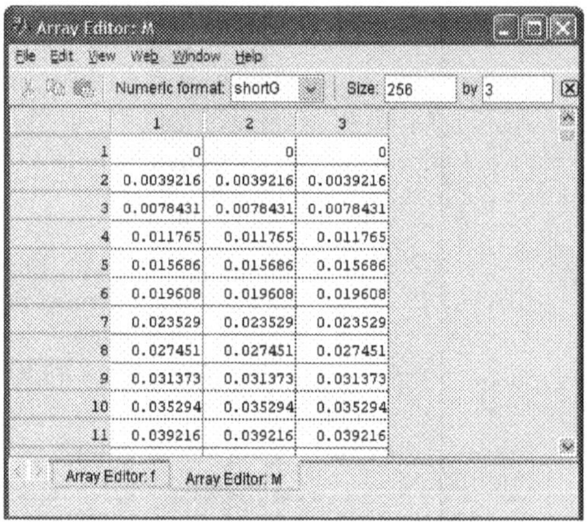

Figure 2.3(c) *Array editor holding the colormap* **M**

As the execution says, the image matrix possesses the pixel size 218×256 thereby making sense of being a two dimensional array. Needless to quote that the **f** is now holding the theory discussed digital image matrix $f[m,n]$. The command **whos** does not provide ample information about the image stored in **f**. Referring to the section 6.1, one can take the help of the function **imfinfo** to ascertain other relevant information about the image. The image dip.bmp is an indexed or color one but that is not manifested by the function **whos**. The moment we know that the image dip.bmp is an indexed one, a consequential question is to have the colormap of the indexed image. Let us execute the following:

>>[f,M]=imread('dip.bmp'); ↵

The function **imread** now has two output arguments **f** and **M**. The **f** and **M** hold the digital image matrix and the colormap matrix respectively. If the **f** is only considered as the image matrix ignoring the colormap, the gray version of the color image is taken into account.

There is one more option for viewing the data class and the image matrix or array size. From MATLAB command window menu bar (section 1.2), one can click the menu *View → Workspace*. Maybe the Workspace browser is already open depending on your computer settings. The workspace browser is shown in the figure 2.3(a). Looking into the browser, one can also find the image matrix or colormap size as well as the data class. Not only that, selecting a variable name (for example, **M** is selected in the figure 2.3(a)) and doubleclicking the variable can even display the contents of the image gray or color level values. Figures 2.3(b) and 2.3(c) show the contents of the intensity image matrix **f** and the colormap matrix **M** respectively for the image dip.bmp. Thus the image reader of MATLAB can read any other softcopy digital image as presented in the table 2.A.

2.8 Color theory and colorspace conversion functions

All practical image objects are colored but most image processing techniques start with the intensity or gray form of the image. Our eyes are more sensitive to the color variations rather than the gray level variations in an image. It is an established fact that all colors can be derived from the three basic colors ñ red, green, and blue.

These three colors are called the primary colors. If we mix any two primary colors, the resulting color is a secondary one and there are three secondary colors namely $\left\{\begin{array}{l} yellow = red + green \\ cyan = green + blue \\ magenta = red + blue \end{array}\right\}$.

In MATLAB we apply two notations for color manipulation ñ in terms of the integer numbers and decimal fractional numbers. If it is integer form, we call the integer as the color level. For example if we choose [0,255] scale, it means any color level marked by an integer from 0 to 255 is possible and there are 256 color levels. The first and the last integers (0 and 255) refer to the complete absence and complete presence of the color respectively. A single pixel in a color image must be having any value from this scale if it is chosen. Let us see the following examples of different color levels in a single pixel in [0,255] scale:

red=0, green=0, and blue=0 $\Rightarrow$ complete absence $\Rightarrow$ black

red=255, green=255, and blue=255 $\Rightarrow$ complete presence $\Rightarrow$ white

red=255, green=255, and blue=0 $\Rightarrow$ secondary color $\Rightarrow$ yellow

red=122, green=55, and blue=110 $\Rightarrow$ other color levels $\Rightarrow$ requires to see the colormap

Ö Ö . and so on.

The decimal fractional form basically normalizes the integer form in the scale [0,1]. Any color level in this scale must be having a decimal fractional value from 0 to 1. Let us see just mentioned color examples in this regard (divide each level by the 255):

red=0, green=0, and blue=0 $\Rightarrow$ complete absence $\Rightarrow$ black

red=1, green=1, and blue=1 $\Rightarrow$ complete presence $\Rightarrow$ white

red=1, green=1, and blue=0 $\Rightarrow$ secondary color $\Rightarrow$ yellow

red=0.4784, green=0.2157, and blue=0.4314 $\Rightarrow$ other color levels $\Rightarrow$ requires to see the colormap

Ö Ö . and so on.

The red-green-blue split of color in a pixel of a digital image is from the viewpoint of the color composition. Another form of the color representation is called the hue-saturation-intensity (HSI). This form characterizes the three components (i.e. red-green-blue) the way human perceives the sensation of a color. We know that all color light waves are electromagnetic waves. The hue component of a color is related with the wavelength of the color wave. The saturation component is the deciding factor about the purity of the color. The hue and saturation together is called the chromaticity of the color. The intensity of the color refers to the brightness.

Assuming the red (R), green (G), and blue (B) components of a color pixel are normalized between 0 and 1, the hue (H), saturation (S), and intensity components (I) are given by the following relationship:

$$H = \left\{\begin{array}{ll} \theta & for \quad B \le G \\ 360 - \theta & for \quad B > G \end{array}\right\} \text{ where } \theta = \cos^{-1}\left[\frac{2R - G - B}{2\sqrt{(R-G)^2 + (R-B)(G-B)}}\right] \text{ in degrees}$$

$$S = 1 - \frac{3\min(R,G,B)}{R+G+B}$$

$$I = \frac{R+G+B}{3}$$

The H can be normalized between 0 and 1 by dividing 360. The expressions regarding the S and I are already normalized.

There are two more color representations namely YCbCr and NTSC. Both of them can be derived from the fundamental RGB components. The first one is used in the digital video system and the other is the television standard of the United States. Their components are Y - Cb - Cr and Y - I - Q for the YCbCr and NTSC systems respectively. The Y is termed as the luminance (related to the intensity) in both cases. The descriptions of the other four components are as follows: $Cb \Leftrightarrow$ difference between the blue component and a reference value, $Cr \Leftrightarrow$ difference between the red component and a reference value, $I \Leftrightarrow$ hue, and $Q \Leftrightarrow$ saturation. The two color spaces are derived from the basic RGB components employing the following relationships:

from RGB to YCbCr: $\begin{bmatrix} Y \\ Cb \\ Cr \end{bmatrix} = \begin{bmatrix} 16 \\ 128 \\ 128 \end{bmatrix} + \begin{bmatrix} 65.481 & 128.553 & 24.966 \\ -37.797 & -74.203 & 112 \\ 112 & -93.786 & -18.214 \end{bmatrix} \begin{bmatrix} R \\ G \\ B \end{bmatrix}$,

from RGB to NTSC: $\begin{bmatrix} Y \\ I \\ Q \end{bmatrix} = \begin{bmatrix} 0.299 & 0.587 & 0.114 \\ 0.596 & -0.274 & -0.322 \\ 0.211 & -0.523 & 0.312 \end{bmatrix} \begin{bmatrix} R \\ G \\ B \end{bmatrix}$, and

$$\text{from NTSC to RGB:} \begin{bmatrix} R \\ G \\ B \end{bmatrix} = \begin{bmatrix} 1 & 0.956 & 0.621 \\ 1 & -0.272 & -0.647 \\ 1 & -1.106 & 1.703 \end{bmatrix} \begin{bmatrix} Y \\ I \\ Q \end{bmatrix}.$$

MATLAB also possesses conversion functions regarding the color space transformations. The image type and the color space literally coexist. Followings are the list of such functions with brief descriptions:

Function name	Brief descriptions
gray2ind	abbreviation of gray to (2) indexed, converts intensity image to indexed image, common syntax: [X,M]=gray2ind(f), where f is the digital image matrix comes from the intensity function, the output arguments X and M are the intensity matrix and the colormap matrix respectively, the M is L×3 matrix were L is the number of levels in X, the default level L is 64, each row in M represents color description of each level, all three elements (in order RGB) in a row are scaled to [0,1], the data type of f can be logical, double or unsigned 8 or 16 bit integers, and any required level L (such as 128 or 256) can be obtained by using the syntax [X,M]=gray2ind(f,L)
ind2gray	abbreviation of the indexed to (2) gray, converts indexed image to intensity image, the reverse counter part of just mentioned gray2ind, the common syntax is f=ind2gray(X,M), the meanings of the symbols are the same as those of gray2ind
rgb2gray	abbreviation of RGB (rgb) to (2) gray, converts RGB image to intensity image, the common syntax is g=rgb2gray(f), where f is the three dimensional array with three pages (subsection 10.12.1) which corresponds to the RGB image, the pages 1, 2, and 3 are red, green, and blue respectively, g is a rectangular matrix representing the digital or discrete image intensity function
rgb2ind	abbreviation of RGB (rgb) to (2) indexed, converts RGB image to indexed image whose common syntax is [g,M]=rgb2ind(f,L), where f is a three dimensional array with three pages containing the RGB components, L and M have the same meanings as do in gray2ind, g is a rectangular matrix representing the digital or discrete image intensity function
ind2rgb	abbreviation of the indexed image to (2) RGB (rgb) image, the common syntax is f=ind2rgb(g,M), this is reverse function of just mentioned rgb2ind, and the symbols have the meanings as of rgb2ind
hsv2rgb	abbreviation of the hue, saturation, and value to (2) RGB (rgb) image, converts hue-saturation-value color space to the basic red-green-blue color space, the common syntax is g=hsv2rgb(f), where f and g both are three dimensional array representing the image, and only change does happen in the colormap
ntsc2rgb	abbreviation of NTSC (ntsc) to (2) RGB (rgb), converts NTSC color values to RGB color values, and the common syntax is g=ntsc2rgb(f), symbol meanings same as those of hsv2rgb
rgb2hsv	abbreviation of RGB (rgb) to (2) hue-saturation-value, converts RGB color values to HSV color space, and the reverse function of hsv2rgb
rgb2ntsc	abbreviation of RGB (rgb) image to (2) NTSC (ntsc) image, it is the reverse function of ntsc2rgb
rgb2ycbcr	abbreviation of RGB (rgb) image to (2) YCbCr (ycbcr) image, RGB color values to YCbCr colorspace, the common syntax is g=rgb2ycbcr(f), where f and g both are three dimensional array representing image, and only change does happen in colormap
ycbcr2rgb	abbreviation of YCbCr (ycbcr) image to (2) RGB (rgb) image, it is the reverse function rgb2ycbcr

One can access to more help on any of these functions from the MATLAB command prompt. For example, execute help ind2rgb for the help of ind2rgb.

2.9 Colorbar generation

Our objective in this section is to generate some color bars from the user definition. The generations give a clear concept of the color theory implemented in MATLAB. A single image pixel is so tiny that it is unable to show the color effects visually. Instead we choose a number of pixels (say 50×30) which are in a digital image. This represents one bar for our discussion. There are 1500 pixels and each of them has three color components ñ red, green, and blue. In MATLAB notation 100% or full colorness is indicated by 1 and complete absence or 0% is indicated by 0. This is maintained for all of the three components. Let us say a pixel has purely or completely red color so it has the numeric color code [1 0 0]. The other two components are absent that is why we set 0 for the green and blue components of the single pixel. Similarly a pixel with purely green or blue color has the numeric code [0   1   0] or [0   0   1] respectively. Let us implement the following examples for the colorbar generation. Since the text is written in black and white form, we are unable to show you the colorful bars but MATLAB figure window will not disappoint you.

✦ ✦ Example 1

Let us generate a red colorbar or digital image like the description in the figure 2.4(a). The implementation is as follows:

MATLAB Command

```
>>R=ones(50,30); ↵
>>c=[1 0 0]; ↵
>>imshow(R,c) ↵
```

Upon execution, you should see a red colorbar displayed in the figure window of MATLAB. The command **ones(50,30)** generates a matrix of ones of the size 50×30 (section 10.4) and assigns the image matrix to the workspace variable R. The c is a three element row matrix containing the color code for the red (which is the colormap). The function **imshow** displays the image (section 2.5) assuming every element in the matrix R has the same color code c.

A digital image of pixel size 50×30 in which every pixel is red

Figure 2.4(a) *Description of a red colorbar*

A digital image of pixel size 50×30 in which every pixel is red	A digital image of pixel size 50×30 in which every pixel is green

Figure 2.4(b) *Description of a red and a green colorbars side by side*

✦ ✦ Example 2

Let us generate two colorbars side by side – one for the red and the other for the green as required in the figure 2.4(b). One can implement that as follows:

```
>>R=ones(50,30); ↵
>>G=2*ones(50,30); ↵
>>T=[R G]; ↵
>>c=[1 0 0;0 1 0]; ↵
>>imshow(T,c) ↵
```

A digital image of pixel size 50×30 in which every pixel is red	A digital image of pixel size 50×30 in which every pixel is green	A digital image of pixel size 50×30 in which every pixel is black

Figure 2.4(c) *Description of a red, a green, and a black colorbars side by side*

The command G=2*ones(50,30); generates a matrix of the size 50×30 and assigns that to the variable G in which every element is 2 (this happens because of the multiplication by 2). The matrices R and G are placed side by side (section 10.6) and assigned to the workspace variable T by the command T=[R G];. In the whole matrix T there are only two elements ñ 1 and 2. The 1 and 2 correspond to the red and green colors whose codes are [1   0   0] and [0   1   0] respectively. Now the colormap takes the form of a three column rectangular matrix. Each row corresponds to one color code thereby providing $\begin{bmatrix} 1 & 0 & 0 \\ 0 & 1 & 0 \end{bmatrix}$ whose MATLAB code is [1 0 0;0 1 0] and which is assigned to c.

The last line displays the expected colorbars in the MATLAB figure window.

✦ ✦ Example 3

Now we intend to display three colorbars as shown in the figure 2.4(c). The first two bars are drawn from the example 2 and the third bar is a black one. The color black means the absence of every basic component hence its color code is [0 0 0]. Their generation command is as follows:

```
>>R=ones(50,30); ↵          ← R holds a matrix of 1s of order 50×30
>>G=2*ones(50,30); ↵        ← G holds a matrix of 2s of order 50×30
>>B=3*ones(50,30); ↵        ← B holds a matrix of 3s of order 50×30
>>T=[R G B]; ↵
>>c=[1 0 0;0 1 0;0 0 0]; ↵
>>imshow(T,c) ↵             ← Displays the color digital image
```

In the third line of above command B=3*ones(50,30); generates a matrix of the size 50×30 and assigns that to the variable B in which every element is 3 indicating the black color level. The complete digital image matrix T

24

placing the three bars side by side is obtained by T=[R G B];. Placing the three color codes row by row, we have

the complete colormap matrix $\begin{bmatrix} 1 & 0 & 0 \\ 0 & 1 & 0 \\ 0 & 0 & 0 \end{bmatrix}$ whose MATLAB statement is seen in the fifth line.

Table 2.D Color names and their red (R), green (G), and blue (B) component values

Color name	[R G B]	Color name	[R G B]
Aquamarine	[0.26 0.72 0.73]	Maroon	[0.51 0.02 0.25]
Coral	[0.97 0.4 0.25]	Medium aquamarine	[0.2 0.53 0.51]
Dark green	[0.15 0.25 0.09]	Midnight blue	[0.08 0.11 0.33]
Dark khaki	[0.72 0.68 0.35]	Mint cream	[0.96 1 0.98]
Dark olive green	[0.29 0.25 0.09]	Navy blue	[0.08 0.02 0.4]
Dark salmon	[0.88 0.55 0.42]	Old lace	[0.99 0.95 0.89]
Dark sea green	[0.55 0.70 0.51]	Plum	[0.73 0.23 0.56]
Deep pink	[0.96 0.16 0.53]	Saddle brown	[0.49 0.19 0.09]
Deep sky blue	[0.23 0.73 1]	Salmon	[0.88 0.55 0.42]
Forest green	[0.31 0.57 0.35]	Sandy brown	[.93 0.6 0.3]
Ghost white	[0.97 0.97 1]	Tan	[0.85 0.69 0.47]
Gold	[0.83 0.63 0.09]	Tomato	[0.97 0.33 0.19]
Khaki	[0.68 0.66 0.43]	Turquoise	[0.26 0.78 0.86]
Lavender blush	[0.99 0.93 0.96]	Violet	[0.55 0.22 0.79]
Lawn green	[0.53 0.97 0.09]	Wheat	[0.95 0.85 0.66]
Lemon chiffon	[1 0.97 0.78]		

♦ ♦ Example 4

Table 2.D presents the MATLAB color component values for the commonly known practical colors. The three colorbars of the figure 2.4(c) are now to be composed of aquamarine, white, and navy blue for which one can conduct the following:

```
>>A=ones(50,30); ↵          ← matrix of 1s of order 50×30 for the aquamarine
>>W=2*ones(50,30); ↵        ← matrix of 2s of order 50×30 for the white
>>N=3*ones(50,30); ↵        ← matrix of 3s of order 50×30 for the navy blue
>>T=[A W N]; ↵
>>c=[0.26 0.72 0.73;1 1 1;0.08 0.02 0.4]; ↵
>>imshow(T,c) ↵             ← Displays the color digital image
```

The workspace variables A, W, and N hold the required bar matrices for the aquamarine, white, and navy blue color respectively. The whiteness appears from the 100% presence of all three components for this reason white has the code [1 1 1]. Choosing the component values from the table 2.D, the colormap matrix becomes $\begin{bmatrix} 0.26 & 0.72 & 0.73 \\ 1 & 1 & 1 \\ 0.08 & 0.02 & 0.4 \end{bmatrix}$ – the color code matrix is seen in the fifth line of above command.

MATLAB reserves specific letter for specific color. For example, we know that the red color has the code [1 0 0]. We can mention the same color specification just writing 'r' where the r is reserved for the red. But the imshow does not accept this, other MATLAB function such as plot (used for graphing y versus x) does. Similar usage is seen for few more colors: g for green, k for black, y for yellow, c for cyan, m for magenta, b for blue, and w for white.

However we close the chapter with the demonstration of the colorbar generation.

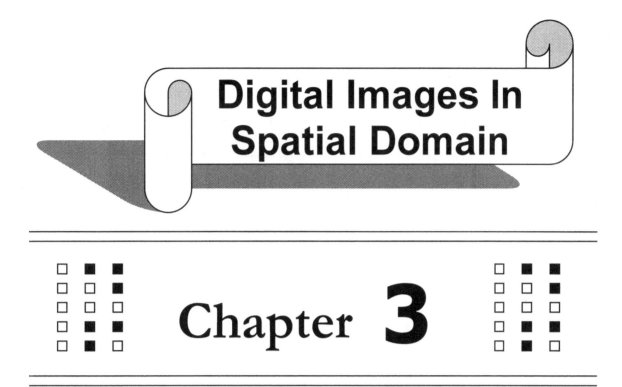

At the very heart of the digital image processing, pixels are the constituent elements. Intuitive meaning of a digital image is not well understood without the spatial or pixel oriented manipulations. Control on the spatial domain in a sense is the control on the digital image. The subject matter in this chapter is to address the know-how details of the spatial domain manipulation techniques to the implementation context of MATLAB. Even though the manipulations are simple but they pave the way for the advanced and sophisticated imaging applications. However the chapter explains the following:

- ♦ ♦ Digital image pixelsí selection, control, and manipulation
- ♦ ♦ Intensity image gray levelsí scaling-transformation-thresholding and discrete differentiation
- ♦ ♦ Geometric transformation basics of a digital image in the light of affine transform
- ♦ ♦ Important computer graphics manipulation such as rotating, resizing, or cropping digital image
- ♦ ♦ Spatial merging of multiple images and two dimensional convolution basics
- ♦ ♦ Single pixel or block-oriented computational style of a digital image and the image arithmetic

3.1 Pixelís neighborhood selection from a digital image

The digital image processing can occur in the spatial or its frequency domain. The spatial domain processing means manipulating image pixelís color or gray level subject to user-required condition but without image transform. A digital image whether it is standstill or moving is nothing but the aggregation of thousands of pixels. Pixel primitiveís understanding in a sense renders complete handle on the digital image. In this section we address how one can access different neighbors of a pixel lying in the image matrix $f[m,n]$ in MATLAB environment. The variation of m and n (always positive integers) comes from the size of the image matrix, which can be read off from MATLAB workspace browser or using the command **size**. We assume that the image matrix $f[m,n]$ is assigned to the workspace variable **f**. Let us say any pixel p in the given digital image has the coordinates (m , n) and its gray level value is $f[m,n]$. Its surrounding pixelís coordinates are given as follows:

$$\begin{array}{ccccc}
\bullet & \bullet & \bullet & \bullet & \bullet \\
\bullet & \bullet\,(m-1,n-1) & \bullet\,(m-1,n) & \bullet\,(m-1,n+1) & \bullet \\
\bullet & \bullet\,(m,n-1) & \bullet\,(m,n) & \bullet\,(m,n+1) & \bullet \\
\bullet & \bullet\,(m+1,n-1) & \bullet\,(m+1,n) & \bullet\,(m+1,n+1) & \bullet \\
\bullet & \bullet & \bullet & \bullet & \bullet
\end{array}$$

$\bullet$ represents one pixel

♣♣ The four neighbors of p symbolized by $N_4(p)$ – according to the image processing textbook notation

This set of four pixels has the pixel coordinates $(m-1,n)$, $(m,n-1)$, $(m,n+1)$, and $(m+1,n)$ and takes the diamond shape •·• in which the center pixel has the coordinates (m,n). One can pick up the $N_4(p)$ from the image matrix f using the command f(m-1,n), f(m,n-1), f(m,n+1), and f(m+1,n) respectively.

♣♣ The four diagonal neighbors of p symbolized by $N_D(p)$

The pixel coordinates for the $N_D(p)$ are $(m+1,n+1)$, $(m-1,n-1)$, $(m-1,n+1)$, and $(m+1,n-1)$ and their shape looks like •·• in which the center pixel has the coordinates (m,n). One can pick up the $N_D(p)$ from the image matrix using the command f(m+1,n+1), f(m-1,n-1), f(m-1,n+1), and f(m+1,n-1) respectively.

♣♣ The 8 neighbors of p symbolized by $N_8(p)$

The $N_8(p)$ takes the form •·•·• in which the center pixel has the coordinates (m,n). It is the combination of $N_4(p)$ and $N_D(p)$. There are 8 pixels in the set (4 from $N_4(p)$ and 4 from $N_D(p)$) whose coordinates are identical to those of the last two sets.

♣♣ User-defined connectivity

Not necessarily the connectivity of the pixels follows above mentioned neighboring. Depending on the image processing problem, one may need mixed connectivity for example the shape • in which the upper left pixel has the coordinates (m,n) and for which the MATLAB selectivity command is f(m,n+1), f(m+1,n), and f(m+2,n+1) for the upper right, lower left, and lower right pixel respectively. This kind of pixel selection happens in the pattern recognition problems.

♣♣ Distance measures between two pixels

Suppose we have two pixels coordinated by (m,n) and (k,l) in the image matrix $f[m,n]$ and their Euclidean distance is given by $D=\sqrt{(m-k)^2+(n-l)^2}$. In MATLAB code we implement the Euclidean distance using the command D=sqrt((m-k)^2+(n-l)^2); in which the workspace variable D holds the distance.

There are other types of distances seen between two pixels as well. The D_4 distance or city block distance between the two pixels is defined as the $|m-k|+|n-l|$ whose MATLAB code is given by the command abs(m-k)+abs(n-l). You can assign this distance to some variable D as we did for the Euclidean distance. Another distance called the D_8 distance or chessboard distance between the two pixels is defined as the $\max(|m-k|,|n-l|)$ whose MATLAB code is max(abs(m-k),abs(n-l)).

Note that above mentioned neighborhood is not defined at the edges or borders of the image. The reader is referred to the subsections 6.1.3 and 10.3.3 for pixel characteristics and pixel selection using the for-loop.

3.2 Gray level scaling and transformation

Given a digital image matrix function $f[m,n]$, the gray level scaling or transformation remaps the image energy according to the user-defined function and we obtain another image $g[m,n]$ in the new domain. The transformation can be linear or nonlinear and happens for every pixel in the image. The knowledge of the gray level range is very important in the transformation. In image processing textbooks we often find the gray level transformation function in graphical form.

Referring to the figure 3.1(a), an image $f[m,n] = \begin{bmatrix} 0 & 255 & 3 \\ 3 & 234 & 1 \\ 5 & 213 & 4 \end{bmatrix}$ in [0,255] is to be transformed to

$g[m,n]$ in [0,255] in accordance with $g[m,n] = c\,f[m,n]$ where c is a

scalar (say $c = 0.3$). So our $g[m,n]$ becomes $\begin{bmatrix} 0 & 76.5 & 0.9 \\ 0.9 & 70.2 & 0.3 \\ 1.5 & 63.9 & 1.2 \end{bmatrix}$

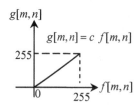

Figure 3.1(a) *Gray level transformation as* $g[m,n] = c\,f[m,n]$

following the scaling with 0.3 (multiplying every pixel element by 0.3). But the scaling changed the range as well. Now the [0,255] of $f[m,n]$ is mapped to [0×0.3,255×0.3] or [0,76.5] for $g[m,n]$. Because of the fractional number multiplication, the gray level becomes fractional. In order to turn them discrete, rounding is carried out – if the fractional part is greater than or equal to 0.5, it is taken as

1. Therefore the $g[m,n]$ should be $\begin{bmatrix} 0 & 77 & 1 \\ 1 & 70 & 0 \\ 2 & 64 & 1 \end{bmatrix}$ and we implement that as follows:

```
>>f=[0 255 3;3 234 1;5 213 4]; ↵   ← f[m,n] matrix is assigned to f
>>g=0.3*f; ↵                        ← g[m,n] = 0.3 f[m,n] is conducted and g holds the result
>>g=round(g) ↵                      ← rounding is carried out and the result is assigned to g again

g =
        0   77    1
        1   70    0
        2   64    1
```

MATLAB function round can perform the rounding towards the nearest integer whose input argument is a rectangular matrix in general. The values held by g are double precision. To convert them as the unsigned 8-bit integer for the image display in [0,255], one can use the command uint8(g). The maximum value in $g[m,n]$ is 77 and the gray levels from 78 to 255 remain idle. This is the effect of scaling however the scaling factor more than 1 brings different situation.

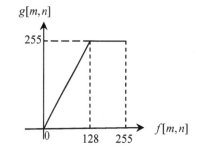

Figure 3.1(b) *Gray level transformation function ñ piecewise linear*

Let us say the scalar c is 1.4 and the $g[m,n]$ becomes

$\begin{bmatrix} 0 & 357 & 4.2 \\ 4.2 & 327.6 & 1.4 \\ 7 & 298.2 & 5.6 \end{bmatrix}$ following the scaling which fits out the maximum 255. One solution to this problem is to

divide every gray level by the maximum gray level in $g[m,n]$ so that the gray levels become in [0,1] and then multiply by 255 in order to convert in [0,255]. Rounding is necessary for obtaining the final image matrix and the command you need is round(255*g/max(max(g))) – section 10.10 for max.

As another transformation function, let us see the piecewise linear transformation function of the figure 3.1(b). When the gray level values are between 0 and 128, they are scaled by a slope $\frac{255}{128}$ and if they are greater than 128, they are sealed to 255. Applying this transformation to the example matrix of $f[m,n]$, one obtains

$\begin{bmatrix} 0 & 255 & 5.9766 \\ 5.9766 & 255 & 1.9922 \\ 9.9609 & 255 & 7.9688 \end{bmatrix}$ and then rounding results $g[m,n] = \begin{bmatrix} 0 & 255 & 6 \\ 6 & 255 & 2 \\ 10 & 255 & 8 \end{bmatrix}$. We implement the gray level

transformation as follows:

```
>>g=round(255*f/128); ↵   ← g holds the f[m,n] scaled by 255/128 and then followed by rounding
>>[R,C]=find(g>=255); ↵
>>for k=1:length(R) g(R(k),C(k))=255; end ↵
>>g ↵                     ← Calling g to see what it holds
```

g =

0	255	6
6	255	2
10	255	8

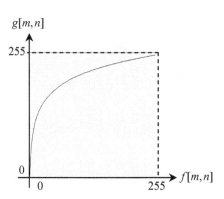

In the second line of above implementation, we used function find (section 10.7) to find position indexes in g at which the gray levels are greater than or equal to 255 and those row and column indexes are stored in the output arguments of the find as R and C respectively. In the third line, pixels greater than 255 are replaced by 255 using a for-loop (subsection 10.3.3) according to the number of elements present in R or C. The command g(R(k),C(k)) corresponds to the pixel of $g[m,n]$ whose coordinates are stored as the k-th element in R and C (R for m and C for n).

Figure 3.1(c) *Logarithmic transformation of the gray level*

Figure 3.1(d) *Logarithmic transformation on the gray levels of man.jpg*

Apart from the linear transformation, other definitive functional transformation is also possible. Let us say the $g[m,n]$ in [0,255] is obtained using a logarithmic transformation from $f[m,n]$ in accordance with the relationship $g[m,n] = \dfrac{255\log_2(1+f[m,n])}{\log_2(1+f[m,n])|_{max}}$ where $f[m,n]$ in [0,255]. The plot of the transformation function is shown in the figure 3.1(c). Applying the logarithmic transformation (and rounding as well), we have $g[m,n] =$

$\begin{bmatrix} 0 & 255 & 64 \\ 64 & 251 & 32 \\ 82 & 247 & 74 \end{bmatrix}$ whose implementation is as follows:

```
>>R=log2(1+f); ↵        ← R holds the log₂(1+f[m,n]) operation result
>>g=255*R/max(max(R)); ↵ ← g holds the computed result of g[m,n]
>>g=round(g) ↵          ← g holds the rounded gray levels
```

with annotations: ← R holds the $\log_2(1+f[m,n])$ operation result; ← g holds the computed result of $g[m,n]$; ← g holds the rounded gray levels

g =

0	255	64
64	251	32
82	247	74

The function $\log_2 x$ has MATLAB code log2(x). The denominator $\log_2(1+f[m,n])|_{max}$ in the transform means the maximum value in the matrix $\log_2(1+f[m,n])$. Figure 3.1(a) transformation with c =0.3 turns the whiter region to black. Figure 3.1(b) transformation increases the less numbered gray levels thereby turning the black zone to whiter. Similar visual effect can also be generated using the logarithmic transform of the figure 3.1(c).

So far we mentioned the transformation related only to the modular image matrix. Now we intend to present the gray level transformation conducted on a practical image. Let us consider the gray version man.jpg of section 2.3. Making the image available in the working directory, we apply the said logarithmic transformation to force the blacker gray levels of the man.jpg closer to white as follows:

```
>>f=imread('man.jpg'); ↵   ← Reading the RGB image and the result is assigned to f
>>f=rgb2gray(f); ↵          ← turning the RGB f to intensity or black and white f, this is f[m,n]
>>f=double(f); ↵            ← turning the unsigned 8-bit integer data of f to the double class for
                               computation reason
>>R=log2(1+f); ↵            ← R holds the log₂(1+f[m,n]) operation result
>>g=255*R/max(max(R)); ↵    ← g holds the computed result of g[m,n] using the logarithmic
                               transform of the figure 3.1(c)
>>g=round(g); ↵             ← g holds the rounded gray levels
>>imshow(uint8(g)) ↵        ← turning contents of g to unsigned 8-bit integer and displaying
```

Pictured in the figure 3.1(d) is the result of the logarithmic transformation. The transformational effect becomes evident looking into the original image of man.jpg displayed in the figure 6.1(a).

3.3 Digital image gray level thresholding

Thresholding a digital image is commonly applied to the image segmentation. In section 8.3 we demonstrate the thresholding using the MATLAB built-in function. Here we intend to introduce the programming concept of thresholding. Given a digital image $f[m,n]$, one may need to apply different threshold to the image. Most digital intensity images encountered are usually of two types, either in [0,1] (inbetween values are fractional) or fixed number gray level for instance [0,255] (inbetween values are positive integer). A threshold is user-defined color or gray level in accordance with the said image gray data variation. Let us go through the following examples.

✦✦ Example 1

Let us apply a threshold $T = 0.6$ to the modular image $f[m,n] = \begin{bmatrix} 0.23 & 0.54 & 0.89 \\ 0.71 & 0.31 & 0.43 \\ 0.67 & 0.29 & 0.97 \end{bmatrix}$ such that the

thresholded image $g[m,n] = \begin{cases} 1 & if & f[m,n] > T \\ 0 & if & f[m,n] \leq T \end{cases}$. This kind of thresholding happens in the binary image generation

from the intensity one and obviously the given image is in [0,1] scale. Our $g[m,n]$ should be $\begin{bmatrix} 0 & 0 & 1 \\ 1 & 0 & 0 \\ 1 & 0 & 1 \end{bmatrix}$ and for

which the command is as follows:

MATLAB Command

```
>>f=[0.23 0.54 0.89;0.71 0.31 0.43;0.67 0.29 0.97]; ↵ ← Assigning f[m,n] to f
>>g=f; ↵                          ← Assigning f to g to have the size of g as that of f
>>[R,C]=find(f>0.6); ↵
>>for k=1:length(R) g(R(k),C(k))=1; end ↵
>>[R,C]=find(f<=0.6); ↵
>>for k=1:length(R) g(R(k),C(k))=0; end ↵
>>g ↵                             ← Calling g to see what it holds

g =
        0   0   1
        1   0   0
        1   0   1
```

The details of the functions find and for-loop are presented in sections 10.7 and 10.3.3 respectively. The third line of above command looks for the position indexes in f where $f[m,n] > 0.6$ is satisfied and assigns those row and column indexes to the variables R and C respectively. Using a for-loop, we select all these indexes stored in R or C and set the threshold accordingly. In a similar fashion, the fourth and fifth lines find the position indexes and set the threshold for the condition $f[m,n] \leq 0.6$ respectively.

Figure 3.2(a) *The man.jpg image after thresholding*

✦✦ Example 2

Example 1 presents a single threshold but this example implements multiple thresholds. The example 1 $f[m,n]$ is now thresholded to obtain

$g[m,n]$ such that $g[m,n] = \begin{cases} 0 & if & 0 \leq f[m,n] \leq 0.3 \\ 0.5 & if & 0.3 < f[m,n] \leq 0.6 \\ 1 & if & f[m,n] > 0.6 \end{cases}$ and we should be having $g[m,n] = \begin{bmatrix} 0 & 0.5 & 1 \\ 1 & 0.5 & 0.5 \\ 1 & 0 & 1 \end{bmatrix}$. The

reader is referred to subsection 10.3.1 for logical operator. Multiple threshold needs using the function find several times. The threshold condition $0 \leq f[m,n] \leq 0.3$ is broken into $0 \leq f[m,n]$ and $f[m,n] \leq 0.3$ to be fed in the function find. However the implementation is as follows:

```
>>f=[0.23 0.54 0.89;0.71 0.31 0.43;0.67 0.29 0.97]; ↵      ← Assigning f[m,n] to f
>>g=f; ↵                              ← Assigning f to g to have the size of g as that of f
>>[R,C]=find(0<=f&f<=0.3); ↵          ← Finding indexes for 0 ≤ f[m,n] ≤ 0.3
>>for k=1:length(R) g(R(k),C(k))=0; end ↵  ← Applying threshold 0 for 0 ≤ f[m,n] ≤ 0.3
>>[R,C]=find(0.3<f&f<=0.6); ↵         ← Finding indexes for 0.3 < f[m,n] ≤ 0.6
>>for k=1:length(R) g(R(k),C(k))=0.5;end ↵ ← Applying threshold 0.5 for 0.3 < f[m,n] ≤ 0.6
```

```
>>[R,C]=find(f>0.6); ↵          ← Finding indexes for f[m,n] > 0.6
>>for k=1:length(R) g(R(k),C(k))=1; end ↵   ← Applying threshold 1 for f[m,n] > 0.6
>>g ↵                           ← Calling g to see what it holds
```

g =

```
        0     0.5000    1.0000
   1.0000     0.5000    0.5000
   1.0000          0    1.0000
```

❖ ❖ Example 3

We wish to apply threshold on the gray version man.jpg of section 2.3 (original image in figure 6.1(a)). Obtain the image, place it in your working directory, and conduct the following:

```
>>f=imread('man.jpg'); ↵     ← Reading the image and assigned to f as 3D array
>>f=rgb2gray(f); ↵           ← Turning the RGB image to gray one and assigned to f
```

So the workspace variable f holds the theory discussed matrix $f[m,n]$. From the workspace browser, we find the f data being unsigned 8-bit integer, which ranges from 0 to 255 (table 2.B). The threshold description must be in terms of the positive integer not as fractional number like previous examples. Let us decide the threshold function as $g[m,n]=\begin{Bmatrix} 0 & if & 0 \le f[m,n] \le 150 \\ 255 & if & 150 < f[m,n] \le 255 \end{Bmatrix}$ and perform the following:

```
>>g=f; ↵                         ← Assigning f to g to have the size of g as that of f
>>[R,C]=find(0<=f&f<=150); ↵     ← Finding indexes for 0 ≤ f[m,n] ≤ 150
>>for k=1:length(R) g(R(k),C(k))=0; end ↵ ← Applying threshold 0 for 0 ≤ f[m,n] ≤ 150
>>[R,C]=find(150<f&f<255); ↵     ← Finding indexes for 150 < f[m,n] ≤ 255
>>for k=1:length(R) g(R(k),C(k))=255; end ↵ ← Applying threshold 255 for 150 < f[m,n] ≤ 255
>>imshow(g) ↵                    ← Displaying the threshold image stored in g
```

Figure 3.2(a) presents the thresholded image we intended for.

❖ ❖ Ready made tool of MATLAB

In section 8.3 we address how one can obtain a binary image from a given digital image employing the threshold technique and MATLAB built-in function.

3.4 Discrete differentiation of a digital image

Differentiation or finding the gradient of a digital image $f[m,n]$ happens in two directions – m and n directed gradients, where m and n are the digital image pixel coordinates and which are solely integer numbers. Different gradients are defined as follows:

$$m \text{ directed gradient: } G_m = \frac{\partial f[m,n]}{\partial m} = f[m+1,n] - f[m,n]$$

$$n \text{ directed gradient: } G_n = \frac{\partial f[m,n]}{\partial n} = f[m,n+1] - f[m,n]$$

$$\text{magnitude gradient: } G = \sqrt{G_m^2 + G_n^2}$$

How the pixel is selected for the gradient finding is shown in the figure 3.2(b). The m and n directed gradients are just the difference of the gray levels between two consecutive pixels along the column and row directions respectively. At the end or last pixel the gradients are not defined. One solution is to repeat the last gradient so that the original image and its gradient are identical in size.

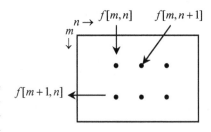

Figure 3.2(b) *Pixel selection for the gradient finding of a digital image*

As we have been doing, let us choose the modular image $f[m,n]=\begin{bmatrix} 9 & 45 & 43 & 9 \\ 4 & 32 & 45 & 6 \\ 8 & 21 & 34 & 6 \end{bmatrix}$ in [0,255] scale. Applying the expressions presented, the first two gradients are computed as $G_m=\begin{bmatrix} -5 & -13 & 2 & -3 \\ 4 & -11 & -11 & 0 \end{bmatrix}$ and $G_n=\begin{bmatrix} 36 & -2 & -34 \\ 28 & 13 & -39 \\ 13 & 13 & -28 \end{bmatrix}$ respectively. But one problem is there in the computation of $\sqrt{G_m^2 + G_n^2}$ due to the non-identical sizes of G_m and G_n. Repeating the last row and column of the

G_m and G_n provides us $\begin{bmatrix} -5 & -13 & 2 & -3 \\ 4 & -11 & -11 & 0 \\ 4 & -11 & -11 & 0 \end{bmatrix}$ and $\begin{bmatrix} 36 & -2 & -34 & -34 \\ 28 & 13 & -39 & -39 \\ 13 & 13 & -28 & -28 \end{bmatrix}$ respectively. Having found the

identical size of the G_m and G_n, the magnitude gradient computation on pixel by pixel becomes $G =$

$\begin{bmatrix} 36.3456 & 13.1529 & 34.0588 & 34.1321 \\ 28.2843 & 17.0294 & 40.5216 & 39 \\ 13.6015 & 17.0294 & 30.0832 & 28 \end{bmatrix}$. Our objective is to obtain these gradients and display them as an

image. Let us proceed with the following:

MATLAB Command

```
>>f=[9 45 43 9;4 32 45 6;8 21 34 6]; ↵      ← Entering f[m,n] matrix to f
>>g=diff(f); ↵              ← g holds Gm without the repetition of the last row
>>Gm=[g;g(end,:)]; ↵        ← Gm holds Gm considering the repetition of the last row (section 10.6)
>>g=diff(f')'; ↵            ← g holds Gn without the repetition of the last column
>>Gn=[g g(:,end)]; ↵        ← Gn holds Gn considering the repetition of the last column (section 10.6)
>>G=sqrt(Gm.^2+Gn.^2); ↵    ← G holds G = √(Gm²+Gn²) (section 10.2 for .^ operation)
```

Displaying the contents:

```
>>Gm ↵              |  >>Gn ↵                 |  >>G ↵

Gm =                |  Gn =                   |  G =
   -5  -13   2  -3  |     36   -2  -34  -34   |     36.3456  13.1529  34.0588  34.1321
    4  -11  -11   0 |     28   13  -39  -39   |     28.2843  17.0294  40.5216  39.0000
    4  -11  -11   0 |     13   13  -28  -28   |     13.6015  17.0294  30.0832  28.0000
```

The MATLAB function **diff** finds the difference of the consecutive elements along the column direction when its input argument is a rectangular matrix. The last row and column in the matrix **g** are selected by the command **g(end,:)** and **g(:,end)** respectively. To conduct the discrete difference in the row direction of $f[m,n]$, we first transpose the $f[m,n]$ by the command **f'** and then apply **diff**. Following the **diff** operation, again transposition is conducted by the command **diff(f')'** to obtain G_n without the repetition of the last column. The rest procedure is to display the G_m, G_n, and G as an intensity image by mapping the minimum and maximum of each to black and white color respectively and for which we employ the function **imshow** for example **imshow(Gm,[ ])** for the G_m.

Figure 3.3(a) G_m gradient image of the man.jpg

Figure 3.3(b) G_n gradient image of the man.jpg

Figure 3.3(c) G gradient image of the man.jpg

Consequentially, the next implication is to apply the gradient computation to a practical digital image. Let us consider the gray version man.jpg of section 2.3. Having placed the image in your working directory, we find the G_m, G_n, and G gradient images of the image as follows:

```
>>f=imread('man.jpg'); ↵   ← Reading the RGB image and assigned to f
```

```
>>f=rgb2gray(f); ↵          ← Turning the RGB image to intensity image and assigned to f
>>f=double(f); ↵            ← Changing the data class to double for computation reason
```

Then, we exercise the second through sixth lines of aforementioned MATLAB command to obtain the gradient image matrices Gm, Gn, and G respectively. Finally, the commands imshow(Gm,[ ]), imshow(Gn,[ ]), and imshow(G,[ ]) present the figures 3.3(a), 3.3(b), and 3.3(c) for different gradients respectively.

3.5 Geometric transform basics of a digital image

The geometric transformation is the part and parcel of digital image processing especially in the computer graphics. The principal reason that lies in the geometric transformation is whatever image we have, we fit the image in 2D monitor screen and in finite number of pixels. A geometric transform involves two operations namely $\begin{Bmatrix} \text{pixel coordinate transformation} \\ \text{color or gray level interpolation} \end{Bmatrix}$. For the color or gray level interpolation, usually one of the three methods namely $\begin{Bmatrix} \text{nearest neighborhood interpolation} \\ \text{linear interpolation} \\ \text{bicubic interpolation} \end{Bmatrix}$ is applied ([22] can be helpful). By definition, the geometric transform T is a vector function that maps the pixel coordinates (m,n) of a digital image function $f[m,n]$ to the pixel coordinates (m',n') of another digital image function $f[m',n']$. The mapping requirement is completely user-defined, the way user likes to view the image. The (m',n') and $f[m',n']$ are related to the pixel coordinate transformation and gray level interpolation respectively. The problem statement here is to find (m',n') and $f[m',n']$ from the given (m,n) and $f[m,n]$ respectively.

The simpler type of geometric transform is the affine transform and it is defined in general in terms of three unknown constants for each directed pixel as follows:

vertically directed: $m' = a_0 + a_1 m + a_2 n$ and

horizontally directed: $n' = b_0 + b_1 m + b_2 n$.

If a digital image $f[m,n]$ undergoes to translation, rotation, scaling, or skewing, we can find the affine transform constant sets $\begin{Bmatrix} a_0 \\ a_1 \\ a_2 \end{Bmatrix}$ and $\begin{Bmatrix} b_0 \\ b_1 \\ b_2 \end{Bmatrix}$ from the user definition.

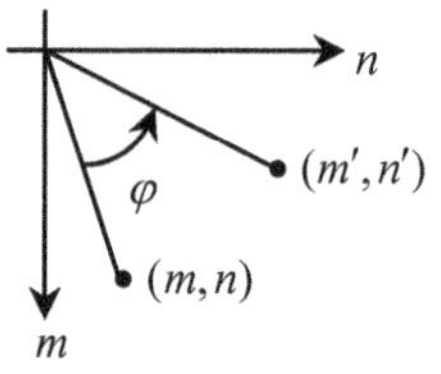

Figure 3.4(a) *An image pixel (m,n) undergoes to a rotation to take the new position (m',n')*

♦ ♦ Rotation of a digital image $f[m,n]$

Rotation of an image about the origin is equivalent to the rotation of any image pixel about the origin (figure 3.4(a)). Let us say the pixel coordinated by (m,n) undergoes a counter clockwise rotation of φ radians about the origin and takes a new position coordinated by (m',n'). Simple geometry allows us to write the following: $\begin{Bmatrix} m' = m\cos\varphi - n\sin\varphi \\ n' = m\sin\varphi + n\cos\varphi \end{Bmatrix}$ or in matrix form, one can write $\begin{bmatrix} m' \\ n' \end{bmatrix} = \begin{bmatrix} \cos\varphi & -\sin\varphi \\ \sin\varphi & \cos\varphi \end{bmatrix} \begin{bmatrix} m \\ n \end{bmatrix}$ where $T = \begin{bmatrix} \cos\varphi & -\sin\varphi \\ \sin\varphi & \cos\varphi \end{bmatrix}$. The vector function T maps the pixel coordinate (m,n) to (m',n'). Both the (m,n) and (m',n') are positive integers as far as the digital image is concern but the computation results fractional values. We round the computed values to the nearest integer. Digital images have rectangular periphery but unwanted triangular region appears at every borderline of the image due to the rotation.

To see the computation, let us rotate the digital image $f[m,n] = \begin{bmatrix} 8 & 5 & 5 & 4 \\ 9 & 4 & 0 & 1 \\ 7 & 21 & 14 & 21 \end{bmatrix}$ about the upper left element (which is 8) by 30^0 counterclockwise. The element 14 in the given image has the pixel coordinates (2,2) (assuming the 8 has the coordinates (0,0)). With the given angle, the T becomes $\begin{bmatrix} 0.866 & -0.5 \\ 0.5 & 0.866 \end{bmatrix}$ and we have the transformed pixel coordinates $\begin{bmatrix} m' \\ n' \end{bmatrix} = \begin{bmatrix} 0.866 & -0.5 \\ 0.5 & 0.866 \end{bmatrix} \begin{bmatrix} m \\ n \end{bmatrix} = \begin{bmatrix} 0.7321 \\ 2.7321 \end{bmatrix}$. Similar calculation applies to every pixel in the image with the same T. By the way, the matrix T is also called the affine matrix. Since no fractional parts exist in the digital pixel domain, rounding provides us $\begin{bmatrix} m' \\ n' \end{bmatrix} = \begin{bmatrix} 1 \\ 3 \end{bmatrix}$. These computations are only for the (m,n) to (m',n') mapping. For the gray level $f[m,n]$ to $f[m',n']$ mapping, let us choose the nearest neighborhood approach. In this approach, we apply the matrix inverse of the operator T to go back to the $\begin{bmatrix} m \\ n \end{bmatrix}$ domain

considering the rounded value. The matrix inverse of the T is given by $T^{-1} = \begin{bmatrix} \cos\varphi & \sin\varphi \\ -\sin\varphi & \cos\varphi \end{bmatrix}$ and we have

$\begin{bmatrix} m \\ n \end{bmatrix} = T^{-1} \begin{bmatrix} m' \\ n' \end{bmatrix}$. For the numerical example, the $\begin{bmatrix} 1 \\ 3 \end{bmatrix}$ in (m',n') now takes the fractional computed value $\begin{bmatrix} 2.3660 \\ 2.0981 \end{bmatrix}$

which becomes $\begin{bmatrix} 2 \\ 2 \end{bmatrix}$ after rounding toward the nearest integer (according to the interpolation method). The

conclusion we make from the computation is the pixel $(m',n')=(1,3)$ in the transform domain has the gray level value $f[m',n']=14$ from $(m,n)=(2,2)$ of the original domain. Similar computation provides all gray levels at every pixel in the whole image, which is the hidden algorithm of the MATLAB function imrotate as will be discussed in section 3.6.

♦ ♦ Change of scale of the image $f[m,n]$

The scaling is important when image taken on different area is displayed on a common picture frame. The scaling also has m and n directed components, let us say a and b respectively. Both of them can be more or less

than 1. The scaling relationship, T vector, and T^{-1} vector are given by $\begin{Bmatrix} m' = am \\ n' = bn \end{Bmatrix}$, $\begin{bmatrix} a & 0 \\ 0 & b \end{bmatrix}$, and $\begin{bmatrix} \dfrac{1}{a} & 0 \\ 0 & \dfrac{1}{b} \end{bmatrix}$

respectively which are observed in the MATLAB function imresize of section 3.7.

♦ ♦ Skewing or shearing the image $f[m,n]$ by an angle φ

A digital image can be skewed or sheared in the m or n direction by an angle φ (also called the vertical and horizontal shearing respectively) and their formulations are as follows:

Vertical skewing:

The pixel coordinate transform relationship: $\begin{Bmatrix} m' = m + n\tan\varphi \\ n' = n \end{Bmatrix}$, T vector: $\begin{bmatrix} 1 & \tan\varphi \\ 0 & 1 \end{bmatrix}$, and T^{-1} vector:

$\begin{bmatrix} 1 & -\tan\varphi \\ 0 & 1 \end{bmatrix}$.

Horizontal skewing:

The pixel coordinate transform relationship: $\begin{Bmatrix} m' = m \\ n' = m\tan\varphi + n \end{Bmatrix}$, T vector: $\begin{bmatrix} 1 & 0 \\ \tan\varphi & 1 \end{bmatrix}$, and T^{-1} vector:

$\begin{bmatrix} 1 & 0 \\ -\tan\varphi & 1 \end{bmatrix}$.

♦ ♦ Ready made tool of MATLAB for the geometric transformation

We cited the affine matrix T order being 2×2 but MATLAB toolbox intakes the matrix T order as 3×3 one and then perform the geometric transformation. For the horizontal skewing, the theory discussed T is

$\begin{bmatrix} 1 & 0 \\ \tan\varphi & 1 \end{bmatrix}$ but to be applicable in MATLAB it should be written as $\begin{bmatrix} 1 & 0 & 0 \\ \tan\varphi & 1 & 0 \\ 0 & 0 & 1 \end{bmatrix}$. It means the addition of one

row and column of zeroes but the lower right element in the T is 1. Applying MATLAB approach, one can rewrite above mentioned affine transform matrices as follows:

Type	Geometric transform equations	MATLAB affine matrix, T
Scale change	$\begin{Bmatrix} m' = am \\ n' = bn \end{Bmatrix}$	$\begin{bmatrix} a & 0 & 0 \\ 0 & b & 0 \\ 0 & 0 & 1 \end{bmatrix}$
Rotation by an angle φ	$\begin{Bmatrix} m' = m\cos\varphi - n\sin\varphi \\ n' = m\sin\varphi + n\cos\varphi \end{Bmatrix}$	$\begin{bmatrix} \cos\varphi & -\sin\varphi & 0 \\ \sin\varphi & \cos\varphi & 0 \\ 0 & 0 & 1 \end{bmatrix}$
Horizontal skewing by φ	$\begin{Bmatrix} m' = m \\ n' = m\tan\varphi + n \end{Bmatrix}$	$\begin{bmatrix} 1 & 0 & 0 \\ \tan\varphi & 1 & 0 \\ 0 & 0 & 1 \end{bmatrix}$

Vertical skewing by φ	$\left\{\begin{array}{l} m' = m + n\tan\varphi \\ n' = n \end{array}\right\}$	$\begin{bmatrix} 1 & \tan\varphi & 0 \\ 0 & 1 & 0 \\ 0 & 0 & 1 \end{bmatrix}$
Translation by (m_0, n_0)	$\left\{\begin{array}{l} m' = m + m_0 \\ n' = n + n_0 \end{array}\right\}$	$\begin{bmatrix} 1 & 0 & 0 \\ 0 & 1 & 0 \\ m_0 & n_0 & 1 \end{bmatrix}$

MATLAB function imtransform (abbreviation of the image transform) can conduct any of just mentioned geometric transforms on a digital image. Let us see the following example.

Example

The image man.jpg of section 2.3 is to be skewed vertically by 25^0. The affine matrix T (according to MATLAB definition) for the problem becomes $\begin{bmatrix} 1 & \tan 25^0 & 0 \\ 0 & 1 & 0 \\ 0 & 0 & 1 \end{bmatrix}$ whose code is [1 tan(pi*25/180) 0;0 1 0;0 0 1]. Place the image in your working directory and carry out the following:

MATLAB Command

```
>>f=imread('man.jpg'); ↵                      ← Reading the image and assigned to f
>>T=maketform('affine',[1 tan(pi*25/180) 0;0 1 0;0 0 1]); ↵
>>g=imtransform(f,T); ↵
>>imshow(g) ↵
```

The image man.jpg is originally an RGB image. The function imtransform works for the RGB image as well as for the intensity one. The function maketform (abbreviation of the make transform) has two input arguments, the first and second of which are the reserve word 'affine' for the affine transform and the code for the affine matrix respectively. The output of maketform is assigned to the workspace variable T which essentially represents the theory discussed T. The third line of above command is the application of the geometric transform on the image stored in f with the help of the vector operator T and the result is assigned to another workspace variable g. The last line command displays the image as shown in the figure 3.4(b). The unwanted region in the image is made black (or equivalently padding the unwanted region by zeroes) by default. You can check the image data class in the workspace browser if it is necessary.

Figure 3.4(b) *The image man.jpg is skewed vertically by 25^0*

Thus one can apply any other previous mentioned geometric transform to a digital image with the help of the imtransform. Nonetheless a lot more options are hidden in the function, execute help imtransform to learn more about the function.

3.6 Rotating a digital image

Image rotation is very important in today's computer animation. Rotation of characters or images on a TV scene is common. Once we have the digital image matrix $f[m,n]$, we can rotate the image in accordance with the user specified angle using the MATLAB function imrotate (abbreviation of the image rotate).

Extra region →

Figure 3.5(a) *Rotation of the letter H without background correction*

Figure 3.5(b) *Rotation of the letter H by 15^0 counter clockwise about its center*

Figure 3.5(c) *Rotation of the letter H by 15^0 clockwise about its center*

Let us consider the H image of the figure 8.1(b) which is to be rotated about the center of the letter by 15^0 counterclockwise and carry out the following:

MATLAB Command

```
>>H=[zeros(50,10) [ones(20);zeros(10,20);ones(20)] zeros(50,10)]; ↵  ← H⇔ f[m,n]
>>N=imrotate(H,15); ↵   ← N holds the resulting image followed by the rotation
>>imshow(N) ↵
```

The first line in the command is the generation of the H image matrix as is done in section 8.1 and assigned the matrix to the workspace variable H. The second line of the command is the application of the function imrotate on H. There are two input arguments in the function – the first and second of which are the name of the image matrix and the angle in degrees by which it is to be rotated respectively. The counterclockwise rotation is indicated by the positive number whereas the negative numbers confirm the clockwise rotation of the image. The third line in the command displays the image of the figure 3.5(a). The image does not appear to be the expected one. When we rotate the image about the center of the image, extra region as indicated in the same figure appears because our

Figure 3.6(a) *The contents of the test.bmp image*

Figure 3.6(b) *The rotated test.bmp image*

Figure 3.6(c) *Cropping the unwanted black region of the image in the figure 3.6(b)*

image matrix is always rectangular. Another dilemma is the function imrotate sets the extra region to 0 which is black in MATLAB convention. We apply some artifice to obtain the correct background image. We first generate the H image taking $\begin{Bmatrix} 1 & for & foreground \\ 0 & for & background \end{Bmatrix}$ by complementing the generated H and then complement the image followed by the rotation as follows:

```
>>N=imrotate(~H,15);  ↵
>>imshow(~N)  ↵
```

The execution results the image of the figure 3.5(b) as expected.

Again let us say we want to rotate the H image by 15^0 clockwise about its center. The angle argument now should be −15. Therefore, the following commands yield the image output as shown in the figure 3.5(c).

```
>>N=imrotate(~H,-15);  ↵
>>imshow(~N)  ↵
```

The H image matrix is in the workspace. We wish to form a movie from the rotated H images that displays the letter H rotating counterclockwise about its center. Close the MATLAB figure window and let us conduct the following easy commands:

```
>>for k=15:15:180 N=imrotate(~H,k); imshow(~N), end  ↵
```

The for-loop (subsection 10.3.3) counter index k generates integers starting from 15 to 180 with a step 15. This k controls the angle of rotation in degrees in the second argument of the function imrotate. For sure, you see the movie on execution of above commands.

Now we wish to rotate the gray version test.bmp of section 2.3 by 30^0 counter clockwise about its center. We assume that you made the image available in your working directory and let us cnduct the following:

```
>>[X,M]=imread('test.bmp');  ↵
>>imshow(X,M)  ↵
>>Y=ind2gray(X,M);  ↵
>>N=imrotate(Y,30);  ↵
>>imshow(N)  ↵
```

Using the function imfinfo of section 6.1 reveals that the image is an indexed one (section 2.4). The first line in above command is to read the color image test.bmp employing the image reader imread and assign the intensity image matrix and colormap matrix to the workspace variables X and M respectively. The second line in the command displays the color image from X and M at the MATLAB figure window whose gray version is shown in the figure 3.6(a). The MATLAB function ind2gray returns the gray image matrix to Y from the X and M in the third line. In the fourth line we rotated the image matrix held in Y by 30^0 counterclockwise and assigned the output to N. The last line results the expected output as seen in the figure 3.6(b).

We explained the theory behind the image rotation in section 3.5. The gray level interpolation methods involved in the image rotation are $\begin{Bmatrix} \text{nearest neighborhood interpolation} \\ \text{bilinear interpolation} \\ \text{bicubic interpolation} \end{Bmatrix}$ whose MATLAB indicatory statements are

$\begin{Bmatrix} \text{nearest} \\ \text{bilinear} \\ \text{bicubic} \end{Bmatrix}$ respectively. If we wanted to rotate the image with specific interpolation method for instance bicubic the fourth line command in the last implementation would be N=imrotate(Y,30,'bicubic'); which includes one more input argument for the interpolation method and the default one is the nearest neighborhood interpolation. Referring to the figure 3.6(b), extra black region appears if we want to accommodate the whole-rotated image. Extra region means more pixel numbers required. If we restrict the rotated image to the actual pixel size of the given test.bmp, one more argument called crop is appended in the function imrotate. Let us implement that as follows:

```
>>N=imrotate(Y,30,'bicubic','crop'); ↵
>>imshow(N) ↵
```

The outcome is the image of the figure 3.6(c). Other options of the imrotate can be accessed by executing help imrotate at the command prompt.

3.7 Resizing or scaling a digital image

Resizing a digital image means increasing or decreasing the pixel size of the image keeping the visual information unaltered. It is one kind of geometric transform as mentioned in the section 3.5. When you stretch or contract some window with the help of mouse, have you ever thought how the size change is happening? If you go through the following implementations, you find the answer. Let us start with the image of the letter H of the figure 8.1(b):

MATLAB Command

```
>>H=[zeros(50,10) [ones(20);zeros(10,20);ones(20)] zeros(50,10)]; ↵ ← H holds the image matrix
```

Suppose we do not know the size of the image matrix H and the pixel size of H is known as follows:

```
>>size(H) ↵

ans =
        50    40
```

The command size says that the image pixel size is 50 pixels×40 pixels or you can see the workspace browser. Let us say we intend to form an H letter image of the size 25 pixels×20 pixels from the image stored in H. Therefore, we implement the following:

```
>>N=imresize(H,[25 20]); ↵        ← N holds the resized image
```

The MATLAB function imresize (abbreviation of the <u>image</u> <u>resize</u>) helps us resize or scale any image matrix to that of user required pixel size. The size is requiring row and column pixel numbers 25 and 20 respectively and we put them as a two element row matrix. The imresize has two input arguments – the first one is the name of the image matrix and the second is the user required pixel size here it is [25 20]. Let us display the resized image stored in N:

```
>>imshow(N) ↵
```

On execution, you see the image of the letter H halved both in horizontally and in vertically compared to the one in the figure 8.1(b). Not only the function reduces the image size but also it enlarges the image. Let us say we want to enlarge the image of H 5 times in each direction hence we should have the pixel dimension of the new image as 250×200. On that account we carry out the following:

```
>>N=imresize(H,[250 200]); ↵
>>imshow(N) ↵
```

Above execution should show you a very big size H letter at the figure window as expected. Mentioning the resizing factor by a single number also works equally. For the last example we could have executed N=imresize(H,5); to obtain the 5 fold image of H. If the command were N=imresize(H,1/3);, we would have the one third reduced image of the H in both directions.

What if we have a practical softcopy image like the test.bmp of section 2.3. Let us carry out the following making the test.bmp available in your working directory:

```
>>[X,M]=imread('test.bmp'); ↵
>>Y=ind2gray(X,M); ↵          ← Y⇔ f[m,n]
>>size(Y) ↵
```

ans =
119 140

Referring to above execution, the first line is to read the image test.bmp and assign the intensity image matrix and colormap matrix to **X** and **M** respectively. The second line converts the **X** and **M** so obtained to gray image matrix and assigns that to **Y**. The third line is displaying the pixel size of the test.bmp which is 119×140 and whose image is in the figure 3.6(a). Let us say we want to enlarge the image 2 times in the row side and 2.5 times in the column side wherefrom the required second input argument of the **imresize** should be [119×2   140×2.5] or [238   350] hence we conduct the following:

>>N=imresize(Y,[238 350]); ↵   ← N holds the resized image
>>imshow(N) ↵

Above execution should display the expected enlarged image in the figure window of MATLAB. For space reason, we excluded its inclusion. Concerning the section 3.5, scaling also needs gray level interpolation. The interpolation

methods supported by the function **imresize** are $\left\{\begin{array}{l}\text{nearest neighborhood interpolation}\\\text{bilinear interpolation}\\\text{bicubic interpolation}\end{array}\right\}$ whose MATLAB associated

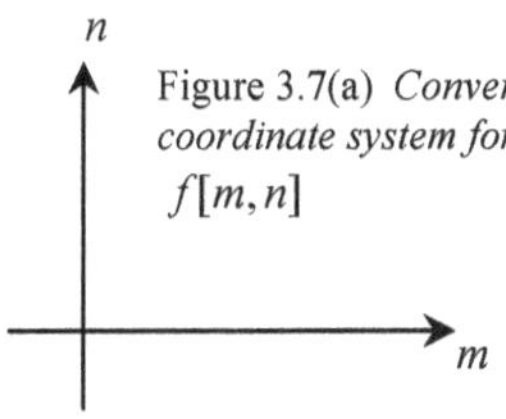

n

Figure 3.7(a) *Conventional coordinate system for* $f[m,n]$

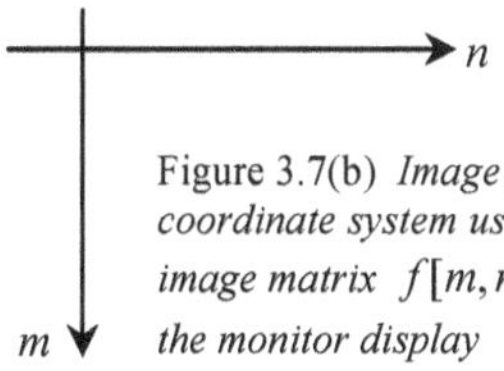

m

n

Figure 3.7(b) *Image processing coordinate system used in the image matrix* $f[m,n]$ *and in the monitor display*

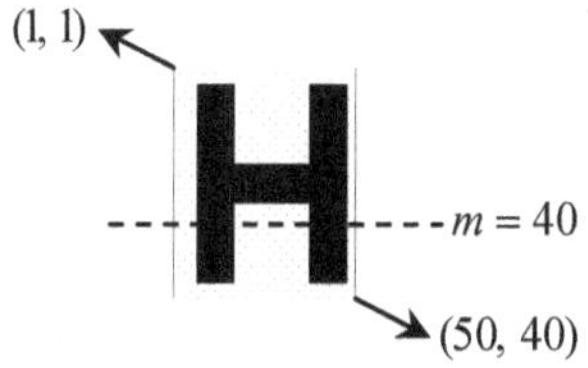

m

(1, 1)

— — $m = 40$

(50, 40)

Figure 3.7(c) *Pixel coordinates relative to the image H*

statements are $\left\{\begin{array}{l}\text{nearest}\\\text{bilinear}\\\text{bicubic}\end{array}\right\}$ respectively. Let us say we wanted to resize the image in the last example using the

bilinear interpolation method. For that the command would be **N=imresize(Y,[238 350],'bilinear');** and the default method is the nearest neighborhood interpolation. The interpolation method appears as the third input argument of the function under the single inverted comma. Resizing indication using a single scalar (like the H) is also possible.

When you see some computer animated movie, sometimes you see an image object is gradually becoming reduced or enlarged. Now you experience how the moviemakers do it. For simplicity let us consider the image of the letter H and carry out the following by first closing the MATLAB figure window:

>>H=[zeros(50,10) [ones(20);zeros(10,20);ones(20)] zeros(50,10)]; ↵ ← H holds the image matrix
>>for k=1:0.1:8 N=imresize(H,1/k); imshow(N), end ↵

Upon successful execution, you see the letter H becoming gradually smaller in size. The first line is just the generation of the letter H image matrix. In the second line we used a for-loop whose counter index **k** changes from 1 to 8 with a step 0.1. The **k** controls the image size of the H. For example when **k** is 8, the image pixel size of the H is reduced to 1/8 in both horizontal and vertical directions. For every value of **k**, we resize the image and display it that is how the movie is being made. The **end** is the terminatory statement of the for-loop.

Figure 3.8(a) *Image of the H after cropping*

Figure 3.8(b) *Cropped image of the figure 3.6(a)*

3.8 Cropping a digital image

Image cropping means that we discard some portion of a given image in terms of the pixel numbers of the image on user required specifications. The placements of m and n coordinate data in the conventional coordinate and in the image processing systems are different. The difference is illustrated in the figures 3.7(a) and 3.7(b).

Let us consider the H letter image of the figure 8.1(b), the image has the pixel size 50×40 (from previous section). Referring to the figure 3.7(c), the upper left and lower right corners of the image correspond to the pixel positions (1,1) and (50,40) respectively. In the same figure let us say we want to discard the down portion of the image indicated by the dotted line corresponding to the pixel line $m = 40$ so our new image should be constructed from the pixel coordinates (1,1) to the pixel coordinates (40,40). We can place the target pixel coordinates as a four element row matrix as [1   1   40   40] (observing minimum m, maximum m, minimum n, and maximum n

38

respectively). The MATLAB function imcrop (abbreviation of the <u>image</u> <u>crop</u>) can crop the image at hand and we implement that as follows:

```
>>H=[zeros(50,10) [ones(20);zeros(10,20);ones(20)] zeros(50,10)]; ↵ ←H holds the image matrix
>>N=imcrop(H,[1 1 40 40]); ↵              ← N holds the image matrix followed by the cropping
>>imshow(N) ↵
```

The imcrop has two input arguments – the first one is the image matrix and the second is the image pixel information as a four element row matrix needed for the cropping. The last line command displays the image as shown in the figure 3.8(a). The function becomes useful for the images when we obtain scanned image. Unnecessary portion of a scanned image can easily be discarded by the imcrop. As a softcopy image, let us consider the image of the figure 3.6(a) which has the file name test.bmp and is an indexed one (section 2.3). Making the image available in the working directory, we perform the following:

```
>>[X,M]=imread('test.bmp'); ↵←Reading the image, X holds intensity matrix, N holds colormap matrix
>>Y=ind2gray(X,M); ↵          ← Y holds the gray version of the test.bmp from the X and M
>>size(Y) ↵                   ← Displaying the pixel size of Y

ans =
        119   140
```

| Image of H | Image of L |

Figure 3.8(c) *Images of H and L side by side*

Let us say we intend to crop the image stored in Y observing the notation of the figure 3.7(c) with the pixel coordinates (11,17) and (119,60) from the upper left and lower right corners of the image respectively whence the necessary implementation is as follows:

```
>>N=imcrop(Y,[11 17 119 60]); ↵ ← N holds the image followed by the cropping
>>imshow(N) ↵
```

We see the output image due to above implementation as displayed in the figure 3.8(b). Thus you can crop any other digitally stored image such as jpeg, tiff, gif, Ö etc with the aid of the function imcrop.

Figure 3.8(d) *Images of H and L side by side displayed by the subplot*

matrix of ones

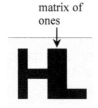

Figure 3.8(e) *Image displayed by the second method*

Figure 3.8(f) *Images of H and L displayed with a separation of 10 ones*

3.9 Displaying various digital images in a single window

Referring to the sections 8.1 and 2.3, we present how to obtain the binary images for H, L, and O and the softcopy image test.bmp respectively. Our objective in this section is to display some or all of those images in a single window. We suggest that the reader go through the section 10.6 for the matrix appending or concatenating. The first step of the implementation is to have the image matrix for each image in the workspace of MATLAB. Assume that we assign each image matrix to the corresponding name for example the matrix of O to O. Let us see the following examples.

♦ ♦ Example A

In this example we wish to see the binary images of H and L side by side as shown in the figure 3.8(c). We solve the problem in two ways ñ the first option uses the built-in MATLAB function called subplot and the second approach is the formation of the entire image matrix and then displaying it.

First method:

The function subplot splits the figure window in subwindows based on user definition. It can accept three positive integer numbers as the input arguments, the first and second of which indicate the number of subwindows in the horizontal and the number of subwindows in the vertical directions respectively. For example, 22 means two subwindows horizontally and two subwindows vertically, 32 means three subwindows horizontally and two subwindows vertically, Ö and so on. The third integer in the input argument numbered consecutively just offers the control on the subwindows so generated. If the first two digits are 32, there should be 6 subwindows and they are numbered and controlled using 1 through 6. According to the figure 3.8(c) we need one row and two columns of subwindow so the first two digits should be 12. The 121 and 122 give the control on the images of H and L respectively. Figure 3.8(d) presents the turnout of the following implementation as needed.

MATLAB Command

```
>>H=[zeros(50,10) [ones(20);zeros(10,20);ones(20)] zeros(50,10)]; ↵   ← H holds the matrix of H
>>L=[zeros(50,10) [ones(40,20);zeros(10,20)]]; ↵                       ← L holds the matrix of L
>>subplot(121),imshow(H) ↵                                            ← Displaying only H
>>subplot(122),imshow(L) ↵                                            ← Displaying only L
```

Image of H	Image of L
Image of O	

Figure 3.9(a) *User requirement for displaying the images of the letters H, L, and O*

Figure 3.9(b) *Displaying the images of the letters H, L, and O by the* subplot

Figure 3.9(c) *Displaying the images of the letters H, L, and O by the matrix method*

Second method:

Looking into the workspace browser, the pixel sizes of the images of H and L are 50×40 and 50×30 respectively. Even though the row numbers of the two image matrices are identical (which is 50), the images displayed are unequal in height as shown in the figure 3.8(d). The reason is image displayed by each subplot executes independently. In this method we form an image matrix that holds H and L side by side. The condition is the numbers of rows of H and L must be identical for the placement. Fortunately they are identical, and it is 50. Let us carry out the following:

```
>>N=[H L]; ↵
>>imshow(N) ↵
```

We place the H and L image matrices side by side by the command [H L];, assign the resultant image matrix to N, and then display it like the figure 3.8(e). We did not insert any separation between the two matrices that is why the two images appear to be continuous in the figure 3.8(e) but one point is certain that they are having the same height. The background of the image is white which corresponds to the pixel value 1 of MATLAB (since N in [0,1]) thereupon we inject a matrix of ones (section 10.4) having the same height 50 between the H and L matrices as indicated by the arrow in the figure 3.8(e). The selection of the width of the one-matrix is userís and it depends how much separation we need between the H and L. Let us say the width is composed of 10 ones. Therefore the size of the one-matrix should be 50×10, and it is generated by the command ones(50,10). The N with the added one-matrix is composed by the following and the figure 3.8(f) shows the implementation (assuming that the previous window is closed):

```
>>N=[H ones(50,10) L]; ↵
>>imshow(N) ↵
```

Image of H	Image of L
Image of O	Image of test.bmp

Figure 3.9(d) *User requirement for displaying the images of the letters H, L, and O and test.bmp*

♣ ♦ Example B

In this example we wish to see the images of the letters H, L, and O as illustrated in the figure 3.9(a). Last example mentioned methods are presented in the following.

First method:

Looking into the upper H and L of the figure 3.9(a), one can say that there should be 2 subwindows in the column direction. The H-L and the O are in two rows. The placement of H-L can occur in 2×2 subwindows which are labeled by the numbers 221, 222, 223, and 224. The numbers 221 and 222 take care of H and L images respectively whereas the 223 and 224 remain unaccounted for. The second row of the figure window is supposed to display the O image in the middle. That could happen if there were three images in the second row of the figure in which the second one is the O. For the sake of O, there should be 2×3 subwindows and they are labeled as 231, 232, 233, 234, 235, and 236. Out of the six numbers, only the 235 is taking care of O and the rest five remain unaccounted for. We assume that you did not delete the matrices H and L from example A and carry out the following first closing the existing figure window:

>>subplot(221),imshow(H) ↵

>>subplot(222),imshow(L) ↵

Now is the turn for the generation of the image matrix O and run the M-file of the figure 8.1(i) in your working path. But before running, delete the last line command imshow(M) from the M-file in the figure 8.1(i) otherwise that will corrupt the standing subplot window. Note that the O image matrix is in the variable M hence we perform the following:

>>O=M; ↵   ← Assigning the image matrix from M to O

>>subplot(235),imshow(O) ↵

Figure 3.9(b) is the expected output.

Second method:

Notice that the image of the O in the last figure is not having the same size as those of the H and L. The reason is we are applying dissimilar subwindows – 2×2 and 2×3. If there were 4 or 6 images, we could have fit them perfectly with the same size. From the workspace browser, the matrix size of O is 41×41. In the example A,

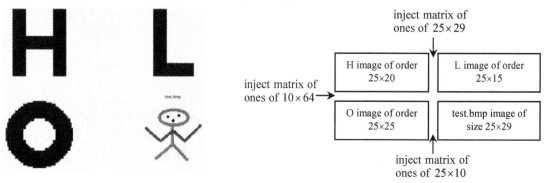

Figure 3.9(e) *Displaying the images of the letters H, L, and O and test.bmp by subplot*

Figure 3.9(f) *Specific requirement for the complete image matrix of the four objects*

the variable N of the second method following the insertion of ones has the size 50×80 (workspace browser). The O would have been best displayed if the size of the O were 50×50 (height of H or L). Again there should be some separation between the H-L image and the O image, let us make it equivalent to 10 ones for which we need the command ones(10,80). Out of the 80 columns in the H-L image (which is stored in N from the example A), we keep 50 for the O itself and 15 on either side of the O. Hence on either side of the O, we have 50×15 ones so that both sides remain white. We apply the function imresize (section 3.7) to resize the O from 41×41 to 50×50. We proceed as follows by closing the last figure window:

>>O=imresize(O,[50,50]); ↵

>>T=[ones(50,15) O ones(50,15)]; ↵

>>I=[N;ones(10,80);T]; ↵

>>imshow(I) ↵

The resized O is again assigned to O in the first line of above command. In the second line, the matrices of ones of order 50×15 are placed on either side of the O and assigned the resulting matrix to T. The third line places the matrix N, separatory one-matrix of order 10×80, and T one above the other and assigns the resultant matrix to I. On execution of the last line, we obtain the image of the figure 3.9(c).

Figure 3.9(g) *Displaying the images of the four objects using matrix method*

♦ ♦ Example C

This example places the images of four objects H, L, O, and test.bmp as mentioned before in accordance with the figure 3.9(d).

First method:

It is obvious that the four images need 2×2 subwindows and we perform the following:

>>subplot(221),imshow(H) ↵   ← Displaying only H

>>subplot(222),imshow(L) ↵   ← Displaying only L

```
>>subplot(223),imshow(O) ↵          ← Displaying only O
>>subplot(224),imshow('test.bmp') ↵  ← Displaying only test.bmp
```
MATLAB responds with the figure 3.9(e).

Second method:
As far as we look for the complete image matrix of the four objects, the size of each matrix needs to be mentioned. When we resize an image, the ratio of the horizontal to vertical pixel numbers had better be preserved. For example the H of order 50×40 has the ratio $\frac{50}{40}$. To avoid distortion, one can resize the H according to $\frac{50}{40}$ for instance to 25×20 or 100×80. Of coarse the resizing can happen to any pixel size but with other ratio image distortion might appear. We intend to construct the complete image matrix as specified in the figure 3.9(f). Presumably the matrices for the H, L, O, and Y (for test.bmp from the last paragraph of section 3.8) are there in the workspace and we perform the following (close the last figure window):

```
>>H=imresize(H,[25,20]); ↵   ← resizing the H to 25×20 and assigning to H
>>L=imresize(L,[25,15]); ↵   ← resizing the L to 25×15 and assigning to L
>>U=[H ones(25,29) L]; ↵     ← forming upper subwindow matrix and assigning to U
>>O=imresize(O,[25,25]); ↵   ← resizing the O to 25×25 and assigning to O
>>Y=imresize(Y,[25,29]); ↵   ← resizing the Y to 25×29 and assigning to Y
>>T=[O ones(25,10) Y]; ↵     ← forming lower subwindow matrix and assigning to T
>>I=[U;ones(10,64);T]; ↵     ← forming the complete image matrix I
>>imshow(I) ↵
```

With all these steps we end up with the image of the figure 3.9(g). If the reader intends to include some title, that can be added by going through the Insert menu of the figure window. In order to display the image in another window instead of closing the last one, the command figure,imshow(I) can be exercised. The procedure we exercised can be applied to any other image format as well.

3.10 Two dimensional convolution in spatial domain

We know that a two dimensional (2D) discrete function takes the form of a rectangular matrix. The geometry of the two dimensional function is shown in figure 4.1(a). Formally the definition of the two dimensional discrete convolution of two discrete functions $f[m,n]$ and $g[m,n]$ is given by $f[m,n]*g[m,n]$ $= \sum_{q=-\infty}^{q=\infty}\sum_{p=-\infty}^{p=\infty} f[p,q]g[m-p,n-q]$. For the image processing, we do not have the infinite summation limits instead the finite convolution. The discrete integer variables m and n represent the image pixels coordinates. The variables p and q are the dummy variables of the summation. For the finiteness we can write

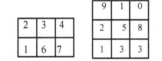

Figure 3.10(a) *Masks for matrices*
$f[m,n]$ and $g[m,n]$

Figure 3.10(b) *Matrix $g[m,n]$ is flipped horizontally and vertically*

the summation formula as $\sum_{q=0}^{Q-1}\sum_{p=0}^{P-1} f[p,q]g[m-p,n-q]$ where $f[m,n]$ or $g[m,n]$ starts at $m=0$ and $n=0$ (most textbook notation). If the m or n starts at 1 which is MATLABís notion, the formula becomes then $\sum_{q=1}^{Q}\sum_{p=1}^{P} f[p,q]g[m-p,n-q]$. However the finite convolution of the two functions can be computed by sliding one function over the horizontally and vertically flipped version of the other. If $f[m,n]$ and $g[m,n]$ (since they are matrices) have the orders $M \times N$ and $P \times Q$ respectively, the order of the resultant convolved matrix $C[m,n]$ is $(M+P-1)\times(N+Q-1)$ regardless of the textbook or MATLAB notation.

Numerically subjectiveness is our approach hence let us consider the two discrete functions as $f[m,n]= \begin{bmatrix} 2 & 3 & 4 \\ 1 & 6 & 7 \end{bmatrix}$ and $g[m,n]= \begin{bmatrix} 9 & 1 & 0 \\ 2 & 5 & 8 \\ 1 & 3 & 3 \end{bmatrix}$ for the convolution, where $m \geq 1$ and $n \geq 1$ (assuming MATLAB notation). A mask as shown in figure 3.10(a) represents each matrix. We flip the matrix $g[m,n]$ horizontally and vertically to have the mask of the figure 3.10(b) and slide the mask of $f[m,n]$ over the flipped version of $g[m,n]$ to have different elements of the resulting convolution matrix. The sliding operation to obtain the first and second rows of convolution matrix is presented schematically in the figure 3.10(c). Anyhow the whole convolution matrix

42

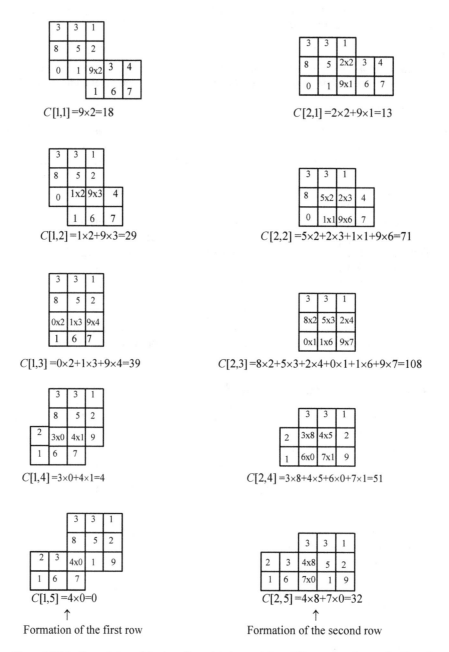

$C[1,1]=9\times2=18$

$C[2,1]=2\times2+9\times1=13$

$C[1,2]=1\times2+9\times3=29$

$C[2,2]=5\times2+2\times3+1\times1+9\times6=71$

$C[1,3]=0\times2+1\times3+9\times4=39$

$C[2,3]=8\times2+5\times3+2\times4+0\times1+1\times6+9\times7=108$

$C[1,4]=3\times0+4\times1=4$

$C[2,4]=3\times8+4\times5+6\times0+7\times1=51$

$C[1,5]=4\times0=0$

Formation of the first row

$C[2,5]=4\times8+7\times0=32$

Formation of the second row

Figure 3.10(c) *Computation of the two dimensional convolution sliding one mask over the flipped version of the other (employing the MATLAB index notation)*

is given by $C[m,n]=\begin{bmatrix}18 & 29 & 39 & 4 & 0\\13 & 71 & 108 & 51 & 32\\4 & 26 & 71 & 104 & 68\\1 & 9 & 28 & 39 & 21\end{bmatrix}$. The orders of $f[m,n]$ and $g[m,n]$ are 2×3 and 3×3 respectively therefore the order of $C[m,n]$ should be (2+3−1)×(3+3−1) or 4×5. The MATLAB function **conv2** (abbreviation of the <u>conv</u>olution in two (2) dimensions) can compute the convolution from given functions $f[m,n]$ and $g[m,n]$. Let us apply the MATLAB counterpart as follows:

MATLAB Command

>>f=[2 3 4;1 6 7]; ↵   ← The matrix $f[m,n]$ is assigned to f

```
>>g=[9 1 0;2 5 8;1 3 3];  ↵        ← The matrix  g[m,n]  is assigned to g
>>C=conv2(f,g)  ↵                  ← Assigning the  C[m,n] = f[m,n]* g[m,n]  to C

C =
        18   29   39    4    0
        13   71  108   51   32
         4   26   71  104   68
         1    9   28   39   21
```

The function conv2 has two input arguments, the first and second of which are the discrete functions $f[m,n]$ and $g[m,n]$ in the form of rectangular matrix respectively. The next legitimate question is what the domain of $C[m,n]$ is. The numbers of the rows and coulmns answer that the domains are $0 \le m \le 3$ and $0 \le n \le 4$ or $1 \le m \le 4$ and $1 \le n \le 5$ according to the image processing textbook or MATLAB notation respectively. Observe that the domain of $C[m,n]$ is greater than those of $f[m,n]$ and $g[m,n]$. The convolution $f[m,n]* g[m,n]$ or $g[m,n]* f[m,n]$ produces the same result, so to say conv2(f,g)=conv2(g,f).

In image processing sometimes we emphasize the convolved matrix size to be the same as that of the original image size. The function conv2 offers the flexibility by taking a third string input argument namely 'same' in conv2. But the third input argument of conv2 follows the first matrix for example conv2(f,g,'same') returns the convolved matrix size as 2×3 because $f[m,n]$ is of 2×3 contrarily conv2(g,f) returns 3×3 size. Let us verify that as follows:

```
>>C=conv2(f,g,'same')  ↵                    >>C=conv2(g,f,'same')  ↵

C =                                          C =
        71  108   51                                 71  108   51
        26   71  104                                 26   71  104
                                                      9   28   39
```

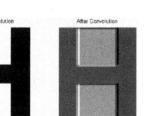

Figure 3.10(d) *Effect of spatial convolution on the binary image letter H*

Figure 3.10(e) *Effect of the spatial convolution on the practical image man.jpg*

✦ ✦ Application of the two dimensional convolution in digital images

The ongoing discourse paves the way of visualizing the upshot of the two dimensional discrete convolution on the digital images. Let us consider the binary image matrix of the letter H of the figure 8.1(b), which we generate by the following command:

MATLAB Command

```
>>H=[zeros(50,10) [ones(20);zeros(10,20);ones(20)] zeros(50,10)];  ↵
```

The contents of the H is our theory discussed $f[m,n]$ and now we need the $g[m,n]$. The selection of $g[m,n]$ mask depends on the user and let us assume that $g[m,n] = \begin{bmatrix} 0 & 0.01 & 0 \\ 0.05 & 0.1 & -0.2 \\ 0.15 & 0.1 & 0 \end{bmatrix}$ and conduct the following:

```
>>g=[0 0.01 0;0.05 0.1 -0.2;0.15 0.1 0];  ↵      ← Entering the mask  g[m,n]  to g
>>C=conv2(H,g,'same');  ↵                        ← Assigning the  C[m,n]  to C
```

To display the images, we seek the help from the function subplot as discussed in section 3.9 therefrom we have:

```
>>subplot(121),imshow(H),title('Before Convolution')  ↵
>>subplot(122),imshow(mat2gray(C)),title('After Convolution')  ↵
```

Execution of above two lines returns the output as shown in the figure 3.10(d). The original binary image of H has been blurred following the convolution. The white background becomes grayish and the deep black limb loses its deep darkness.

Let us take another example, the man.jpg image of the section 2.3. Making the image available in the working directory, let us carry out the following for the image details (subsection 6.1.1):

>>imfinfo('man.jpg') ↵

ans =
    Filename: 'man.jpg'
        ⋮
      etc

From the execution, we find the image is a true color one and convert the image to a gray one as follows:

>>X=imread('man.jpg'); ↵← Reading the image as a three dimensional array and assigned to X
>>Y=rgb2gray(X); ↵   ← Turning the array to gray image and assigned to Y

Therefore the Y so obtained is the theory discussed function $f[m,n]$. Let us choose the same mask $g[m,n]$ as we did for the H example. We perform the convolution and display the images (close previous figure window or use the command figure) by the following:

>>C=conv2(Y,g,'same'); ↵
>>subplot(121),imshow(Y),title('Before Convolution') ↵
>>subplot(122),imshow(mat2gray(C)),title('After Convolution') ↵

MATLAB response is depicted in the figure 3.10(e) in which you find the man.jpg image has been blurred due to the convolution. In both examples we used the function mat2gray to convert the gray level values between 0 and 1 because the convolution results an image matrix whose elements are other than between 0 and 1. If the gray values are to be applicable for the function imshow, the conversion is essential.

3.11 Pixel oriented computation of a digital image

The basic idea of pixel oriented computation is we pick up every pixel and its gray level from a digital image and whatever manipulation is carried out, we return the pixelís associated gray level to the same pixel. Of coarse we select a neighborhood size around the pixel in order to conduct the pixel oriented computation.

For isolated point detection in an image, we employ the mask $\begin{bmatrix} -1 & -1 & -1 \\ -1 & 8 & -1 \\ -1 & -1 & -1 \end{bmatrix}$ (the chosen mask size is 3×3) at every pixel in the

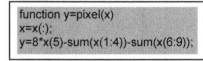

```
function y=pixel(x)
x=x(:);
y=8*x(5)-sum(x(1:4))-sum(x(6:9));
```

digital image. It means every pixelís gray value in the image is multiplied by 8 and its 8 neighborsí gray values are subtracted from the multiplication. Let us say the modular image matrix is

Figure 3.11(a) *The contents of the function file pixel*

$f[m,n] = \begin{bmatrix} 34 & 43 & 21 & 54 \\ 34 & 234 & 21 & 23 \\ 78 & 234 & 21 & 23 \end{bmatrix}$. Also we assume that the undefined

elements within the mask at the border of the image is 0. The upper left pixelís gray level 34 of the example image turnouts the computation as 34×8–43–34–234=–39. Again the second row element 21 gives us 21×8–43–21–54–23–23–21–234–234=–485. Performing similar computation for all pixels, we end up with the matrix $g[m,n] =$

$\begin{bmatrix} -39 & 0 & -207 & 367 \\ -351 & 1386 & -485 & 44 \\ 122 & 1484 & -367 & 119 \end{bmatrix}$ – this is what we expect from the pixel

Figure 3.11(b) *Pixel oriented computation on the test.bmp*

oriented computation. The first step of the problem is to write the mask operation in an M-file. Open the MATLAB M-file Editor (section 1.3), type the statements of the figure 3.11(a) in the Editor, save the file by the name pixel in your working directory, and carry out the following:

MATLAB Command

>>f=[34 43 21 54;34 234 21 23;78 234 21 23]; ↵ ← Assigning $f[m,n]$ to f
>>g=nlfilter(f,[3 3],'pixel') ↵   ← The result is assigned to g, which is $g[m,n]$

```
g =
       -39        0     -207      367
      -351     1386     -485       44
       122     1484     -367      119
```

The MATLAB function nlfilter can perform the pixel oriented computation. There are three input arguments in the function, the first, second, and third of which are the given digital image matrix, mask size as two element row matrix, and the function file name under quote according to which the pixel oriented computation is needed. The input argument of the function file pixel (you can name the file of your choice) is x, which picks up 3×3 block at every pixel element in the image. The command x=x(:); turns the block x as a column vector in which the 5th one is the center element in the mask. The elements 1 through 4 and 6 through 9 in x are to be subtracted from the 8 times of the middle element whose MATLAB code follows the last line in the file. The return of the nlfilter is a matrix of the same size as that of $f[m,n]$ taking into account every pixel.

To see the application in a practical image, let us consider the image test.bmp (indexed image) of section 2.3. We intend to apply aforementioned isolated point detection on the gray version test.bmp using the same mask. Making the image available in your working directory, let us carry out the following:

```
>>[X,M]=imread('test.bmp'); ↵     ← Reading intensity matrix X and colormap matrix M
>>f=ind2gray(X,M); ↵              ← Turning the indexed image to gray one and assigned to f
>>g=nlfilter(f,[3 3],'pixel'); ↵  ← g holds the image followed by pixel oriented processing
>>imshow(g,[ ]) ↵                 ← Displaying the image g by mapping minimum to 0 and maximum to 1
```

Figure 3.11(b) presents the image shown by MATLAB figure window.

3.12 Block oriented computation of a digital image

Sometimes a digital image matrix is split in blocks to which resembling computation is exercised. The idea can be expressed as we pick up one block from the image matrix, do necessary manipulation, and put the block back to the matrix from where it was taken. Let us say we have the digital image matrix $f[m,n] =$

$$\begin{bmatrix} 4 & 5 & 0 & 5 & 5 & 8 \\ 7 & 3 & 2 & 2 & 1 & 3 \\ 3 & 0 & 2 & 6 & 8 & 9 \\ 4 & 7 & 7 & 1 & 3 & 2 \end{bmatrix}$$. The dimension of the matrix is 4×6. One can split the matrix in various order, by way

of illustration 2×2, 2×3, 4×3, Ö etc no further than the dimension of $f[m,n]$. Let us decide the split order being

2×3 accordingly the subimages or modular matrices are $\begin{bmatrix} 4 & 5 & 0 \\ 7 & 3 & 2 \end{bmatrix}$, $\begin{bmatrix} 5 & 5 & 8 \\ 2 & 1 & 3 \end{bmatrix}$, $\begin{bmatrix} 3 & 0 & 2 \\ 4 & 7 & 7 \end{bmatrix}$, and

$\begin{bmatrix} 6 & 8 & 9 \\ 1 & 3 & 2 \end{bmatrix}$. We can apply any function to these blocks either user-defined or built-in with the help of the

MATLAB function blkproc (abbreviation of the block processing). Assume that we intend to square every element in each block. Hence the modular blocks become $\begin{bmatrix} 16 & 25 & 0 \\ 49 & 9 & 4 \end{bmatrix}$, $\begin{bmatrix} 25 & 25 & 64 \\ 4 & 1 & 9 \end{bmatrix}$, $\begin{bmatrix} 9 & 0 & 4 \\ 16 & 49 & 49 \end{bmatrix}$, and

$\begin{bmatrix} 36 & 64 & 81 \\ 1 & 9 & 4 \end{bmatrix}$ respectively and placing the blocks in order results the matrix $\begin{bmatrix} 16 & 25 & 0 & 25 & 25 & 64 \\ 49 & 9 & 4 & 4 & 1 & 9 \\ 9 & 0 & 4 & 36 & 64 & 81 \\ 16 & 49 & 49 & 1 & 9 & 4 \end{bmatrix}$.

Let us implement the computation by the following:

MATLAB Command

```
>>f=[4 5 0 5 5 8;7 3 2 2 1 3;3 0 2 6 8 9;4 7 7 1 3 2]; ↵     ← Assignment of f[m,n] to f
>>N=blkproc(f,[2 3],'x.^2') ↵
```

```
N =
        16    25     0    25    25    64
        49     9     4     4     1     9
         9     0     4    36    64    81
        16    49    49     1     9     4
```

The function blkproc has three input arguments ñ the image matrix f, submatrix dimension as a two element row matrix (here it is 2×3), and the function needs to be performed respectively. Squaring every element in each block x has the MATLAB code x.^2 which is put inside the single inverted comma. The final outcome of blkproc is assigned to some variable N whose size is the same as that of $f[m,n]$. As another example, we take sine on all elements in each block by the command blkproc(f,[2 3],'sin') because $\sin x$ has the MATLAB code sin(x) or sin.

♣ ♣ Illustration of the digital image compression with the help of blkproc

The application of the function blkproc becomes very lucid from the example we are going to address. The two dimensional discrete cosine transform of a digital image is illustrated in section 4.3. The basic theory of the transform is as follows:

$$f[m,n] \xrightarrow{\textit{Forward discrete cosine transform}} F[u,v] \xrightarrow{\textit{Inverse discrete cosine transform}} f[m,n]$$

$$\text{digital image matrix} \qquad \text{forward transform matrix} \qquad \text{digital image matrix}$$

46

When we take the two dimensional forward transform of the image matrix $f[m,n]$, we obtain the forward transform matrix $F[u,v]$ of the same size as that of $f[m,n]$. If we discard some forward transform coefficients and set 0 to those coefficients, still we recover the image but the zero setting happens on block by block. This is our problem statement.

To be more precise and proceed with one example, we divide whole image matrix $f[m,n]$ in terms of 8×8 matrix block like $\begin{bmatrix} 8\times 8 \ block & 8\times 8 \ block & \dots \\ & \vdots & \\ & & 8\times 8 \ block \end{bmatrix}$ and take two dimensional forward discrete cosine transform on every 8×8 block using the formula of section 4.3. In doing so each transformed 8×8 block takes the matrix shape $\begin{bmatrix} 4\times 4 \ block & 4\times 4 \ block \\ 4\times 4 \ block & 4\times 4 \ block \end{bmatrix}$. Let us set zero to the elements intersecting the 5th row through the 8th row and the 5th column through the 8th column of each 8×8 block so that every 8×8 transform block appears to be $\begin{bmatrix} 4\times 4 \ block & 4\times 4 \ block \\ 4\times 4 \ block & 4\times 4 \ block \ of \ 0 \end{bmatrix}$. In order for the recovery, we take two dimensional inverse discrete cosine transform using the formula of section 4.3 on newly formed every 8×8 block. At the beginning example we squared every element in each block by the command 'x.^2' in fact any workspace-defined function, built-in function, or user-written M-file function can be the third input argument of the blkproc. From section 4.3 we know that the forward and inverse counterparts of the transform are dct2 and idct2 respectively.

Let us implement the block oriented processing on the gray version man.jpg of section 2.3 (original display in figure 6.1(a)). Obtain the image in your working directory, open the M-file Editor from MATLAB command window (section 1.3), write the codes in the editor as shown below on the right side, and save the file by the name mfile in the same directory. Let us execute the following:

```
>>f=imread('man.jpg'); ↵
>>f=rgb2gray(f); ↵
>>F=blkproc(f,[8 8],'dct2'); ↵
>>M=blkproc(F,[8 8],'mfile'); ↵
>>N=blkproc(M,[8 8],'idct2'); ↵
>>imshow(mat2gray(N)) ↵
```

Contents of the function mfile:
```
function B=mfile(A)
A(5:8,5:8)=0;
B=A;
```

The first and second lines of above command are to read the RGB image and convert from the RGB to gray image respectively thereby storing the digital image matrix $f[m,n]$ to the workspace variable f. In the third line we applied two dimensional discrete cosine transform with the help of dct2 on every 8×8 block of the image matrix $f[m,n]$ stored in f and kept the transform to some matrix F. In the fourth line, our written function mfile is applied to each 8×8 block of F for the zero insertion and we stored the result to the workspace variable M. For the recovery, we applied the two dimensional inverse discrete cosine transform with the help of the idct2 to every 8×8 block of M and assigned the result to the workspace variable N. Since the matrix elements stored in N are not between 0 to 1 due to the coefficient discarding, we mapped the recovered N element values between 0 and 1 with the help of the function mat2gray and thus imshow shows the output like the figure 3.11(c). Looking into the figure, one can say that there is not enough difference at least visually between the original image of the figure 6.1(a) and the image recovered after

Figure 3.11(c) *Image recovery of the man.jpg after discarding one fourth of the forward discrete cosine transform coefficients*

discarding one fourth forward transform coefficients. To mention about the function file mfile, the blkproc processes every 8×8 matrix, which is assigned to the input argument A of the mfile and from which the elements intersecting the 5th row through the 8th row and the 5th column through the 8th column of each block is picked up by the command A(5:8,5:8) and set to zero by the command A(5:8,5:8)=0;. The command B=A; is just for the functional return of the mfile.

We summarize our observation that discarding one fourth of the image transform coefficients, we are able to recover a digital image. This is the hidden idea of any lossy image compression scheme like jpeg or others. How many discrete cosine transform coefficients we can discard without image distortion are certainly a matter of exploration. The last six line MATLAB commands remain same for the 8×8 block. If we want to discard more coefficients, which essentially explains more compression, all we need is change the mfile contents. Three examples are presented in the following.

Example A

Out of the 64-transform coefficients in every 8×8 block, we want to discard the 5th row through the 8th row of the block like $\begin{bmatrix} 4\times4\ block & 4\times4\ block \\ 4\times4\ block\ of\ 0 & 4\times4\ block\ of\ 0 \end{bmatrix}$. The change needed in the mfile is as follows:

```
function B=mfile(A)
A(5:8,:)=0;
B=A;
```

Save the M-file following the change and let us execute the last three lines of the MATLAB command. We should see the acceptable image like the one in the figure 3.11(c). Discarding half transform coefficients, we compressed the man.jpg image to Ω of its original size.

Example B

Out of the four 4×4 blocks in every 8×8 block, we set three blocks to zero like $\begin{bmatrix} 4\times4\ block & 4\times4\ block\ of\ 0 \\ 4\times4\ block\ of\ 0 & 4\times4\ block\ of\ 0 \end{bmatrix}$. The natural question is how one can pick up the elements from each 4×4 block. In example A we picked up two down 4×4 blocks hence the command for these two down blocks are the same. For the third 4×4 block, we have to pick up the elements intersecting the 1st row through the 4th row and the 5th column through the 8th column. It all takes place in the mfile as follows:

```
function B=mfile(A)
A(5:8,:)=0;
A(1:4,5:8)=0;
B=A;
```

Again let us execute the three lines of the MATLAB command from which still we see the acceptable image thereby compressing the image to one fourth of its original size.

Example C

Now we keep only the first 2×2 transform coefficients in each 8×8 block so that the block takes the matrix shape as $\begin{bmatrix} \begin{bmatrix} 2\times2\ block & 2\times2\ block\ of\ 0 \\ 2\times2\ block\ of\ 0 & 2\times2\ block\ of\ 0 \end{bmatrix} & 4\times4\ block\ of\ 0 \\ 4\times4\ block\ of\ 0 & 4\times4\ block\ of\ 0 \end{bmatrix}$. The element

Figure 3.11(d) *Image recovery of the man.jpg after discarding 60 out of 64 forward discrete cosine transform coefficients*

selection for the zero in the mfile should occur from the intersection of the 3rd through the 8th both for the row and column directions hence the M-file content is as follows:

```
function B=mfile(A)
A(3:8,:)=0;
A(:,3:8)=0;
B=A;
```

Figure 3.11(d) shows the recovered image following the three linesí execution, which compresses the image to 1/16 of its original size. At the point we see some distortion in the image.

Anyhow we selected the 8×8 rectangular block for the illustration. In a similar fashion one can investigate the coefficients for other size block and diagonal discarding as well as for the other transforms.

3.13 Digital image arithmetic in spatial domain

Digital image arithmetic means basic mathematical operations such as addition, subtraction, multiplication Ö etc conducted on the digital image considering the whole image as a single variable. We know that a digital image is mainly a two or three dimensional array hence the image arithmetic relates the computation very much so. We quote few arithmetic operations in the following.

✦ ✦ Addition or subtraction of digital images

Image addition can be regarded as the matrix addition. For instance we have the digital image matrices $f[m,n]=\begin{bmatrix} 27 & 86 & 250 \\ 30 & 21 & 196 \end{bmatrix}$ and $g[m,n]=\begin{bmatrix} 7 & 236 & 8 \\ 43 & 21 & 86 \end{bmatrix}$ – each one having 256 gray levels in [0,255]. Following the addition we end up with the resultant matrix as $h[m,n] = \begin{bmatrix} 34 & 322 & 258 \\ 73 & 42 & 282 \end{bmatrix}$. With the help of the MATLAB

function imadd (abbreviation of the <u>im</u>age <u>add</u>ition), the image addition is performed as follows:

MATLAB Command

```
>>f=[27 86 250;30 21 196]; ↵      ← Assigning f[m,n] to f
>>g=[7 236 8;43 21 86]; ↵         ← Assigning g[m,n] to g
>>h=imadd(f,g) ↵                  ← h[m,n] is formed by adding f and g and assigned to h


h =
    34  322  258
    73   42  282
```

Due to the addition, the gray levels of the resultant image matrix become different for example each image with 256 levels in [0,255] causes to have 511 levels in [0,510]. This can be overcome either using mat2gray or using imshow with the empty matrix argument (chapter 2). The function imadd has two input arguments ñ the image matrices f and g. The important point is that the two matrices must be of identical order (the same pixel size).

There are two supplied images in MATLAB by the names saturn.tif and text.tif. Their individual display can be seen by executing the command imshow('saturn.tif') or imshow('text.tif'). We intend to add them for which we conduct the following:

```
>>f=imread('saturn.tif'); ↵       ← Reading saturn.tif and assigned to f
>>g=imread('text.tif'); ↵         ← Reading text.tif and assigned to g
```

Looking into the MATLAB workspace browser, we find that the sizes of the f and g are 328×438 and 256×256 respectively. Because of nonidentical size, they can not be added. Also another discrepancy is noticed about the data class. The data classes of the text.tif and saturn.tif are logical and unsigned 8-bit integer (section 2.7) respectively. Image addition can not occur until both data classes are identical and their data ranges are [0,1] and [0,255] respectively. Individually one data in one image may not be pronounced in others. For example the 1 in logical data displays white within the image but in [0,255] scale that appears as black. So we turn the logical array to double class for computation reason and multiply by 255 to make 255 as white. We resize the image stored in f to the pixel size 256×256 with the help of the imresize (section 3.7) for the addition reason and the discrepancies are overcome as follows:

```
>>f=imresize(f,[256 256]); ↵      ← resizing the image stored in f to 256×256 and assigned to f
>>h=imadd(double(f),255*double(g)); ↵  ← h[m,n] is formed by adding f and g and assigned to h
>>imshow(h,[ ]) ↵                 ← Displaying h
```

Figure 3.12(a) *The addition of the images saturn.tif and text.tif*

Figure 3.12(b) *The subtraction of the image text.tif from the saturn.tif*

Figure 3.12(c) *Linear combination of three images*

Figure 3.12(a) shows the addition image. The image subtraction is very similar to the addition just like matrix subtraction of two identical data class and size matrices. The MATLAB function imsubtract (abbreviation of the <u>im</u>age <u>subtract</u>) can perform the image subtraction for the last two images as follows:

```
>>h=imsubtract(double(f),255*double(g)); ↵   ← h holds the subtraction result
>>imshow(h,[ ]) ↵                            ← Displaying h
```

Presented figure 3.12(b) shows the subtraction of the g (text.tif) from the f (saturn.tif). Some other options are also included in the two functions (execute help imsubtract or help imadd for that).

The two said functions can handle only two images. If you have a number of images to be added or subtracted, you can employ the MATLAB function imlincomb (abbreviation of the <u>im</u>age <u>lin</u>ear <u>comb</u>ination). The linear combination of two images $f[m,n]$ and $g[m,n]$ can be written as $af[m,n] + bg[m,n]$ where a and b are the user defined scalars. Again the linear combination of three images $f[m,n]$, $g[m,n]$, and $r[m,n]$ can be written as $af[m,n]+bg[m,n]+cr[m,n]$ where the multipliers of the images are scalars. It is assumed that all component images are of the same pixel size and of the same data class. Different scalar values render different visual perceptions in the resulting image. For example, $\begin{Bmatrix} a=1 \\ b=1 \end{Bmatrix}$ means addition of $f[m,n]$ and $g[m,n]$, $\begin{Bmatrix} a=1 \\ b=-1 \end{Bmatrix}$ means subtraction of $g[m,n]$ from $f[m,n]$, $\begin{Bmatrix} a=1 \\ b=0.1 \end{Bmatrix}$ means the dominant effect of $f[m,n]$ but some shadow-like presence of $g[m,n]$, and so on.

Let us see one implementation on the imlincomb. The workspace variable g is holding the text.tif as a logical array from previous implementation. Let us turn it (as well as the f) in [0,255] and as double precision data class image by the following:

>>g=255*double(g); ↵   ← g holds $g[m,n]$ of size 256×256 of double precision data in [0,255]

>>f=double(f); ↵   ← f holds $f[m,n]$ of size 256×256 of double precision data in [0,255]

There is one more supplied image in MATLAB called cameramen.tif (execute imshow('cameraman.tif') to see the image). Let us say this image is $r[m,n]$ hence we obtain:

>>r=imread('cameraman.tif'); ↵   ← r holds $r[m,n]$ of size 256×256 unsigned 8-bit integer data

>>r=double(r); ↵   ← Turning the data class of r to double and assigned to r

We have three images $f[m,n]$, $g[m,n]$, and $r[m,n]$ stored to the workspace variables f, g, and r respectively of the same size (256×256) and of the same data class (double). We intend to perform the operation $0.8f[m,n]-0.3g[m,n]+0.5r[m,n]$ for which the following can be executed:

>>h=imlincomb(0.8,f,-0.3,g,0.5,r); ↵   ← h holds $0.8f[m,n]-0.3g[m,n]+0.5r[m,n]$

>>imshow(h,[ ]) ↵   ← Displaying the contents of h as an image

Figure 3.12(c) shows the linear combination of the three images. As implemented, the function imlincomb has six input arguments, the first two of which are the scalar multiplier 0.8 of the image $f[m,n]$ and the image matrix itself respectively. Similar convention is followed for the other two images consecutively. Thus you can linearly combine images as many as you need. The function is useful for designing user-defined foreground and background. Execute help imlincomb to see other options in the function.

Given two images $f[m,n]$ and $g[m,n]$, their absolute difference image is defined as $|f[m,n]-g[m,n]|$ for which the MATLAB function imabsdiff (abbreviation of the <u>im</u>age <u>abs</u>olute <u>diff</u>erence) can be employed like the imadd or imsubtract.

❖ ❖ Multiplication or division of digital images

Figure 3.12(d) *Division of the image saturn.tif by cameraman.tif*

Multiplication or division of two identical size images is completely pixel by pixel operation. Considering the modular image earlier we presented in this section, the multiplication and division of the images $f[m,n]$ and $g[m,n]$ are

$$\begin{bmatrix} 189 & 20296 & 2000 \\ 1290 & 441 & 16856 \end{bmatrix}$$ and

$$\begin{bmatrix} 3.8571 & 0.3644 & 31.25 \\ 0.6977 & 1 & 2.2791 \end{bmatrix}$$ respectively. To elucidate the operation, the upper left pixel is obtained by 27×7=189 and $\frac{27}{7}$=3.8571

Figure 3.12(e) *Complement image of the test.bmp without considering colormap*

Figure 3.12(f) *Complement image of the test.bmp considering colormap*

for the multiplication and division respectively. The respective functions for the MATLAB implementation are immultiply (abbreviation of the <u>im</u>age <u>multiply</u>) and imdivide (abbreviation of the <u>im</u>age <u>divide</u>). From the last implementation, the variables f and r are holding the images saturn.tif and cameraman.tif respectively. The division of the image saturn.tif by the cameraman.tif is carried out as follows:

>>h=imdivide(f,r); ↵   ← h holds the division of f by r

>>imshow(h,[ ]) ↵

Figure 3.12(d) shows the division result of the two images. In a similar fashion you can also perform the image multiplication. To learn more about the functions, execute help imdivide or help immultiply.

♦ ♦ Complement of digital images

The complement set definition of the set theory applies to finding the complement of a digital image. The complement image is very much dependent on the digital image data class. Because different data class has different data range. Let us say an unsigned 8-bit integer image whose data range is in between 0 and 255 (table 2.B). The maximum value of the gray level in the image is 255. The complement of the image $f[m,n] = \begin{bmatrix} 27 & 86 & 250 \\ 30 & 21 & 196 \end{bmatrix}$ in the [0,255] scale is obtained by subtracting every element of $f[m,n]$ from 255 which

returns $\begin{bmatrix} 228 & 169 & 5 \\ 225 & 234 & 59 \end{bmatrix}$. This is implemented by the MATLAB function imcomplement (abbreviation of the image complement) as follows:

```
>>f=[27 86 250;30 21 196]; ↵      ← Entering f[m,n] in [0,255] to f as double class
>>f=uint8(f); ↵                   ← Turning contents of the f to unsigned 8-bit integer
>>h=imcomplement(f) ↵             ← Applying the function and result is put to h

    h =
         228   169    5
         225   234   59
```

For the intensity image, the complement effect turns the white to black and vice versa as well as the inbetween gray levels. Let us see the effect on the indexed test.bmp image (figure 2.2(a) of section 2.3). Having available the image in the working directory, we conduct the following:

```
>>f=imread('test.bmp'); ↵     ← Reading test.bmp and assigned the intensity matrix of the indexed
                                image to f where f class is uint8 (from workspace browser)
>>h=imcomplement(f); ↵        ← h holds the complement of the test.bmp in [0,255]
>>imshow(h) ↵                 ← Displaying the h
```

Presented figure 3.12(e) is the complement image output due to above execution. Another data class we use for the intensity image is double in [0,1] whose inbetween values are fractional. For this kind of image, every gray level value in the image is subtracted from 1 to obtain the complement image. The complement image gray level values are also fractional in [0,1]. Now we exercise two output arguments for the indexed test.bmp as follows:

```
>>[f,m]=imread('test.bmp'); ↵   ← f and m hold the intensity and colormap matrices respectively
>>f=ind2gray(f,m); ↵            ← turning the indexed image to gray image from f and m
```

The last f holds double class data in [0,1] (workspace browser) not the unsigned 8-bit integer however we take the complement image of f and assign the resulting image to h as follows:

```
>>h=imcomplement(f); ↵
>>imshow(h) ↵
```

Figure 3.12(f) is the display due to the last line execution that differs from the pervious one. The reason is we excluded the color information from the image of the figure 3.12(e). If the image data class is logical, the complement operation turns 0 to 1 and 1 to 0. Execute help imcomplement to see more details about the function.

In this short context we do not intend to address all spatial domain problems. We bring an end to the chapter with the discussion of the digital image arithmetic.

Digital Image Transforms

Chapter 4

Digital image transform is important in the sense that image data compression is primarily based on the image transform. Application of the image compression surrounds daily life such as in video-conferencing, medical data storing, wired or wireless transmission of pictures, finger print storing, smart cart reading, and many more. Image data analysis and image feature extraction also require image transform. With the increasing demand of compressed images and devoted effort of engineers and researchers, different image transforms have been evolved. We outline fundamental image transforms often found in most textbooks on the following captions:

♦ ♦ Two dimensional discrete Fourier transform, discrete cosine transform, and Hadamard transform in forward and inverse domains

♦ ♦ Two dimensional forward and inverse Hotelling transforms with elaborate discourse on the eigenvalue-eigenvector of a square matrix and covariance of random variables

♦ ♦ Hough transform and its implication in the line detection in a raster image

♦ ♦ Two dimensional forward and inverse wavelet transforms with detail block diagrams and computational flow

♦ ♦ Methods of displaying the transform spectrum or the transform in various options

4.1 Two dimensional discrete Fourier transform

In this section we introduce the computational style of two dimensional (2D) discrete Fourier transform (DFT) in MATLAB. The Fourier transform basically decomposes digital image information as a sum of modular sinusoids. Since a digital black and white image takes the form of a rectangular matrix, we apply first the transform to a rectangular matrix and then the transform to practical images in the next section. The geometry of the image matrix function $f[m, n]$ is shown in the figure 4.1(a). The independent integer variables m and n correspond to the position index of the image pixels. They can vary from 1 to M and 1 to N respectively where the image $f[m, n]$ has the size $M \times N$ pixels. The $f[m, n]$ matrix elements are the gray level values of the black and white image at any particular pixel coordinates (m , n).

♦♦ Two dimensional forward discrete Fourier transform

The forward two dimensional discrete Fourier transform $F[u, v]$ of the image matrix $f[m, n]$ is expressed as $F[u, v] = \sum_{n=1}^{N} \sum_{m=1}^{M} f[m, n] e^{-j\frac{2\pi(u-1)(m-1)}{M}} e^{-j\frac{2\pi(n-1)(v-1)}{N}}$. Since the transform $F[u, v]$ is discrete, it takes the form of a rectangular matrix of order $M \times N$ as well. The spatial (related to the pixel position) frequency variables u and v vary from 1 to M and 1 to N respectively.

Let us take the example of the image matrix as $f[m, n] =$

$$\begin{bmatrix} 10 & 3 & -5 & 6 \\ 0 & 7 & 11 & 4 \\ -3 & 8 & 9 & 7 \end{bmatrix}, \text{ where } \begin{Bmatrix} M = 3 \\ N = 4 \end{Bmatrix}.$$ We calculate few forward

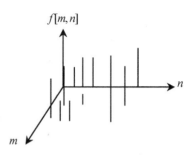

Figure 4.1(a) *Geometry of a discrete image signal* $f[m, n]$

discrete Fourier transform coefficients of the image matrix as follows:

$F[1, 1] = \sum_{n=1}^{4} \sum_{m=1}^{3} f[m, n] = 57$, $\qquad F[1, 2] = \sum_{n=1}^{4} \sum_{m=1}^{3} f[m, n] e^{-j\frac{\pi(n-1)}{2}} = (10+0-3) e^0 + (3+7+8) e^{-j\frac{\pi}{2}} + (-5+11+9) e^{-j\pi} + (6+4+$

$7) e^{-j\frac{3\pi}{2}} = -8 - j$, $\qquad F[2, 1] = \sum_{n=1}^{4} \sum_{m=1}^{3} f[m, n] e^{-j\frac{2\pi(m-1)}{3}} = (10+3-5+6) e^0 + (0+7+11+4) e^{-j\frac{2\pi}{3}} + (-3+8+9+7) e^{-j\frac{4\pi}{3}} = -7.5 -$

$j 0.866$, $F[2, 2] = \sum_{n=1}^{4} \sum_{m=1}^{3} f[m, n] e^{-j\frac{2\pi(m-1)}{3}} e^{-j\frac{\pi}{2}(n-1)} = 24.7679 + j 4.134$, and so on. Computing the other coefficients, we

end up with the two dimensional forward discrete Fourier transform (2D DFT) of the image matrix as

$$F[u, v] = \begin{bmatrix} 57 & -8 - j & -13 & -8 + j \\ -7.5 - j0.866 & 24.7679 + j4.134 & 0.5 - j7.7942 & 28.2321 - j5.866 \\ -7.5 + j0.866 & 28.2321 + j5.866 & 0.5 + j7.7942 & 24.7679 - j4.134 \end{bmatrix}.$$ Our objective is to obtain these

Fourier transform coefficients $F[u, v]$ in MATLAB from the image matrix $f[m, n]$. The MATLAB counterpart of the transform is fft2 (abbreviation of the fast Fourier transform in 2 dimension). Let us carry out the image transform as follows:

MATLAB Command

```
>>f=[10 3 -5 6;0 7 11 4;-3 8 9 7]; ↵
>>F=fft2(f) ↵


F =
        57.0000              -8.0000 - 1.0000i    -13.0000            -8.0000 + 1.0000i
        -7.5000 - 0.8660i    24.7679 + 4.1340i    0.5000 - 7.7942i    28.2321 - 5.8660i
        -7.5000 + 0.8660i    28.2321 + 5.8660i    0.5000 + 7.7942i    24.7679 - 4.1340i
```

The first line in above command is to assign the image matrix $f[m, n]$ to the workspace variable f and the second line is to apply the function fft2 on the f and then assign the transform coefficients to the workspace variable F. Our objective is served as we mentioned.

In most image processing texts, you find the pixel variation from 0 to $M - 1$ or $N - 1$ with the Fourier exponent kernel $e^{-j\frac{2\pi u m}{M-1}}$ or $e^{-j\frac{2\pi n v}{N-1}}$. If we say that the pixels are changing from 1 to M or N (which is more logical), then the Fourier kernel we provided applies. Employing either expression does not change the image information content. However, the forward transform expression could have been written as $F[u, v] = \sum_{n=0}^{N-1} \sum_{m=0}^{M-1} f[m, n] e^{-j\frac{2\pi u m}{M-1}} e^{-j\frac{2\pi n v}{N-1}}$ for the pixel variation from 0 to $M - 1$ or $N - 1$. Also note that the spatial frequency variables u and v assume the same variations as the pixel variables m and n do.

The nature of the discrete Fourier transform is complex because of the complex exponential kernel. To analyze the image property based on the transform domain, sometimes it is required that we separate various components of the complex discrete Fourier transform. Considering the complex number $x + jy$ in rectangular form, its real, imaginary, magnitude, and phase angle in radians are given by x, y, $\sqrt{x^2 + y^2}$, and $\tan^{-1}\frac{y}{x}$ respectively. Hence one can separate the real, imaginary, magnitude, and phase angle parts from the computed

$F[u, v]$ coefficients for the numerical image $f[m, n]$ as $\mathrm{Re}\{F[u, v]\} = \begin{bmatrix} 57 & -8 & -13 & -8 \\ -7.5 & 24.7679 & 0.5 & 28.2321 \\ -7.5 & 28.2321 & 0.5 & 24.7679 \end{bmatrix}$,

$\mathrm{Im}\{F[u, v]\} = \begin{bmatrix} 0 & -j & 0 & +j \\ -j0.866 & j4.134 & -j7.7942 & -j5.866 \\ +j0.866 & j5.866 & +j7.7942 & -j4.134 \end{bmatrix}$, $|F[u, v]| = \begin{bmatrix} 57 & 8.0623 & 13 & 8.0623 \\ 7.5498 & 25.1106 & 7.8102 & 28.835 \\ 7.5498 & 28.835 & 7.8102 & 25.1106 \end{bmatrix}$, and

$\angle F[u, v] = \begin{bmatrix} 0 & -3.0172 & 3.1416 & 3.0172 \\ -3.0266 & 0.1654 & -1.5067 & -0.2049 \\ 3.0266 & 0.2049 & 1.5067 & -0.1654 \end{bmatrix}$ (angles in $[-\pi, \pi]$ not in $[0, 2\pi]$) respectively. The

complex $F[u, v]$ coefficients in rectangular form are held by the variable F in MATLAB workspace. Let us carry out the extraction as follows:

>>R=real(F) ↵   >>I=imag(F) ↵

R =   I =
    57.0000   -8.0000 -13.0000   -8.0000   0 -1.0000   0   1.0000
    -7.5000 24.7679   0.5000 28.2321   -0.8660   4.1340 -7.7942 -5.8660
    -7.5000 28.2321   0.5000 24.7679   0.8660   5.8660   7.7942 -4.1340

>>A=abs(F) ↵   >>P=angle(F) ↵

A =   P=
    57.0000   8.0623 13.0000   8.0623   0 -3.0172   3.1416   3.0172
    7.5498 25.1106   7.8102 28.8350   -3.0266   0.1654 -1.5067 -0.2049
    7.5498 28.8350   7.8102 25.1106   3.0266   0.2049   1.5067 -0.1654

As we implemented, the MATLAB functions real, imag, abs, and angle can pick up the real, imaginary, magnitude, and phase angle (in radians) components from the discrete Fourier transform matrix $F[u, v]$ and assign those to the workspace variables R, I, A, and P respectively. These assignees can be employed for further processing. If the phase angle were needed in degrees, we could use the command P=180/pi*angle(F).

♦ ♦ Flipping the two dimensional discrete Fourier transform coefficients about the half indices

Let us consider the one dimensional discrete Fourier transform $F[u]$ of a discrete function $f[m]$. From the properties of the discrete Fourier transform we know that both discrete functions have the sample number indexed from 0 to $M-1$. The Fourier spectrum (real, imaginary, Ö etc) $F[u]$ is even or odd function about the half-number indexed sample. The significant frequency components of $F[u]$ are located at the smaller and larger values of u (for example, $u = 0, 1, 2, Ö$ and $u = M-1$, $M-2, Ö$). Moreover the largest magnitude spectrum values occur at the edges of the u domain, for example, at $u = 0$ and $M-1$. If the function $f[m]$ contains too many low frequency components, the graph of $|F[u]|$ versus u only shows the variations at the edges. For

better display reason we flip the $|F[u]|$ versus u about the half index (for odd sample number about $u = \dfrac{M+1}{2}$

and for even sample number between $\dfrac{M}{2}$ and $\dfrac{M}{2}+1$ of $F[u]$) as follows:

With this sort of flipping the significant u components gather in the middle of the domain which exhibits more perceptibleness in frequency. Let us turn our attention to the MATLAB function fftshift that performs just mentioned half indexed flipping. Let us say we have the odd and even sample number row matrices x=[10 2 1 1 2] and y=[10 2 1 1 2 10] respectively. Following the half indexed flipping, one should obtain the flipped matrices as [1 2 10 2 1] and [1 2 10 10 2 1] for the x and y matrices respectively whose implementations are shown below:

for the odd number sample,   **for the even number sample,**
        >>x=[10 2 1 1 2]; ↵   >>y=[10 2 1 1 2 10]; ↵
        >>fftshift(x) ↵   >>fftshift(y) ↵

ans =   ans =
    1   2 10   2   1   1   2 10 10   2   1

Now we concentrate on the half indexed flipping in the two dimensional transform. The half indexed flipping happens in the direction of the discrete spatial frequency u as well as in the direction of v for the two dimensional discrete Fourier transform. The flipping is illustrated in the figure 4.1(b). The black region in the figure consolidates most significant spatial frequency components present in $F[u,v]$. The half indexed flipping of

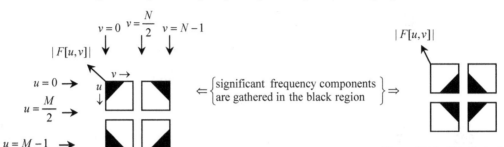

Figure 4.1(b) *Magnitude spectrum distribution of F[u, v] over u and v domains*

Figure 4.1(c) *Magnitude distribution of F[u, v] after half indexed flipping over both u and v domains*

$|F[u,v]|$ about $\left(\dfrac{M}{2},\dfrac{N}{2}\right)$ concentrates all significant frequency components around $\left(\dfrac{M}{2},\dfrac{N}{2}\right)$ which is easier to

discern (figure 4.1(c)). We know that $|F[u,v]|$ is $\begin{bmatrix} 57 & 8.0623 & 13 & 8.0623 \\ 7.5498 & 25.1106 & 7.8102 & 28.835 \\ 7.5498 & 28.835 & 7.8102 & 25.1106 \end{bmatrix}$ for aforementioned

modular image $f[m, n]$. The half indexed flipping on $|F[u,v]|$ first in the u and then in the v directions should

provide us $\begin{bmatrix} 7.5498 & 28.835 & 7.8102 & 25.1106 \\ 57 & 8.0623 & 13 & 8.0623 \\ 7.5498 & 25.1106 & 7.8102 & 28.835 \end{bmatrix}$ and $\begin{bmatrix} 7.8102 & 25.1106 & 7.5498 & 28.8350 \\ 13 & 8.0623 & 57 & 8.0623 \\ 7.8102 & 28.835 & 7.5498 & 25.1106 \end{bmatrix}$

respectively. In the MATLAB workspace the assignee A is holding $|F[u,v]|$ values from previous implementation. The expected flipping can easily be carried out with the furtherance of the **fftshift** function as follows:

    >>fftshift(A) ↵

    ans =
        7.8102   25.1106   7.5498   28.8350
       13.0000   8.0623   57.0000   8.0623
        7.8102   28.8350   7.5498   25.1106

✦ ✦ Two dimensional inverse discrete Fourier transform

Two dimensional (2D) inverse discrete Fourier transform (IDFT) is the recovery of the main image matrix $f[m, n]$ from the transform matrix $F[u, v]$. Resembling computation like the forward counterpart applies to the inverse two dimensional discrete Fourier transform whose formulation is given by $f[m, n] = \dfrac{1}{MN}\sum_{v=1}^{N}\sum_{u=1}^{M}F[u,v]e^{j\frac{2\pi(u-1)(m-1)}{M}}e^{j\frac{2\pi(n-1)(v-1)}{N}}$. Starting from the transform matrix $F[u, v]$ obtained in previous discussion,

let us recover the image information at the pixel (2,3) in other words $f[2,3] = 11$ of the $f[m, n]$ image matrix which

is computed as $f[2,3] = \dfrac{1}{12}\sum_{v=1}^{4}\sum_{u=1}^{3}F[u,v]e^{j\frac{2\pi(u-1)}{3}}e^{j\pi(v-1)}$ with the $m = 2$, $n = 3$, $M = 3$, and $N = 4$. Expanding the

double sum, we have $f[2,3] = \dfrac{1}{12}[57+(-7.5-j0.866)e^{j\frac{2\pi}{3}}+(-7.5+j0.866)e^{j\frac{4\pi}{3}}+(-8-j)e^{j\pi}+(24.7679+$

$j4.134)e^{j\frac{2\pi}{3}}e^{j\pi}+(28.2321+j5.866)e^{j\frac{4\pi}{3}}e^{j\pi}-13e^{j2\pi}+(0.5-j7.7942)e^{j\frac{2\pi}{3}}e^{j2\pi}+(0.5+j7.7942)e^{j\frac{4\pi}{3}}e^{j2\pi}+(-8+j)\times$

$e^{j3\pi}+(28.2321-j5.866)e^{j\frac{2\pi}{3}}e^{j3\pi}+(24.7679-j4.134)e^{j\frac{4\pi}{3}}e^{j3\pi}]=11$. Thus coefficient by coefficient calculation can

return us the whole original image matrix $f[m, n]$. The MATLAB function that enjoins the two dimensional inverse discrete Fourier transform is ifft2 (abbreviation of the inverse fast Fourier transform in 2 dimension). From the forward computation, we have the $F[u, v]$ assigned to F in the workspace of MATLAB. Let us conduct the following to obtain the $f[m, n]$:

>>ifft2(F) ↵

ans =

10	3	-5	6	← The exact recovery of $f[m, n]$
0	7	11	4	
-3	8	9	7	

As we expected from the transform.

4.2 Two dimensional discrete Fourier transform on an image

We assume that the reader has gone through previous section because most functions therefrom are drawn here. To apply the two dimensional discrete Fourier transform to a black and white image, the first step is you have to have the image matrix available in MATLAB workspace.

Considering the H image of the section 8.1, we wish to apply the two dimensional forward discrete Fourier transform on the image and to display the real, imaginary, magnitude, and phase angle components of the transform as another image. Let us carry out the following:

$v \rightarrow$
u
$\downarrow$

  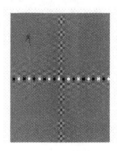

Figure 4.1(d) *Real spectrum of the binary image H*

Figure 4.1(e) *Half indexed flipping of the real spectrum of the binary image H*

Figure 4.1(f) *Imaginary spectrum of the binary image H following the half indexed flipping*

MATLAB Command

>>H=[zeros(50,10) [ones(20);zeros(10,20);ones(20)] zeros(50,10)]; ↵   ← H⇔ $f[m, n]$

>>F=fft2(H); R=real(F); I=imag(F); A=abs(F); P=angle(F); ↵   ← F⇔ $F[u, v]$

The first line of above command generates the image matrix and assigns to H. In the second line there are five different commands, the first of which takes the two dimensional discrete Fourier transform of the image matrix H and assigns that to F. The next four commands of which pick up the real, imaginary, magnitude, and phase components of the transform and assign those to the workspace variables R, I, A, and P respectively.

Employing the MATLAB function imshow displays each component of the transform as a digital image. To make sure that the image matrix elements are in accordance with the format of the imshow, let us see what the minimum and maximum values (section 10.10) of the elements in the real spectrum R are:

>>min(min(R)) ↵   >>max(max(R)) ↵

ans =   ans =

-508.2482   800

Above implementation says that the real spectrum of the transform held in R has the range from ñ508.2482 to 800.

We map the spectrum values considering $\begin{Bmatrix} -508.2482 \text{ as } 0 \\ 800 \text{ as } 1 \end{Bmatrix}$ with the addition of one more argument in the imshow as follows:

>>imshow(R,[-508.2482 800]) ↵

The second argument of the imshow is a two element row matrix indicating the minimum and maximum values present in the real spectrum R respectively. Figure 4.1(d) presents the real spectrum of the binary image H at the maximized window. It is apparent from the figure that the uppermost point on the left is white and that is not from the whiteness of the paper instead from the real spectrum values. The size of the real spectrum matrix Re{ $F[u, v]$ }

is the same as that of $f[m, n]$ (50×40 from workspace browser). The directive increments for the u and v are also shown by the arrows in figure 4.1(d). This convention is followed by the other component spectrum as well. The white in the real spectrum corresponds to 1 in [0,1] scale or in other words to the maximum 800 in [ñ508.2482,800] in actual data. Let us see what the value of the Re{ $F[u, v]$ } at coordinates (u , v)=(1,1) is by the following:

>>R(1,1) ↵

ans =
     800

It means the first element in the real spectrum matrix R is 800 as expected. The command imshow(R,[-508.2482 800]) is equivalent to the imshow(R,[ ]). Now we perform the half indexed flipping on the R, assign the output to R1, and then display the flipped real spectrum R1 as presented in the figure 4.1(e) by the following (maximize the window):

>>R1=fftshift(R); imshow(R1,[ ]) ↵

Referring to the last figure, significant pixel energy now gathers at the center of the spectrum unlike the cornered energy occupancy in the direct real spectrum. The procedure and functional application-style for the real spectrum will be engaged to the other three spectrums in the following.

  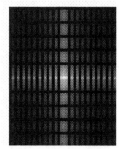

Figure 4.1(g) *Magnitude spectrum of the binary image H following the half indexed flipping*

Figure 4.1(h) *Phase spectrum of the binary image H following the half indexed flipping*

Figure 4.1(i) *Magnitude spectrum of the binary image H in the logarithmic scale* $\log_{10}(1+|F[u,v]|)$ *following the half indexed flipping*

We apply the half indexed flipping to the imaginary, magnitude, and phase spectrums stored in the variables I, A, and P from earlier implementation and assign the flipped versions to the workspace variables I1, A1, and P1 respectively as follows:

>>I1=fftshift(I); imshow(I1,[ ]) ↵   ← Flipped imaginary spectrum of H in the figure 4.1(f)
>>A1=fftshift(A); imshow(A1,[ ]) ↵   ← Flipped magnitude spectrum of H in the figure 4.1(g)
>>P1=fftshift(P); imshow(P1,[ ]) ↵   ← Flipped phase angle spectrum of H in the figure 4.1(h)

The turnouts of above executions are depicted each at the maximized window. MATLAB keeps one window open for the implementation of the imshow that is why above spectra are displayed in the same figure window. If the reader wants all four spectra to be displayed in separate windows, the MATLAB command figure can be exercised before imshow with a comma, for example, the imaginary one has the following syntax:

>>I1=fftshift(I); figure, imshow(I1,[ ]) ↵

Again if we wish to display all four spectra in a single window but in four subwindows, the MATLAB function subplot (section 3.9) can be exercised as follows:

>>R1=fftshift(R); subplot(221),imshow(R1,[ ]) ↵   ← shown in upper left subwindow
>>I1=fftshift(I); subplot(222),imshow(I1,[ ]) ↵   ← shown in upper right subwindow
>>A1=fftshift(A); subplot(223),imshow(A1,[ ]) ↵   ← shown in lower left subwindow
>>P1=fftshift(P); subplot(224),imshow(P1,[ ]) ↵   ← shown in lower right subwindow

However upon execution of above commands, the reader would see the figures 4.1(e), 4.1(f), 4.1(g), and 4.1(h) in a single window. If you wish to add title or name of the figure, that can be added from the figure window menu bar (for example, Insert → Title for the figure caption) by bringing mouse pointer first to the specific subwindow.

Very often the magnitude spectrum of a digital image receives priority or much addressed compared to the other spectrums in the image processing. The reason is the spectrum is related with the image gray level energy of the original image. Above all the range of the transform values is wide in the magnitude spectrum. For example, let us see the minimum and maximum values of aforementioned magnitude spectrum for the letter H:

>>min(min(A)) ↵   >>max(max(A)) ↵

ans =   ans =
            0   800

When displayed as a black and white image, the variation from 0 (black) to 800 (white) requires employing 801 gray levels if every integer variation is counted. But the function imshow has the default gray level number 256. Most of the values in the magnitude spectrum of the figure 4.1(g) are around 800 that is why we wee see a bright rectangular spot at the center of the spectrum. Logarithmic operation on the magnitude spectrum ($\log_{10} | F[u,v] |$) can reduce the wide range to a close one. But the problem is theoretically $\log_{10} 0$ is minus infinity so what we do is

we add 1 to all elements in the spectrum and apply the logarithmic operation. Thus we avoid the minus infinity situation and map the magnitude spectrum values from 0–800 to 1–801. Since $\log_{10} 800 = 2.9031$ and $\log_{10} 801 = 2.9036$, a third digit error is introduced in doing so – for practical reasons that can be ignored. Mathematically one can describe the operation as $\log_{10}(1+| F[u,v] |)$. Let us perform the operation $\log_{10}(1+| F[u,v] |)$ on the magnitude spectrum $| F[u,v] |$ stored in A and assign the result to the workspace variable A2 as follows:

>>A2=log10(1+A); ↵

The common logarithm $\log_{10} x$ has the MATLAB counterpart log10(x). Let us see the magnitude spectrum (close the previous window or use the command figure) in the logarithmic scale by the following:

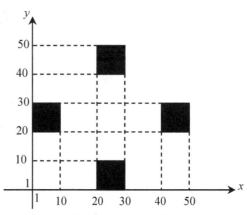

Figure 4.2(a) *A binary image of four square blocks*

>>imshow(fftshift(A2),[ ]) ↵

The result is the spectrum of the figure 4.1(i). The higher spatial frequencies of the spectrum ($\log_{10}(1+| F[u,v] |)$ values for the increasing u and v) are dormant in the standard scale depiction of the figure 4.1(g). Due to the logarithmic operation, the high frequency portion (increasing radius from the center) of the spectrum becomes conspicuous. Just to explore, the minimum and maximum in the logarithmic spectrum are obtained as:

>>min(min(A2)) ↵   >>max(max(A2)) ↵

ans =   ans =
            0   2.9036

The wide range of the image magnitude spectrum values 0-800 is now mapped to 0-2.9036 because of the $\log_{10}(1+| F[u,v] |)$ operation. If the spectrum $| F[u,v] |$ does not possess the 0 minimum value and the minimum value is greater than 1, there is no need to add 1. The reader can directly perform the $\log_{10}(| F[u,v] |)$ operation. But we confirm that the minimum value in the $| F[u,v] |$ is 1. The reason is when x changes from 0 to 1, $\log_{10} x$ changes from $-\infty$ to 0, an abrupt change in the gray level value turns the significant frequency components trivial. Let us say the minimum value in $| F[u,v] |$ is 0.1. To turn the minimum element to 1, we add 0.9 to all elements of $| F[u,v] |$ prior to the logarithmic operation. In that case we actually perform $\log_{10}(0.9+| F[u,v] |)$ not $\log_{10}(1+| F[u,v] |)$. The important point is even in the logarithmic domain we want to have the minimum value in the spectrum as 0. The function fftshift does not affect the spectrum element values rather position indices.

The two dimensional Fourier transform is the fundamental transform of the digital image processing for which we presented above elaborate implementation. The terminology, notation, and variable we exercised so far will be applied to few more image examples in the following.

♦ ♦ Example A

Let us find the half indexedly flipped real, imaginary, logarithmic magnitude, and phase spectrums of the four large square dot image of the figure 4.2(a).

A practical digital image literally contains thousands of pixels so taking the origin at (0,0) or (1,1) does not matter a lot in the image representation. Referring to figure 4.2(a), the square dots have the corner coordinates as follows – left square: $\begin{cases}(1,20)\\(10,20)\\(10,30)\\(1,30)\end{cases}$, right square: $\begin{cases}(40,20)\\(50,20)\\(50,30)\\(40,30)\end{cases}$, lower square: $\begin{cases}(20,1)\\(30,1)\\(30,10)\\(20,10)\end{cases}$, and upper square: $\begin{cases}(20,40)\\(30,40)\\(30,50)\\(20,50)\end{cases}$.

First we form a matrix X of ones of order 50×50 in order to construct the binary image (section 8.1) background of the figure 4.2(a) by writing **ones(50)** assuming $\left\{\begin{array}{l}\text{0 for foreground}\\\text{1 for background}\end{array}\right\}$. MATLAB has its solitary way of representing matrices for example the left square dot has the x variation from 1 to 10 and the y variation from 20 to 30. The elementsí selection for the left square can take place by writing X(1:10,20:30) in MATLAB. What we do is just place 0 for these elements by writing X(1:10,20:30)=0. Similarly the other three square dots can be selected and set to zero by writing X(40:50,20:30)=0, X(20:30,1:10)=0, and X(20:30,40:50)=0 for the right, lower, and upper square respectively. However the formal presentation of the commands is as follows:

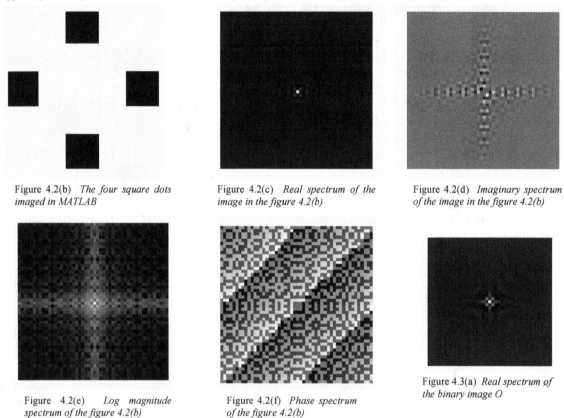

Figure 4.2(b) *The four square dots imaged in MATLAB*

Figure 4.2(c) *Real spectrum of the image in the figure 4.2(b)*

Figure 4.2(d) *Imaginary spectrum of the image in the figure 4.2(b)*

Figure 4.2(e) *Log magnitude spectrum of the figure 4.2(b)*

Figure 4.2(f) *Phase spectrum of the figure 4.2(b)*

Figure 4.3(a) *Real spectrum of the binary image O*

MATLAB Command

```
>>X=ones(50); X(1:10,20:30)=0; X(40:50,20:30)=0; ↵
>>X(20:30,1:10)=0; X(20:30,40:50)=0; ↵
>>figure,imshow(X) ↵
```

Presented in the figure 4.2(b) is the MATLAB display of the image. Now we exercise various commands for the spectrumsí finding as follows where the variables have their usual meanings:

```
>>F=fft2(X); R=real(F); I=imag(F); A=abs(F); P=angle(F); ↵
>>R1=fftshift(R); figure,imshow(R1,[ ]) ↵   ← command for the flipped real spectrum
>>I1=fftshift(I); figure,imshow(I1,[ ]) ↵   ← command for the flipped imaginary spectrum
```

In implementing so we end up with the figures 4.2(c) and 4.2(d) for the real and imaginary spectrums respectively each at the maximized window. Prior to taking the logarithmic spectrum stored in A, we should be vigilant about the minimum value of the magnitude spectrum $|F[u,v]|$ and let us find it as follows:

```
>>m=min(min(A)) ↵   ← minimum value of |F[u,v]| is assigned to the workspae variable m
```

```
m =
      0.0094
```

The difference between 1 and 0.0094 is 0.9906 therefore we add 0.9906 (equivalent to 1-m) to the magnitude spectrum held in A and apply the logarithm as follows:

```
>>A1=log10(1-m+A); ↵   ← A1 holds the logarithmic magnitude spectrum of the image
```

It is advisable to store the minimum value of $|F[u,v]|$ to some variable m and use 1-m in the logarithmic computation. The problem is when MATLAB displays the decimal numbers, it truncates the numbers after 4 decimal places in short format which does not appear on the screen. Those ignored decimal parts can again raise the problem of considering the $|F[u,v]|$ values being less than 1. However let us see the rest two spectrums, which are the logarithmic magnitude and the phase, of the four square dots as follows:

>>figure,imshow(fftshift(A1),[ ]) ↵   ← command for the flipped log magnitude spectrum

>>P1=fftshift(P); figure,imshow(P1,[ ]) ↵ ← command for the flipped phase spectrum

Figures 4.2(e) and 4.2(f) show the implementational results for the log-magnitude and phase spectrums at the maximized window respectively.

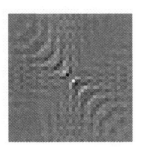

Figure 4.3(b) *Imaginary spectrum of the binary O*

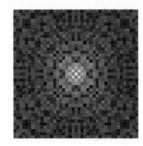

Figure 4.3(c) *Log magnitude spectrum of the binary O*

Figure 4.3(d) *Phase spectrum of the binary O*

Figure 4.3(e) *Real spectrum of the binary image L*

Figure 4.3(f) *Imaginary spectrum of the binary L*

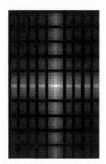

Figure 4.3(g) *Log magnitude spectrum of the binary L*

Figure 4.3(h) *Phase spectrum of the binary L*

✦ ✦ Example B

Referring to the binary image of the letter O from section 8.1, the generated image remains stored in the variable **M** after running the M-file code of the figure 8.1(i). Assign the **M** to **X** by writing **X=M;** in the MATLAB command prompt and exercise the last seven line commands to obtain the figures 4.3(a), 4.3(b), 4.3(c), and 4.3(d) for the real, imaginary, log magnitude, and phase spectra of the image O respectively (each at maximized window).

✦ ✦ Example C

The letter L binary image is also picked up from section 8.1. Having generated the matrix of L, execution of the command **X=L;** and the last seven lines of the example A is required to provide the pictures of the figures 4.3(e), 4.3(f), 4.3(g), and 4.3(h) for the real, imaginary, log magnitude, and phase spectra of the binary image L respectively (each at the maximized window).

Figure 4.3(i) *Real spectrum of the binary image L using 8 gray level display*

✦ ✦ Example D

Depending on the image analysis problem, we may seek for alternate display of a digital image pertaining to the gray level. The function **imshow** offers 256 default gray level display. Despite the gap reduction between the minimum and maximum gray level values by the logarithmic operation, it might be required that we employ the fixed gray level such as 4, 8, 16, Ö etc. Let us consider the real spectrum for the letter L of the example C and find its minimum and maximum gray level values as follows:

>>min(min(R)) ↵   >>max(max(R)) ↵

ans =   ans =

-194.7936   800

In many formerly gray level mappings we utilized the function mat2gray but did not mention the formula behind the mapping. We wish to introduce the gray level mapping formula from one range [R_{min} , R_{max}] to another [N_{min} , N_{max}], which is given by $N = \dfrac{(N_{max} - N_{min})R + N_{min}R_{max} - N_{max}R_{min}}{R_{max} - R_{min}}$. The N and R correspond to the latter and the former domain gray level values respectively.

Assume that we intend to display the real spectrum of L by 8 gray levels within the range [−194.7936,800]. But the function imshow does not accept the range and the gray level number together. If the gray level data is in [0,1], the imshow accepts the gray level number. Therefore we need the real spectrum values mapping as $\begin{Bmatrix} -194.7936 \\ 800 \end{Bmatrix} \Rightarrow \begin{Bmatrix} 0 \\ 1 \end{Bmatrix}$ for which R_{min} =−194.7936, R_{max} =800, N_{min} =0, and N_{max} =1. The R indicates any gray level value in the real spectrum matrix R. Plugging the range limits, the formula reduces to $N = \dfrac{R + 194.7936}{994.7936}$ that means all values in the real spectrum is added with 194.7936 and divided by the 994.7936. This is the computation that the MATLAB function mat2gray (abbreviation of the <u>mat</u>rix <u>2</u> (to) <u>gray</u> level) performs in obtaining the data in [0,1] as follows:

>>N=mat2gray(R); ↵

So the N contains the real spectrum as fractional number in [0,1] for the image L. Just to verify whether MATLAB mapped the new real spectrum matrix N correctly:

>>min(min(N)) ↵   >>max(max(N)) ↵

ans =   ans =
0   1

As we expected. To display the flipped real spectrum of L using 8 gray levels, all we need is the following:

>>imshow(fftshift(N),8) ↵

Now the second argument of imshow is not a two element matrix instead a single positive integer (8) indicating the required number of gray levels. However the figure 4.3(i) presents the 8 gray level display of the flipped real spectrum. The other spectrums (imaginary, log magnitude, or phase) can also be displayed at different gray levels.

♦ ♦ Example E

To display the real spectrum in the log-magnitude scale for the binary image L, the main point of consideration is the spectrum has the negative values (from the example D). The logarithm of a negative number is complex for example the minimum of Re{ $F[u,v]$ } is ñ194.7936 and $\log_{10}(-194.7936)$ =2.2896+ j 1.3644. The complex number has no significance in the gray level mapping. The solution is we first map the values from 1 to some specific value using the example D mentioned formula and then apply the logarithmic operation as we did before.

♦ ♦ Example F

The image examples chosen so far are mainly the binary ones but most practical images are colored. Now we wish to include the transform computation and visualization for one practical digital image. Considering gray form test.bmp of section 2.3 and making it available in the working directory, we exercise the following:

>>[Y,M]=imread('test.bmp'); ↵   ← Y and M hold the intensity and colormap matrices respectively
>>X=ind2gray(Y,M); ↵   ← turning the indexed image to gray one from Y and M

From the workspace browser, the X data for the image test.bmp is double class and in [0,1] including the fractional number from 0 to 1. The next step is to apply the last seven line commands of the example A for obtaining various spectrums. The image format does not have to be the .bmp, in fact any other digitally stored image files (table 2.A) can also be processed for viewing various image spectrums in a similar fashion.

♦ ♦ Color display of the Fourier spectrum

For analysis reason, color display of various spectrum is more meaningful. In section 9.10 we address how to turn a black and white or gray image to color one. In all these display we possess the black and white image of any mentioned spectrum. Let us consider the flipped imaginary spectrum of the four square dots from example A which is stored in the workspace variable I1. Our objective is to display the figure 4.2(d) in color form. We draw the function grayslice from the section 9.10 and implement the color display with 16 levels as follows:

>>g=grayslice(I1,16); ↵
>>imshow(g,jet(16)) ↵   ← MATLAB figure window shows the colored spectrum

4.3 Two dimensional discrete cosine transform

The formula frame defined for the two dimensional discrete Fourier transform is based on the complex exponential thereby involving all image processing calculations complex whether the domain is direct or inverse. The involvement of two components of a complex number naturally requires significant computational load and memory space. The transform kernel connected with the two dimensional (2D) discrete cosine transform (DCT) are solely the cosine functions which bring about the computations on real numbers. Anyhow the two dimensional forward discrete cosine transform $F[u,v]$ of a digital image matrix $f[m,n]$ is given by $F[u,v]=$

$$\sum_{n=1}^{N}\sum_{m=1}^{M}w[u,v]f[m,n]\cos\frac{\pi(2m-1)(u-1)}{2M}\cos\frac{\pi(2n-1)(v-1)}{2N}, \quad \text{where} \quad w[u,v]=\begin{cases} \sqrt{\dfrac{1}{MN}} & when \ u=1 \ and \ v=1 \\ \sqrt{\dfrac{2}{MN}} & when \ u=1 \ and \ v\geq 2 \ or \\ & v=1 \ and \ u\geq 2 \\ \sqrt{\dfrac{4}{MN}} & else \end{cases},$$

$w[u,v]$ is called the weight factor of the transform, m and u vary from 1 to M, and n and v vary from 1 to N.

As an elementary image example, we consider the modular image matrix exercised in section 4.1. Of coarse, both the image matrix $f[m,n]$ and DCT transform matrix $F[u,v]$ have the identical order that is $M\times N$.

Let us compute few discrete cosine transform coefficients as follows: $F[1,1]=\dfrac{1}{\sqrt{12}}\sum_{n=1}^{4}\sum_{m=1}^{3}f[m,n]=16.4545$, $F[2,1]=$

$$\sqrt{\frac{2}{12}}\sum_{n=1}^{4}\sum_{m=1}^{3}f[m,n]\cos\frac{\pi(2m-1)}{6}=\frac{1}{\sqrt{6}}[(10+3-5+6)\cos\frac{\pi}{6}+(0+7+11+4)\cos\frac{\pi}{2}+(-3+8+9+7)\cos\frac{5\pi}{6}] \ = \ -2.4749,$$

$$F[3,3] \ = \ \frac{2}{\sqrt{12}}\sum_{n=1}^{4}\sum_{m=1}^{3}f[m,n]\cos\frac{\pi(2m-1)}{3}\cos\frac{\pi(2n-1)}{4} \ = \ \frac{2}{\sqrt{12}}[\{10\cos\frac{\pi}{3}+0\cos\frac{3\pi}{3}-3\cos\frac{5\pi}{3}\}\cos\frac{\pi}{4}+\{3\cos\frac{\pi}{3}+$$

$$7\cos\frac{3\pi}{3}+8\cos\frac{5\pi}{3}\}\cos\frac{3\pi}{4}+\{-5\cos\frac{\pi}{3}+11\cos\frac{3\pi}{3}+9\cos\frac{5\pi}{3}\}\cos\frac{5\pi}{4}+\{6\cos\frac{\pi}{3}+4\cos\frac{3\pi}{3}+7\cos\frac{5\pi}{3}\}\cos\frac{7\pi}{4}]= 6.7361,$$

and so on. Thus we obtain the whole forward two dimensional discrete cosine transform matrix as $F[u,v]=$

$$\begin{bmatrix} 16.4545 & -3.3030 & -2.5981 & -2.6938 \\ -2.4749 & 8.1892 & 10.9602 & -1.4787 \\ -1.8371 & 2.1905 & 6.7361 & -3.7796 \end{bmatrix}$$ – a clumsy computation indeed. The MATLAB function **dct2**

(abbreviation of the discrete cosine transform in 2 dimensions) can help us bypass so much computation for the two dimensional discrete cosine transform. Let us conduct the computation of $F[u,v]$ as follows:

MATLAB Command

```
>>f=[10 3 -5 6;0 7 11 4;-3 8 9 7]; ↵
>>F=dct2(f) ↵

F =

        16.4545   -3.3030   -2.5981   -2.6938
        -2.4749    8.1892   10.9602   -1.4787
        -1.8371    2.1905    6.7361   -3.7796
```

The first line is the assignment of the image matrix $f[m,n]$ to **f**, the second line is the application of the **dct2** on **f**, and the computed result is stored to the workspace variable **F** which essentially represents the $F[u,v]$. Most image processing texts use the notation of the independent variableís change from 0. The modified expression could be

$$F[u,v]=\sum_{n=0}^{N-1}\sum_{m=0}^{M-1}w[u,v]f[m,n]\cos\frac{\pi(2m+1)u}{2M}\cos\frac{\pi(2n+1)v}{2N}, \quad \text{where} \quad w[u,v]=\begin{cases} \sqrt{\dfrac{1}{MN}} & when \ u=0 \ and \ v=0 \\ \sqrt{\dfrac{2}{MN}} & when \ u=0 \ and \ v\geq 1 \ or \\ & v=0 \ and \ u\geq 1 \\ \sqrt{\dfrac{4}{MN}} & else \end{cases} \quad \text{and}$$

$\begin{cases} 0\leq m \ or \ u \leq M-1 \\ 0\leq n \ or \ v \ \leq N-1 \end{cases}$. Either expression provides the same transform coefficients for the $F[u,v]$.

♣ ♣ Two dimensional inverse discrete cosine transform

Along with the forward transform, the inverse discrete cosine transform is also there for the recovery of $f[m,n]$ from $F[u,v]$. The two dimensional (2D) inverse discrete cosine transform (IDCT) has the associated

formulation $f[m,\ n]=\sum\limits_{v=1}^{N}\sum\limits_{u=1}^{M}w[u,v]F[u,v]\cos\dfrac{\pi(2m-1)(u-1)}{2M}\cos\dfrac{\pi(2n-1)(v-1)}{2N}$ with aforementioned weight factor

$w[u,v]$. We recover at least one gray level from the last numerical $F[u,v]$ for example $f[2,3]=$

$\sum\limits_{v=1}^{4}\sum\limits_{u=1}^{3}w[u,v]F[u,v]\cos\dfrac{\pi(u-1)}{2}\cos\dfrac{5\pi(v-1)}{8} = \dfrac{16.4545}{\sqrt{12}}+\sqrt{\dfrac{2}{12}}(-2.4749\cos\dfrac{\pi}{2}-1.8371\cos\pi)+\sqrt{\dfrac{2}{12}}(-3.3030\cos\dfrac{5\pi}{8})+$

$\dfrac{2}{\sqrt{12}}(8.1892\cos\dfrac{\pi}{2}\cos\dfrac{5\pi}{8}+ \quad 2.1905\cos\pi\cos\dfrac{5\pi}{8}) \quad + \quad \sqrt{\dfrac{2}{12}}(-2.5981\cos\dfrac{5\pi}{4})+\dfrac{2}{\sqrt{12}}(10.9602\cos\dfrac{\pi}{2}\cos\dfrac{5\pi}{4}+$

$6.7361\cos\pi\cos\dfrac{5\pi}{4})+\sqrt{\dfrac{2}{12}}(-2.6938\cos\dfrac{15\pi}{8})+\dfrac{2}{\sqrt{12}}(-1.4787\cos\dfrac{\pi}{2}\cos\dfrac{15\pi}{8}-3.7796\cos\pi\cos\dfrac{15\pi}{8}) =11.$ In one pixel so

much calculation is involved for sure 12 pixelsí recovery would take not less than one hour. In a practical image we have thousands of pixels so you can imagine how much time a computer saves. Anyhow the MATLAB function idct2 (abbreviation of the inverse discrete cosine transform in 2 dimensions) can relieve us from the lengthy calculation. Found two dimensional forward discrete cosine transform coefficients for the modular image are stored in the workspace variable F, let us apply the function as follows:

MATLAB Command

```
>>idct2(F) ↵
```

$v \rightarrow$

```
ans =                               ← Exact recovery of f[m, n]
    10.0000    3.0000   -5.0000    6.0000
    -0.0000    7.0000   11.0000    4.0000
    -3.0000    8.0000    9.0000    7.0000
```

u
$\downarrow$

Due to the machine accuracy, very small decimal parts appear in the inverse transform. For practical reasons they can be truncated or rounded.

Figure 4.4(a) Two dimensional discrete cosine transform of the binary image H

♣ ♣ Two dimensional discrete cosine transform on a digital image

For the discrete cosine transform, all we have is the real coefficients. Let us apply the two dimensional forward discrete cosine transform (2D DCT) to the binary image H of section 8.1 by the following:

MATLAB Command

```
>>H=[zeros(50,10) [ones(20);zeros(10,20);ones(20)] zeros(50,10)]; ↵        ← H⇔ f[m, n]
>>R=dct2(H); ↵                                                              ← R⇔ F[u,v]
>>imshow(R,[ ]) ↵                          ← Displaying the R by first mapping in [0,1] by [ ]
```

The 2D DCT of the binary image H as a digital image is shown in the figure 4.4(a). Unlike the two dimensional discrete Fourier transform, the significant spatial frequencies are located close to the edges $u=1$ and $v=1$. Most frequency concentrations happen around $(1,1)$ in the u-v plane of the figure 4.4(a). How the transform can be applied to a practical image is addressed in section 4.2 (example F). Instead of applying the fft2, the reader needs to exercise dct2 for the digital image stored in X.

4.4 Digital image transform matrices

Often practiced digital image processing transforms partake one common thought that any digital image matrix $f[m,n]$ of order $M \times N$ can be transformed to the forward transform matrix $F[u,v]$ of order $M \times N$ with the aid of two transform matrices T_1 and T_2 of orders $M \times M$ and $N \times N$ respectively. This kind of the transform matrix can be found for the two dimensional discrete Fourier transform, two dimensional discrete cosine transform, and two dimensional Hadamard transform (section 4.5). Attached figure 4.4(b)

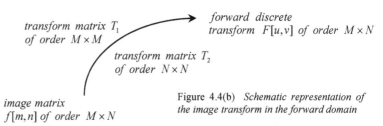

transform matrix T_1 of order $M \times M$

forward discrete transform $F[u,v]$ of order $M \times N$

transform matrix T_2 of order $N \times N$

image matrix $f[m,n]$ of order $M \times N$

Figure 4.4(b) Schematic representation of the image transform in the forward domain

presents the schematic representation of the common two dimensional discrete image transform in the forward domain. The image transform matrices are derived basically from the kernel of the related transform. One can define the transform relationship in terms of the matrix multiplication as $F[u,v] = T_1 \, f[m, n] \, T_2$. Note that both the T_1 and T_2 are a square matrix and their orders come from the row and column pixel numbers of the image matrix $f[m, n]$ respectively. The main advantage of using the transform matrices is we can avoid the summation computational form in the computation of the forward discrete transform. Forward transform is the analysis phase of the image processing while on the contrary the inverse transform is the synthesis phase. Figure 4.4(c) shows the schematics of the inverse discrete transform in the act of the matrix expression $f[m, n] = T_1 \, F[u,v] \, T_2$. Now we explain how these transform matrices can be reached and applied to a digital image.

✦ ✦ Discrete Fourier transform matrix

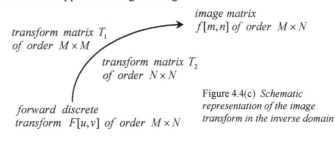

The discrete Fourier transform matrix T is computed from the complex exponential function $T[m,n] = e^{-\frac{j2\pi(m-1)(n-1)}{N}}$, where each of the m and n can vary from 1 to N and N comes from the row or column directed pixel number in the given

Figure 4.4(c) *Schematic representation of the image transform in the inverse domain*

digital image matrix $f[m,n]$. As an example, let us say the N is 3. When $\begin{Bmatrix} m = 1 \\ n = 1 \end{Bmatrix}$ and $\begin{Bmatrix} m = 2 \\ n = 3 \end{Bmatrix}$, we have $T[1,1] = 1$

and $T[2,3] = e^{-\frac{j2\pi(2-1)(3-1)}{3}} = -0.5 + j\,0.8660$. Thus inserting all m and n results the discrete Fourier transform matrix

of order 3×3 as $\begin{bmatrix} 1 & 1 & 1 \\ 1 & -0.5 - j0.866 & -0.5 + j0.866 \\ 1 & -0.5 + j0.866 & -0.5 - j0.866 \end{bmatrix}$ considering the m and n as the position indexes of the

matrix elements. In a similar computation one can obtain the discrete Fourier transform matrix of order 4×4 as

$\begin{bmatrix} 1 & 1 & 1 & 1 \\ 1 & -j & -1 & j \\ 1 & -1 & 1 & -1 \\ 1 & j & -1 & -j \end{bmatrix}$. Our objective is to obtain the discrete Fourier transform matrix for which we employ the

MATLAB function **dftmtx** (abbreviation for the <u>d</u>iscrete <u>F</u>ourier <u>t</u>ransform <u>m</u>atri<u>x</u>) with the input argument N. Let us obtain the 4×4 discrete Fourier transform matrix and assign that to T as follows:

MATLAB Command

```
>>T=dftmtx(4) ↵

T =
        1.0000        1.0000        1.0000        1.0000
        1.0000     0 - 1.0000i       -1.0000     0 + 1.0000i
        1.0000       -1.0000        1.0000       -1.0000
        1.0000     0 + 1.0000i       -1.0000     0 - 1.0000i
```

Our objective is served. Now we wish to verify that the transform matrix particularly substitutes the summational

computation. Recall from section 4.1 that we transformed the digital image $f[m, n] = \begin{bmatrix} 10 & 3 & -5 & 6 \\ 0 & 7 & 11 & 4 \\ -3 & 8 & 9 & 7 \end{bmatrix}$ to the

2D Fourier transform matrix $F[u, v] = \begin{bmatrix} 57 & -8 - j & -13 & -8 + j \\ -7.5 - j0.866 & 24.7679 + j4.134 & 0.5 - j7.7942 & 28.2321 - j5.866 \\ -7.5 + j0.866 & 28.2321 + j5.866 & 0.5 + j7.7942 & 24.7679 - j4.134 \end{bmatrix}$

with the use of the two dimensional summation formula. We should end up with the same $F[u, v]$ transform matrix if we utilize the transform matrices as follows:

```
>>f=[10 3 -5 6;0 7 11 4;-3 8 9 7]; ↵
>>T1=dftmtx(3); T2=dftmtx(4); ↵
>>F=T1*f*T2 ↵

F =
```

57.0000	-8.0000 - 1.0000i	-13.0000	-8.0000 + 1.0000i
-7.5000 - 0.8660i	24.7679 + 4.1340i	0.5000 - 7.7942i	28.2321 - 5.8660i
-7.5000 + 0.8660i	28.2321 + 5.8660i	0.5000 + 7.7942i	24.7679 - 4.1340i

The T1 and T2 in above command correspond to the Fourier transform matrices T_1 and T_2 of orders 3×3 (because the number of rows in $f[m, n]$ is 3) and 4×4 (because the number of columns in $f[m, n]$ is 4) respectively. We generate them by writing the commands dftmtx(3) and dftmtx(4) respectively. The operator * indicates the matrix multiplication. The command F=T1*f*T2 is equivalent to implementing $F[u,v] = T_1 \ f[m, n] \ T_2$.

Having found the forward transform, the matrix concept applies to the $F[u,v]$ evenly to obtain the inverse transform for which the necessary formula is $f[m, n] = \dfrac{\overset{*}{T_1} F[u,v] \overset{*}{T_2}}{MN}$, where $\overset{*}{T_1}$ and $\overset{*}{T_2}$ are the complex conjugates of the matrices T_1 and T_2 respectively. Also the M and N refer to the numbers of rows and columns in the transform matrix $F[u, v]$ respectively. Let us recover the original image matrix $f[m, n]$ from the stored $F[u, v]$ in F employing the Fourier transform matrices as follows:

>>f=conj(T1)*F*conj(T2)/12 ↵

f =

10	3	-5	6
0	7	11	4
-3	8	9	7

So we successfully recovered the $f[m, n]$ from $F[u, v]$. The MATLAB function conj takes the complex conjugate on all elements in a matrix for instance the conj(T1) returns $\begin{bmatrix} 1 & 1 & 1 \\ 1 & -0.5 + j0.866 & -0.5 - j0.866 \\ 1 & -0.5 - j0.866 & -0.5 + j0.866 \end{bmatrix}$.

♦ ♦ Discrete cosine transform matrix

The discrete cosine transform matrix of order $N \times N$ is given by the expression $T = \left[w[n]\cos\dfrac{\pi(2m-1)(n-1)}{2N} \right]^*$ along with the weight factor $w[n] = \begin{cases} \dfrac{1}{\sqrt{N}} & when \ n=1 \\ \sqrt{\dfrac{2}{N}} & else \end{cases}$, where both the m and n are the positive integers and can vary from 1 to N and the operator * indicates the matrix transpose not the complex conjugate. To provide with an example, let us obtain the discrete cosine transform matrix for $N = 3$. From the expression of T, one can easily write $T = \begin{bmatrix} \dfrac{1}{\sqrt{3}} & \sqrt{\dfrac{2}{3}}\cos\dfrac{\pi}{6} & \sqrt{\dfrac{2}{3}}\cos\dfrac{\pi}{3} \\ \dfrac{1}{\sqrt{3}} & \sqrt{\dfrac{2}{3}}\cos\dfrac{\pi}{2} & \sqrt{\dfrac{2}{3}}\cos\pi \\ \dfrac{1}{\sqrt{3}} & \sqrt{\dfrac{2}{3}}\cos\dfrac{5\pi}{6} & \sqrt{\dfrac{2}{3}}\cos\dfrac{5\pi}{3} \end{bmatrix}^* = \begin{bmatrix} 0.5774 & 0.5774 & 0.5774 \\ 0.7071 & 0 & -0.7071 \\ 0.4082 & -0.8165 & 0.4082 \end{bmatrix}$

considering the m and n are the position indices of the matrix elements in T. It should be pointed out that the transposition takes place following the computation of the matrix elements for all m and n's. The corresponding MATLAB function we have is dctmtx (abbreviation for the discrete cosine transform matrix) whose input argument can be the N. Let us find the 3×3 discrete cosine transform matrix as follows:

MATLAB Command
>>T=dctmtx(3) ↵

T =

0.5774	0.5774	0.5774
0.7071	0.0000	-0.7071
0.4082	-0.8165	0.4082

With the help of the discrete cosine transform matrix we can also transform the image matrix $f[m, n]$ of order $M \times N$ to the forward discrete cosine transform matrix $F[u, v]$ of order $M \times N$ that necessitates to use the matrix expression $F[u,v] = T_1 \ f[m, n] \ T_2^{\ *}$, where T_1 and T_2 are the discrete cosine transform matrices of orders $M \times M$

and $N \times N$ respectively. Note that we need the transposition of the T_2. Concerning the section 4.3, we transformed the image matrix $f[m, n] = \begin{bmatrix} 10 & 3 & -5 & 6 \\ 0 & 7 & 11 & 4 \\ -3 & 8 & 9 & 7 \end{bmatrix}$ to the forward transform matrix $F[u,v] =$

$\begin{bmatrix} 16.4545 & -3.3030 & -2.5981 & -2.6938 \\ -2.4749 & 8.1892 & 10.9602 & -1.4787 \\ -1.8371 & 2.1905 & 6.7361 & -3.7796 \end{bmatrix}$ utilizing the two dimensional summation formula. Our aim here is to

attain the identical image transform matrix employing the discrete cosine transform matrices T_1 and T_2 for which we conduct the following:

MATLAB Command

```
>>f=[10 3 -5 6;0 7 11 4;-3 8 9 7]; ↵
>>T1=dctmtx(3); T2=dctmtx(4); ↵
>>F=T1*f*T2' ↵

F =
        16.4545  -3.3030  -2.5981  -2.6938
        -2.4749   8.1892  10.9602  -1.4787
        -1.8371   2.1905   6.7361  -3.7796
```

Since the row and column directed pixels in the $f[m, n]$ are 3 and 4, we require the T_1 and T_2 of orders 3×3 and 4×4 which are generated in the second line of above command by writing T1=dctmtx(3); and T2=dctmtx(4); respectively. The operator ' indicates the matrix transpose of the matrix T2. The command F=T1*f*T2' is the straightforward implementation of the matrix expression $F[u,v] = T_1\, f[m,\,n]\, T_2{}^*$.

The next legitimate expectation is to invert the transform matrix $F[u,v]$ with the intermediacy of the matrix expression $f[m,\,n] = T_1{}^*\, F[u,v]\, T_2$ so that we are successful in obtaining the original image matrix $f[m,\,n]$. Now the transposition of T_1 is required unlike the forward counterpart. The $F[u,v]$ coefficients are present in the workspace, let us see how MATLAB replaces the inverse two dimensional summation computation:

```
>>T1'*F*T2 ↵

ans =
        10.0000   3.0000  -5.0000   6.0000
        -0.0000   7.0000  11.0000   4.0000
        -3.0000   8.0000   9.0000   7.0000
```

which is exactly the same as the original image matrix $f[m, n]$.

✦ ✦ Hadamard transform matrix

The number of rows or columns of a Hadamard transform matrix, which is essentially a square matrix of order $N \times N$, must follow $N = 2^m$ where $m = 1, 2, 3\ddot{\rm O}$ etc. The lowest order Hadamard matrix is of order 2×2 for

which $N = 2$ and $m = 1$ and is given by $H_{2\times2} = \begin{bmatrix} 1 & 1 \\ 1 & -1 \end{bmatrix}$. Advantage of recursive relationship is taken to form the

Hadamard matrices of other orders. Letting H_N represent the Hadamard matrix of order $N \times N$, the recursive

relationship is given by $H_N = \begin{bmatrix} H_{N/2} & H_{N/2} \\ H_{N/2} & -H_{N/2} \end{bmatrix}$ hence $H_{4\times4} = H_4 = \begin{bmatrix} H_2 & H_2 \\ H_2 & -H_2 \end{bmatrix} = \begin{bmatrix} \begin{bmatrix} 1 & 1 \\ 1 & -1 \end{bmatrix} & \begin{bmatrix} 1 & 1 \\ 1 & -1 \end{bmatrix} \\ \begin{bmatrix} 1 & 1 \\ 1 & -1 \end{bmatrix} & -\begin{bmatrix} 1 & 1 \\ 1 & -1 \end{bmatrix} \end{bmatrix} =$

$\begin{bmatrix} 1 & 1 & 1 & 1 \\ 1 & -1 & 1 & -1 \\ 1 & 1 & -1 & -1 \\ 1 & -1 & -1 & 1 \end{bmatrix}$. Similarly the Hadamard matrix of order 8×8 can be generated by $\begin{bmatrix} H_4 & H_4 \\ H_4 & -H_4 \end{bmatrix}$. To

generate the Hadamard matrix of order $N \times N$, we use the command hadamard(N). Formation of different Hadamard matrices is shown exercising the function as follows:

MATLAB Command

for the matrix of order 2×2,
>>H=hadamard(2) ↵

H =
     1   1
     1 -1

for the matrix of order 4×4,
>>H=hadamard(4) ↵

H =
     1   1   1   1
     1 -1   1 -1
     1   1 -1 -1
     1 -1 -1   1

for the matrix of order 8×8,
>>H=hadamard(8) ↵

H =
     1   1   1   1   1   1   1   1
     1 -1   1 -1   1 -1   1 -1
     1   1 -1 -1   1   1 -1 -1
     1 -1 -1   1   1 -1 -1   1
     1   1   1   1 -1 -1 -1 -1
     1 -1   1 -1 -1   1 -1   1
     1   1 -1 -1 -1 -1   1   1
     1 -1 -1   1 -1   1   1 -1

4.5 Two dimensional discrete Hadamard transform

The formal definition employing the two dimensional summation of the Hadamard transform can be found in [20]. We present here only the matrix method for the computation of the transform. In the last section we defined the Hadamard matrices whose row or column directed pixel number can only be the power of 2.

♦ ♦ Two dimensional forward Hadamard transform

The forward two dimensional Hadamard transform $F[u, v]$ of the image $f[m, n]$ can be defined in terms of the matrix multiplication as $F[u, v] = H_1 \, f[m, n] \, H_2$. Both the image matrix $f[m, n]$ and the transform matrix $F[u, v]$ are of order $M \times N$. Also the M or N must be the power of 2, for example, 4×8, 256×256 Ö etc not any arbitrary image size. The Hadamard matrices H_1 and H_2 have the orders $M \times M$ or $N \times N$ respectively. As an example, we can consider the image matrix $f[m, n] = \begin{bmatrix} 2 & -5 & 3 & 8 \\ 4 & 7 & 23 & 56 \end{bmatrix}$ where $M = 2$ and $N = 4$ hence the Hadamard matrices H_1 and H_2 for the transform should be of orders 2×2 and 4×4 respectively. Employing the matrices of previous section we have $F[u, v] = \begin{bmatrix} 1 & 1 \\ 1 & -1 \end{bmatrix} \begin{bmatrix} 2 & -5 & 3 & 8 \\ 4 & 7 & 23 & 56 \end{bmatrix} \times$

$\begin{bmatrix} 1 & 1 & 1 & 1 \\ 1 & -1 & 1 & -1 \\ 1 & 1 & -1 & -1 \\ 1 & -1 & -1 & 1 \end{bmatrix} = \begin{bmatrix} 98 & -34 & -82 & 42 \\ -82 & 38 & 54 & -18 \end{bmatrix}$ following the matrix multiplication. Since there is no built-in function for the transform, we exercise the matrix approach as follows:

MATLAB Command
```
>>f=[2 -5 3 8;4 7 23 56]; ↵
>>H1=hadamard(2); H2=hadamard(4); ↵
>>F=H1*f*H2 ↵

F =
        98  -34  -82   42
       -82   38   54  -18
```
In the first line of above command we assign the new image matrix $f[m, n]$ to the worspace variable f. The Hadamard matrices of orders 2×2 and 4×4 are generated and assigned to the workspace variables H1 and H2 by writing H1=hadamard(2); and H2=hadamard(4); respectively. The command F=H1*f*H2 implements the forward transform $F[u, v] = H_1 \, f[m, n] \, H_2$ calculation.

♣ ♣ Two dimensional inverse Hadamard transform

As a sequel of the transform, we obtain the inverse Hadamard transform from the $F[u, v]$ using the matrix relationship $f[m, n] = \dfrac{H_1 F[u,v] H_2}{MN}$. Let us apply the matrix formula in the computed transform: $\dfrac{1}{2 \times 4} \begin{bmatrix} 1 & 1 \\ 1 & -1 \end{bmatrix}$

$$\times \begin{bmatrix} 98 & -34 & -82 & 42 \\ -82 & 38 & 54 & -18 \end{bmatrix} \begin{bmatrix} 1 & 1 & 1 & 1 \\ 1 & -1 & 1 & -1 \\ 1 & 1 & -1 & -1 \\ 1 & -1 & -1 & 1 \end{bmatrix} = \begin{bmatrix} 2 & -5 & 3 & 8 \\ 4 & 7 & 23 & 56 \end{bmatrix}$$ – the image matrix we started with. In

MATLAB we implement the matrix computation as follows:
```
>>H1*F*H2/8 ↵
```

```
ans =
        2   -5   3    8
        4    7  23   56
```

♣ ♣ Hadamard transform on a digital image using the matrix concept

One issue arises while taking the transform that the row or column pixel number in the generated or stored image must be the power of 2. Let us consider the binary L image from section 8.1:
```
>>L=[zeros(50,10) [ones(40,20);zeros(10,20)]]; ↵
>>size(L) ↵
```

```
ans =
        50   30
```

The image pixel size is 50×30. If we concentrate on the number forming from the power of 2, we have 2, 4, 8, 16, 32, 64, Ö etc. The closest size based on the power of 2 for the image could be 64×32. To feed the image to the Hadamard transform, we need to resize the image with the help of the MATLAB function imresize (section 3.7) as follows:
```
>>N=imresize(L,[64 32]); ↵
>>H1=hadamard(64); H2=hadamard(32); ↵
>>F=H1*N*H2; ↵
```

The first line in above command is to resize the image L to the pixel size 64×32 and assign the output image matrix to N. In the second line we generated the Hadamard matrices of orders 64 and 32 and assign the matrices to H1 and H2 respectively. The third line is just the computation of the Hadamard transform on the resized image of the L. Like the discrete cosine transform, the transform coefficients are all real. The transform display as an image can happen using the command imshow(F,[ ]).

4.6 Hotelling transform

The Hotelling transform is based on the local gray level statistical properties of a digital image. The transform has other names as well – eigenvector, principal component, or discrete Karhunen- Lo'eve (K-L) transform. To understand the theory of the Hotelling transform, we need to understand the concepts of eigenvalueñ eigenvector of matrix algebra and covariance of discrete random variables of statistics. In the following two subsections first we discuss the two concepts and then the transform is introduced in the third subsection.

4.6.1 Eigenvalues and eigenvectors of a square matrix

The concept of the eigenvalue-eigenvector is only applicable for the square matrix. If A is a square matrix of order $N \times N$, λ is a scalar, and I is an identity matrix of order $N \times N$, then the equation $|\lambda I - A| = 0$ is called the characteristic equation of the matrix A which is a polynomial of degree N and has N roots designated as λ_1, λ_2, Ö, λ_N. These roots of the characteristic equation are called the eigenvalues of the matrix A. Let us determine the eigenvalues of the square matrix $A = \begin{bmatrix} 3 & 4 & 5 \\ 4 & -3 & -1 \\ 0 & 0 & 3 \end{bmatrix}$. The characteristic equation of the matrix A is

$$|\lambda I - A| = \lambda \begin{bmatrix} 1 & 0 & 0 \\ 0 & 1 & 0 \\ 0 & 0 & 1 \end{bmatrix} \tilde{n} \begin{bmatrix} 3 & 4 & 5 \\ 4 & -3 & -1 \\ 0 & 0 & 3 \end{bmatrix} = (\lambda - 3)(\lambda + 5)(\lambda - 5) = 0$$ consequently the eigenvalues of A are −5, 3,

and 5. In MATLAB the function **eig** (from the <u>eig</u>envalue) can help us find the eigenvalues of a square matrix taking the matrix as its input argument whose implementation for the example matrix is as follows:

MATLAB Command

```
>>A=[3 4 5;4 -3 -1;0 0 3]; ↵
>>E=eig(A) ↵

E =
     5
    -5
     3
```

The eigenvalues of A as a column matrix are assigned to the workspace variable **E**. Depending on the nature of A, eigenvalues can be real or complex however the **eig** is suitable for handling complex eigenvalues in general.

There are N eigenvalues in the characteristic polynomial $|\lambda I - A|$. For each eigenvalue, there is a matrix X of order $N \times 1$ which satisfies the matrix equation $A X = \lambda X$. If the equation is satisfied by the vector X, then X is called an eigenvector of the matrix A. Matrix multiplication of A and X results the order of $A X$ as $N \times 1$ again the order of matrix λX is also $N \times 1$. For the N eigenvalues we must have N eigenvectors. The eigenvalues are unique but the eigenvectors are not. The reader is referred to [2] and [23] for theoretical finding of the eigenvectors in general.

Let us consider the matrix $A = \begin{bmatrix} 2 & 2 & 0 \\ 2 & 1 & 1 \\ -7 & 2 & -3 \end{bmatrix}$ for the eigenvector illustration. The order of A is 3×3

hence there are three eigenvalues and three eigenvectors of A. It is given that the eigenvalues of A are $\begin{Bmatrix} 3 \\ 1 \\ -4 \end{Bmatrix}$.

Also given $\begin{bmatrix} 0.0747 \\ -0.2242 \\ 0.9717 \end{bmatrix}$, $\begin{bmatrix} -0.6667 \\ -0.3333 \\ 0.6667 \end{bmatrix}$, and $\begin{bmatrix} -0.4364 \\ 0.2182 \\ 0.8729 \end{bmatrix}$ are the eigenvectors of A. We introduce now how these
$for\ \lambda = -4 \quad for\ \lambda = 1 \quad\quad for\ \lambda = 3$

eigenvectors can be obtained from MATLAB. One can place these three eigenvectors of A to form another square

matrix $Y = \begin{bmatrix} 0.0747 & -0.6667 & -0.4364 \\ -0.2242 & -0.3333 & 0.2182 \\ 0.9717 & 0.6667 & 0.8729 \end{bmatrix}$ (let us call it eigenmatrix). MATLAB does not return individual

eigenvector instead the eigenmatrix Y. Let us carry out the following to find eigenvalues and eigenvectors of A:

only for the eigenvalues,

```
>>A=[2 2 0;2 1 1;-7 2 -3]; ↵
>>E=eig(A) ↵

E =
    -4.0000
     3.0000
     1.0000
```

for the eigenvalues and eigenvectors,

```
>>[Y X]=eig(A) ↵

Y =
     0.0747   -0.6667   -0.4364
    -0.2242   -0.3333    0.2182
     0.9717    0.6667    0.8729
X =
    -4.0000        0        0
         0    3.0000        0
         0        0    1.0000
```

for picking up the second eigenvector,

```
>>Y(:,2) ↵

T =
    -0.6667
    -0.3333
     0.6667
>>diag(X) ↵

ans =
    -4.0000
     3.0000
     1.0000
```

Referring to above execution, the function **eig** returns only the eigenvalues as a column matrix if the number of output arguments is one or empty. When the function is utilized in collaboration with two output arguments [Y X], we obtain two square matrix outputs, the first of which is the eigenmatrix (Y) and the other of which is a diagonal matrix placing the eigenvalues in the diagonal. If you want to pick up the second eigenvector from Y, the command Y(:,2) can be exercised. Similarly the command Y(:,3) stands for the third eigenvector. The eigenvalues as a column matrix can be picked up from the diagonal matrix X by MATLAB function **diag**. Note that the eigenvalues are not placed in ascending or descending order but they correspond with the eigenvectors for example the eigenvector $\begin{bmatrix} 0.0747 \\ -0.2242 \\ 0.9717 \end{bmatrix}$ in the Y matrix is for $\lambda = -4$, and so is the others. All eigenvectors returned by the **eig** are

normalized for example the first eigenvector $\begin{bmatrix} 0.0747 \\ -0.2242 \\ 0.9717 \end{bmatrix}$ has the magnitude $\sqrt{0.0747^2 + (-0.2242)^2 + 0.9717^2} = 1$.

The reader can verify that each eigenvalue-eigenvector set satisfy the matrix equation $A\ X = \lambda\ X$.

4.6.2 Covariance of random variables

A random variable observation data is arranged as the rows or columns in a rectangular matrix. If the observations are placed as columns in the rectangular matrix, then the number of columns in the matrix can be taken as the number of the random variables. Having placed two or more random variables in a rectangular matrix, the covariance among columns in the rectangular matrix provides a relationship between the random variables or about their tendency to vary together rather than independently. The covariance of several random variables is a

matrix. Let us say the columns in the matrix $A = \begin{bmatrix} A_{11} & A_{12} & \cdots & A_{1N} \\ A_{21} & A_{22} & \cdots & A_{2N} \\ \vdots & \vdots & \ddots & \vdots \\ A_{M1} & A_{M2} & \cdots & A_{MN} \end{bmatrix}$ represent the observations of N

random variables where M is the number of observations for each. Then the covariance matrix of A is given by

$$V = \begin{bmatrix} V_{11} & V_{12} & \cdots & V_{1N} \\ V_{21} & V_{22} & \cdots & V_{2N} \\ \vdots & \vdots & \ddots & \vdots \\ V_{N1} & V_{N2} & \cdots & V_{NN} \end{bmatrix} \text{ where } V_{ij} = \frac{\sum_{k=1}^{M}(A_{ki} - \overline{A_i})(A_{kj} - \overline{A_j})}{M-1}, \ A_1 = \begin{bmatrix} A_{11} \\ A_{21} \\ \vdots \\ A_{M1} \end{bmatrix}, \ A_2 = \begin{bmatrix} A_{12} \\ A_{22} \\ \vdots \\ A_{M2} \end{bmatrix} \ddot{O} \dots, \text{ and } A_N = \begin{bmatrix} A_{1N} \\ A_{2N} \\ \vdots \\ A_{MN} \end{bmatrix},$$

and $\overline{A_j}$ is the mean of the jth column of A. The diagonal elements of V are the variances of each column in A, the off-diagonal elements of A are covariance of the columns of A, V is a symmetric matrix of order $N \times N$, and A is of order $M \times N$ in general (later on A is assumed to be our theory discussed digital image matrix $f[m, n]$).

To elucidate with a numerical example, let us consider $A = \begin{bmatrix} -2 & 6 & 6 \\ 4 & 30 & 1 \\ 1 & -4 & -4 \\ 5 & 0 & 5 \end{bmatrix}$ where $M = 4$ and $N = 3$. The

order of V must be 3×3 and V prescribes the matrix form $\begin{bmatrix} V_{11} & V_{12} & V_{13} \\ V_{21} & V_{22} & V_{23} \\ V_{31} & V_{32} & V_{33} \end{bmatrix}$. Since V is a symmetric

matrix, we have $V_{12} = V_{21}$, $V_{13} = V_{31}$, and $V_{23} = V_{32}$. The means for the columns are $\overline{A_1} = \frac{1}{4}(-2+4+1+5) = 2$, $\overline{A_2} = 8$, and

$\overline{A_3} = 2$ on that $V_{11} = \frac{\sum_{k=1}^{4}(A_{k1} - \overline{A_1})^2}{4-1} = \frac{(-2-2)^2 + (4-2)^2 + (1-2)^2 + (5-2)^2}{4-1} = 10$, $V_{22} = \frac{\sum_{k=1}^{4}(A_{k2} - \overline{A_2})^2}{4-1} = 232$, $V_{33} = \frac{\sum_{k=1}^{4}(A_{k3} - \overline{A_3})^2}{4-1}$

$= 20.6667$, $V_{21} = \frac{\sum_{k=1}^{4}(A_{k1} - \overline{A_1})(A_{k2} - \overline{A_2})}{4-1} = \frac{(-2-2)(6-8)+(4-2)(30-8)+(1-2)(-4-8)+(5-2)(0-8)}{4-1} = 13.3333$, $V_{31} =$

$\frac{\sum_{k=1}^{4}(A_{k1} - \overline{A_1})(A_{k3} - \overline{A_3})}{4-1} = \tilde{n}1$, and $V_{32} = \frac{\sum_{k=1}^{4}(A_{k2} - \overline{A_2})(A_{k3} - \overline{A_3})}{4-1} = 6$ therefore $V = \begin{bmatrix} 10 & 13.3333 & -1 \\ 13.3333 & 232 & 6 \\ -1 & 6 & 20.6667 \end{bmatrix}$.

The MATLAB function **cov** (abbreviation of the <u>cov</u>ariance) helps us find the covariance of the random variable observations placed in the matrix A as follows:

MATLAB Command

```
>>A=[-2 6 6;4 30 1;1 -4 -4;5 0 5]; ↵
>>V=cov(A) ↵

V =
          10.0000      13.3333      -1.0000
```

$$
\begin{array}{ccc}
13.3333 & 232.0000 & 6.0000 \\
-1.0000 & 6.0000 & 20.6667
\end{array}
$$

The first line in above command is the assignment of the observation matrix to A and in the second line the function cov applies to A and assigns the return of the function to V which is what we want.

4.6.3 Applying eigen and covariance matrices to Hotelling transform

Prior to taking the Hotelling transform on a digital square image of pixel size $N \times N$, the first deliberation is pixels located on a column are assumed as the random variable observation. Referring to the figure 4.5(a), there are N random pixel variables in the digital image matrix $f[m, n]$ with N observations for each. Like others Hotelling transform also has the forward and inverse counterparts. Let us discuss them in the following.

♦ ♦ Forward Hotelling transform

The forward Hotelling transform $F[u, v]$ for the square digital image $f[m, n]$ of order $N \times N$ is defined by the matrix expression $F[u, v] = T\ (\ f[m, n] - C\ )$, where the orders of $F[u, v]$, T, and C are all $N \times N$. The matrices T and C related with the transform are obtained as follows:

⇒ first we find the covariance matrix V from the image matrix $f[m, n]$ considering the column pixels as the random variable observation (last subsection) employing the figure 4.5(a)

⇒ then we find the eigenmatrix of V (last subsection) which is our transform matrix T

⇒ all elements in the first column of C is the mean value of the first column of the image matrix $f[m, n]$ similarly all elements in the second column of C is the mean value of the second column of $f[m, n]$, and so on.

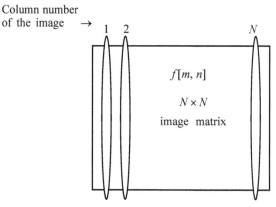

Column number of the image →

Figure 4.5(a) *Picking up the columns from a digital image* $f[m, n]$ *for the Hotelling transform*

All the while our approach has been through the numerical example. Let us consider the square image

matrix $f[m, n] = \begin{bmatrix} 6 & 4 & 4 \\ 9 & 0 & 2 \\ 6 & 7 & 3 \end{bmatrix}$ which has the covariance matrix $V = \begin{bmatrix} 3 & -5.5 & -1.5 \\ -5.5 & 12.3333 & 2 \\ -1.5 & 2 & 1 \end{bmatrix}$. The eigenmatrix of

the last V, which is essentially the T, is $\begin{bmatrix} -0.7255 & 0.5456 & 0.4195 \\ -0.2176 & 0.3963 & -0.8919 \\ -0.6529 & -0.7384 & -0.1688 \end{bmatrix}$. The matrix C is derived from the

mean of each column of $f[m, n]$ as $\begin{bmatrix} 7 & 3.6667 & 3 \\ 7 & 3.6667 & 3 \\ 7 & 3.6667 & 3 \end{bmatrix}$ therefore the forward Hotelling transform of the image

matrix $f[m, n]$ is calculated as $F[u, v] = T\ (\ f[m, n] - C\ ) = \begin{bmatrix} -0.7255 & 0.5456 & 0.4195 \\ -0.2176 & 0.3963 & -0.8919 \\ -0.6529 & -0.7384 & -0.1688 \end{bmatrix} \times$

$\left\{ \begin{bmatrix} 6 & 4 & 4 \\ 9 & 0 & 2 \\ 6 & 7 & 3 \end{bmatrix} - \begin{bmatrix} 7 & 3.6667 & 3 \\ 7 & 3.6667 & 3 \\ 7 & 3.6667 & 3 \end{bmatrix} \right\} = \begin{bmatrix} 1.3973 & -0.8443 & -1.2711 \\ 1.9022 & -4.4989 & -0.6140 \\ -0.6551 & 1.9272 & 0.0854 \end{bmatrix}$. Our expectation from MATLAB

is we should have the forward transform matrix $F[u, v]$ starting from the image matrix $f[m, n]$. Unfortunately there is no built-in function in MATLAB for the Hotelling transform but with the existing function, the forward transform computation can easily be conducted without too much programming as follows:

MATLAB Command

```
>>f=[6 4 4;9 0 2;6 7 3]; ↵
>>V=cov(f); [T,E]=eig(V); ↵
>>M1=mean(f); C=repmat(M1,3,1); ↵
>>F=T*(f-C) ↵
```

F =

```
    1.3973    -0.8443    -1.2711
    1.9022    -4.4989    -0.6140
   -0.6551     1.9272     0.0854
```

The first line in above command is the assignment of the image matrix $f[m, n]$ to f. In the second line there are two commands: the first of which (V=cov(f);) computes the covariance matrix of the image matrix $f[m, n]$ and assigns the result to the variable V and the second of which ([T,E]=eig(V);) computes the eigenmatrix T from the covariance matrix V and keeps the output to the variable T. Even though the eigenvalues held in the diagonal matrix E are not necessary, the E must be present as the output argument to make the function **eig** suitable for eigenmatrix finding according to MATLAB format. Again in the third line there are two commands. The command (M1=mean(f);) finds the mean of each column of the image matrix $f[m, n]$ and keeps the resultant output to the variable M1 so the M1 contains the row matrix [7 3.6667 3] for the given $f[m, n]$. The next command in the third line (C=repmat(M1,3,1);) generates $\begin{bmatrix} 7 & 3.6667 & 3 \\ 7 & 3.6667 & 3 \\ 7 & 3.6667 & 3 \end{bmatrix}$ taking [7 3.6667 3] as the input and keeps the output in the variable C. The details of the MATLAB function **repmat** are presented in section 10.8. The last line command F=T*(f-C) is the direct implementation of $F[u, v] = T (f[m, n] - C)$ conformably the variable F holds the forward Hotelling transform $F[u, v]$ as we calculated (the operator * represents the matrix multiplication) before.

♣ ♦ Inverse Hotelling transform

To mention the synthesis phase, we should be able to recover the original image matrix $f[m, n]$ from the computed forward transform $F[u, v]$. The matrix formula that brings about the synthesis is $f[m, n] = T^* F[u, v] + C$ where T^* is the transpose of the transform matrix T and whose implementation from previously obtained matrices is as follows:

```
>>f=T'*F+C ↵
```

f =

```
    6.0000    4.0000    4.0000
    9.0000    0.0000    2.0000
    6.0000    7.0000    3.0000
```

It is obvious that the MATLAB reformation is the image matrix we started with. The command T' means the transpose of T.

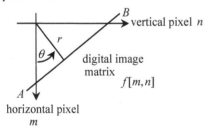

Figure 4.5(b) *Mapping the line AB present in the digital image $f[m,n]$ to a single point (r,θ)*

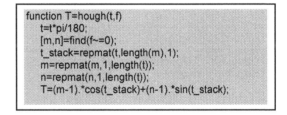

Figure 4.5(c) *The M-file for the Hough transform*

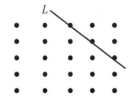

Figure 4.5(d) *The raster image $f[m,n]$ of 5×5 pixels having three nonzero gray values connected by the line L*

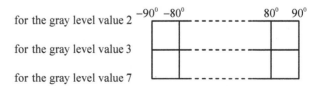

Figure 4.5(e) *Contents of the T matrix for the example 1*

4.7 The Hough transform

The Hough transform detects straight lines present in a raster or black and white image and maps the line to a point. A raster image has gray levels numbered from 0 to some specific integer. The transform considers only the nonzero gray levels in the digital image. If a digital image possessed few gray levels, the Hough transform would not be necessary. Gray levels changing within close variations make us find an algorithm. For a digital image in [0,255], the gray levels 2, 3, or 6 appears as almost equal contrast in the image. Concerning the figure 4.5(b), let us assume that the digital image matrix $f[m,n]$ has the same or nonzero gray level values along the straight line AB. We map the line AB to the single point (r,θ) with the geometry shown in the figure, and the equation employed for the mapping is $r = m\cos\theta + n\sin\theta$. The θ ranges from ñ90^0 to +90^0 due to the geometric position of it in the m-n domain. For every pixel in the image we have one sinusoidal curve but of coarse with various phase and amplitude. The reader chooses θ variation with some steps. For example, the θ can change from ñ90^0 to +90^0 with a step of 10^0.

The algorithm employed in the Hough transform is as follows:

$\Rightarrow$ select the θ variation step from ñ90^0 to +90^0 for the mapping

$\Rightarrow$ find the nonzero gray level in the image $f[m,n]$ located at the pixel (m,n) and store the position indexes in an array

$\Rightarrow$ compute r for every position index for all θ variations using $r = m\cos\theta + n\sin\theta$

$\Rightarrow$ store all computed r ís in a rectangular matrix T as rows, T is the Hough transform matrix

$\Rightarrow$ finally plot all rows of the rectangular matrix against the same predecided θ variations

So one can say that the transform is basically a plot of many r ís against θ but ensuring one r and one sinusoidal for one nonzero gray level. There is no built-in function in MATLAB for the Hough transform but we present the necessary M-file source codes for the transform with the following illustrations.

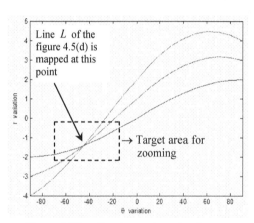

Figure 4.5(f) *Hough transform for the image matrix of the example 1*

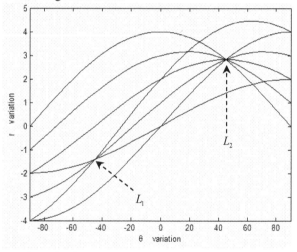

Figure 4.5(g) *Hough transform for the image matrix of the example 2*

❖ ❖ Example 1

Let us consider the 5×5 raster image matrix $f[m,n] = \begin{bmatrix} 0 & 0 & 2 & 0 & 0 \\ 0 & 0 & 0 & 3 & 0 \\ 0 & 0 & 0 & 0 & 7 \\ 0 & 0 & 0 & 0 & 0 \\ 0 & 0 & 0 & 0 & 0 \end{bmatrix}$ in which the gray levels can

vary from 0 to 255. The nonzero elements in the matrix occupy the position indexes (1,3) for 2, (2,4) for 3, and (3,5) for 7. When $f[m,n]$ is displayed as a black and white image within the gray level scaled from 0 to 255, there will not be that much difference in the image contrast for these three nonzero gray levels since they are close to each other with respect to 255. Figure 4.5(d) presents the relative positions of the nonzero pixels connected by the straight line L. We intend to map the line L of the m-n spatial domain to a single point in the r-θ domain in the Hough space ñ that is our expectation from MATLAB.

First we open a new M-file from the File menu of the MATLAB Command Window, type the M-file source codes of the figure 4.5(c) in the M-file editor, and save the file by the name hough in our working path. The M-file function hough has two input arguments ñ t and f. The t can be a row matrix indicating θ variations from ñ

90^0 to 90^0 with some step angle and f is the raster image matrix whose element should be positive integers including 0. Let us assume that the θ step size is 10^0. The number of the output arguments of the function hough is one, which is T. The return to the T is a rectangular matrix which in essence is the rectangular matrix for r of the algorithm. The first row of the T is the value of the r for different θ computed by $r = m\cos\theta + n\sin\theta$ only for the gray level value 2 in the image $f[m,n]$. The second row of the T is the value of the r for different θ computed by $r = m\cos\theta + n\sin\theta$ only for the gray level value 3 in the image $f[m,n]$. Thus other nonzero pixels in the $f[m,n]$ are handled. From ñ90^0 to 90^0 with the step 10^0, there are 19 points therefore the matrix T must be of order 3×19. The pictorial representation of the matrix T is presented in the figure 4.5(e). According to the algorithm, we generate a row matrix t (there is no symbol θ in the workspace that is why we use t for θ) from ñ 90^0 to $+90^0$ with the step 10^0 by executing the following command:

MATLAB Command

>>t=-90:10:90; ↵

We enter the image matrix $f[m,n]$ to the workspace variable f by the following:

>>f=[0 0 2 0 0;0 0 0 3 0;0 0 0 0 7;0 0 0 0 0;0 0 0 0 0]; ↵

Then we call the function hough as follows:

>>T=hough(t,f); ↵

After that we plot each row of the Hough transform matrix T against the same θ variation as follows:

>>plot(t,T) ↵

The figure 4.5(f) is the Hough space output we expected in which the line L of the figure 4.5(d) is mapped at the arrow-indicated point. There are three nonzero pixels in the image $f[m,n]$ that is why there are three sinusoids in the Hough space figure. Looking into the workspace browser, we make sure that the size of the Hough transform matrix is 3×19. On execution of the command plot, you do not see the Hough space plot as we presented but for sure the graph without the axes labeling appears. From the menu bar of the MATLAB figure window, click the Insert using mouse then X Label.

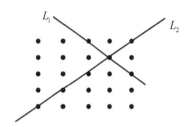

Figure 4.5(h) *The raster image $f[m,n]$ of 5×5 pixels having three nonzero gray values connected by the line L_1 and five nonzero gray values connected by the line L_2*

The blinking cursor appears in the middle of the horizontal axis of the plot and type there \theta variation. The command \theta is used for the generation of the symbol θ in the graphics. Again click the Insert then Y Label and type r variation at the blinking cursor. The horizontal axis of the figure may not be set to ñ90 to 90. In order to set the horizontal axis variation from ñ90 to 90, click the Edit in the menu bar and then Axes Properties. The Axes Property Editor window appears. In that window select Edit Properties for Axes then X. Uncheck the limits from Auto and type ñ90 and 90 in the prompt box. Finally click the Edit plot icon (section 1.3) in the menu bar of the figure window.

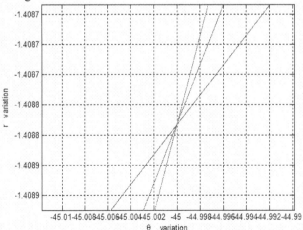

Figure 4.6(a) *Zooming the target area of the figure 4.5(f) six times*

Figure 4.6(b) *The display of the hand written image object stored as digital.jpg*

As an engineer or a scientist, we need to be deterministic in our analysis. Having available the Hough space graph, at what (r,θ) point the line L is mapped to. Let us include the grid lines in the graph of the figure 4.5(f) by the following:

>>grid ↵

Click the Zoom In icon located in the menu bar of the figure window and select the targeted area with the help of the mouse as shown in the figure 4.5(f). Zoom the meeting point of the three sinusoids several times so that the reader can read off the r-θ directly from the figure 4.5(f). You see the horizontal and vertical axesí accuracy is increased every time you zoom in. We zoomed the intersection point six times to obtain the graph of the figure 4.6(a). Looking into the zoomed graph, one can easily say that the line L is mapped to the point $(r, \theta)=(-1.4088, -45^0)$ in the Hough space.

✦ ✦ Example 2

The 5×5 raster image matrix $f[m,n] = \begin{bmatrix} 0 & 0 & 2 & 0 & 8 \\ 0 & 0 & 0 & 3 & 0 \\ 0 & 0 & 5 & 0 & 7 \\ 0 & 4 & 0 & 0 & 0 \\ 1 & 0 & 0 & 0 & 0 \end{bmatrix}$ contains two lines L_1 and L_2 as shown in

the figure 4.5(h). There are seven nonzero elements in the matrix indexed as (1,3) for 2, (1,5) for 8, (2,4) for 3, (3,3) for 5, (3,5) for 7, (4,2) for 4, and (5,1) for 1. We should have seven sinusoids − three of which intersect to map the L_1 and other five of which intersect to map the L_2 in the r-θ domain of the Hough space ñ that is what we expect from MATLAB. Let us take another step angle (5^0) for θ and conduct the implementation as follows:

MATLAB Command
```
>>t=-90:5:90; ↵
>>f=[0 0 2 0 8;0 0 0 3 0;0 0 5 0 7;0 4 0 0 0;1 0 0 0 0]; ↵
>>T=hough(t,f); ↵
>>plot(t,T,'k-') ↵
```
Figure 4.5(g) depicts the Hough transform for the image in the figure 4.5(h) in which the indicatory arrows show the required mapping. We added the labeling in the graph as we did in the example 1. Note that the function plot has three input arguments. The first two are obvious but the third one has k and -. The k means all curves graphed by the plot is black and the - means the graph lines are continuous not broken lines. From ñ90^0 to 90^0 with the step 5^0, there are 37 points hence the matrix T must have the size 7×37 (can be verified from the workspace browser). The pixel indexed by (2,4) is common to both lines from what cause the sine curve of it is also shared by the two points. We performed the zooming similar to the example 1 to obtain the points $(-1.4142, -45^0)$ and $(2.8284, 45^0)$ where the lines L_1 and L_2 mapped to respectively in the Hough space.

✦ ✦ Example 3

Examples 1 and 2 illustrate simplistic images to explain the theory behind the Hough transform. Extra factors need to be addressed when dealing with practical images. Let us say we have the digital.jpg image in our working path from section 2.3. Carrying out the command imshow('digital.jpg') displays the image of the figure 4.6(b). Subsection 6.1.1 described function imfinfo applying on the image (execute imfinfo('digital.jpg')) displays the image details that is how the digital.jpg is a true color image and has the pixel size 276×688. Let the function imread read off the image:

```
>>X=imread('digital.jpg'); ↵        ← The color image is stored as a 3D array in X
```
For the Hough transform, a gray image is required in lieu of the individual color component therefore we perform the following:

```
>>f=rgb2gray(X); ↵
```

The function rgb2gray converts the color image stored in 3D array X to the gray image and assigns to the workspace variable f. It is worthy to mention that just one word Digital is occupying the whole image. If we do not reduce the image size, one thick line in the image yields a series of intersecting points in the Hough space which is not desired at all. One can reduce the image in f by 5 times with the help of the MATLAB function imresize as follows (section 3.7):

```
>>N=imresize(f,1/5); ↵
```
Hence the variable N holds the resized image whose Hough transform we are seeking for. From the workspace browser, the data class of N is uint8 which is in [0,255] from table 2.B. Exercising the commands max(max(N)) and min(min(N)) reveal that the minimum and maximum gray level values present in the image N are 255 and 145 respectively. Another

Figure 4.6(c) *Hough transform for the hand written image object Digital of the example 3*

captious point is that 0 corresponds to the background in the last two examples and in the written M-file hough. But the 255 corresponds to the white background in MATLAB notation whereas 0 bears out the black foreground for the digital.jpg. Under the circumstance one needs the complement image in order to keep the function hough operational. We subtract all gray levels from 255 to have the complement. Since numeric operation requires double class data, their conversion from uint8 to double is a prerequisite and that happens as follows:

>>f=255-double(N); ↵

Let us choose the Hough space θ variation from ñ90^0 to +90^0 with a step 15^0 as follows:

>>t=-90:15:90; ↵

Finally we seek for the Hough transform matrix and its graphical display as follows:

>>T=hough(t,f); ↵

>>plot(t,T,'k-') ↵

Figure 4.6(c) is the picture of the Hough transform for the hand written image object with proper axes labeling and setting. There are so many closely located sinusoids that you do not see the lines indicatory points in the Hough plot. A bright white dot distinctly displays one intersecting point in the plot. Click the Zoom In icon from Figure Window menu bar and zoom any desired zone to see the intersecting points in the Hough plot as we did before.

If the image contains large pixel size, the function plot is not feasible for the Hough transform. In that case we quantize the r values to some specific number like the θ ís and form a rectangular matrix of ones where the rows and columns correspond to the numbers of r ís and θ ís respectively and calculate each r employing previously mentioned formula. We change the 1s to 0s at the quantized r ís position and then display the rectangular matrix as an image. That is left as an exercise for the reader. However we bring an end to the Hough transform discourse.

Forward discrete Fourier or cosine transform

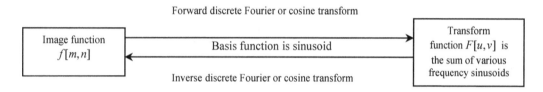

Figure 4.6(d) *Schematics of the Fourier or cosine transform*

Forward discrete wavelet transform

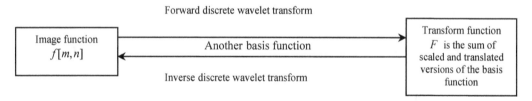

Figure 4.6(e) *Schematics of the wavelet transform*

4.8 Two dimensional discrete wavelet transform

Recall the two dimensional discrete Fourier or cosine transform in which the forward discrete transform function $F[u,v]$ is entirely a function of the spatial frequency u or v. There is no information about the pixel or spatial variable m or n in $F[u,v]$. The function $F[u,v]$ is expressionally the superposition of various frequency sinusoids relating to the frequency u and/or v. Hence the basis functions are all sinusoids in the transform whereas the wavelet transform uses other kinds of basis functions not necessarily the sinusoids for example Haar, Daubechies, etc. The treatment of the wavelet transform needs extensive discourse for which the reader is referred to [60]-[77]. Nevertheless we elucidate the transform to the context of the two dimensional discrete image transform. The schematical difference between the conventional Fourier or cosine and the wavelet transforms is presented in the figures 4.6(d) and 4.6(e). The basis function of the wavelet transform is termed as the analyzing wavelet or mother wavelet. The scaled and translated versions of the mother wavelet are called the members of the wavelet family. In the next subsection we introduce necessary terms involved in the two dimensional discrete wavelet transform.

4.8.1 Terms used in the discrete wavelet transform

The following important terms need to be addressed while applying the two dimensional discrete wavelet transform to a digital image.

76

♣♣ Image matrix dimension or pixel size

In order to apply the wavelet transform, previously mentioned digital image matrix function $f[m,n]$ ís pixel size must be the power of two for example 4×4, 32×64, 256×256, Ö etc. Let us say the digital image matrix $f[m,n]$ is of order $M \times N$, the M or N can be written as 2^m where m =2, 3, 4 Ö etc.

♣♣ Analyzing wavelet type for the transform

It is compulsory that the reader has to select the mother wavelet required for the transform. Not all mother wavelets can be applied to calculate the discrete wavelet transforms. The wavelets which are expressible in terms of the low and high pass filter coefficients are only applicable for the transform. Let us carry out the following in MATLAB:

MATLAB Command

```
>>help waveinfo ↵
    WAVEINFO Information on wavelets.
    WAVEINFO provides information for all the wavelets
    within the toolbox.
    WAVEINFO('wname') provides information for the wavelet
    family whose short name is specified by the string
    'wname'.
    Available family short names are:
    'haar'   : Haar wavelet.
         ⋮
       etc.
```

Above execution exhibits available wavelets and their short names found in MATLAB for example **haar** for the Haar wavelet (in the 8-th line). In order to learn about any specific wavelet for example Haar, one needs to execute the short name under the single inverted comma with the help of the MATLAB function **waveinfo** as follows:

```
>>waveinfo('haar') ↵
HAARINFO Information on Haar wavelet.
        Haar Wavelet
        General characteristics: Compactly supported
        wavelet, the oldest and the simplest wavelet.
        scaling function phi = 1 on [0 1] and 0 otherwise.
        wavelet function psi = 1 on [0 0.5[, = -1 on [0.5 1] and 0 otherwise.
        Family          Haar
        Short name      haar
        Examples        haar is the same as db1
        Orthogonal      yes
        Biorthogonal    yes
        Compact support yes
        DWT             possible
             ⋮
        etc.
```

The Haar wavelet characteristics are displayed. From the displayed characteristics, one can infer that the discrete wavelet transform (**DWT**) is achievable considering the Haar as the mother wavelet.

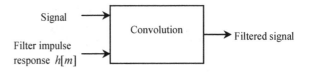

Figure 4.6(f) *The block diagram of the filtering operation*

$$
\begin{array}{rrrr}
f[m] \rightarrow & 7 & 8 & 9 \\
h[m] \rightarrow & & 2 & -3 \\
\hline
& 14 & 16 & 18 \\
& & -21 & -24 & -27 \\
\hline
& 14 & -5 & -6 & -27
\end{array}
$$

Figure 4.6(g)   *Convolution of the $f[m]$ and $h[m]$ by the polynomial multiplication*

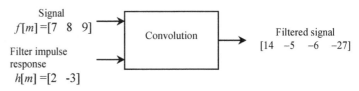

Figure 4.6(h) *The filtering operation on the discrete signal*

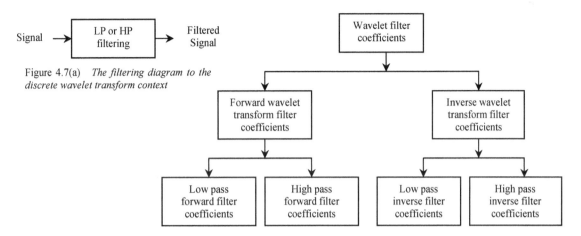

Figure 4.7(a) *The filtering diagram to the discrete wavelet transform context*

Figure 4.7(b) *Different types of filter coefficients employed in the two dimensional discrete wavelet transform*

❖ ❖ The downsampling of a one dimensional discrete signal

The downsampling is the part and parcel of the discrete wavelet transform and required in the forward transform. Due to the separability of the two dimensional discrete wavelet transform, only one dimensional operation is carried out either in the row or column direction in two stages but one at a time. To illustrate the downsampling, let us consider the one dimensional discrete signal $f[m]$=[4 -4 7 0 4 8 1 3] whose length is the power of 2 (here 2^3=8) and it must have to be for the sake of the 2D discrete wavelet transform. Mathematically the downsampling by a factor of 2 is turning the $f[m]$ to $f[2m]$. Skipping every alternate sample of $f[m]$ can provide the $f[2m]$ as follows:

$$f[m]=[4 \ -4 \ 7 \ 0 \ 4 \ 8 \ 1 \ 3] \quad \boxed{2\downarrow} \quad f[2m]=[-4 \ 0 \ 8 \ 3]$$

❖ ❖ The upsampling of a one dimensional discrete signal

Upsampling is the reverse process of the downsampling. Upsampling of a one dimensional discrete signal by a factor of 2 is the insertion of a single zero between the samples. Mathematically the operation turns the $f[m]$ to $f\left[\dfrac{m}{2}\right]$. For example, we have the one dimensional discrete signal $f[m]$=[4 -4 7 0 4] whose upsampled version by a factor of 2 is schematized as follows:

$$f[m]=[4 \ -4 \ 7 \ 0 \ 4] \quad \boxed{2\uparrow} \quad f\left[\frac{m}{2}\right]=[4 \ 0 \ -4 \ 0 \ 7 \ 0 \ 0 \ 0 \ 4]$$

❖ ❖ What are the lowpass and highpass filterings in the wavelet transform?

A digital or discrete filter can be characterized either in the time or spatial domain or in their frequency domains. We describe the filter in the spatial domain to be congruous for the discrete wavelet transform. The impulse response of the filter must be known for the transform application. For example, one filter can have impulse response $h[m]$ =$2\,\delta[m]-3\,\delta[m-1]$ or in coefficient form $h[m]$ =[2 −3] where $h[m]$ exists only for m =0 and m =1 and $\delta[m]$ is the unit sample function. A specific discrete filter has specific impulse response $h[m]$ (low or high pass). Figure 4.6(f) depicts basic spatial domain filtering operation on a discrete function $f[m]$.

The convolution operation can be defined as the polynomial multiplication of digital signal $f[m]$ and digital filter impulse response $h[m]$ in other words the formulation is given by $\sum_k f[m-k]h[k]$ or $\sum_k h[m-k]f[k]$.

To illustrate by an example, let us say the signal is $f[m]$=[7 8 9] and the filter has aforementioned impulse response $h[m]$. Figure 4.6(g) presents the polynomial multiplication for the example at hand supplemented with the figure 4.6(h). The length of the filtered signal is given by the length of $f[m]$ +length of $h[m]$ −1. To the context of the discrete wavelet transform, figure 4.7(a) is applicable in which the impulse response $h[m]$ depends on the wavelet type selection and is left as a choice for the user. The shorts LP and HP in the block diagram of the wavelet transform are used for the lowpass and highpass filterings. But in the discrete wavelet transform the forward and

78

inverse transforms may not involve the same filter coefficients. Each type of the transforms has the lowpass and highpass filter coefficients. Figure 4.7(b) shows the filter coefficientsí tree structure that the transform can have.

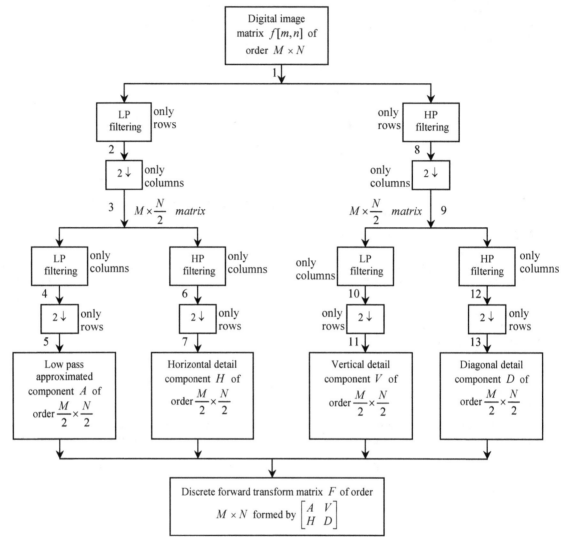

Figure 4.7(c) *Block diagram of the forward two dimensional discrete wavelet transform*
*Note that the numbers 1 through 13 beside the flow lines are not related with the block diagram of the transform. We utilize them for the computation of the transform (due to space reason).

♦ ♦ How can we obtain the wavelet filter coefficients?

Wavelet filter coefficients mean the impulse responses of the filters deriving from the mother wavelet selected for the transform computation. Although we do not explicitly employ the filter coefficients when implementing the transform in MATLAB, the knowledge of the filter coefficients might be known for the analysis reason. Now we mention how the wavelet filter coefficients can readily be obtained from MATLAB. The Haar wavelet has the short name haar in MATLAB and let us execute the following:

MATLAB Command

```
>>[LF,HF,LI,HI]=wfilters('haar') ↵

LF =
      0.7071   0.7071
HF =
     -0.7071   0.7071
LI =
      0.7071   0.7071
```

HI =
$$0.7071 \quad -0.7071$$

The MATLAB function wfilters (abbreviation of the wavelet filters) can display different types of filter coefficients as mentioned in the figure 4.7(b). The function has four output arguments namely LF, HF, LI, and HI. They represent the forward lowpass, forward highpass, inverse lowpass, and inverse highpass filter impulse responses respectively. The reader can use any other name of his choice as the output arguments. As another example, let us consider the Daubechies wavelet of order 2 whose MATLAB short name is db2. Its various filter impulse responses can be obtained as follows:

>>[LF,HF,LI,HI]=wfilters('db2') ↵

LF =
$$-0.1294 \quad 0.2241 \quad 0.8365 \quad 0.4830$$
HF =
$$-0.4830 \quad 0.8365 \quad -0.2241 \quad -0.1294$$
LI =
$$0.4830 \quad 0.8365 \quad 0.2241 \quad -0.1294$$
HI =
$$-0.1294 \quad -0.2241 \quad 0.8365 \quad -0.4830$$

Pointing the associated terms out, we quote the two dimensional discrete wavelet transform in next subsection.

4.8.2 Two dimensional forward discrete wavelet transform

The two dimensional discrete wavelet transform recurrently requires downsampling, upsampling, lowpass filtering, and highpass filtering. Even though the transform thoroughly takes care of the two dimensional discrete signal or image matrix but the hidden arithmetic is one dimensional on account of the separability of the transform. Each of the four operations applies to one dimension which in essence the row or column of the digital image matrix $f[m,n]$. The computation is carried out in two stages but one at a time. However the figure 4.7(c) schematically illustrates the two dimensional forward discrete wavelet transform applied to a digital image.

Our objective in the transform is to obtain the forward transform matrix F from the digital image function $f[m,n]$ like the other transforms. The order of the transform matrix F is the same as that of the $f[m,n]$ that is no less ñ no more operation.

The block diagram of the figure 4.7(c) helps us find the two dimensional forward discrete wavelet transform of $f[m,n]$. Let us consider the modular image matrix $f[m,n] = \begin{bmatrix} 36 & 4 & -6 & 23 \\ 65 & 32 & -34 & 21 \\ 74 & 43 & 21 & 0 \\ 67 & -32 & 28 & -3 \end{bmatrix}$ and compute

the discrete transform with respect to the Haar wavelet whose forward and inverse filter coefficients are given by $\begin{cases} \text{for lowpass, } h_0[m] = [0.7071 \quad 0.7071] \\ \text{for highpass, } h_1[m] = [-0.7071 \quad 0.7071] \end{cases}$ and $\begin{cases} \text{for lowpass, } h_0[m] = [0.7071 \quad 0.7071] \\ \text{for highpass, } h_1[m] = [0.7071 \quad -0.7071] \end{cases}$ respectively (found

before). Now we explain how different computations are carried out in the numbered flow lines of the figure 4.7(c).

♦ ♦ Flow line 1 of the figure 4.7(c)

Here we have just the digital image matrix function $f[m,n]$ we start with.

♦ ♦ Flow line 2 of the figure 4.7(c)

The first row of $f[m,n]$ is [36   4   -6   23]. The convolution of the first row of $f[m,n]$ with the lowpass forward filter coefficients $h_0[m] = [0.7071 \quad 0.7071]$ is [25.4558   28.2843   −1.4142   12.0208   16.2635]. Similarly the convolutions of the second, third, and fourth rows of $f[m,n]$ with the same filter coefficients provide [45.9619 68.5894 −1.4142 −9.1924 14.8492], [52.3259 82.7315 45.2548 14.8492 0], and [47.3762   24.7487   −2.8284   17.6777   −2.1213] respectively. We have

$$\begin{bmatrix} 25.4558 & 28.2843 & -1.4142 & 12.0208 & 16.2635 \\ 45.9619 & 68.5894 & -1.4142 & -9.1924 & 14.8492 \\ 52.3259 & 82.7315 & 45.2548 & 14.8492 & 0 \\ 47.3762 & 24.7487 & -2.8284 & 17.6777 & -2.1213 \end{bmatrix}$$ placing the convolution result in a matrix form – this is the

flow in the line 2 of the figure 4.7(c).

80

♦♦ Flow line 3 of the figure 4.7(c)

It is lucid from the order of $f[m,n]$ that $M=4$ and $N=4$. We must have a matrix of order 4×2 by

downsampling only the columns of the matrix obtained from previous step, which is $\begin{bmatrix} 28.2843 & 12.0208 \\ 68.5894 & -9.1924 \\ 82.7315 & 14.8492 \\ 24.7487 & 17.6777 \end{bmatrix}$ – this

is the flow in the line 3 of the figure 4.7(c).

♦♦ Flow line 4 of the figure 4.7(c)

Each of the first and second columns of the matrix in the flow line 3 is convolved with aforementioned

lowpass filter coefficients to yield $\begin{bmatrix} 20 & 8.5 \\ 68.5 & 2 \\ 107 & 4 \\ 76 & 23 \\ 17.5 & 12.5 \end{bmatrix}$ – this is the flow in the line 4 of the figure 4.7(c).

♦♦ Flow line 5 of the figure 4.7(c)

Downsampling the rows of the matrix of flow line 4 by a factor 2, we obtain $\begin{bmatrix} 68.5 & 2 \\ 76 & 23 \end{bmatrix}$ (flow in the

line 5 of the figure 4.7(c)) hence the lowpass approximated component of the transform is $A = \begin{bmatrix} 68.5 & 2 \\ 76 & 23 \end{bmatrix}$.

♦♦ Flow line 6 of the figure 4.7(c)

This flow line takes input from the flow line 3 which holds $\begin{bmatrix} 28.2843 & 12.0208 \\ 68.5894 & -9.1924 \\ 82.7315 & 14.8492 \\ 24.7487 & 17.6777 \end{bmatrix}$. For the highpass

filtering along the columns of the last matrix using the forward filter coefficients [−0.7071 0.7071], convolutions

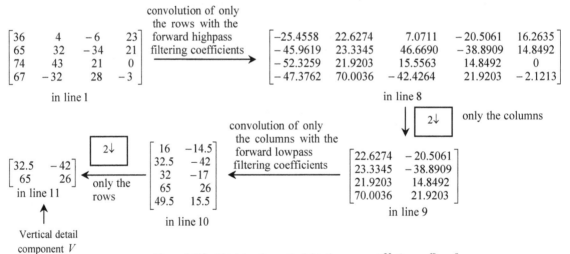

Figure 4.7(d) *Obtaining the vertical detail component V from* $f[m,n]$

Figure 4.7(e) *Obtaining the diagonal detail component D from* $f[m,n]$

of the two columns with the filter coefficients provide $\begin{bmatrix} -20 \\ -28.5 \\ -10 \\ 41 \\ 17.5 \end{bmatrix}$ and $\begin{bmatrix} -8.5 \\ 15 \\ -17 \\ -2 \\ 12.5 \end{bmatrix}$ respectively therefore the line 6

conveys $\begin{bmatrix} -20 & -8.5 \\ -28.5 & 15 \\ -10 & -17 \\ 41 & -2 \\ 17.5 & 12.5 \end{bmatrix}$.

◆ ◆ **Flow line 7 of the figure 4.7(c)**

On downsampling the rows of the matrix found in the line 6 by a factor of 2, one obtains the horizontal detail matrix H as $\begin{bmatrix} -28.5 & 15 \\ 41 & -2 \end{bmatrix}$.

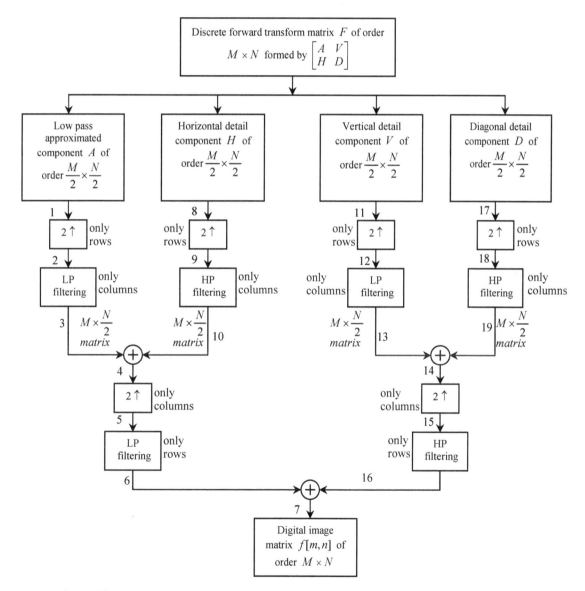

Figure 4.7(f) *Block diagram of the inverse two dimensional discrete wavelet transform*
*Note that the numbers 1 through 19 beside the flow lines are not related with the block diagram of the transform. We utilize them for the computation of the inverse transform (due to space reason).

♦♦ Flow lines 8, 9, 10, 11, 12, and 13 of the figure 4.7(c)

We conducted computation for the left branch of the tree of the figure 4.7(c). The right partís computation is similar to that of the left one. Figures 4.7(d) and 4.7(e) present the related intermediate matricesí flow for the right part of the tree.

At the point, we finished the computation of the two dimensional forward discrete wavelet transform of the modular image matrix $f[m,n]$ with respect to the Haar wavelet as

$$
\begin{bmatrix} 68.5 & 2 \\ 76 & 23 \end{bmatrix} \xrightarrow[\text{rows}]{\text{only}} \begin{bmatrix} 68.5 & 2 \\ 0 & 0 \\ 76 & 23 \end{bmatrix} \xrightarrow[\text{columns}]{\substack{\text{lowpass} \\ \text{filtering} \\ \text{only}}} \begin{bmatrix} 48.4368 & 1.4142 \\ 48.4368 & 1.4142 \\ 53.7401 & 16.2635 \\ 53.7401 & 16.2635 \end{bmatrix}
$$

A in line 1 → 2↑ → in line 2 → in line 3

$$
\begin{bmatrix} -28.5 & 15 \\ 41 & -2 \end{bmatrix} \xrightarrow[\text{rows}]{\text{only}} \begin{bmatrix} -28.5 & 15 \\ 0 & 0 \\ 41 & -2 \end{bmatrix} \xrightarrow[\text{columns}]{\substack{\text{highpass} \\ \text{filtering} \\ \text{only}}} \begin{bmatrix} -20.1525 & 10.6066 \\ 20.1525 & -10.6066 \\ 28.9914 & -1.4142 \\ -28.9914 & 1.4142 \end{bmatrix}
$$

H in line 8 → 2↑ → in line 9 → in line 10

$$
+ \rightarrow \begin{bmatrix} 28.2843 & 12.0208 \\ 68.5894 & -9.1924 \\ 82.7315 & 14.8492 \\ 24.7487 & 17.6777 \end{bmatrix}
$$

in line 4

$$
\begin{bmatrix} 32.5 & -42 \\ 65 & 26 \end{bmatrix} \xrightarrow[\text{rows}]{\text{only}} \begin{bmatrix} 32.5 & -42 \\ 0 & 0 \\ 65 & 26 \end{bmatrix} \xrightarrow[\text{columns}]{\substack{\text{lowpass} \\ \text{filtering} \\ \text{only}}} \begin{bmatrix} 22.9810 & -29.6985 \\ 22.9810 & -29.6985 \\ 45.9619 & 18.3848 \\ 45.9619 & 18.3848 \end{bmatrix}
$$

V in line 11 → 2↑ → in line 12 → in line 13

$$
\begin{bmatrix} -0.5 & 13 \\ -34 & -5 \end{bmatrix} \xrightarrow[\text{rows}]{\text{only}} \begin{bmatrix} -0.5 & 13 \\ 0 & 0 \\ -34 & -5 \end{bmatrix} \xrightarrow[\text{columns}]{\substack{\text{highpass} \\ \text{filtering} \\ \text{only}}} \begin{bmatrix} -0.3536 & 9.1924 \\ 0.3536 & -9.1924 \\ -24.0416 & -3.5355 \\ 24.0416 & 3.5355 \end{bmatrix}
$$

D in line 17 → 2↑ → in line 18 → in line 19

$$
+ \rightarrow \begin{bmatrix} 22.6274 & -20.5061 \\ 23.3345 & -38.8909 \\ 21.9203 & 14.8492 \\ 70.0036 & 21.9203 \end{bmatrix}
$$

in line 14

$$
\begin{bmatrix} 28.2843 & 12.0208 \\ 68.5894 & -9.1924 \\ 82.7315 & 14.8492 \\ 24.7487 & 17.6777 \end{bmatrix} \xrightarrow[\text{columns}]{\text{only}} \begin{bmatrix} 28.2843 & 0 & 12.0208 \\ 68.5894 & 0 & -9.1924 \\ 82.7315 & 0 & 14.8492 \\ 24.7487 & 0 & 17.6777 \end{bmatrix} \xrightarrow[\text{rows}]{\substack{\text{lowpass} \\ \text{filtering} \\ \text{only}}} \begin{bmatrix} 20 & 20 & 8.5 & 8.5 \\ 48.5 & 48.5 & -6.5 & -6.5 \\ 58.5 & 58.5 & 10.5 & 10.5 \\ 17.5 & 17.5 & 12.5 & 12.5 \end{bmatrix}
$$

in line 4 → 2↑ → in line 5 → in line 6

$$
\begin{bmatrix} 22.6274 & -20.5061 \\ 23.3345 & -38.8909 \\ 21.9203 & 14.8492 \\ 70.0036 & 21.9203 \end{bmatrix} \xrightarrow[\text{columns}]{\text{only}} \begin{bmatrix} 22.6274 & 0 & -20.5061 \\ 23.3345 & 0 & -38.8909 \\ 21.9203 & 0 & 14.8492 \\ 70.0036 & 0 & 21.9203 \end{bmatrix} \xrightarrow[\text{rows}]{\substack{\text{highpass} \\ \text{filtering} \\ \text{only}}} \begin{bmatrix} 16 & -16 & -14.5 & 14.5 \\ 16.5 & -16.5 & -27.5 & 27.5 \\ 15.5 & -15.5 & 10.5 & -10.5 \\ 49.5 & -49.5 & 15.5 & -15.5 \end{bmatrix}
$$

in line 14 → 2↑ → in line 15 → in line 16

$$
\text{The image matrix we started with} \rightarrow \begin{bmatrix} 36 & 4 & -6 & 23 \\ 65 & 32 & -34 & 21 \\ 74 & 43 & 21 & 0 \\ 67 & -32 & 28 & -3 \end{bmatrix} \leftarrow +
$$

Figure 4.7(g) *Numerical recovery of the original image matrix* $f[m,n]$ *from the quadruplet* $\{ A, H, V, D \}$

$$F = \begin{bmatrix} A & V \\ H & D \end{bmatrix} = \begin{bmatrix} 68.5 & 2 & 32.5 & -42 \\ 76 & 23 & 65 & 26 \\ -28.5 & 15 & -0.5 & 13 \\ 41 & -2 & -34 & -5 \end{bmatrix}, \quad \text{where} \quad A = \begin{bmatrix} 68.5 & 2 \\ 76 & 23 \end{bmatrix}, \quad V = \begin{bmatrix} 32.5 & -42 \\ 65 & 26 \end{bmatrix},$$

$H = \begin{bmatrix} -28.5 & 15 \\ 41 & -2 \end{bmatrix}$, and $D = \begin{bmatrix} -0.5 & 13 \\ -34 & -5 \end{bmatrix}$ – we expect this computation from MATLAB. The MATLAB function

dwt2 (abbreviation of the discrete wavelet transform in two (2) dimensions) can implement the whole transform computation as follows:

MATLAB Command

```
>>f=[36 4 -6 23;65 32 -34 21;74 43 21 0;67 -32 28 -3]; ⏎
>>[A,H,V,D]=dwt2(f,'haar') ⏎


A =
        68.5000    2.0000
        76.0000   23.0000
H =
       -28.5000   15.0000
        41.0000   -2.0000
V =
        32.5000  -42.0000
        65.0000   26.0000
D =
        -0.5000   13.0000
       -34.0000   -5.0000
```

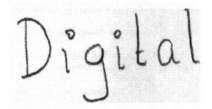

Figure 4.8(a) *Lowpass approximate component* A *of the wavelet transform of the digital.jpg*

The first line in above command is the assignment of the modular image matrix $f[m,n]$ to the workspace variable f. The function dwt2 has two input arguments, the first and second of which are the digital image matrix name and the wavelet type respectively. The wavelet type must be placed using short name and under the single inverted comma. Our selected Haar wavelet is recognized by the short name 'haar'. Other wavelets capable of exhibiting discrete wavelet transform have also specific short names (mentioned before). The number of the output arguments of the function dwt2 is four ñ A, H, V, and D and they represent the transform associated matrices A, H, V, and D respectively. That is what we promised to reveal.

4.8.3 Two dimensional inverse discrete wavelet transform

Having known the quadruplet $\{ A, H, V, D \}$ from the forward discrete wavelet transform, an algorithm for the two dimensional inverse discrete wavelet transform must be available for the synthesis of $f[m,n]$ from the quadruplet for which we present the block diagram of the figure 4.7(f). In subsection 4.8.1 we introduced all related terms of the forward or inverse transform. Figure 4.7(g) shows the numerical flow being numbered according to the inverse transform block diagram 4.7(f) so that we are able to reconstruct the original image $f[m,n]$ eventually. It is important to mention that the filter coefficients employed are the inverse ones. After all our immediate concern is the MATLAB implementation and that is rendered as follows:

MATLAB Command

```
>>A=[68.5 2;76 23]; H=[-28.5 15;41 -2]; V=[32.5 -42;65 26]; D=[-0.5 13;-34 -5]; ⏎
>>f=idwt2(A,H,V,D,'haar') ⏎


f =
        36.0000    4.0000    -6.0000   23.0000
        65.0000   32.0000   -34.0000   21.0000
        74.0000   43.0000    21.0000   -0.0000
        67.0000  -32.0000    28.0000   -3.0000
```

Figure 4.8(b) *Horizontal detail component* H *of the wavelet transform of the digital.jpg*

The first line in the command is just the entering of the quadruplet $\{ A, H, V, D \}$ to the respective variable. The MATLAB function idwt2 simulates the two dimensional inverse discrete wavelet transform (abbreviation of the inverse discrete wavelet transform in two (2) dimensions). There are five input arguments in the function, the first four of which are the quadruplet matrices in the presented order and the fifth of which is the type of the mother wavelet in terms of the MATLAB short name (presented formerly). Mentioning the mother wavelet type is a requisite both for the forward and inverse counterparts of the transform. In next subsection we implement the transform on a practical digital image.

84

4.8.4 Two dimensional discrete wavelet transform on an image

To apply the two dimensional forward discrete wavelet transform, we choose the hand written digital.jpg (gray version) from the example 3 of section 4.7. The image has the size 276×688. There is a function called nextpow2 in MATLAB which finds the next power of 2 of a number. Let us find the next power of 2 both for the horizontal and vertical pixel numbers as follows:

MATLAB Command

>>nextpow2(276) ↵   >>nextpow2(688) ↵

ans =   ans =
9   10

Figure 4.8(c) *Vertical detail component* V *of the wavelet transform of the digital.jpg*

Figure 4.8(d) *Diagonal detail component* D *of the wavelet transform of the digital.jpg*

We know that $2^8=256$, $2^9=512$, and $2^{10}=1024$. The horizontal pixel size 276 is in between 2^8 and 2^9 and the vertical pixel size 688 is in between 2^9 and 2^{10}. Since making the size of the image as the power of 2 is mandatory for the transform, let us choose the image size as 256×512. We take the help of the function imresize to obtain the requisite size (section 3.7). Making the digital.jpg available in the working directory, let us compute the wavelet transform for the image as follows:

>>Y=imread('digital.jpg'); ↵   ← Reading the true color image and assigned to Y
>>f=rgb2gray(Y); ↵   ← Converting the true color image Y to the gray image f
>>f=imresize(f,[256,512]); ↵   ← Resizing the gray image f to the size 256×512 and assigning the resized image again to f which is $f[m,n]$

>>[A,H,V,D]=dwt2(f,'haar'); ↵   ← Finding the wavelet transform quadruplet $\{A,H,V,D\}$ considering the Haar as the mother wavelet

From the workspace browser, the data class of the wavelet transform quadruplet is double. We display the lowpass approximate component A of the transform as a digital image by first mapping the data in [0,1] by the following:

>>figure,imshow(A,[ ]) ↵

Figure 4.8(a) presents the output from above execution. The other three members of the quadruplet are displayed like the figures 4.8(b), 4.8(c), and 4.8(d) for the H, V, and D respectively as follows:

>>figure,imshow(H,[ ]) ↵
>>figure,imshow(V,[ ]) ↵
>>figure,imshow(D,[ ]) ↵

The order of the resized $f[m,n]$ or digital.jpg is 256×512 therefore each of the quadruplet has the order 128×256 (can be checked from the workspace browser). If you wish to display the whole quadruplet as a single image, following command can be exercised:

>>F=[A V;H D]; ↵   ← Forming the forward transform matrix F from the quadruplet (section 10.6 for the matrix composite)

>>figure,imshow(F,[ ]) ↵   ← Displaying the F as a single image (not presented for space reason)

In the displayed image we find only the A component as prominent, the other three almost appear as the black zone that means their gray level values are very close to 0 in [0,1] scale for the whole composite image. Individual mapping in [0,1] may show the details of each component but not in the composite F image. Anyhow one can easily retrieve the original digital.jpg image by the inverse command idwt2(A,H,V,D,'haar'). For the other kind of the mother wavelet, for example the Daubechies wavelet of order 4, all you need is execute [A,H,V,D]=dwt2(f,'db4') or idwt2(A,H,V,D,'db4') where db4 is the short name of the analyzing wavelet.

As another wavelet transform example, let us consider the indexed dip.bmp (gray version) of section 2.3, make the image available in the working directory, and perform the following:

>>[X,M]=imread('dip.bmp'); ↵   ← Reading the image, X⇔intensity matrix and M⇔colormap
>>f=ind2gray(X,M); ↵   ← Turning the indexed image to gray image f

From the workspace browser, the size of the f is 218×256. Let us resize the image to the pixel size 256×256 for the transform reason as follows:

>>f=imresize(f,[256,256]); ↵   ← The resized gray image is again assigned to f

Now is the time for the analyzing wavelet selection (say the mother wavelet is the Daubechies of order 4) whence the transform quadruplet is obtained as:

>>[A,H,V,D]=dwt2(f,'db4'); ↵

The image display of the quadruplet components can occur as conducted for the Haar example. Anyhow we close the section with this implementation.

4.9 Mesh or surface plot of two dimensional image transforms

The two dimensional discrete transform $F[u, v]$ whichever it is Fourier, cosine, or Hadamard is essentially the function of two spatial frequencies u and v. The plot of $F[u, v]$ versus u and v is a three dimensional plot which in general results a surface on the u-v domains. Figure 4.8(e) shows the geometry of the transform space in general. For example, if we have discrete Fourier transform, we can graph Re{ $F[u, v]$ }, Im{ $F[u, v]$ }, | $F[u, v]$ |, or $\angle F[u, v]$ in the axis of $F[u, v]$ on the base variations of u and v.

Let us consider the binary image H of section 8.1. Our objective is to view the half indexedly flipped discrete Fourier magnitude spectrum (section 4.2) for the H image as a surface plot for which we conduct the following:

>>H=[zeros(50,10) [ones(20);zeros(10,20);ones(20)] zeros(50,10)]; ↵

>>F=fft2(H); A=abs(F); A=fftshift(A); ↵

>>mesh(A) ↵

The first line in above command is the generation of the binary image matrix for H. In the second line the commands F=fft2(H); and A=abs(F); take two dimensional discrete Fourier transform of H and assign the output to F (which is $F[u, v]$) and take the absolute value of the transform and assign that to A (which is (| $F[u, v]$ |) respectively. We flip the magnitude spectrum | $F[u, v]$ | half indexedly and again assign the result to A by the command A=fftshift(A);. The third line command mesh(A) results the mesh plot of the figure 4.8(g) in which the input argument A is in general a rectangular matrix. The arrows in the figure indicate the relative directions of the u, v, and | $F[u, v]$ | in three dimensional space. The matrix order of | $F[u, v]$ | or A is 50×40 (found in the workspace browser) and the u and v correspond to the 50 and 40 respectively. The MATLAB function mesh sets the u and v limits from 1 to 50 and from 1 to 40 by default indicated by the order of the matrix held in A. We can set the u and v limits according to our choice but the u and v must be a row matrix of lengths 50 and 40 respectively.

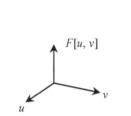

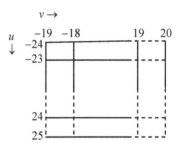

Figure 4.8(e) *Geometry of the transform space in general*

Figure 4.8(f) *Arranging the u-v grid of the mesh plot for the half indexedly flipped magnitude spectrum* | $F[u, v]$ |

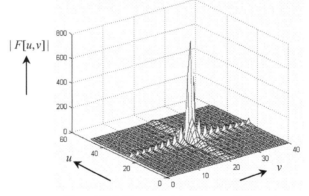

Figure 4.8(g) *The mesh plot of the magnitude spectrum* | $F[u, v]$ | *for the binary image H*

The spectrum is flipped about the half index both in the u and v directions. We can form a row matrix of integers from ñ24 to 25 with the increment 1 to make sense with the flipped spectrum and that also covers 50 points in the u direction:

>>u=-24:25; ↵

In a similar fashion we form a row matrix of integers from ñ19 to 20 with the increment 1 that covers 40 points in the v direction:

86

>>v=-19:20; ↵

Just mentioned *u* and *v* grid rearrangement is depicted in the figure 4.8(f). We execute the following to display the mesh figure 4.9(a):

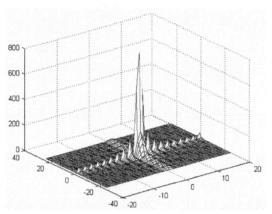

Figure 4.9(a) *The mesh plot with the arrangement of the u - v grid of the figure 4.8(f)*

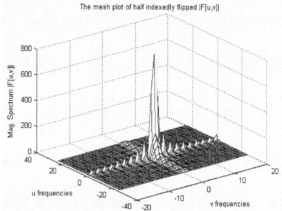

Figure 4.9(b) *Mesh plot of the figure 4.9(a) with different labeling*

>>mesh(v,u,A) ↵

Now we have three input arguments in the **mesh** function ñ the first, second, and third of which are the *v* directed spatial frequency variation as a row matrix, the *u* directed spatial frequency variation as a row matrix, and half indexedly flipped spectrum as a rectangular matrix respectively. To obtain a complete graph, we need to include different labeling. In the window of the figure 4.9(a), click **Insert** → **Z Label** from the menu bar. The cursor starts blinking in the middle of $|F[u, v]|$ axis of the figure 4.9(a) due to the last action. You type there **Mag. Spectrum |F[u,v]|**. In the same window again click **Insert** → **X Label**, type **v frequencies** at the blinking cursor, click **Insert** → **Y Label**, type **u frequencies** at the blinking cursor, and click **Insert** → **Title**, type **The mesh plot of half indexedly flipped |F[u,v]|** at the blinking cursor. The result is the mesh plot of the figure 4.9(b) with different axes and title labeling. When you insert the text objects following the blinking action of the cursor, you can move the text object by dragging the object using the mouse pointer to any suitable position in the graphics window.

The *u* and *v* grid numbers are even (50 and 40 respectively) for this reason asymmetric distribution is associated with the row matrix

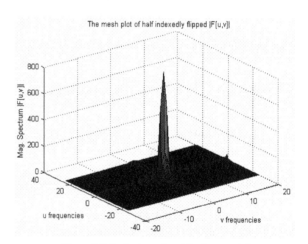

Figure 4.9(c) *Surface plot of the figure 4.9(b)*

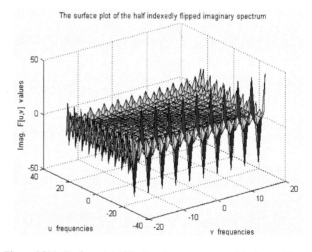

Figure 4.9(e) *Surface plot of the imaginary spectrum of the image H*

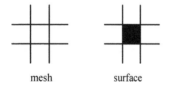

Figure 4.9(d) *The elementary grids for the mesh and surface plots*

generation for u and v (u=-24:25; and v=-19:20; respectively). Of coarse the u and v depend on the original image pixel size. Let us say the size of A were 51×41, under the circumstance the command for the odd number frequencies would be u=-25:25; and v=-20:20; thereby providing a symmetric distribution in the u - v domain. Even if the pixel numbers are even, only one pixelís translation does not alter the surface shape a lot as far as thousands of pixels in a practical image are concern.

Whatever commands are executed for the mesh can be executed for the MATLAB function surf (abbreviation for the surface) to view the surface plot. For instance, we exercise the following in lieu of mesh(v,u,A):

>>surf(v,u,A) ↵

The outcome is the surface plot of the figure 4.9(c) for the same problem. In the mesh plot, the $|F[u, v]|$ values are covered by a net or mesh while on the contrary a surface is used for the covering when the function surf is used. The difference between a mesh and a surface on a tiny grid is depicted in the figure 4.9(d).

The two dimensional Fourier magnitude spectrum is not the only surface plot we have, any other two dimensional transform spectrum can also be graphed as a surface in a similar fashion. For instance, we graph the surface plot of the half indexedly flipped imaginary spectrum of the binary image H as follows:

>>I=imag(F); ↵

>>surf(v,u,I) ↵

The figure 4.9(e) pictures the surface plot of the imaginary spectrum of the H image. Also we inserted the X, Y, and Z labels and title as v frequencies, u frequencies, and Imag. F[u,v] values and The surface plot of the half indexedly flipped imaginary spectrum by clicking the Insert from the figure window as we did before.

For any other transform, we have to have the transform matrix $F[u, v]$ available first. Let us say we are attentive to viewing the surface plot of the two dimensional discrete cosine transform (section 4.3) for the binary H image. The all real function $F[u, v]$ is obtained as follows:

>>F=dct2(H); ↵   ← F holds $F[u, v]$

>>surf(F) ↵

For sure the last line command should display the surface plot of $F[u, v]$ (not displayed for space reason). Since the half index symmetry is not present in the discrete cosine transform, there is no need to apply the fftshift function.

As a practical image example, let us graph the surface plot of the half indexedly flipped Fourier magnitude spectrum of test.bmp (gray one) from section 2.3. Placing the image in the working path, we execute the following:

>>[Y,M]=imread('test.bmp'); ↵   ←Reading the indexed image, where Y⇔intensity image matrix and
                                 M⇔colormap matrix

>>f=ind2gray(Y,M); ↵   ← Turning the indexed image to gray image, where f⇔ $f[m, n]$

>>F=fft2(f); ↵   ← F holds the 2D DFT of $f[m, n] \Leftrightarrow F[u, v]$

>>A=abs(F); ↵   ← $|F[u, v]|$ is assigned to A

Looking into the workspace browser, the size of A or F is 119×140 therefore aforementioned u and v vectors are generated as follows:

>>u=-59:59; ↵   ← 119=59 (for negative)+1(for 0)+59(for positive) integers

>>v=-69:70; ↵   ← 140=69 (for negative)+1(for 0)+70(for positive) integers

>>surf(v,u,fftshift(A)) ↵   ← Displays the surface plot (not presented for space reason)

The surface plot is much like the one in the figure 4.9(c) anyway we bring an end to the section.

4.10 Image transform with padding and truncation

As many as five digital image transforms we introduced so far. All digital image transforms share one common strategy that is they possess a forward transform matrix. What image information is hidden in different portions of the transform matrix can be investigated by deliberately setting some portion of the transform matrix to zero. In this regard padding and truncation operations are significant. Or we may need them to increase the size of the original digital image matrix to transform it on the power of 2 length basis.

The padding of a digital image means adding some zeroes to the image matrix so that its size is increased. It goes without mentioning that the padding must be carried out in horizontal and vertical pixel directions of the digital image. Both the forward and inverse transforms can be padded or truncated. Recall the two dimensional forward and inverse Fourier and cosine transformsí MATLAB functions fft2, ifft2, dct2, and idct2 (sections 4.1 and 4.3). Each of the four functions has the padding and truncating options indicated by appending two more input arguments in the function.

Let us say we have a digital image matrix $f[m,n] = \begin{bmatrix} 7 & 9 & 3 \\ 2 & 3 & 1 \end{bmatrix}$. We intend to form a matrix

$\begin{bmatrix} 7 & 9 & 3 & 0 \\ 2 & 3 & 1 & 0 \\ 0 & 0 & 0 & 0 \end{bmatrix}$ from the $f[m,n]$ which is the padding of the image $f[m,n]$ to the size 3×4 (appending one row

and one column of zeroes) and then apply the two dimensional forward discrete Fourier transform so that the transform has also the size 3×4. Let us carry out that as follows:

MATLAB Command

>>f=[7 9 3;2 3 1]; ↵   ← Assigning $f[m,n]$ to f
>>fft2(f,3,4) ↵

ans =

25.0000	5.0000 -12.0000i	1.0000	5.0000 +12.0000i
16.0000 - 5.1962i	0.9019 - 8.3660i	1.0000	6.0981 + 6.6340i
16.0000 + 5.1962i	6.0981 - 6.6340i	1.0000	0.9019 + 8.3660i

With the command fft2(f), the return would be of size 2×3 but now the transform return is of the size 3×4. The function fft2 has three input arguments, the second and third of which intake the requisite row and column numbers respectively to which the $f[m,n]$ to be padded. The row and column numbers (3 and 4) must be greater than those of the original ones (2 and 3) in $f[m,n]$.

Instead of taking the Fourier transform on the whole image matrix $f[m,n]$, we may seek for the transform up to specific row and column numbers in the image matrix ñ this is called the truncation. Considering

$f[m,n] = \begin{bmatrix} 7 & 9 & 3 & 0 \\ 2 & 3 & 1 & 0 \\ 0 & 0 & 0 & 0 \end{bmatrix}$, we wish to compute the transform only on the first 2×2 portion of $f[m,n]$ that is

$\begin{bmatrix} 7 & 9 \\ 2 & 3 \end{bmatrix}$, which is termed as the truncation of $f[m,n]$ to 2×2. Therefore the forward transform matrix must be of

order 2×2 whose implementation is as follows:

>>f=[7 9 3 0;2 3 1 0;0 0 0 0]; ↵   ← Assigning the last $f[m,n]$ to f
>>fft2(f,2,2) ↵   ← the 2nd and 3rd input arguments of fft2 indicate truncation order

ans =
    21   -3
    11   -1

The truncation is accomplished. In contrast to the padding, the second and third input arguments (2 and 2) of the fft2 are less than the actual image size (3 and 4) for the truncation. We illustrated the padding and truncation on the forward transform, the same can happen in the inverse Fourier transform as well. The provision for similar padding and truncation is also included in the discrete cosine transform functions dct2 and idct2. For the other types of transforms, padding and truncation can be brought about by deleting or appending specific rows and/or columns before applying the transform (sections 10.5 and 10.6). With the padding and truncation discourse, we bring an end to the chapter.

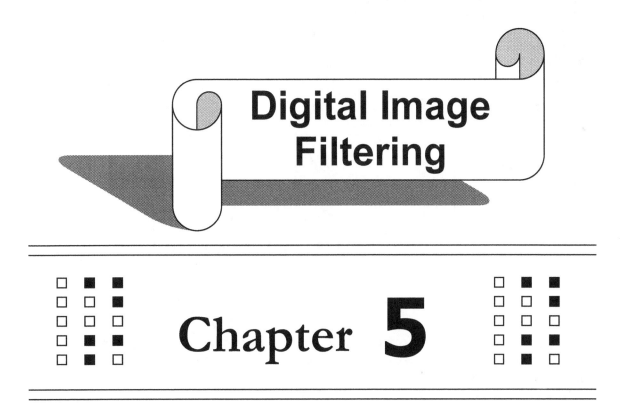

Digital Image Filtering

Chapter 5

In this chapter we concentrate on the implementation of the digital image filters often exercised in diversified image processing applications. Sampling two wide applications, filtering a digital image is principally required for the image enhancement and restoration. Generally speaking, there are two approaches practiced for the digital image filter design. The first approach is the spatial domain approach through which mask based design maneuvering takes place on the digital image matrix without taking any transform. The second one transforms the digital image and any design criterion is applied in the transform domain. Apart from these two approaches, a digital image is also filtered based on its local characteristics. However followings are the headings that are highlighted in this discourse:

- ❖ ❖ The concept of the digital image filtering along with different types
- ❖ ❖ Important approaches for image filter design ñ in spatial and in spatial frequency domains
- ❖ ❖ Design of the four basic ideal filters accompanying the Butterworth counterpart
- ❖ ❖ Two dimensional median, homomorphic, and minimum square error (Wiener) filters
- ❖ ❖ Mask for filtering and mask-oriented filtering applying the built-in or user defined alternative

5.1 Digital image filtering

Digital image filtering is required to improve the image quality or restoring the digital image which is corrupted by some noise. Sometimes filtering is applied even for generating special visual effects on some movie scenes. Image filter design can take place in the spatial or transform domain. In the spatial domain approach we do not transform the image instead user defined masks or blocks are employed for the filtering. Figure 5.1(a) shows the basic approach for the image filter design in the spatial domain. Mostly two dimensional discrete convolution (section 3.10) is applied as the mathematical tool to reach to the filtered digital image from the unfiltered one. On the contrary in the transform domain approach, we first transform the digital image $f[m,n]$ using two dimensional forward discrete Fourier or other transform (chapter 4). Image filter function design solely happens in the transform or spatial frequency domain. Following the filter design, the two dimensional inverse discrete transform is applied to obtain the image back in the spatial domain. Figure 5.1(b) depicts the block diagram of digital image filter

90

design using the transform domain approach. The term frequency primarily applies to the Fourier transform context. The Fourier transform decomposes the digital image information $f[m,n]$ as a sum of $M \times N$ modular sinusoids. These modular sinusoids are nicknamed as the frequency component. The ideal image filter classification is based on the rejection, retainment, or modification of the frequency components. In next section we address how one can design the ideal digital image filters in spatial frequency domain.

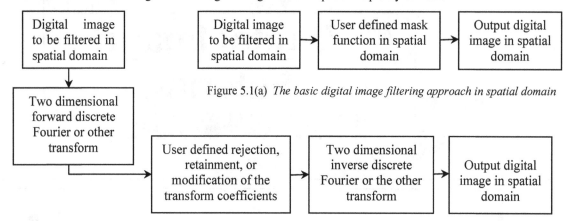

Figure 5.1(a) *The basic digital image filtering approach in spatial domain*

Figure 5.1(b) *The basic digital image filtering approach in the transform domain*

5.2 Ideal digital image filters in spatial frequency domain

Referring to section 4.1, any digital image matrix $f[m,n]$ for a digital gray image has two dimensional forward discrete Fourier transform $F[u,v]$. If the image $f[m,n]$ has $M \times N$ pixels, so does the size of $F[u,v]$. The u and v are called the spatial frequencies of the image. We can deliberately set some u and v frequency components to zero to see the ideal filtering effect. Depending on the u-v domain selection, we have four types of filter ñ lowpass, highpass, bandpass, and bandstop. Since the $F[u,v]$ has the half index symmetry, customarily we describe the filter definition in terms of the half indexedly flipped version of the transform (section 4.1). Let us say $H[u,v]$ is the half indexedly flipped version of the forward discrete transform $F[u,v]$. The u and v can vary from 1 to M and from 1 to N respectively (MATLAB notation). But the $H[u,v]$ is defined in terms of the center

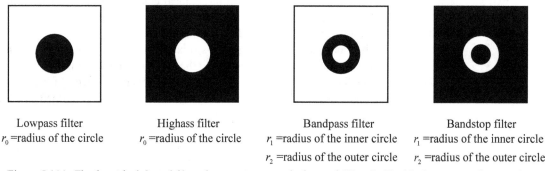

Lowpass filter	Highass filter	Bandpass filter	Bandstop filter
r_0 =radius of the circle	r_0 =radius of the circle	r_1 =radius of the inner circle	r_1 =radius of the inner circle
		r_2 =radius of the outer circle	r_2 =radius of the outer circle

Figure 5.1(c) *The four ideal digital filter characteristics on the base of $H[u,v]$. The black region is the transform pass region for each filter*

position on the u-v domain. The center position takes place at the coordinates $\left(\dfrac{M+1}{2}, \dfrac{N+1}{2}\right)$, which falls inbetween the u or v nodes for even M or N. On that the radial distance between any point on the base of $F[u,v]$ and the central point is given by $r = \sqrt{\left(u - \dfrac{M+1}{2}\right)^2 + \left(v - \dfrac{N+1}{2}\right)^2}$. All ideal image filters have the user defined spatial cutoff frequency (s) based on the r and the definitions of the four types of the filter are as follows:

Ideal lowpass filter: $H[u,v] = \begin{cases} 1 & for\ r \leq r_0 \\ 0 & for\ r > r_0 \end{cases}$ where r_0 is the user defined lowpass cutoff frequency

Ideal highpass filter: $H[u,v] = \begin{cases} 0 & for\ r \leq r_0 \\ 1 & for\ r > r_0 \end{cases}$ where r_0 is the user defined highpass cutoff frequency

Ideal bandpass filter: $H[u,v] = \begin{cases} 1 & for\ r_1 \leq r \leq r_2 \\ 0 & elsewhere \end{cases}$ where r_1 and r_2 are the user defined lower and

upper cutoff frequencies respectively

Ideal bandstop filter: $H[u,v] = \begin{cases} 0 & for\ r_1 \leq r \leq r_2 \\ 1 & elsewhere \end{cases}$ where r_1 and r_2 are the user defined lower and

upper cutoff frequencies respectively

Figure 5.1(c) depicts the schematic representations of the four ideal filters based on the u-v domain of the $H[u,v]$ in which the black region corresponds to the passband or the region where $H[u,v]=1$. Since multiple programming statements are to be written, we need an M-file (section 1.3) to design the ideal digital filters.

We wish to design an ideal lowpass radially symmetric digital filter like the figure 5.1(c) of cutoff frequency $r_0=10$ and of the size 40×40. This is actually two dimensional forward transform matrix $F[u,v]$ size and should also be the image pixel size. To begin the design, we form a matrix of ones of the same size as that of $F[u,v]$. With the

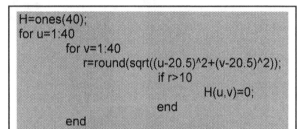

```
H=ones(40);
for u=1:40
        for v=1:40
                r=round(sqrt((u-20.5)^2+(v-20.5)^2));
                        if r>10
                                H(u,v)=0;
                        end
        end
end
```

Figure 5.1(d) *M-file statements for the ideal lowpass two dimensional digital filter design*

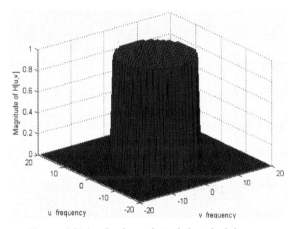

Figure 5.2(a) *Surface plot of the ideal lowpass filter function $H[u,v]$ at a cutoff frequency 10*

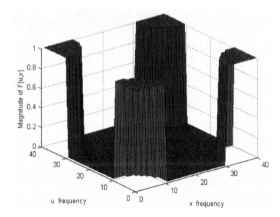

Figure 5.2(b) *Surface plot of the ideal lowpass filter function $F[u,v]$ at a cutoff frequency 10*

size 40×40, the center point coordinate in the u-v domain is given by (20.5,20.5) hence the variable distance is $r = \sqrt{(u-20.5)^2 + (v-20.5)^2}$ whose MATLAB code is given by **sqrt((u-20.5)^2+(v-20.5)^2)**. Since the value of u or v is positive integer, we round the r towards the nearest integer with the help of MATLAB function **round**. The whole u-v domain is selected by using two for-loops whose counter index controls the spatial frequency position in $H[u,v]$ where u or v varies from 1 to 40 (decided from user defined matrix size of $F[u,v]$). However the complete code of the $H[u,v]$ design is given in the figure 5.1(d). Type the MATLAB statements in the M-file editor (sections 1.3 and 10.3) and run the file. The workspace variable **H** is holding the two dimensional filter transform function $H[u,v]$ for the lowpass filter. The **H** is rather a matrix and does not bear any information regarding the u or v. MATLAB by default assumes the number of points as the domain variation. For example with the 40 points in the u direction (can be seen in the workspace browser), the u coordinates are chosen from 1 to 40. Since the design concerns the half indexedly flipped one, we can form a row vector from ñ19.5 to 19.5 with increment 1 to make sense with the design. This can happen by first generating a row matrix from 1 to 40 with

92

increment 1 and then subtracting 20.5 from every element whose equivalent MATLAB command is [1:40]-20.5. Anyhow the reader can view the surface plot (section 4.9) of the designed $H[u,v]$ by the following commands:

>>U=[1:40]-20.5; ↵
>>V=[1:40]-20.5; ↵
>>surf(V,U,H) ↵

Figure 5.2(a) presents the surface plot of the lowpass two dimensional digital filter we designed. We inserted v frequency, u frequency, and Magnitude of H[u,v] by first clicking the Insert menu and then X Label, Y Label, and Z Label respectively from the figure window. Also you need to click the Edit plot icon (section 1.3) following the labeling. Let us not forget that the H is holding the half indexedly flipped version of the filter transfer

```
H=ones(40);
for u=1:40
        for v=1:40
                r=round(sqrt((u-20.5)^2+(v-20.5)^2));
                if r<10
                        H(u,v)=0;
                end
        end
end
U=[1:40]-20.5;
V=[1:40]-20.5;
surf(V,U,H)
F=fftshift(H);
```

Figure 5.2(c) *M-file statements for the ideal highpass two dimensional digital filter design*

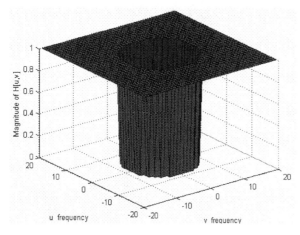

Figure 5.2(d)   *Surface plot of the highpass filter function $H[u,v]$ at a cutoff frequency $r_0=10$*

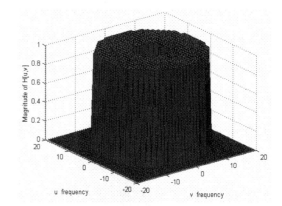

Figure 5.2(e) *Surface plot of the bandpass filter function $H[u,v]$ at cutoff frequencies $r_1=5$ and $r_2=15$*

function. To obtain it back in the original domain of u-v, one should take the help of the MALAB function fftshift (section 4.1) as follows:

>>F=fftshift(H); ↵

The actual lowpass filter transfer function $F[u,v]$ to be applicable for the image filtering is now held by the workspace variable F for which the u or v variation is from 1 to 40. However we can obtain the surface plot of the actual lowpass filter function as we did for the $H[u,v]$ by executing surf(F). Figure 5.2(b) shows the surface plot of $F[u,v]$ which is what we intended to design. *It is important to mention that when filtering some image function, we apply the $F[u,v]$ not the $H[u,v]$*.

We elaborately quoted the design procedure for an ideal two dimensional digital lowpass filter. The design procedure for the other three filter types is very

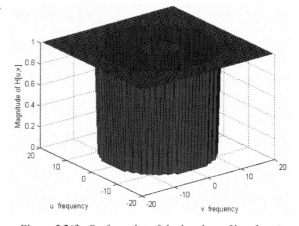

Figure 5.2(f) *Surface plot of the bandstop filter function $H[u,v]$ at cutoff frequencies $r_1=5$ and $r_2=15$*

similar to that of the lowpass. Only do we change the cut-off frequency condition (s) which is incorporated in the logical expression of the if-end statement presented in the figure 5.1(d). However we illustrate the complete codes for the three other ideal filters in the following so that the reader feels convenient with the design.

♣♦ Highpass example

Design an ideal highpass two dimensional digital image filter of size 40×40 whose highpass cutoff spatial frequency is $r_0 = 10$. The complete M-file codes for the highpass filter design is presented in the figure 5.2(c). Running the codes of the figure, one obtains the surface plot of the $H[u,v]$ transfer function for the highpass filter as graphed in the figure 5.2(d). The programming statements are identical with that of the lowpass one (figure 5.1(d)) except the logical expression r<10.

♣♦ Bandpass example

Design an ideal bandpass two dimensional digital image filter of size 40×40 whose bandpass cutoff spatial frequencies are $r_1 = 5$ and $r_2 = 15$ respectively. The programming statements are identical with that of the lowpass (figure 5.1(d)) or highpass (figure 5.2(c)) one but the condition beside the if must be r>15|r<5. Figure 5.2(e) portraits the surface plot of the $H[u,v]$ function for the filter.

♣♦ Bandstop example

Design an ideal bandstop two dimensional digital image filter of size 40×40 whose bandstop cutoff spatial frequencies are $r_1 = 5$ and $r_2 = 15$ respectively. For the design, all we need is change the if condition of previous statements to r<15&r>5 which should result the surface plot of $H[u,v]$ as shown in the figure 5.2(f).

Once again in all examples the variable F holds the actual filter function $F[u,v]$. While applying the fftshift function, the odd number size of the input argument of the function shifts the whole transform by 1 sample thereby resulting a slight distortion. To avoid that, we suggest the reader to take the filter size as the even number.

♣♦ Ideal lowpass filtering applied to a digital image

Let us consider the softcopy digital image dip.bmp of section 2.3 and obtain the image in our working directory. We intend to apply the ideal lowpass filtering on the gray image at a cutoff frequency $r_0 = 20$. Applying the function imfinfo of subsection 6.1.1, the image is an indexed one whose gray version is displayed in figure 6.1(c). The lowpass concept is associated with the transfom domain approach for which the schematics of the figure 5.1(b) applies. According to the block diagram, first the image needs being read off and we do so as follows:

>>[Y,Mp]=imread('dip.bmp'); ↵ ← Reading the indexed image, where Y⇔intensity image matrix and
Mp⇔colormap matrix

>>f=ind2gray(Y,Mp); ↵   ← Turning the indexed image to gray image, where f⇔ $f[m,n]$

The next step is to take the two dimensional forward discrete Fourier transform of f with the help of fft2 (section 4.1) and assign the transform to the workspace variable G which is essentially the theory discussed $F[u,v]$ of the section 4.1 for the digital image:

>>G=fft2(f); ↵

The design of the two dimensional lowpass digital filter needs the filter size to be decided which comes from the size of G. Let us find it as follows:

>>[M,N]=size(G); ↵

Therefore the filter size must be M×N (M=218 and N=256 can be checked from the workspace browser) instead of the beginning exampleís 40×40. Involving the M or N means implementing the programming in a general way. Recall that in the first line of the M-file statements in the figure 5.1(d), we had H=ones(40); now the

```
H=ones(M,N);
for u=1:M
        for v=1:N
                r=round(sqrt((u-(M+1)/2)^2+(v-(N+1)/2)^2));
                if r>20
                        H(u,v)=0;
                end
        end
end
F=fftshift(H);
```

Figure 5.3(a) *M-file statements for the ideal lowpass two dimensional digital filter design for the image dip.bmp*

statement should be H=ones(218,256); in order to meet the dip.bmp image specification. The last counter values of for-loops must be M and N for the u and v respectively. The radial distance $\sqrt{\left(u - \dfrac{M+1}{2}\right)^2 + \left(v - \dfrac{N+1}{2}\right)^2}$ has the

MATLAB code sqrt((u-(M+1)/2)^2+(v-(N+1)/2)^2). The other change we need is in the statement related to the cutoff frequency which dwells beside the if statement. Since the user defined cutoff spatial frequency is 20, the command now should be r>20. However we provide the complete codes for the filter design in the figure 5.3(a). Make necessary modifications in previous M-file statements and run the M-file. On that execution the lowpass filter transfer function $F[u,v]$ is being held by the variable **F** in the workspace. Let us call the two dimensional forward discrete Fourier transform of the image dip.bmp as $G[u,v]$ which is held in the variable **G**. Multiplication

Figure 5.3(b) *Ideal lowpass filtering on the image dip.bmp at cutoff frequency 20*

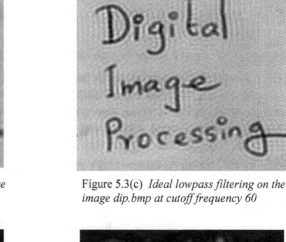

Figure 5.3(c) *Ideal lowpass filtering on the image dip.bmp at cutoff frequency 60*

Figure 5.3(d) *Ideal highpass filtering on the image dip.bmp at cutoff frequency 10*

Figure 5.3(e) *Ideal bandpass filtering on the image dip.bmp at the lower and upper cutoff frequencies $r_1 = 5$ and $r_2 = 15$ respectively*

in the spatial frequency domain results the ideal lowpass image filtering and it is just the mathematical operation $G[u,v]\ F[u,v]$. Note that the multiplication is scalar that is multiplication of the like positional elements of the identical size matrics $G[u,v]$ and $F[u,v]$. The MATLAB statement for the $G[u,v]\ F[u,v]$ is **G.*F** (section 10.2). Anyhow let us carry out the following:

```
>>T=G.*F; ↵
>>R=abs(ifft2(T)); ↵
>>imshow(R,[ ]) ↵
```

The first line in above command is the assignment of the filtered transfer function $G[u,v]\ F[u,v]$ to the workspace variable **T**. After that, one needs to take the two dimensional inverse discrete Fourier transform in accordance with the figure 5.1(b). The command ifft2 takes the inverse Fourier transform (section 4.1) of **T** followed by taking the absolute value with the help of the MATLAB command **abs**. The nature of the Fourier forward or inverse transform is complex. Depending on the gray level energy concentration as well as the spatial frequency maneuvering, we may end up with the complex number gray level that is not feasible at all. This is the rationale for taking the absolute value. Anyhow, the outcome is assigned to the workspace variable **R** which is our recovered image ensuing the ideal lowpass filtering. The last line command shows the recovered image as presented in the figure 5.3(b) by mapping the gray level in [0,1] (section 2.5). Comparing to the original image in the figure 6.1(c), image blurring becomes visible due to the lowpass filtering. To see the effect of another spatial frequency, let us consider the spatial cutoff frequency of the lowpass filter to be 60. For that, change the statement beside the if to r>60 in the M-file of the figure 5.3(a) and run the M-file following saving. The last three linesí execution results in the figure 5.3(c) which shows the ideal lowpass filtered dip.bmp image at spatial cutoff frequency 60 ñ the conclusion one can draw is the image becomes less blurry as the lowpass spatial cutoff frequency of the filter increases.

♣ ♣ Ideal highpass filtering applied to the digital image dip.bmp

We intend to apply the ideal two dimensional highpass filtering to the digital image dip.bmp at a cutoff spatial frequency $r_0 = 10$. In the codes of the lowpass which are located in the figure 5.3(a), just replace the r>20 with r<10 beside the if statement and run the M-file and all relevant statements afterward. The reader should see the ideal highpass filtered image as shown in the figure 5.3(d).

♣ ♣ Ideal bandpass or bandstop filtering applied to the digital image dip.bmp

To see the ideal bandpass filtering effect on the dip.bmp, let us choose the lower and upper spatial cutoff frequencies as $r_1 = 5$ and $r_2 = 15$ respectively. Now we turn the logical if expression of the figure 5.3(a) to r>15|r<5 for the required bandpass filter however presented figure 5.3(e) is the aftereffect of the ideal bandpass filtering. Analogously one can investigate the effect of the ideal bandstop filtering on the digital image.

5.3 Butterworth digital image filtering

The design of the Butterworth filter takes place in the spatial frequency domain for which the general block diagram of the figure 5.1(b) is equally applicable. The filter differs from the ideal counterpart as discussed in the last section to the expressional context of the half indexedly flipped transfer function $H[u,v]$. We presented the

definition of the four basic types of the ideal filter in terms of the radial distance r in the spatial frequency or the u - v domain from the center point $\left(\dfrac{M+1}{2}, \dfrac{N+1}{2}\right)$ in the last section as well. Let us consider the ideal lowpass filter which

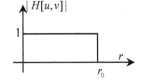

Figure 5.4(a) *Ideal lowpass image filter along the radial direction r*

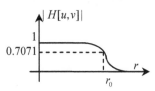

Figure 5.4(b) *Butterworth lowpass image filter along the radial direction r*

has the transfer function $H[u,v] = \begin{cases} 1 & for \ r \le r_0 \\ 0 & for \ r > r_0 \end{cases}$. In any direction around the center point on the u - v plane, the

$H[u,v]$ has a sharp transition (figure 5.4(a)) from 1 to 0 at the spatial cutoff frequency r_0. In the Butterworth lowpass filter this sharpness is smoothed by introducing some inverse squared distance function with respect to the cutoff frequency r_0. Figure 5.4(b) shows a typical characteristic of the Butterworth lowpass filter. However the transfer function of the Butterworth lowpass filter in the spatial frequency domain is given by $H[u,v] =$

$\dfrac{1}{1 + (\sqrt{2} - 1)\left(\dfrac{r}{r_0}\right)^{2n}}$ where r_0 and n are called the spatial cutoff frequency and the order of the filter respectively.

Of coarse, both the r_0 and n are user defined. Customarily, the cutoff frequency r_0 of the Butterworth filter is

defined as the spatial frequency at which the $H[u,v]$ is down to $\dfrac{1}{\sqrt{2}}$ or 0.7071 of its maximum value.

As an example, let us design a digital two dimensional lowpass Butterworth filter of order 2 at a cutoff frequency 10. These two parameters are not enough for the design. Since the design befalls in the spatial frequency domain, the image pixel size or in other words the u - v size must have to be known in advance. Let us assume that the image or its transform size is 30×40. Our objective is to find just mentioned half indexedly flipped transfer function $H[u,v]$ from these specifications.

In the last section, we designed the ideal lowpass filter and the others using two for-loop concept. Here in this problem vectorization of the for-loop (section 10.11) is employed. Vectorization of the for-loop is efficient in computation to the context of execution time because of the digital imageís large pixel number. With the required

specification, the $H[u,v]$ becomes $\dfrac{1}{1 + 0.4142\left(\dfrac{r}{10}\right)^4}$ with $r = \sqrt{\left(u - \dfrac{M+1}{2}\right)^2 + \left(v - \dfrac{N+1}{2}\right)^2}$ where $M = 30$ and

$N = 40$. Let us present the complete code for the lowpass Butterworth filter design as follows:

MATLAB Command
```
>>M=30; u=[1:M]'; ↵
>>N=40; v=[1:N]; ↵
```

```
>>U=repmat(u,1,N); ↵
>>V=repmat(v,M,1); ↵
>>r=sqrt((U-(M+1)/2).^2+(V-(N+1)/2).^2); ↵
>>H=1./(1+0.4142*(r/10).^4); ↵
>>F=fftshift(H); ↵
```

In above command the M=30; and N=40; are just the assignment of the transfer functioní u and v directed size respectively. The u and v are positive integer. Because of the size 30×40, they change from 1 to 30 and from 1 to 40 with the step 1 which are generated by the command u=[1:30]'; and v=1:40; respectively. But the u and v must

be a column and a row vectors respectively. The U and V hold $\begin{bmatrix} 1 & 1 & & 1 \\ 2 & 2 & & 2 \\ 3 & 3 & \cdots & 3 \\ \vdots & \vdots & & \\ 30 & 30 & & 30 \end{bmatrix}$ and $\begin{bmatrix} 1 & 2 & 3 & \cdots & 40 \\ 1 & 2 & 3 & \cdots & 40 \\ & & \vdots & & \\ 1 & 2 & 3 & \cdots & 40 \end{bmatrix}$

respectively. Both of them must be of the same size as that of the required $H[u,v]$ which is here 30×40. The size as well as the contents of a matrix can be verified from the workspace browser (doubleclick the concern variable to see the array editor). The fifth line in the command is the MATLAB code for the radial distance r. The transfer function $\dfrac{1}{1+0.4142\left(\dfrac{r}{10}\right)^4}$ has the code

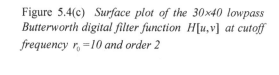

1./(1+0.4142*(r/10).^4) but we do not use the vector code unlike the ideal lowpass counterpart instead we employ the scalar code (section 10.2). However the variable H holds the half indexedly flipped lowpass Butterworth filter transfer function $H[u,v]$. To obtain the unflipped or actual transfer function $F[u,v]$, we exercise the last line command. Now the F can be applied to any image of the size 30×40 in the spatial frequency domain. If the reader is interested in viewing the surface plot of the $H[u,v]$, the following command like the ideal lowpass counterpart can be executed:

Figure 5.4(c) *Surface plot of the 30×40 lowpass Butterworth digital filter function $H[u,v]$ at cutoff frequency $r_0 =10$ and order 2*

```
>>U=[1:30]-15.5; V=[1:40]-20.5; ↵
>>surf(V,U,H) ↵
```

Observe that we changed the contents of the workspace variables U and V for the graphing reason. Presented figure 5.4(c) is the surface plot of the designed lowpass digital Butterworth filter (last section for the label insertion). Comparing the last graph to the ideal counterpart of the figure 5.2(a), the sharp transition is smoothed to some degree ñ that is what is required from the design.

♦ ♦ Butterworth lowpass filtering applied to the digital image dip.bmp

Without the application to a practical digital image, the theory does not become meaningful. Let us apply just discussed lowpass Butterworth digital filter of order $n =2$ and having cutoff frequency $r_0 =10$ to the gray version dip.bmp of section 2.3 as follows (obtain the image in your working directory):

```
>>[Y,Mp]=imread('dip.bmp'); ↵    ←Reading the indexed image, where Y⇔intensity image matrix and
                                    Mp⇔colormap matrix
>>f=ind2gray(Y,Mp); ↵             ← Turning the indexed image to gray image, where f⇔ f[m,n]
>>G=fft2(f); ↵                    ← 2D DFT on the image f and G holds the transform G[u,v]
>>[M,N]=size(G); ↵                ← Deciding the filter size from the size of G
>>u=[1:M]'; v=[1:N]; ↵  ← Generating aforementioned column and row vectors u and v respectively
>>U=repmat(u,1,N); ↵              ← Generating U from the same column vector u
>>V=repmat(v,M,1); ↵              ← Generating V from the same row vector v
>>r=sqrt((U-(M+1)/2).^2+(V-(N+1)/2).^2); ↵     ← Computation of the radial distance r
>>H=1./(1+0.4142*(r/10).^4); ↵             ← Computation of the H[u,v] for the filter
>>F=fftshift(H); ↵        ← F holds the unflipped counterpart of the filter which is F[u,v]
```

>>T=G.*F; ↵   ← T holds filtered image transform followed by the operation $G[u,v]$ $F[u,v]$
>>R=abs(ifft2(T)); ↵   ← R holds the inverse 2D DFT on T followed by the absolute value
>>imshow(R,[ ]) ↵   ← Displaying the contents of R first turning the gray levels to [0,1]

Successful execution should show you the image of the figure 5.4(d) as the expected output.

❖ ❖ Butterworth highpass filtering applied to the digital image dip.bmp

A Butterworth highpass filter has the transfer function $H[u,v] = \dfrac{1}{1+(\sqrt{2}-1)\left(\dfrac{r_0}{r}\right)^{2n}}$ where r, r_0, and n

have their usual meanings as mentioned previously. Note that the r and r_0 interchanged the numerator and denominator positions compared to the lowpass counterpart. Let us apply the highpass Butterworth filter at $r_0 = 10$ and of order 2 to the image dip.bmp. Because of the different expression for the $H[u,v]$, the MATLAB code should be H=1./(1+0.4142*(10./r).^4);. The rest of the programming is exactly identical with that of the lowpass counterpart. Figure 5.4(e) presents the dip.bmp image upon the application of the Butterworth highpass filtering.

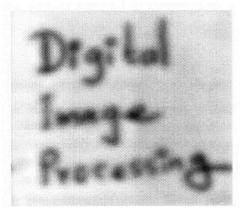

Figure 5.4(d) *Butterworth lowpass filtering on the image dip.bmp at cutoff frequency* $r_0 = 10$ *and order* $n = 2$

Figure 5.4(e) *Butterworth highpass filtering on the image dip.bmp at cutoff frequency* $r_0 = 10$ *and order* $n = 2$

5.4 Median filtering of a digital image

The median filtering functions solely on the local statistical properties of a digital image. One can say that the filtering occurs in the spatial or pixel domain as schematized in the figure 5.1(a). Further discussions on the median gray level and filtering are presented in subsections 6.1.4 and 7.4.1.

If we have a set of digital image pixel gray or color levels, the median of the set is defined as the half of the values in the set are less than the median and the half are greater than the median. When applied to a digital image, the filtering obligates to select a specific neighborhood or block size and the user has to supply the block size which is also called the mask.

Let us say we have the modular digital image matrix $f[m,n] = \begin{bmatrix} 6 & -5 & 3 & 4 & 2 \\ 0 & -3 & 2 & 9 & 10 \\ 11 & -2 & 1 & -1 & 0 \\ 12 & -6 & 5 & 7 & 33 \end{bmatrix}$ and intend to

perform the median filtering on the image $f[m,n]$ with a mask size of 3×3. The filtering happens to every gray level in the image matrix $f[m,n]$ but the original gray level is not altered at all during the filtering. At the edge points if the mask fits out of $f[m,n]$, the rest elements inside the neighborhood or mask are taken as zero. In MATLAB notation the first element 6 in $f[m,n]$ has the position index (1,1). Placing the 3×3 mask on the first

element results in $\begin{bmatrix} 0 & 0 & 0 \\ 0 & 6 & -5 \\ 0 & 0 & -3 \end{bmatrix}$. We first sort the set of the values in order to perform the median filtering on the

block which is [0 0 0 0 0 0 −5 −3 6]. The median is the 5th element because we have the odd number (here it is 9) of elements. Therefore the median value 0 occupies the position indexed by (1,1). Few more positional values of the $f[m,n]$ are presented in the following:

position index	elements inside the 3×3 mask	sorted elements inside the mask	the 5th element
(1, 2)	$\begin{bmatrix} 0 & 0 & 0 \\ 6 & -5 & 3 \\ 0 & -3 & 2 \end{bmatrix}$	[-5 -3 0 0 0 0 2 3 6] ↑	0
(2, 1)	$\begin{bmatrix} 0 & 6 & -5 \\ 0 & 0 & -3 \\ 0 & 11 & -2 \end{bmatrix}$	[-5 -3 -2 0 0 0 0 6 11] ↑	0
(2, 2)	$\begin{bmatrix} 6 & -5 & 3 \\ 0 & -3 & 2 \\ 11 & -2 & 1 \end{bmatrix}$	[-5 -3 -2 0 1 2 3 6 11] ↑	1
(3, 4)	$\begin{bmatrix} 2 & 9 & 10 \\ 1 & -1 & 0 \\ 5 & 7 & 33 \end{bmatrix}$	[-1 0 1 2 5 7 9 10 33] ↑	5

Thus one can obtain the median filtered matrix as $\begin{bmatrix} 0 & 0 & 0 & 2 & 0 \\ 0 & 1 & 1 & 2 & 0 \\ 0 & 1 & 1 & 5 & 0 \\ 0 & 0 & 0 & 0 & 0 \end{bmatrix}$ – this is what we expect from MATLAB.

The MATLAB function medfilt2 (abbreviation of the <u>med</u>ian <u>filt</u>ering in two (<u>2</u>) dimensions) can compute the median filtering as follows:

MATLAB Command

```
>>f=[6 -5 3 4 2;0 -3 2 9 10;11 -2 1 -1 0;12 -6 5 7 33]; ↵     ← Assigning f[m,n] to f
>>R=medfilt2(f,[3,3]) ↵                                        ← R is holding the filtered image

R =
     0    0    0    2    0
     0    1    1    2    0
     0    1    1    5    0
     0    0    0    0    0
```

The function medfilt2 has two input arguments, the first and second of which are the digital image matrix and the mask size chosen for the filtering. The mask size argument is coded as the two element row matrix. If we intended to use 5×7 mask size, the command would be medfilt2(f,[5,7]). The command medfilt2(f) filters the image on a default 3×3 mask size.

We wish to median filter the image dip.bmp (gray version) of section 2.3 on a 3×3 mask size for which we adopted the following MATLAB statements assuming that the image is in your working folder:

Figure 5.5(a) *Median filtering of the image dip.bmp*

```
>>[Y,Mp]=imread('dip.bmp'); ↵     ← Reading the indexed image, where Y⇔intensity image matrix and
                                     Mp⇔colormap matrix
>>f=ind2gray(Y,Mp); ↵              ← Turning the indexed image to gray image, where f⇔ f[m,n]
>>R=medfilt2(f); ↵                 ← R is holding the filtered image
>>imshow(R,[ ]) ↵                  ← Displaying the filtered image first turning in [0,1]
```

Figure 5.5(a) depicts the median filtered image. The input image matrix of the medfilt2 must be a rectangular one and it can not be a three dimensional array as happens in the true color image. The data classes that the function supports are logical, unsigned 8-bit integer, unsigned 16-bit integer, and double.

5.5 Homomorphic filtering of a digital image

The reader is referred to [20] for the theory behind the homomorphic filtering. The filtering is applied in the spatial frequency domain but not directly. The block diagram of the homomorphic filtering is shown in the figure 5.5(b). The first phase of the filtering is to take natural logarithm on every gray level in the given digital image matrix $f[m,n]$ (MATLAB counterpart log). Then the two dimensional forward discrete Fourier transform (section 4.1) is applied to obtain $G[u,v]$ in the spatial frequency domain. After that the user selected filter function $F[u,v]$ whose half indexedly flipped version is $H[u,v]$ is computed. The filtering happens to carrying out $G[u,v]\,F[u,v]$. For the recovery two dimensional inverse discrete Fourier transform (section 4.1) is applied to $G[u,v]\,F[u,v]$. Then exponent on every complex element obtained from the inverse transform is conducted to gain the filtered output image matrix $o[m,n]$. All matrices involved in the processing have the same size (the size of the original image matrix). The element in given digital image $f[m,n]$ must not be zero because of $\ln 0 = -\infty$. The nature of the discrete Fourier transform urges to calculate the exponentiation in complex numbers for instance $e^{2+j4} = e^2 \cos 4 + je^2 \sin 4$. We take the absolute value of complex $o[m,n]$ to bring the image back to the spatial domain with the help of the command **abs**. Theoretically speaking $o[m,n]$ should not be complex because of the symmetric nature of $H[u,v]$ but complex number arises due to the digitization and machine accuracy.

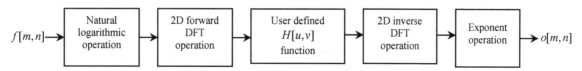

Figure 5.5(b) *Block diagram of the homomorphic filtering*

Now the homomorphic filter term $H[u,v]$ needs to be addressed. The $H[u,v]$ function for the homomorphic filter can be derived from the Butterworth highpass counterpart whose definition is $H[u,v] = \dfrac{1}{1+(\sqrt{2}-1)\left(\dfrac{r_0}{r}\right)^{2n}}$ (symbols have their usual meanings). The modified expression for the homomorphic filter is

given by $H[u,v] = a + \dfrac{b-a}{1+(\sqrt{2}-1)\left(\dfrac{r_0}{r}\right)^{2n}}$, where the parameters a and b are user defined scalars with $a<1$, $b>1$, and $b>a$. Let us choose $a=0.5$, $b=2$, $r_0=10$, $n=2$, and $0 \le r \le 50$. Figure 5.5(c) shows the plot of the $H[u,v]$ versus the radial distance r for the homomorphic filtering.

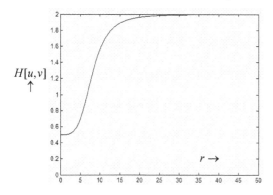

Figure 5.5(c) *Plot of the $H[u,v]$ for the homomorphic filter*

Figure 5.5(d) *The image dip.bmp followed by the homomorphic filtering*

With the expression mentioned, we wish to implement the homomorphic filtering on the gray dip.bmp of section 2.3. All notations and symbols employed in sections 5.2 and 5.3 are drawn here. Plugging the chosen values of the filter parameters a, b, r_0, and n, the homomorphic filter expression becomes

$H[u,v] = 0.5 + \dfrac{1.5}{1+0.4142\left(\dfrac{10}{r}\right)^4}$ which has the scalar form MATLAB code `0.5+1.5./(1+0.4142*(10./r).^4)`.

Assuming the image dip.bmp in our working path, we go for the implementation straightforwardly in accordance with the block diagram 5.5(b) as follows:

MATLAB Command

>>[Y,Mp]=imread('dip.bmp'); ↵ ← Reading the indexed image, where Y⇔intensity image matrix and
Mp⇔colormap matrix

>>f=ind2gray(Y,Mp); ↵   ← Turning the indexed image to gray image, where f⇔ $f[m,n]$ in [0,1]

>>f=log(f); ↵   ← Applying the natural logarithm on f and again assigning the output to f⇔ $\ln\{f[m,n]\}$

>>G=fft2(f); ↵ ← Applying 2D forward DFT on $\ln\{f[m,n]\}$ and assigning the output to G which is $G[u,v]$

>>[M,N]=size(G); ↵   ← Finding the filter size from the size of G

>>u=[1:M]'; v=[1:N]; ↵   ← Finding the column and row vectors u and v respectively for the $H[u,v]$

>>U=repmat(u,1,N); ↵   ← Finding the repetitive matrix U from u

>>V=repmat(v,M,1); ↵   ← Finding the repetitive matrix V from v

>>r=sqrt((U-(M+1)/2).^2+(V-(N+1)/2).^2); ↵ ← Computing radial distance from the center of u - v domain

>>H=0.5+1.5./(1+0.4142*(10./r).^4); ↵   ← Computing $H[u,v]$ from the user defined specification

>>F=fftshift(H); ↵   ← F holds the unflipped version of $H[u,v]$ on u - v domain which is $F[u,v]$

>>T=G.*F; ↵   ← $G[u,v]$ $F[u,v]$ operation is carried out and assigned the output to T

>>o=ifft2(T); ↵   ← Applying 2D inverse DFT on $\{G[u,v]\ F[u,v]\}$ and assigned the output to o

>>o=abs(exp(o)); ↵ ← Exponentiation on the inverse transform followed by the absolute operation

>>imshow(o,[ ]) ↵   ← Displaying the filtered image held in o which is $o[m,n]$ in [0,1]

Depicted figure 5.5(d) shows the output from above execution or homomorphic filtered image. Any digital image $f[m,n]$ can be considered as the product of illuminance and reflectance that is $f[m,n]=i[m,n]\ r[m,n]$ where $i[m,n]$ and $r[m,n]$ are illuminance and reflectance components respectively. Roughly the $i[m,n]$ is related with low spatial frequency components whereas the reflectance is with the high frequency ones. Contrast of an image is associated with the reflectance component of the image object. The logarithmic operation separates the two components of the image. The homomorphic filtering reduces the influence of low frequencies and boosts the high frequencies as plotted in the figure 5.5(c) so that the contrast is improved. The reader can verify that by comparing the original image of dip.bmp displayed in the figure 6.1(c) to that of the homomorphic filtered in figure 5.5(d).

5.6 Minimum mean square error or Wiener filter

The minimum mean square error filter utilizes the local statistical knowledge in filtering a digital image. The filter is also called the Wiener two dimensional adaptive filter. The filter becomes adaptive in the sense that it works on the image zonal characteristics. The image filtering happens through the following algorithm and formulation:

⇒ The computation occurs in the spatial domain i.e. for every pixel element in the image

⇒ The mask $f_b[m,n]$ is chosen from the given digital image matrix $f[m,n]$ where m, n are the image pixel variables

⇒ The mask $f_b[m,n]$ size is user defined say $P \times Q$

⇒ The local mean and variance for the mask $f_b[m,n]$ are given by $\mu = \dfrac{1}{PQ}\sum\limits_{n=0}^{Q-1}\sum\limits_{m=0}^{P-1} f_b[m,n]$ and $\sigma^2 =$

$\dfrac{1}{PQ}\sum\limits_{n=0}^{Q-1}\sum\limits_{m=0}^{P-1}(f_b^{\ 2}[m,n]-\mu^2)$ respectively

⇒ The filtered image $r[m,n]$ for the $f[m,n]$ is given by the expression $r[m,n] = \mu + \dfrac{\sigma^2 - v^2}{\sigma^2}(f[m,n]-\mu)$

where v^2 is user defined noise variance

The expression $\sum\limits_{n=0}^{Q-1}\sum\limits_{m=0}^{P-1} f_b[m,n]$ is equivalent to the sum of all elements in the matrix block $f_b[m,n]$. The complete filtered image $r[m,n]$ has the same size as that of the original image $f[m,n]$. At the edge of the image, we pad the undefined element within the mask with zero.

Let us consider the modular image matrix $f[m,n] = \begin{bmatrix} 11 & 4 & 48 & 33 \\ 5 & 3 & 21 & 56 \\ 98 & 32 & 12 & 66 \\ 99 & 1 & 23 & 29 \end{bmatrix}$ for the Wiener filtering with

mask size 3×3 (meaning P =3 and Q =3) and variance v^2 =3. Our objective is to find the $r[m,n]$ of the size 4×4. In order to gain insight computation, let us calculate two pixel pointsí gray level coordinated (MATLAB notation) by (1,1) and (2,3). For first coordinates, $f_b[m,n]$ becomes $f_b[1,1] = \begin{bmatrix} 0 & 0 & 0 \\ 0 & 11 & 4 \\ 0 & 5 & 3 \end{bmatrix}$ after padding with zeroes. We

have mean of $f_b[1,1] = \mu = \dfrac{23}{9} = 2.5556$, $f_b^2[m,n] - \mu^2 = \begin{bmatrix} 0 & 0 & 0 \\ 0 & 121 & 16 \\ 0 & 25 & 9 \end{bmatrix} - \begin{bmatrix} 6.5309 & 6.5309 & 6.5309 \\ 6.5309 & 6.5309 & 6.5309 \\ 6.5309 & 6.5309 & 6.5309 \end{bmatrix}$, $\sigma^2 = \dfrac{1}{9}$ (sum of

all elements in $f_b^2[m,n] - \mu^2$)=12.4691 therefore the first filtered pixel $r[1,1]$ is $2.5556 + \dfrac{12.4691 - 3}{12.4691}(11 - 2.5556) =$

8.9683. The pixel element (2,3) which is 21 does not need padding and its computation is as follows: $f_b[2,3] =$

$\begin{bmatrix} 4 & 48 & 33 \\ 3 & 21 & 56 \\ 32 & 12 & 66 \end{bmatrix}$, $\mu = 30.5556$, $f_b^2[m,n] - \mu^2 = \begin{bmatrix} 16 & 2304 & 1089 \\ 9 & 441 & 3136 \\ 1024 & 144 & 4356 \end{bmatrix} - \begin{bmatrix} 933.6420 & 933.6420 & 933.6420 \\ 933.6420 & 933.6420 & 933.6420 \\ 933.6420 & 933.6420 & 933.6420 \end{bmatrix}$, $\sigma^2 =$

457.358, and $r[2,3] = 30.5556 + \dfrac{457.358 - 3}{457.358}(21 - 30.5556) = 21.0285$. Slight discrepancy between our computation

and MATLAB return is caused by the number truncation. We truncate μ or other parameters in four decimal accuracy before the computation of $r[2,3]$ but machine conducts the computation with more accuracy. Similar

computation finally results the Wiener filtered $r[m,n]$ matrix as $\begin{bmatrix} 8.9683 & 4.0850 & 47.6079 & 32.7797 \\ 5.0395 & 3.0817 & 21.0285 & 6.0875 \\ 97.8637 & 32.0015 & 12.0786 & 65.6367 \\ 98.8637 & 1.0577 & 22.9665 & 28.9016 \end{bmatrix}$ that

is what we are after. Now focus needs to be given in MATLAB implementation for which we utilize the MATLAB function **wiener2** as follows:

MATLAB Command

```
>>f=[11 4 48 33;5 3 21 6;98 32 12 66;99 1 23 29];  ↵          ← Entering f[m,n] to f
>>r=wiener2(f,[3 3],3)  ↵                                      ← r holds the r[m,n]


r =

        8.9683     4.0850    47.6079    32.7797
        5.0395     3.0817    21.0285     6.0875
       97.8637    32.0015    12.0786    65.6367
       98.8637     1.0577    22.9665    28.9016
```

The function **wiener2** has three input arguments. The first, second, and third of which are the digital image matrix $f[m,n]$, the user defined mask size as the two element row matrix, and the user defined variance respectively. One can use the function **round** to have the fractional numbers as integers because the digital image needs the $r[m,n]$ element to be integer. The reader is referred to chapter 7 for the application of the filtering.

5.7 Mask generation for digital image filtering

Referring to the block diagram in figure 5.1(a), a mask must be generated prior to applying the spatial or pixel domain filtering to any digital image matrix $f[m,n]$. We describe the mask as a modular matrix $h[m,n]$ where $\begin{Bmatrix} 0 \leq m \leq M-1 \\ 0 \leq n \leq N-1 \end{Bmatrix}$ in textbook or $\begin{Bmatrix} 1 \leq m \leq M \\ 1 \leq n \leq N \end{Bmatrix}$ in MATLAB notation. The m and n are the pixel variables and the required size of the mask for filtering is $M \times N$. In this section we address most common masks that can readily be generated in MATLAB derived from the mother function **fspecial** for digital image filtering purpose.

♦ ♦ Mask for the neighborhood averaging

We intend to generate a mask for the neighborhood averaging of size $M \times N$ on that account the mask must have each element as $\dfrac{1}{MN}$. For example, a 4×5 neighborhood averaging mask has the matrix outlook

$\begin{bmatrix} 0.05 & 0.05 & 0.05 & 0.05 & 0.05 \\ 0.05 & 0.05 & 0.05 & 0.05 & 0.05 \\ 0.05 & 0.05 & 0.05 & 0.05 & 0.05 \\ 0.05 & 0.05 & 0.05 & 0.05 & 0.05 \end{bmatrix}$. The MATLAB function **fspecial** offers the provision for generating various

masks. The first input argument of the function indicates the mask name. Specific MATLAB indicatory word is there for specific mask. For instance, the neighborhood averaging mask has the reserve word **average**. The second input argument of the **fspecial** accepts the required mask size as two element row matrix. However the implementation of the mask generation and the assignment to **g** are as follows:

>>g=fspecial('average',[4,5]) ↵   ← **g** is the mask we generated

g =

0.0500	0.0500	0.0500	0.0500	0.0500
0.0500	0.0500	0.0500	0.0500	0.0500
0.0500	0.0500	0.0500	0.0500	0.0500
0.0500	0.0500	0.0500	0.0500	0.0500

◆ ◆ Sobel mask for the horizontal or vertical edge finding

The 3×3 Sobel mask for the horizontal edge detection is given by $h[m,n] = \begin{bmatrix} 1 & 2 & 1 \\ 0 & 0 & 0 \\ -1 & -2 & -1 \end{bmatrix}$ which is

implemented by the preceding function **fspecial** as follows:

for the horizontal mask,   **for the vertical mask,**
>>h=fspecial('sobel') ↵   >>h=h' ↵   ← Assigned to **h** again

h =   h =

1	2	1
0	0	0
-1	-2	-1

1	0	-1
2	0	-2
1	0	-1

The input argument **sobel** of **fspecial** must be placed under the single inverted comma as a string. Note that MATLAB notation is followed rather than the image processing text one (section 3.8). The Sobel mask required for the vertical edge detection can easily be seen by the transposition of $h[m,n]$ that is h' (upper right implementation). If you insist on having the text book form of the mask, the commands flipud(h) and fliplr(h') can be exercised for the horizontal and vertical masks respectively where h=fspecial('sobel').

◆ ◆ Laplacian mask with the parameter α

The two dimensional Laplacian operator $\nabla^2 = \dfrac{\partial^2}{\partial x^2} + \dfrac{\partial^2}{\partial y^2}$ in continuous case is approximated by the 3×3

mask $\dfrac{4}{\alpha+1}\begin{bmatrix} \dfrac{\alpha}{4} & \dfrac{1-\alpha}{4} & \dfrac{\alpha}{4} \\ \dfrac{1-\alpha}{4} & -1 & \dfrac{1-\alpha}{4} \\ \dfrac{\alpha}{4} & \dfrac{1-\alpha}{4} & \dfrac{\alpha}{4} \end{bmatrix}$ where $0 \le \alpha \le 1$. Let us say $\alpha = 0.4$ so the mask should be

$\begin{bmatrix} 0.2857 & 0.4286 & 0.2857 \\ 0.4286 & -2.8571 & 0.4286 \\ 0.2857 & 0.4286 & 0.2857 \end{bmatrix}$. The function **fspecial** can still be employed for the mask generation as follows:

>>h=fspecial('laplacian',0.4) ↵   ← The mask $h[m,n]$ is assigned to the variable h

h =

0.2857	0.4286	0.2857
0.4286	-2.8571	0.4286
0.2857	0.4286	0.2857

The first input argument of the **fspecial** is the mask name (must appear exactly as we mentioned), and the second input argument specifies the α.

◆ ◆ Prewitt mask

Similar to the Sobel mask, the Prewitt mask also has the 3×3 horizontal (related to y derivative approximation) and vertical (related to x derivative approximation) approximate edge finding matrices which are given by $\begin{bmatrix} 1 & 1 & 1 \\ 0 & 0 & 0 \\ -1 & -1 & -1 \end{bmatrix}$ and $\begin{bmatrix} -1 & 0 & 1 \\ -1 & 0 & 1 \\ -1 & 0 & 1 \end{bmatrix}$ respectively. Their implementation employing the function **fspecial**

(the input argument of the function bears 'prewitt') is as follows:

for the horizontal mask,   **for the vertical mask,**

>>h=fspecial('prewitt') ↵   >>h=-h' ↵   ← Assigned to h again

h =   h=

    1   1   1   -1   0   1

    0   0   0   -1   0   1

  -1 -1 -1   -1   0   1

♦ ♦ Normalized and rotationally symmetric Gaussian mask

The formulation of the normalized rotationally symmetric Gaussian mask is given by

$$h[m,n] = \frac{e^{-\frac{r^2}{2\sigma^2}}}{\sum_{n=1}^{N}\sum_{m=1}^{M} e^{-\frac{r^2}{2\sigma^2}}} \quad \text{where} \quad r = \sqrt{\left(m - \frac{M+1}{2}\right)^2 + \left(n - \frac{N+1}{2}\right)^2}$$ and the $M \times N$ is the user defined mask size

(assuming the MATLAB notation). The variance σ^2 is also user defined. The denominator expression is

equivalent to the sum of all elements in the matrix $e^{-\frac{r^2}{2\sigma^2}}$ for different m and n.

Let us generate the mask of the size 4×5 (means M =4 and N =5) for a variance of 3 (means σ^2 =3). With this size, the variations of the m and n should be $1 \le m \le 4$ and $1 \le n \le 5$ where the m and n are integers.

Plugging different m and n, one obtains $h[m,n] = \begin{bmatrix} 0.0288 & 0.0475 & 0.0561 & 0.0475 & 0.0288 \\ 0.0402 & 0.0663 & 0.0783 & 0.0663 & 0.0402 \\ 0.0402 & 0.0663 & 0.0783 & 0.0663 & 0.0402 \\ 0.0288 & 0.0475 & 0.0561 & 0.0475 & 0.0288 \end{bmatrix}$ – this is what we

need from the function **fspecial**. The implementation of the rotationally symmetric Gaussian mask is as follows:

>>h=fspecial('gaussian',[4 5],sqrt(3)) ↵   ← The mask $h[m,n]$ is assigned to the variable h

h =

    0.0288   0.0475   0.0561   0.0475   0.0288

    0.0402   0.0663   0.0783   0.0663   0.0402

    0.0402   0.0663   0.0783   0.0663   0.0402

    0.0288   0.0475   0.0561   0.0475   0.0288

The function **fspecial** is now having three input arguments. The first, second, and third of which are the reserved word for the Gaussian mask as a string, the user defined mask size as a two element row matrix, and the user defined standard deviation respectively. We chose the variance σ^2 hence the standard deviation is $\sigma = \sqrt{3}$ and coded by **sqrt(3)**.

♦ ♦ Rotationally symmetric Laplacian of Gaussian mask

Laplacian of Gaussian is derived from the second derivative (with respect to r) of the Gaussian function

$e^{-\frac{r^2}{2\sigma^2}}$. The implementation is similar to that of the Gaussian but the first indicative input argument of the **fspecial** is **log** (abbreviation of the <u>l</u>aplacian <u>o</u>f <u>g</u>aussian). Another important point is that the sum of all elements in the mask $h[m,n]$ is zero. The generation of a 4×5 size mask with a variance 3 is as follows:

>>h=fspecial('log',[4 5],sqrt(3)) ↵   ← The mask $h[m,n]$ is assigned to the variable h

h =

    0.0194   0.0041   -0.0047   0.0041   0.0194

    0.0108   -0.0163   -0.0314   -0.0163   0.0108

    0.0108   -0.0163   -0.0314   -0.0163   0.0108

    0.0194   0.0041   -0.0047   0.0041   0.0194

♣ ♣ Rotationally symmetric circular disk mask

In this option we generate a rotationally symmetric circular disk mask $h[m,n]$ of size $2M+1 \times 2M+1$, where M is a positive integer radius as well as the pixel width for the generation. The sum of all elements in $h[m,n]$ is equal to 1. Let us generate the mask with the help of the function **fspecial** (first input argument is the reserve word **'disk'** and the second input argument is radius) for a radius 3 pixel (with this radius the size should be 7×7) as follows:

>>h=fspecial('disk',3) ↵   ← The mask $h[m,n]$ is assigned to the variable h

h =

0	0.0003	0.0110	0.0172	0.0110	0.0003	0
0.0003	0.0245	0.0354	0.0354	0.0354	0.0245	0.0003
0.0110	0.0354	0.0354	0.0354	0.0354	0.0354	0.0110
0.0172	0.0354	0.0354	0.0354	0.0354	0.0354	0.0172
0.0110	0.0354	0.0354	0.0354	0.0354	0.0354	0.0110
0.0003	0.0245	0.0354	0.0354	0.0354	0.0245	0.0003
0	0.0003	0.0110	0.0172	0.0110	0.0003	0

♣ ♣ Mask for image contrast enhancement

The 3×3 spatial filter function for image contrast enhancement with the parameter α is given by $h[m,n] = \frac{1}{\alpha+1}\begin{bmatrix} -\alpha & \alpha-1 & -\alpha \\ \alpha-1 & \alpha+5 & \alpha-1 \\ -\alpha & \alpha-1 & -\alpha \end{bmatrix}$. The α between 0 and 1 is user defined. For $\alpha=0.3$, the $h[m,n]$ should be

$\begin{bmatrix} -0.2308 & -0.5385 & -0.2308 \\ -0.5385 & 4.0769 & -0.5385 \\ -0.2308 & -0.5385 & -0.2308 \end{bmatrix}$. The function **fspecial** can return this output by the following:

>>h=fspecial('unsharp',0.3) ↵   ← The mask $h[m,n]$ is assigned to the variable h

h =

-0.2308	-0.5385	-0.2308
-0.5385	4.0769	-0.5385
-0.2308	-0.5385	-0.2308

The function **fspecial** has two input arguments, the first and second of which are the reserve word **'unsharp'** and the value of α respectively.

♣ ♣ Mask for blurring due to uniform linear motion

We address this mask as well as its theory in section 7.3.

♣ ♣ User defined mask

So far we mentioned the built-in spatial masks supplied in the **fspecial** function of the Image Processing Toolbox. In fact the reader can construct, experiment or design his own mask just like matrix entering in MATLAB. There are two basic rules while designing a mask to the context of smoothing and sharpening a digital image. A mask $h[m,n]$ whose values are all positive and whose sum of all elements is equal to 1 renders a smoothing effect on the image. On the contrary a mask $h[m,n]$ whose values include positive as well as negative number and whose sum of all elements is equal to 0 causes a sharpening effect in the image intensity. However we provide some other masks in the following:

a Laplacian mask of order 5×5 for the edge detection: $h[m,n] = \begin{bmatrix} -1 & -1 & -1 & -1 & -1 \\ -1 & -1 & -1 & -1 & -1 \\ -1 & -1 & 24 & -1 & -1 \\ -1 & -1 & -1 & -1 & -1 \\ -1 & -1 & -1 & -1 & -1 \end{bmatrix}$

a 3×3 mask: $h[m,n] = \begin{bmatrix} 1 & 2 & 1 \\ 2 & 4 & 2 \\ 1 & 2 & 1 \end{bmatrix}$ and a 5×5 mask: $h[m,n] = \begin{bmatrix} 1 & 1 & 1 & 1 & 1 \\ 1 & 4 & 4 & 4 & 1 \\ 1 & 4 & 12 & 4 & 1 \\ 1 & 4 & 4 & 4 & 1 \\ 1 & 1 & 1 & 1 & 1 \end{bmatrix}$ used for smoothing a 3×3 mask: $h[m,n] = \begin{bmatrix} -1 & -1 & -1 \\ -1 & 9 & -1 \\ -1 & -1 & -1 \end{bmatrix}$ and a 5×5 mask: $h[m,n] = \begin{bmatrix} 0 & -1 & 1 & -1 & 0 \\ -1 & 2 & -4 & 2 & -1 \\ -1 & -4 & 13 & -4 & -1 \\ -1 & 2 & -4 & 2 & -1 \\ 0 & -1 & 1 & -1 & 0 \end{bmatrix}$ used for the

sharpening.

In the case of smoothing, the sum of all elements being 1 can happen by dividing all elements in the mask by the sum of all elements. For instance, the 3×3 mask for the smoothing is constructed as follows:

>>h=[1 2 1;2 4 2;1 2 1]; ↵   ← Entering the matrix code of $h[m,n]$ and assigning to h

>>h=h/sum(sum(h)) ↵   ← Dividing by the sum of all elements using sum(sum(h)) and
                           assigning the result again to h

h =

```
0.0625    0.1250    0.0625
0.1250    0.2500    0.1250
0.0625    0.1250    0.0625
```

In order to construct a sharpening mask, we need to make sure that the sum of all elements is zero or at least very small quantity epsilon (MATLAB code is eps) owing to the numerical nature of the computation. If sum(sum(h)) is not equal to zero, we can alter some element (s) in the mask to turn the sum to zero.

5.8 Filtering in the spatial domain employing a mask

Filtering of the digital image matrix function $f[m,n]$ employing the mask $h[m,n]$ is basically a two dimensional convolution operation $f[m,n] * h[m,n]$ as presented in section 3.10. But the size of the digital image matrix $f[m,n]$ increases in the m and n directions due to the convolution operation. It is desirable that our image matrix should retain the original size whatever image operation we conduct on. In this regard the MATLAB function imfilter (abbreviation of the image filter) is very useful. The function can return the filtered image size same as that of the original size. Also the complete size option is there in the function. We present two examples on how the filtering can happen using imfilter in the spatial domain (figure 5.1(a)) in the following.

Figure 5.6(a) *Smoothing effect generated on the image text.jpg using a rotationally symmetric Gaussian mask of size 7×7 and standard deviation 8*

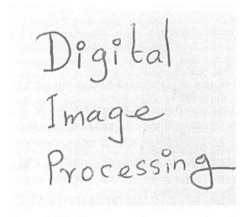

Figure 5.6(b) *Sharpening effect generated on the image dip.bmp using the contrast enhancement mask of the size 3×3 with parameter $\alpha = 0.2$*

✦ ✦ Example 1

Let us apply a rotationally symmetric Gaussian mask of size 7×7 and variance 64 (last section) to the gray text.jpg of section 2.3. Obtain the softcopy image, place it in your working directory, and conduct the following:

MATLAB Command

>>f=imread('text.jpg'); ↵ ← Reading the image and assigned to f, where f is a 3D array (section 10.12)

>>f=rgb2gray(f); ↵   ← Converting the image from RGB to gray one, f holds $f[m,n]$

>>h=fspecial('gaussian',[7 7],8); ↵ ← Filter mask $h[m,n]$ is generated and assigned to h

>>g=imfilter(f,h); ↵   ← g holds filtered $f[m,n]$ by $h[m,n]$ or $f[m,n] * h[m,n]$ result

>>imshow(g) ↵   ← Displaying the filtered image held in **g**

The filtering result is displayed in the figure 5.6(a). Compared to the original image (figure 8.5(a)), the text.jpg has been smoothed due to the filtering. The function imfilter has two input arguments. The first of which is the digital image matrix to be smoothed and the second one is the spatial filtering mask which can be any of the ones presented in last section.

♦ ♦ Example 2

In this example we consider the gray version dip.bmp of section 2.3 whose original display is shown in the figure 6.1(c). It is evident from the figure that the image contrast is not so appealing. We pick up the contrast enhancement filter mask of the size 3×3 with parameter α =0.2 from last section. Placing the image in the working directory, let us conduct the following:

MATLAB Command

>>[Y,Mp]=imread('dip.bmp'); ↵ ← Reading the indexed image, where Y⇔intensity image matrix and
                                            Mp⇔colormap matrix

>>f=ind2gray(Y,Mp); ↵   ← Turning the indexed image to gray image, where f⇔ $f[m,n]$ in [0,1]

>>h=fspecial('unsharp',0.2); ↵ ← Filter mask $h[m,n]$ is generated and assigned to h

>>g=imfilter(f,h); ↵   ← g holds filtered $f[m,n]$ by $h[m,n]$ or $f[m,n] * h[m,n]$ result

>>imshow(g) ↵   ← Displaying the filtered image held in g

Figure 5.6(b) presents the result of the last line execution which self explains the increased contrast compared to the original one.

Thus the reader can choose any mask either from the fspecial built-in or own-designed and apply the mask with help of the imfilter to see the filtering effect on the digital image. However as an introductory text, we do not wish to include all filters applied to the digital images. We present some other image processing toolbox functions as regards to the digital image filtering in the following before we close the chapter.

Function	Its purpose
ordfilt2	It performs two dimensional order statistical filtering
fsamp2	It designs two dimensional finite impulse response filter using frequency sampling
ftrans2	It designs two dimensional finite impulse response filter using frequency transformation
fwind1	It designs two dimensional finite impulse response filter using one dimensional window method
fwind2	It designs two dimensional finite impulse response filter using two dimensional window method
deconvreg	It removes the blurring in an image using regularized filter
deconvwnr	It removes the blurring in an image using Wiener filter
imtophat	It performs top hat filtering
firdemo	It demonstrates two dimensional finite impulse response filtering and filter design
nrfiltdemo	It demonstrates the noise reduction filtering

MATLAB command prompt assistance is available for just mentioned functions with the use of the command help for example help ordfilt2 for the first function in the list.

Digital Image Properties and Edges

Chapter 6

The chapter outlines two headings ñ digital image properties and digital image edges. By image properties we mean the properties of the pixels and color levels. A digital image is entirely deterministic pertaining to the pixel numbers and color levels. It is possible to access precisely to these pixels and color levels by virtue of the well-written MATLAB image processing functions. In the first section we attempt to explain how one obtains the common digital image data statistics whether it is related with the pixel or color level starting from a softcopy image. In second section we concentrate on the methods of finding image edges from a digital image. Edge detection is an essential process in digital video processing for instance the separation of the foreground from the background in an image. However the focus we have given is on the followings:

- ♦ ♦ Procedure for obtaining the comprehensive image details and accessing to pixel position and gray or color levels
- ♦ ♦ Vital statistics such as mean, standard deviation, etc of gray/color levels present in an image
- ♦ ♦ Equipped tools for edge detection in a digital image applying different methods and options
- ♦ ♦ Statistical texture feature computation in a digital image

6.1 Properties of a digital image

A digital image is usually stored in a softcopy file. Even though we have different formats for digital image storage, image analysis and image data manipulation require that we know various properties of the image. In this section our aim is to focus how one can know the image properties if a softcopy image file is supplied. We present the subtitle in terms of questionnaire form so that the reader can comfortably grasp the section content.

6.1.1 How to know about the description of a digital image?

In MATLAB there is a function called imfinfo (abbreviation of the <u>im</u>age <u>f</u>ormatís <u>info</u>rmation) that assists us to know about the digital image description. To utilize the function, the first step is to obtain the softcopy file of the image either in floppy, CD, or any other digital means. Place the file in your working path with the help of the Microsoft Windows Explorer. If you want to see the list of files present in your working path from MATLAB Command Window, execute the command dir. Well, you can have the image file name, storage format type, file size, and generation date from the Microsoft Windows Explorer but for the image processing reason we may need more information. Suppose we have the file man.jpg (obtain the softcopy file by going through section 2.3) and intend to see its description. Let us carry out the following:

MATLAB Command

>>imfinfo('man.jpg') ↵

ans =

Filename: 'man.jpg'	← The name of the softcopy image file
FileModDate: '24-Sep-2004 08:17:02'	← Image file generation date and timing
FileSize: 5398	← Image file size is 5398 Bytes
Format: 'jpg'	← Image file format is jpeg
FormatVersion: ' '	
Width: 253	
Height: 361	
BitDepth: 24	
ColorType: 'truecolor'	
FormatSignature: ' '	
Comment: { }	

Figure 6.1(a) *The image man.jpg*

A number of descriptions of the image are exhibited by MATLAB and above left indicatory arrows show some of the descriptions about the image file. We had better display the image man.jpg by the following:

>>imshow('man.jpg') ↵

The function imfinfo also manifests the width and height of the image as 253 and 361 respectively. Figure 6.1(a) shows the MATLAB display of the image in which the pixels associated with the width and height are also shown or in other words the image has the size 361 pixels×253 pixels. How do we relate the theory discussed digital image function $f[m,n]$ with the displayed image? The m and n correspond to the 361 and 253 respectively. Therefore the m and n vary from 1 to 361 and from 1 to 253 respectively if you consider MATLAB notation. Adhering to the text book notation, the m and n vary from 0 to 360 and 0 to 252 respectively.

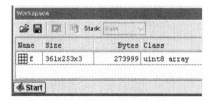

Figure 6.1(b) *Workspace browser of MATLAB*

The color level information in a digital image are coded in terms of the bits for example 2, 8, 16, 24, 32, Ö etc bits. The more is the number of bits, the better is the resolution of the image. The bit depth displayed by the imfinfo indicates that the image is having 24 bit color resolution.

As the color type displayed by the imfinfo, we find that the image color is a true color one. It means every pixel of the man.jpg within 361×253 pixel size has three components namely red, green, and blue thereby

necessitating to have $r[m,n] = \begin{bmatrix} A\ matrix\ of\ size\ 361\times253 \\ representing\ red\ values \end{bmatrix}$, $g[m,n] = \begin{bmatrix} A\ matrix\ of\ size\ 361\times253 \\ representing\ green\ values \end{bmatrix}$, and

$b[m,n] = \begin{bmatrix} A\ matrix\ of\ size\ 361\times253 \\ representing\ blue\ values \end{bmatrix}$ for the three components respectively. These three together are delivering the

digital image matrix $f[m,n]$ as a three dimensional array (subsection 10.12.1) or the triplet $\begin{Bmatrix} r[m,n] \\ g[m,n] \\ b[m,n] \end{Bmatrix}$ of sections

2.2 and 2.4. For this reason we find the size of the variable to which the image is assigned as 361×253×3. Each

pixel in the image has 24-bit description or each color level has $\dfrac{24}{3}$ =8 bit description. That means each color level

can vary from 1 to 2^8=256 or 0 to 255 according to MATLAB or textbook notation respectively. Execute help imfinfo in MATLAB Command prompt to learn more about the imfinfo.

The man.jpg is a true color or RGB (section 2.4) one. Another important type digital image is the indexed image whose discussion follows in the subsection 6.1.2.

♦ ♦ Deciding a digital image type

Given a digital softcopy image, we might be interested to know about the image type out of the four –

$$\left. \begin{array}{l} \text{binary} \\ \text{intensity} \\ \text{indexed} \\ \text{RGB or true color} \end{array} \right\}$$ on the definition of section 2.4. There are MATLAB functions by the names isbw

(abbreviation of is the image black and white), isgray (abbreviation of is the image gray), isind (abbreviation of is the image indexed), and isrgb (abbreviation of is the image RGB) for the four mentioned image types respectively. If the return of any of the four functions is true, the output is 1 otherwise 0. But the important point is the image reader imread of MATLAB (section 2.7) has to be conducted first to apply these functions. Aforementioned image man.jpg is a RGB one, let us test that as follows:

>>f=imread('man.jpg'); ↵   ← Image reading is assigned to the workspace variable f
>>isrgb(f) ↵

ans =
    1

6.1.2 How to obtain the digital image matrix $f[m,n]$?

Having known the basic image descriptions, obtaining the digital image matrix $f[m,n]$ is the next step of digital image analysis. All computational manipulations are conducted on the $f[m,n]$ so this is an important start up. The image reader function imread can read any specific image which is in accordance with MATLAB available formats (table 2.A). On the last execution, the imread reads the image and assigns the reading data to the workspace variable f. Until we are aware of the size of f, we can not decide about the dimension of $f[m,n]$. To know about the size, we execute the command size as follows:

>>size(f) ↵

ans =
    361 253   3

The 361 and 253 so displayed refer to the height and width of the man.jpg (figure 6.1(a)) in terms of the pixels respectively. The third digit 3 means that the f is a three dimensional array. If the image were black and white, the 3 would be absent. When we scanned the man.jpg, we had done it in the color format that is why the 3 is appearing. Another option of viewing the size of f is click the View in the MATLAB Menu Bar and then Workspace. Or maybe the workspace browser window is already open in your system. Figure 6.1(b) shows the contents of the workspace browser in which you find the 361×253×3 as the matrix size of the f under the category Size.

Individual color images that is red, green, and blue may need to be separated. They are also structured in the same order. Let us carry out the following:

>>R=f(:,:,1); G=f(:,:,2); B=f(:,:,3); ↵

The command R=f(:,:,1); picks up the red component of the image from the three dimensional array f and assigns that to R where R is a two dimensional array or rectangular matrix. Similarly the other two commands pick up the green and blue components of the image and assign those to G and B respectively. If you wish to display the red color component image matrix which is stored in R, execute the command imshow(R). Similar command also follows for the G and B images. Each of the matrices R, G, and B follows the size of f and has the size 361×253. You can also verify the size of R, G, or B from the workspace browser of the figure 6.1(b).

The next question is what the data type of the matrix element is and the command class can check that:

>>class(R) ↵   >>class(G) ↵   >>class(B) ↵

ans =   ans =   ans =

uint8   uint8   uint8

The workspace browser of the figure 6.1(b) also shows the data class alongside the size of R, G, or B. On that the elements of the red, green, and blue matricesí are all unsigned 8 bit integer or uint8 (table 2.B). But the arithmetic considering R, G, or B as a matrix can not be performed on the unsigned 8 bit integer format. Any digital image arithmetic mandatorily requires double precision format of the R, G, or B data. We convert the image matrix data class from the unsigned 8 bit integer to double precision format with the help of the function double as follows:

110

>>R=double(R); ↵   >>G=double(G); ↵   >>B=double(B); ↵

Following the conversion, the double precision data is assigned to like variable for example double(R) to R. So to explicate, variables R, G, and B hold the theory-mentioned functions $r[m,n]$, $g[m,n]$, and $b[m,n]$ respectively. Now one can perform image transform, convolution, or any other image analysis on so obtained R, G, and B.

Despite we separate the true color image into individual red, green, and blue components, the black and white (other nicknames are gray, intensity, or monochrome) form is frequently required for many fundamental digital image analyses. The MATLAB function rgb2gray (abbreviation of the red, green, and blue to (2) gray, section 2.8) converts a true color image, which is stored as a three dimensional array, to gray image so that we have a single rectangular matrix for the image. Aforementioned f is holding the three dimensional array therefore we perform the following:

>>f=rgb2gray(f); ↵   ← Again assigned to the same variable f

Here and now the f is having the theory discussed digital image matrix $f[m,n]$ often found in most image processing textbooks. Let us not forget that this f also needs checking for the data type or conversion as we did for the individual component. Looking into the workspace browser, the elements of f are unsigned 8-bit integer ensuring that the elements are all positive integer and vary from 0 to 255 (table 2.B).

Even though the gray image is used for the fundamental study of the digital images, the practical images nowadays are all colored. Not all the images are stored in the true color or RGB format. As another example, let us choose the image dip.bmp (section 2.3), obtain the softcopy image, place the image in the working directory, and carry out the following:

>>imshow('dip.bmp') ↵   ← Figure 6.1(c) shows the output
>>imfinfo('dip.bmp') ↵

ans =

    Filename: 'dip.bmp'
    FileModDate: '25-Sep-2004 07:17:12'
    FileSize: 55822
    Format: 'bmp'
    FormatVersion: 'Version 3 (Microsoft Windows 3.x)'
    Width: 256
    Height: 218
    BitDepth: 8
    ColorType: 'indexed'
    FormatSignature: 'BM'
    NumColormapEntries: 256
    Colormap: [256x3 double]
    RedMask: [ ]
    GreenMask: [ ]
    BlueMask: [ ]
    ImageDataOffset: 1078
    BitmapHeaderSize: 40
    NumPlanes: 1
    CompressionType: 'none'
    BitmapSize: 55808
    HorzResolution: 15748
    VertResolution: 15748
    NumColorsUsed: 0
    NumImportantColors: 0

dip.bmp

Figure 6.1(c) *The image dip.bmp*

mouse pointer
here

Figure 6.1(d) *The pixel location and color level values at the mouse pointer*

The imfinfo execution says that the image is having the size 218 pixels×256 pixels in the directions of the height and width respectively (figure 6.1(a)). Since the red, green, and blue masks are all empty (indicated by [ ]), the image is not a true color one instead an indexed one. This is also evident from the quote 'indexed' of the color type. We are certain that the image dip.bmp is an indexed one, then there should be the intensity image matrix component and the colormap matrix in correspondence with the section 2.4. That requires to hire two output arguments. Our chosen workspace variables f and m refer to the theory discussed intensity function $f[m,n]$ and its associated colormap respectively. Let MATLAB read the image as follows:

>>[f,m]=imread('dip.bmp'); ↵

In the workspace browser, we find the matrix size of f as 218×256 (exactly the pixel size) and the data class as unsigned 8 bit integer indicating the positive integer level variation in [0,255]. Since there are 256 levels in the unsigned 8-bit integer format, the colormap must be possessing 256 level information in which each level has the three basic color information $\begin{Bmatrix} red \\ green \\ blue \end{Bmatrix}$ in [0,1] where 0 and 1 signify complete absence and complete occupancy of the color respectively. That is why the size of the colormap held in the variable m must be 256×3 (workspace browser) in which each row contains the color decomposition for each level.

But again basic image processing needs the digital gray image matrix $f[m,n]$ for which we utilize the conversion function ind2gray (section 2.8) that converts an indexed color image to the gray type as follows:

>>f=ind2gray(f,m); ↵

The workspace variable f is now having the two dimensional digital image matrix $f[m,n]$ we are interested in. The return data class of the f from the ind2gray is double (from the workspace browser) specifying fractional in [0,1]. The 0, fractional, and 1 are for the black, inbetween gray level, and white respectively. Most image processing textbook addresses [0,255] scale rather than [0,1]. Employing the function im2unit8 of the table 2.C, we obtain the f in [0,255] scale as follows:

>>f=im2uint8(f); ↵

Nevertheless the f has to be in the double data class for the sake of the image computation which can happen by executing:

>>f=double(f); ↵

Therefore the assignee f is having the textbook $f[m,n]$ digital image matrix corresponding to the gray version of the color image dip.bmp (figure 6.1(c)) in which the gray levels are positive integer and ranging from 0 to 255. If you call the f, as a matter of fact you call the whole matrix or the gray image dip.bmp.

6.1.3 How to access the pixel color level values?

In this subsection we elucidate how to access the gray or color level values starting from a softcopy image. Let us obtain red, green, and blue component images from the man.jpg image (last subsection) as follows:

>>f=imread('man.jpg'); ↵

>>R=f(:,:,1); G=f(:,:,2); B=f(:,:,3); ↵

Suppose we intend to see the minimum and maximum (section 10.10) red color level values in the image for which we carry out the following:

>>min(min(R)) ↵   >>max(max(R)) ↵

ans =   ans =
     94   251

From the workspace browser data class, each color image has 256 color level variations in [0,255]. In this color level scale, the red has the minimum discrete level value 94 and the maximum discrete level value 251. It also indicates that the red color level from 0 to 93 and from 252 to 255 are absent in the red component image. Similarly one can check that the minimum and maximum color level values for the green and blue components are $\begin{Bmatrix} 93 \\ 234 \end{Bmatrix}$ and $\begin{Bmatrix} 92 \\ 243 \end{Bmatrix}$ respectively.

Suppose we wish to see the first pixelís (the first pixel has the coordinate (1,1) in MATLAB notation, uppermost and leftmost pixel in figure 6.1(a)) red, green, and blue component level values and the commands are as follows:

>>R(1,1) ↵   >>G(1,1) ↵   >>B(1,1) ↵

ans =   ans =   ans =
    193   170   178

The pixel size of the image is 361×253 (workspace browser). The coordinates of the center point in the image are (181,127). At the center point of the image, the three componentsí color level values are as follows:

>>R(181,127) ↵   >>G(181,127) ↵   >>B(181,127) ↵

ans =   ans =   ans =
    200   146   144

The reader is referred to section 10.5 for picking up the matrix elements or in other words color levels at different pixels. What if we convert the image to the black and white form, consequently we have only one color level (which is widely known as the gray level):

>>f=rgb2gray(f); ↵

Now the f is no longer a three dimensional array instead a two dimensional one whose data class is also unsigned 8-bit integer (workspace browser). Let us find its minimum and maximum gray levels as follows:

>>min(min(f)) ↵   >>max(max(f)) ↵

ans =   ans =
    101   237

Therefore the gray form of the man.jpg has the gray level variations from 101 to 237 in [0,255] scale whereas the other gray levels (0 to 100 and 238 to 255) are absent in the gray image. The theory discussed digital image matrix $f[m,n]$ has positive integers only from 101 to 237 for the gray image.

Referring to the indexed dip.bmp of the last subsection, the intensity image matrix f and the colormap matrix m are found again:

>>[f,m]=imread('dip.bmp'); ↵
>>min(min(f)) ↵   >>max(max(f)) ↵

ans =   ans =
    132   255

Workspace browser says that the f data class is unsigned 8-bit integer indicating the scale in [0,255] or 256 intensity levels. Above execution means that the intensity levels from 0 to 131 are absent in the dip.bmp. For every intensity level in f, there is a colormap (section 2.4). We wish to see the colormap for the intensity level 132 for which the implementation is as follows:

>>m(132,:) ↵

ans =
    0.5137   0.5137   0.5137

Above execution indicates that the intensity level 132 has red, green, and blue component values as 0.5137, 0.5137, and 0.5137 respectively each in [0,1]. The indexed color dip.bmp is converted to the gray image as follows:

>>f=ind2gray(f,m); ↵   ← assigned to f again and the f is holding the digital gray image matrix $f[m,n]$
>>min(min(f)) ↵   >>max(max(f)) ↵

ans =   ans =
    0.5176   1

From the workspace browser, the data class of f is double indicating in [0,1] scale. Also above implementation says that the digital image matrix $f[m,n]$ will not have any fractional value less than 0.5176. The lower rightmost pixel (figure 6.1(c) and workspace browser) of the image has the coordinates (218,256) whose intensity value 0.9451 can be found by the command f(218,256). Thus the reader can access to any pixel position or its gray or color value for different types of digital images.

✦ Mouse driven access to pixel in a digital image

From the displayed image, one can view the pixel position and color information with the help of the MATLAB function pixval (abbreviation of the pixel value) by moving the mouse pointer from one point to another in the image. Let us redisplay the image man.jpg with the imshow and execute the pixval in the next command as follows:

>>imshow('man.jpg') ↵
>>pixval ↵

Now let us move onto the MATLAB figure window and move the mouse pointer on the image area. You see the target pointer as shown in the figure 6.1(d). Beneath the image, an extra bar appears at which you see the pixel position as indicated in the same figure. For the man.jpg, we see the theory discussed $r[m,n]=210$, $g[m,n]=175$, and $b[m,n]=179$ at the pixel coordinates $m=152$ and $n=38$ for the three components respectively as shown in the figure. As another tips of the function, bring mouse pointer at any point in the image area, press the left button of the mouse, and move to any other point in the image area keeping the left button pressed. You see the distance between the two points in terms of the pixel coordinates at the bottom bar as well.

6.1.4 How to know about the pixelís color level statistics?

A digital image holds many descriptors as well as precise pixel statistics for example minimum or maximum pixel value, mean or variance Ö etc. One may need to know these descriptors before any image analysis. Considering the man.jpg image of the section 6.1.1 as the test one, we address them in the following:

♣ The number of pixels in a digital image

As the function imfinfo displays, the height and width of the man.jpg are 361 and 253 respectively. Therefore the number of the pixels in the image is 361×253=91333.

♣ The minimum or maximum color level of the pixels in a digital image

The reader is referred to the last subsection for the minimum or maximum pixel value.

♣ The mean pixel color level value in a digital image

Let us say the modular digital image matrix is $f[m,n] = \begin{bmatrix} 5 & 7 \\ 9 & 3 \end{bmatrix}$ whose elementsí mean or average value is 6. We carry out that as follows:

```
>>f=[5 7;9 3]; ↵   ← f holds f[m,n]       >>f=imread('man.jpg'); ↵      ← f holds 3D array
>>mean2(f) ↵                               >>R=f(:,:,1); ↵               ← R holds r[m,n]
                                           >>mean2(R) ↵

ans =
        6                                  ans =
                                                   183.8229
```

The MATLAB function mean2 (abbreviation of the <u>mean</u> in two (<u>2</u>) dimensions) can find the mean of all elements in a rectangular matrix when the matrix is its input argument. We intend to find the mean of the red color level in the man.jpg. Above execution on the right side shows that the red color level has the mean value 183.8229.

♣ The range of the pixel color levels in a digital image

The range of the pixel color levels in a digital image is defined as the difference between the maximum and minimum values in the color level values. For example the red component of the man.jpg image has the minimum and maximum red color levels as 94 and 251 hence the range of the red color level is 157. MATLAB function range can find the range 157 as follows:

```
>>f=imread('man.jpg'); R=f(:,:,1); ↵
>>R=double(R(:)); ↵
>>range(R) ↵

ans =
        157
```

The function range operates on a single row or column matrix but not on a rectangular matrix. If it does, that returns the range for each column. The red component image stored in R is a rectangular matrix which is turned to a column matrix by the command R(:). Also the range operates on double class or decimal data.

♣ The variance and standard deviation of the pixel color levels in a digital image

Assume that Y is a random color level in a digital image matrix with the mean color level m. The variance of the color levels in the digital image is defined as $V(Y) = \dfrac{\sum\limits_{i=1}^{N}(Y_i - m)^2}{N-1}$, where $m = \dfrac{\sum\limits_{i=1}^{N} Y_i}{N}$ and N is the number of pixels in the image. Taking the modular digital image matrix $f[m,n] = \begin{bmatrix} -2 & -8 \\ 0 & -14 \end{bmatrix}$ into account (elements are color levels), the mean and variance of all color levels in $f[m,n]$ are given by m =ñ6 and $V(f[m,n]) = \dfrac{(-2+6)^2 + (-8+6)^2 + (0+6)^2 + (-14+6)^2}{4-1} = 40$ respectively. Let us find that hiring the MATLAB function var (abbreviation of the <u>variance</u>) as follows:

```
>>f=[-2 -8;0 -14]; ↵      ← entering the modular image matrix to f
>>f=f(:); ↵               ← turning the matrix to a column one and assigned that to f again
>>var(f) ↵                ← computing the variance

ans =
        40
```

The command var(f) returns the variance for each column color level in $f[m,n]$ should we not exercise f=f(:);. Let us find the variance of the red color levels of the image man.jpg as follows:

```
>>f=imread('man.jpg'); ↵   ← Reading the image, f is a 3D array
```

```
>>R=f(:,:,1); ↵        ← Picking up the red component image matrix R from f
>>R=R(:); ↵            ← Turning the rectangular matrix R to a column one and assigned to R again
>>R=double(R); ↵       ← Turning the color levels to double class and assigned to R again
>>var(R) ↵
```

ans =
1.1061e+003

In MATLAB notation, the e+003 means 10^3 hence the return 1.1061e+003 is read off as 1.1061×10^3 =1106.1. As executed, the var operates on double class data.

The standard deviation of the random color level in a digital image matrix is straightforwardly defined as the positive square root of the variance that is $\sigma=\sqrt{\dfrac{\sum_{i=1}^{N}(Y_i-m)^2}{N-1}}$, where the symbols have their aforementioned meanings and σ is the standard deviation of the color levels. Its MATLAB counterpart is std (abbreviation of the standard deviation). Let us compute the standard deviation (which should be $\sqrt{1106.1}$ =33.2581) of the red color levels of the image man.jpg as follows:

```
>>std(R) ↵
```

ans =
33.2573

✦ The median value of the color levels in a digital image

In ascending order, the middle element of the color levels in a digital image is called the median. Assuming there are N sorted color levels in the digital image, the median color level is then the $\left(\dfrac{N+1}{2}\right)^{th}$ element if the number of elements is odd or the average of the $\left(\dfrac{N}{2}\right)^{th}$ and $\left(\dfrac{N}{2}+1\right)^{th}$ elements if the number of elements is even. Commonly a digital image possesses an even number of elements. Considering the modular image $f[m,n]=$ $\begin{bmatrix} 7 & -3 \\ -4 & -2 \\ -1 & 0 \end{bmatrix}$ whose sorted values are $\begin{bmatrix} -4 \\ -3 \\ -2 \\ -1 \\ 0 \\ 7 \end{bmatrix}$, the median (average of the 3rd and 4th elements) is ñ1.5. The MATLAB function median can find the median of the color levels from the prototype image as follows:

```
>>f=[7 -3;-4 -2;-1 0]; ↵   ← Entering the image matrix f[m,n] to f
>>f=f(:); ↵                ← Turning the rectangular matrix f to a column one and assigned to f again
>>median(f) ↵              ← Finding the median from f
```

ans =
-1.5000

Now the implementation of the median on the red color levels in the image man.jpg is conducted as follows:

```
>>f=imread('man.jpg'); ↵ ← Reading the image, f is 3D array
>>R=f(:,:,1); ↵          ← Picking up the red component image matrix R
>>R=R(:); ↵              ← Turning the rectangular matrix R to a column one and assigned to R again
>>median(R) ↵            ← Finding the median from R
```

ans =
191

Hence the red component image of the man.jpg has the median color value 191. Turning the rectangular image matrix to a column is necessary because the median also operates on columns. Some MATLAB function needs double precision conversion (for example var) and some does not (for example median). It depends how these functions are written on.

♦ A comprehensive way for the pixel color level statistics

So far we outlined the procedure one at a time for reaching the statistics of digital image pixels. MATLAB offers a lot of flexibility in computation. Some illustrated pixel statistics can be exhibited by the datastats (abbreviation of the <u>data statistics</u>). Let us apply datastats on red color level of man.jpg as follows:

```
>>f=imread('man.jpg'); ↵      ← Reading the image and assigned to f, f is 3D array
>>R=f(:,:,1); ↵               ← Picking up the red component image matrix R
>>R=double(R); ↵              ← Turning the red color levels to double class and assigned to R
>>R=R(:); ↵                   ← Turning the rectangular matrix R to a column one and
                                 assigned to R again because datastats acts on a vector
>>S=datastats(R) ↵            ← The return of the datastats is assigned to S
```

```
S =
      num: 91333        ← The number of the pixels in man.jpg
      max: 251          ← Maximum red color level in man.jpg
      min: 94           ← Minimum red color level in man.jpg
     mean: 183.8229     ← Mean value of the red color levels in man.jpg
   median: 191          ← Median value of the red color levels in man.jpg
    range: 157          ← Range of the red color levels in man.jpg
      std: 33.2573      ← Standard deviation of the red color levels in man.jpg
```

The MATLAB return assigned to S is basically a structure array (subsection 10.12.2). As the execution shows, the first field of the S is num. Let us say we intend to have the pixel numbers of the man.jpg from S for that the command is shown below:

```
>>N=S.num ↵      ← The number of pixels is picked up and assigned to N
```

```
N =
      91333
>>Mx=S.max ↵     ← The maximum red color level is picked up and assigned to Mx
```

```
Mx =
      251
```

Let us explore the pixel statistics for the gray version of the digital dip.bmp image of section 2.3 as follows:

```
>>[f,m]=imread('dip.bmp'); ↵ ← Reading the image, f is intensity matrix, and m is colormap matrix
>>f=ind2gray(f,m); ↵          ← Conversion to gray image and assigned to f again
>>f=f(:); ↵                   ← Turning the gray image matrix f to a column one and assigned to f again
>>S=datastats(f) ↵            ← The return of the datastats is assigned to S
```

```
S =
      num: 55808        ← Number of the pixels in dip.bmp
      max: 1            ← Maximum gray intensity in dip.bmp
      min: 0.5176       ← Minimum gray intensity in dip.bmp
     mean: 0.9471       ← Mean value of the gray intensity in dip.bmp
   median: 0.9647       ← Median value of the gray intensity in dip.bmp
    range: 0.4824       ← Range of the gray intensity in dip.bmp
      std: 0.0775       ← Standard deviation of the gray intensity in dip.bmp
```

6.1.5 How to find the probabilities of a digital image color levels?

Suppose we have an intensity image whose gray levels are numbered from 0 to 255. Within the gray levels, let us consider the modular digital image matrix $f[m,n] = \begin{bmatrix} 4 & 4 & 5 & 6 \\ 4 & 5 & 6 & 255 \\ 2 & 6 & 2 & 255 \end{bmatrix}$. Of the 256 levels, only the gray levels 2, 4, 5, 6, and 255 are present in the image and their frequencies of occurrence are 2, 3, 2, 3, and 2 respectively. The total number of pixels or elements in the matrix is 12 therefore the gray levels have the probabilities 0.1667, 0.25, 0.1667, 0.25, and 0.1666 (found by $\frac{frequency}{total\ no\ of\ pixels}$) respectively. Our objective is to find the probabilities starting from the matrix $f[m,n]$. The MATLAB function tabulate can find the frequency as well as the probability for each gray level in the image matrix as follows:

116

MATLAB Command

```
>>f=[4 4 5 6;4 5 6 255;2 6 2 255]; ↵
```
← Assignment of the image $f[m,n]$ to f

```
>>tabulate(f(:)) ↵
```

Value	Count	Percent
1	0	0.00%
2	2	16.67%
3	0	0.00%
4	3	25.00%
5	2	16.67%
6	3	25.00%
7	0	0.00%
8	0	0.00%
⋮		
254	0	0.00%
255	2	16.67%

   ↑   ↑   ↑
gray level frequency probability

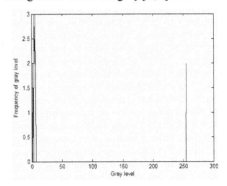

Figure 6.2(a) *The histogram of the modular image matrix $f[m,n]$*

The function **tabulate** does not accept rectangular matrix for this reason we first turn the matrix f to a column one using the command f(:) and then apply the function. The return of the function is displayed as three columns, first, second, and third of which are the gray level value, frequency of the gray level, and probability respectively. Of coarse, the sum of all probabilities must be 1. The elements in $f[m,n]$ must be positive integers excluding 0. To take advantage from the **tabulate**, we add 1 to $f[m,n]$ (mapping from [0,255] to [1,256]). Without an assignee, the return is shown on MATLAB command window. Some variable P can hold the return as follows:

```
>>P=tabulate(f(:)); ↵
```

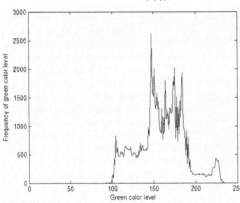

Figure 6.2(b) *The histogram of the green color levels of the image man.jpg*

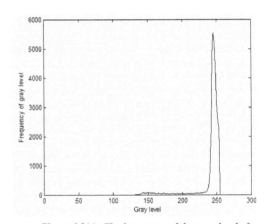

Figure 6.2(c) *The histogram of the gray levels for the gray version of image dip.bmp*

Control on the gray levels, frequencies, and probabilities (as a column matrix) is achievable by executing the commands P(:,1), P(:,2), and P(:,3) respectively.

We find the probabilities for the green color levels of the digital image man.jpg of subsection 6.1.1 as follows:

```
>>f=imread('man.jpg'); ↵
```
← Reading the image and assigned to f, f is 3D array

```
>>G=f(:,:,2); ↵
```
← Picking up green component image G which is earlier mentioned $f[m,n]$

```
>>G=double(G); ↵
```
← Turning the green color levels to double class and again assigned to G

```
>>G=G(:); ↵
```
← Turning the geen image G to a column one and assigned to G again

```
>>P=tabulate(1+G); ↵
```
← The return of **tabulate** is assigned to P, the third column of P holds the probabilites for [0,255]

As another example, let us find the probabilities for the gray levels in the gray version of the dip.bmp image of subsection 6.1.2 when scaled to [0,255] as follows:

```
>>[Y,Mp]=imread('dip.bmp'); ↵
```
← Reading the indexed image, where Y⇔intensity image matrix and Mp⇔colormap matrix

```
>>f=ind2gray(Y,Mp); ↵
```
← Turning the indexed image to gray image, where f⇔ $f[m,n]$ in [0,1]

```
>>f=im2uint8(f); ↵
```
← Turning the f in [0,1] to f in [0,255], and assigned to f again

>>f=double(f); ⏎*   ← Turning the data class of f from unsigned 8-bit integer to double, and assigned to f again

>>P=tabulate(1+f(:)); ⏎   ← Finding the probabilities first turning f to a column matrix, the third column of P holds the probabilites for [0,255]

6.1.6 How to draw the histogram of a digital image?

The histogram of a digital image is defined as the plot of the frequency of the color levels versus the color level. In a simplistic way let us consider the modular image matrix $f[m,n]$ of last subsection. The frequencies of the color levels for this image are presented there as well. The procedure for obtaining the histogram of the modular $f[m,n]$ is as follows:

MATLAB Command

>>f=[4 4 5 6;4 5 6 255;2 6 2 255]; ⏎   ← Assignment of modular image $f[m,n]$ in [0,255] to f

>>P=tabulate(1+f(:)); ⏎   ← Finding the frequency table in [1,256] and assigning that to P

>>x=P(:,1); ⏎   ← Picking up the gray levels from P and assigning to x, where x in [1,256]

>>x=x-1; ⏎   ← Now the x in [0,255] to be consistent with $f[m,n]$

>>y=P(:,2); ⏎   ← Picking up the frequencies from P in [0,255] or [1,256] and assigning to y

>>plot(x,y) ⏎   ← Plotting the histogram with the command plot

Shown figure 6.2(a) is the resulting histogram for the prototype image $f[m,n]$. The function plot has two input arguments – horizontal and vertical data, which are here color levels and frequencies of the color levels respectively. Once the figure is drawn, click Insert from the figure window menu bar and then click Y label. The blinking cursor appears in the middle of the Y-axis, type there **Frequency of gray level**, and click the Edit plot icon (section 1.3). Similarly from the Insert menu, we add the X-axis label **Gray level**.

If a digital image is a true color one, there should be three histograms for each color component ñ red, green, and blue but for the gray image only one type of histogram is associated with. Considering the color man.jpg of subsections 6.1.1 and 6.1.2, the histogram of the green component image is found as follows:

>>f=imread('man.jpg'); ⏎   ← Reading the image and assigned to f, f is a 3D array

>>G=f(:,:,2); ⏎   ← Picking up green component image G in [0,255] which is here $f[m,n]$

>>G=double(G); ⏎   ← Turning the green color levels to double class and again assigned to G

>>G=1+G(:); ⏎   ← Turning the rectangular matrix G to a column one in [1,256] and put to G

>>P=tabulate(G); ⏎   ← Finding the green color frequency table in [1,256] and assigning that to P

>>x=P(:,1); x=x-1; ⏎   ← Picking up green color levels from P and assigning to x, x in [0,255] latter

>>y=P(:,2); ⏎   ← Picking up green level frequencies from P in [0,255] or [1,256] and assigning those to y

>>plot(x,y) ⏎   ← Plotting the green color level histogram using the command plot

Figure 6.2(b) presents the histogram of the green component image of the man.jpg. Employing alike computation, you can plot the histogram of the red or blue color component image for the man.jpg.

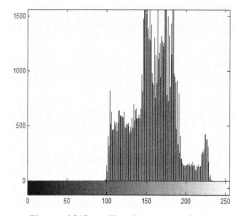 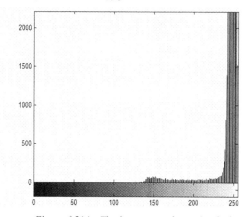

Figure 6.2(d) *The histogram of the green component image of the man.jpg using* imhist

Figure 6.2(e) *The histogram of gray levels for the gray version of dip.bmp using* imhist

As another illustration, let us discover the histogram of the gray levels in [0,255] for the gray version of the dip.bmp (subsection 6.1.2) as follows:

>>[f,m]=imread('dip.bmp'); ⏎   ← Reading the image, f⇔intensity matrix, m⇔colormap matrix

```
>>f=ind2gray(f,m); ↵        ← Turning the indexed image [f,m] to gray image f in [0,1]
>>f=im2uint8(f); ↵          ← Turning the double class f in [0,1] to unsigned 8-bit integer f in [0,255]
>>f=double(f); ↵            ← Turning the gray levels from unsigned 8-bit integer to double class and
                              assigning to f
>>P=tabulate(1+f(:)); ↵     ← Finding the gray level frequency table in [1,256] and assigning that to P
>>x=P(:,1); x=x-1; ↵        ← Picking up gray levels from P and assigning to x, x in [0,255] latter
>>y=P(:,2); ↵               ← Picking up gray level frequencies from P in [0,255] or [1,256] and
                              assigning those to y
>>plot(x,y) ↵               ← Plotting the histogram with the command plot, add labels as we did before
```

Figure 6.2(c) shows the gray level histogram for the monochrome version of the dip.bmp. The implication of histogram is to anticipate the concentration of color or gray levels present in a digital image. For example the figures 6.2(b) and 6.2(c) manifest that most green color and gray levels are occupying the levels from 100 to 240 and 125 to 255 (approximately) respectively.

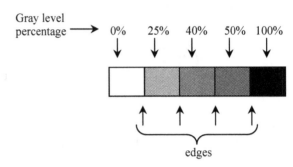

Figure 6.3(a) *The perception of gray level change and edges*

♣ A ready made tool for the histogram of a digital image

Instead of going through all these steps, one can implement the histogram very quickly with the help of the function imhist (abbreviation of the <u>im</u>age <u>hist</u>ogram). Let us carry out that for the green color levels of the man.jpg as follows:

```
>>f=imread('man.jpg'); ↵    ← Reading the image and assigned to f, f is a 3D array
>>G=f(:,:,2); ↵             ← Picking up the green component image matrix G
>>imhist(G) ↵               ← Using the imhist on G
```

Figure 6.2(d) is the outcome from the implementation. For the gray version of the dip.bmp in [0,255], all we manipulate is one component and the procedure is as follows:

```
>>[f,m]=imread('dip.bmp'); ↵   ← Reading the image, f⇔intensity matrix, m⇔colormap matrix
>>f=ind2gray(f,m); ↵           ← Turning the indexed image [f,m] to gray image f in [0,1]
>>f=im2uint8(f); ↵             ← Turning the f in [0,1] to f in [0,255]
>>imhist(f) ↵                  ← Using the imhist on f
```

Figure 6.2(e) depicts the concern histogram. What does the reader infer from the former and latter procedures? The former procedure gives you the control on every color or gray level and its exact frequency of occurrence whereas the latter does not. The latter is discretized by taking the bar plot. A group of levels in the latter for instance 1 to 10 or other are quantified to one level. However itís the choice of the reader which method he prefers to.

Figure 6.3(b) *The edges in the binary H of section 8.1*

6.2 Edge detection in a digital image

As the section title implies, we intend to switch to the edge detection in a digital image. All the while we treated a digital image as a rectangular matrix in which the matrix elements represent either the gray or color level. Edge detection means the detection of the pixel coordinates as well as regions when the gray or color levels change sharply in the image matrix. As a simple example, let us consider modular image $f[m,n] = \begin{bmatrix} 6 & 7 & 19 & 21 \\ 3 & 5 & 20 & 22 \end{bmatrix}$. The

first and second columns in the image having the gray levels ranging from 3 to 7 whereas the third and fourth columns range from 19 to 22. Abrupt change in the gray level is happening at the third column, so this is the edge for the image $f[m,n]$ and that is the numerical understanding. To illustrate the edge associated with gray level, figure 6.3(a) is presented in which uniform gray level slots are juxtaposed. The 0% and 100% represent the white and black regions respectively. Edges appear at two distinct uniform gray level slots indicated by the uparrows as shown in the figure (more references in [20], [22], and [51]).

However there are as many as six methods available in MATLAB for finding the digital image edges. MATLAB function edge can find the edges in a digital image. Given a digital image, abrupt change in the gray level is denoted by 1 (which is white) whereas other region is set at 0 (which is black) thereby forming the edges in the entire image. Let us consider the binary H image of section 8.1 and find the edge of the image as follows:

MATLAB Command

```
>>H=[zeros(50,10) [ones(20);zeros(10,20);ones(20)] zeros(50,10)]; ↵ ← H holds the image matrix
```

```
>>E=edge(H); ↵          ← Edge detected image output is assigned to the workspace variable E
>>imshow(E) ↵
```

The input argument of the **edge** is the digital image matrix which is here H. Figure 6.3(b) shows the result of the third line execution which self explains the edges present in the image. The methods planted in the function **edge** are $\begin{Bmatrix} \text{Sobel operator} \\ \text{Canny} \\ \text{Prewitt} \\ \text{Roberts} \\ \text{Laplacian of Gaussian} \\ \text{Zero cross} \end{Bmatrix}$ whose MATLAB indicatory statements are $\begin{Bmatrix} \text{sobel} \\ \text{canny} \\ \text{prewitt} \\ \text{log} \\ \text{zerocross} \end{Bmatrix}$ respectively. Let us say we intend to find the edges of the same H using the Laplacian of Gaussian method on whose account another input argument **log** (abbreviation of the <u>l</u>aplacian <u>o</u>f the <u>G</u>aussian) coded by the single inverted comma is placed beside the first input argument of **edge** as follows:

```
>>E=edge(H,'log'); ↵
```

Similarly the other five methods can be applied for the edge finding of a digital image. Four more examples are attached in the following.

Figure 6.3(c) *Edges present in the gray version of man.jpg*

Figure 6.3(d) *Edges present in the gray version of the dip.bmp*

Figure 6.3(e) *Edge detection of the image man.jpg applying a threshold 0.3*

✦ Example 1

The image man.jpg of subsection 6.1.1 is a true color one but the function **edge** does not apply for the color images therefore the conversion from the color to gray counterpart is a requisite. Let us conduct the following making the image available in the working directory:

```
>>f=imread('man.jpg'); ↵   ← Reading the image and assigned to f, f is a 3D array
>>f=rgb2gray(f); ↵          ← Turning RGB image to gray image and assigned to f again
>>E=edge(f,'canny'); ↵      ← Edge detected image output is assigned to the workspace variable E
>>imshow(E) ↵
```

We applied aforementioned Canny method for the edge detection which appears as the second input argument of the function observing the MATLAB short name **'canny'**. Figure 6.3(c) is the output from the last line execution.

✦ Example 2

This example brings about the edge finding implementation applying the zero crossing method on the gray version of the indexed dip.bmp as follows:

```
>>[f,m]=imread('dip.bmp'); ↵ ← Reading the image, f⇔intensity
                               matrix, m⇔colormap matrix
>>f=ind2gray(f,m); ↵ ← Turning the indexed image [f,m] to gray
                       image f in [0,1]
>>E=edge(f,'zerocross'); ↵ ← Second argument for the method
>>imshow(E) ↵        ←Figure 6.3(d) presents the execution result
```

Figure 6.3(f) *Horizontal edge detection of the dip.bmp using the Sobel method*

✦ Example 3

Most edge detection methods offer the provision for inserting the threshold as the input argument. Let us choose the example 1 for the threshold insertion (say 0.3). Of coarse, choice of the threshold depends on the edge detection method. For the Canny method, the threshold can be from 0 to 1. The third line command in the example

1 is now modified as E=edge(f,'canny',0.3); taking the threshold into account as the third input argument in the function. The fourth line of the example shows the figure 6.3(e) upon the application of the threshold.

⬧ Example 4

Sobel method has two categories of edge detection ñ vertical and horizontal. The example 2 mentioned image is to be edge detected employing the Sobel method in conjunction with the horizontal one. The third line command in the example 2 now should be E=edge(f,'sobel','horizontal');. The third input argument of the edge is the reserved string horizontal placed inside the single inverted comma. Yet the threshold insertion is possible in the function. In that case the threshold and horizontal appear as the third and fourth input arguments of the function respectively. Anyhow figure 6.3(f) results from the execution of the fourth line command in the example. In a like implementation one can obtain the vertical edge detection using the command E=edge(f,'sobel','vertical');. One can acquire more about the edge by executing:
>>help edge ↵

```
function y=jprobn(f)
[ro,co]=size(f);
m1=min(min(f));  %Finding the minimum gray level in f
m2=max(max(f));  %Finding the maximum gray level in f
V=m1:m2;        %Generating row vector V from min to max
for k=1:length(V)
    for o=1:length(V)
        s=0;
        for m=1:ro
            for n=1:co-1
                if f(m,n)==V(k) & f(m,n+1)==V(o)
                    s=s+1; %s is the repetition counter
                end
            end
        end
        y(k,o)=s;      %Forming joint probability matrix y
    end
end
```

Figure 6.4(a) *The MATLAB codes of the function file **jprobn** for the computation of the → directed joint probability density function*

It should be pointed out that the matrix E following the edge detection is a binary one regardless of the argument and method we apply.

6.3 Texture features in a digital image

When the digital image gray or color level characteristics are repetitive or quasi-repetitive, the texture analysis becomes very useful in identifying remotely sensed imaging applications such as aircraft or satellite imagery. Qualitative evaluation of an image region is the aim of the texture feature analysis in a digital image. Of the three principal approaches – statistical, spectral, and structural, implementations on some features regarding the statistical approach are addressed in the following.

⬧ ⬧ Gray level cooccurrence matrix of a digital image

The gray level cooccurrence matrix of a digital image emerges from the joint probability density function of two pixels located in the image which is a second order statistical measurement of the digital image matrix. The directional position of the two pixels is user defined. The digital image matrix $f[m,n]$ can be of any size but with some specific number of gray levels (integers). For example with the three gray levels – 0, 1, and 2, a 6×5 $f[m,n]$

can be $\begin{bmatrix} 0 & 0 & 1 & 0 & 0 \\ 2 & 1 & 0 & 0 & 0 \\ 0 & 1 & 1 & 1 & 1 \\ 2 & 2 & 1 & 1 & 1 \\ 0 & 1 & 0 & 0 & 0 \\ 0 & 0 & 1 & 2 & 2 \end{bmatrix}$. The next question is how we define the directional position. Let us say the direction

is horizontally rightward or →. It means we deliberate on the gray levels in $f[m,n]$ which are in a row. If the direction is vertically downward or ↓, the gray levels in $f[m,n]$ which are in a column only receive attention. If the direction is diagonal, only the diagonal elements of the image matrix do we consider. The diagonal direction can be upward or downward. Once again these all directionals are user defined.

Let us consider the → direction. With the three gray levels, the gray level possibilities for the example

$f[m,n]$ are 0 with $\begin{bmatrix} 0 \\ 1 \\ 2 \end{bmatrix}$, 1 with $\begin{bmatrix} 0 \\ 1 \\ 2 \end{bmatrix}$, and 2 with $\begin{bmatrix} 0 \\ 1 \\ 2 \end{bmatrix}$. Considering any 0 in $f[m,n]$ also has 0 adjacently in the →

direction, we have the numbers of occurrence 2, 2, 2, and 1 in the first, second, fifth, and sixth rows of the $f[m,n]$ respectively. On that account the total number of occurrence of the gray level 00 in $f[m,n]$ is 2+2+2+1=7. Again in the same direction the occurrence of the gray level 12 in $f[m,n]$ is 1 (only one in the sixth row of $f[m,n]$).

Continuing this way, one ends up with the discrete joint probability density function $P = \begin{matrix} & 0 & 1 & 2 \\ 0 \\ 1 \\ 2 \end{matrix}\begin{bmatrix} 7 & 4 & 0 \\ 3 & 5 & 1 \\ 0 & 2 & 2 \end{bmatrix}$. As

functional form, we write it as $P[i,j]$ where i or j is [0,1,2] from the gray level of $f[m,n]$. If L is the number of gray levels in $f[m,n]$, the size of $P[i,j]$ must be $L \times L$. Here $L = 3$ gives us the size of P being 3×3. The gray level cooccurrence matrix is defined as $C_{ij} = \dfrac{P[i,j]}{\sum\limits_{j=0}^{L-1}\sum\limits_{i=0}^{L-1} P[i,j]}$ just for the normalization in [0,1] scale. The denominator of C_{ij} is equivalent to summing all elements in $P[i,j]$ which is here 24 on account of that

$$C_{ij} = \begin{bmatrix} 0.2917 & 0.1667 & 0 \\ 0.1250 & 0.2083 & 0.0417 \\ 0 & 0.0833 & 0.0833 \end{bmatrix} \text{ for the}$$

modular $f[m,n]$ in [0,2].

Our written function **jprobn** can find the discrete joint probability density function when its input argument is the digital image matrix $f[m,n]$. We expect P matrix from MATLAB as the return of the function **jprobn**. Write the source codes of the figure 6.4(a) in the M-file editor in your working path of MATLAB, save the file by the name **jprobn**, and execute the following:

MATLAB Command

```
>>f=[0 0 1 0 0;2 1 0 0 0;0 1 1 1 1;2 2 1 1 1;0 1 0 0 0;0 0 1 2 2]; ↵ ← Entering f[m,n] to f
>>P=jprobn(f) ↵                    ← Calling the jprobn and its P output is the P[i,j]
```

```
P =

     7     4     0
     3     5     1
     0     2     2
>>C=P/sum(sum(P)) ↵ ← C⇔C_ij


C =

    0.2917    0.1667         0
    0.1250    0.2083    0.0417
         0    0.0833    0.0833
```

The third line in above command is the computation of the required gray level cooccurrence matrix C_{ij} (section 10.9 for **sum**) what we are after.

Most image processing textbooks address the discrete joint probability density function for the vertically downward and diagonally downward directed pixel positions as well. The computed discrete joint probability density functions of the modular

```
function y=jprobm(f)
[ro,co]=size(f);
m1=min(min(f));  %Finding the minimum gray level in f
m2=max(max(f));  %Finding the maximum gray level in f
V=m1:m2;        %Generating row vector V from min to max
for k=1:length(V)
   for o=1:length(V)
      s=0;
      for m=1:ro-1
         for n=1:co
            if f(m,n)==V(k) & f(m+1,n)==V(o)
               s=s+1; %s is the repetition counter
            end
         end
      end
      y(k,o)=s;        %Forming joint probability matrix y
   end
end
```

Figure 6.4(b) *The MATLAB codes of the function file **jprobm** for the computation of the ↓ directed joint probability density function*

```
function y=jprobmn(f)
[ro,co]=size(f);
m1=min(min(f));  %Finding the minimum gray level in f
m2=max(max(f));  %Finding the maximum gray level in f
V=m1:m2;        %Generating row vector V from min to max
for k=1:length(V)
   for o=1:length(V)
      s=0;
      for m=1:ro-1
         for n=1:co-1
            if f(m,n)==V(k) & f(m+1,n+1)==V(o)
               s=s+1; %s is the repetition counter
            end
         end
      end
      y(k,o)=s;        %Forming joint probability matrix y
   end
end
```

Figure 6.4(c) *The MATLAB codes of the function file **jprobmn** for the computation of the joint probability density function for the diagonally downward directional operator* image $f[m,n]$ are given by $P = \begin{array}{ccc} & \begin{matrix} 0 & 1 & 2 \end{matrix} \\ \begin{matrix} 0 \\ 1 \\ 2 \end{matrix} & \begin{bmatrix} 3 & 5 & 4 \\ 5 & 4 & 1 \\ 2 & 1 & 0 \end{bmatrix} \end{array}$ and $P = \begin{array}{ccc} & \begin{matrix} 0 & 1 & 2 \end{matrix} \\ \begin{matrix} 0 \\ 1 \\ 2 \end{matrix} & \begin{bmatrix} 3 & 3 & 3 \\ 3 & 5 & 0 \\ 1 & 2 & 0 \end{bmatrix} \end{array}$ for the vertically and diagonally downward

directions respectively. The modified function files jprobm and jprobmn as presented in the figures 6.4(b) and 6.4(c) can calculate the discrete joint probability density functions for the vertically and diagonally downward directions respectively. Having written them in the M-file in our working directory, they provide us the following:

for the vertically downward: **for the diagonally downward:**

>>P=jprobm(f) ↵   ← P⇔ $P[i,j]$ >>P=jprobmn(f) ↵   ← P⇔ $P[i,j]$

P =   P =

    3   5   4   3   3   3
    5   4   1   3   5   0
    2   1   0   1   2   0

The command C=P/sum(sum(P)) is also equally applicable for finding the C_{ij} matrices which is of prime importance for the following features in a digital image. In the three function files we assumed that the image gray levels are integer and the functions compute the discrete join probability density function from minimum to maximum gray levels in the digital image matrix.

❖❖ Uniformity

Uniformity in the digital image $f[m,n]$ is defined as the $\sum_{j=0}^{L-1} \sum_{i=0}^{L-1} C_{ij}^{2}$ that means squaring every element in the matrix C_{ij} and summing all of them. For the modular image $f[m,n]$, the uniformity along the horizontally rightward direction is 0.1875 whose computation is as follows:

>>f=[0 0 1 0 0;2 1 0 0 0;0 1 1 1 1;2 2 1 1 1;0 1 0 0 0;0 0 1 2 2]; ↵ ← Entering $f[m,n]$ to f

>>P=jprobn(f); C=P/sum(sum(P)); ↵   ← P⇔ $P[i,j]$ and C⇔ C_{ij}

>>sum(sum(C.^2)) ↵   ← Computation using $\sum_{j=0}^{L-1} \sum_{i=0}^{L-1} C_{ij}^{2}$

ans =
    0.1875

❖❖ Entropy

Entropy of the digital image $f[m,n]$ is defined as $-\sum_{j=0}^{L-1} \sum_{i=0}^{L-1} C_{ij} \log_2 C_{ij}$ (base 2 logarithm means in terms of bits). But the problem is any 0 element in C_{ij} causes the logarithm of 0 to appear which is minus infinity. To avoid this situation, we add a very small quantity epsilon (whose MATLAB code is **eps**) to every element in C_{ij} in the logarithmic argument. However the entropy of the prototype $f[m,n]$ along the horizontally rightward directed pixel is 2.5843 and whose computation is as follows:

>>C1=C+eps; ↵
>>-sum(sum(C.*log2(C1))) ↵

ans =
    2.5843

In the first line we added **eps** to every element in C and assigned the result to C1. The log2(x) is equivalent to $\log_2 x$. The scalar or element by element multiplication takes place between C_{ij} and $\log_2 C_{ij}$ (section 10.2).

❖❖ Maximum probability

The maximum probability in cooccurrence matrix C_{ij} is given by $\max_{i,j} C_{ij}$ which means the maximum value in matrix C_{ij}. For the example at hand, the maximum probability is 0.2917 and computed as follows:

>>max(max(C)) ↵   ← Section 10.10 for the max

ans =
    0.2917

♦ ♦ Element difference moment of order k

The element difference moment of order k is defined as $\sum_{j=0}^{L-1} \sum_{i=0}^{L-1} (i-j)^k C_{ij}$. This is a two dimensional computation especially for the part $(i-j)^k$. Element by element multiplication occurs between $(i-j)^k$ and C_{ij}. We seek the help from the MATLAB function **meshgrid** (section 10.11) to compute the function $(i-j)^k$ considering k =2. For the same matrix C_{ij} and the operator, the element difference moment of order 2 is given by 0.4167, and it is computed as follows:

```
>>[i,j]=meshgrid(0:2,0:2); ↵      ← i or j changes from 0 to 2 (gray level) integerwise
>>sum(sum((i-j).^2.*C)) ↵
```

```
ans =
      0.4167
```

When k =2, the moment is called the contrast of the digital image $f[m,n]$. Raising power to every element by 2 is executed by the operator .^ in the foregoing command.

♦ ♦ Inverse element difference moment of order k

The inverse element difference moment of order k is defined as

$\sum_{j=0}^{L-1} \sum_{i=0}^{L-1} \frac{C_{ij}}{(i-j)^k}$ for $i \neq j$. The condition $i \neq j$ makes it difficult to execute

the computation in one line MATLAB statement. Whether it is $\frac{1}{(i-j)^k}$

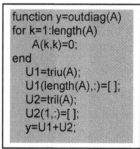

```
function y=outdiag(A)
for k=1:length(A)
    A(k,k)=0;
end
    U1=triu(A);
    U1(length(A),:)=[ ];
    U2=tril(A);
    U2(1,:)=[ ];
    y=U1+U2;
```

Figure 6.4(d)   *The function file* ***outdiag*** *for the removal of the diagonal elements from a square matrix*

or C_{ij}, it takes the shape of a square matrix for different i or j regardless of the number of levels L. The condition $i = j$ appears in the diagonal elements of the **meshgrid** output variables or C_{ij}. If we exclude the diagonal elements from those square matrices, we have the matrices corresponding to $i \neq j$ but the point is due to the removal of the diagonal, the matrix size becomes $L-1 \times L$. For

example, the **meshgrid** output i contains $\begin{bmatrix} 0 & 1 & 2 \\ 0 & 1 & 2 \\ 0 & 1 & 2 \end{bmatrix}$ which becomes $\begin{bmatrix} 0 & 1 & 2 \\ 0 & 1 & 2 \end{bmatrix}$ after the diagonal removal. Our

written M-file **outdiag** as shown in the figure 6.4(d) takes any square matrix as the input argument and returns the matrix excluding the diagonal elements from the matrix. Write the statements in the M-file editor and save the file in the working directory by the name **outdiag**. One can also perform the computation using the for-loop in conjunction with the if-else checking but it is not advisable to use the for-loop for the image computation due to time constraint. However let us compute the inverse element difference moment (the computed moment is given by 0.4167) of order 2 considering the same directional operator, image matrix $f[m,n]$, and C_{ij} as follows:

```
>>[i,j]=meshgrid(0:2,0:2); ↵      ← Forming the meshgrid for all i and j
>>i=outdiag(i); ↵                 ← Removal of the diagonal from i and assign the result again to i
>>j=outdiag(j); ↵                 ← Removal of the diagonal from j and assign the result again to j
>>C=outdiag(C); ↵                 ← Removal of the diagonal from C and assign the result again to C

>>sum(sum(C./(i-j).^2)) ↵         ← Implementation of ∑ ∑ C_ij/(i-j)^k when i ≠ j

ans =
      0.4167
```

♦ ♦ Finding the features in a practical digital image

Ongoing demonstrations present the computation of the texture features in a modular image $f[m,n]$. Now we wish to address the findings of those features in the gray version (in scale [0,255]) of the indexed color dip.bmp (subsection 6.1.2). Aforementioned six features of the digital image considering the horizontally rightward operator and of order 2 for the two moments are computed as follows:

MATLAB Command

```
>>[f,m]=imread('dip.bmp'); ↵      ← Reading the image, f⇔intensity matrix, m⇔colormap matrix
>>f=ind2gray(f,m); ↵              ← Turning the indexed image [f,m] to gray image f in [0,1]
>>f=im2uint8(f); ↵                ← Turning the f in [0,1] to f in [0,255] but unsigned 8-bit integer
```

```
>>f=double(f); ↵          ← Converting the gray levels of f to double class in [0,255] and put to f
>>P=jprobn(f); ↵          ← Finding the joint probability density function P[i, j] and assigned to P
>>C=P/sum(sum(P)); ↵      ← Finding the gray level cooccurrence matrix C_{ij} and assigned to C
>>sum(sum(C.^2)) ↵        ← Finding the uniformity
```

ans =
            0.0147   ← This is the uniformity of the image dip.bmp
```
>>C1=C+eps; ↵             ← Adding negligible value eps to C_{ij} to avoid logarithm of zero
>>-sum(sum(C.*log2(C1))) ↵  ← Finding the entropy of the image dip.bmp
```

ans =
            7.2566   ← This is the entropy of the image dip.bmp
```
>>max(max(C)) ↵           ← Finding the maximum probability
```

ans =
            0.0312   ← This is the maximum probability on C_{ij} of the dip.bmp

We introduced the computations of various features considering that the gray levels vary from 0 to some other positive integer. Conversion format of the dip.bmp says that the gray levels in the image are in [0,255]. We have no idea about the gray level statistics. Let us find the minimum and maximum gray levels present in the dip.bmp as follows:
```
>>L1=min(min(f)) ↵        ← Finding the minimum gray level and assigned that to L1
```

L1 =
            132
```
>>L2=max(max(f)) ↵        ← Finding the maximum gray level and assigned that to L2
```

L2 =
            255

Above execution says that the gray levels in the image dip.bmp are ranging from 132 to 255 (indicates 124 levels). Referring to the MATLAB workspace browser, the size of P or C being 124×124 is for that reason. Previous mentioned jprobm, jprobn, and jprobmn are written for taking care of the range from the minimum to the maximum. With regard to the computation in the actual gray levels, now we have i or j varying from 132 to 255 and the meshgrid computation must be followed accordingly:
```
>>[i,j]=meshgrid(L1:L2); ↵   ← Forming the meshgrid from 132 to 255 for the gray level present
>>sum(sum((i-j).^2.*C)) ↵    ← Computing the element difference moment of order 2
```

ans =
            122.6935   ← This is the element difference moment of order 2 of the dip.bmp
```
>>i=outdiag(i); ↵    ← Removal of the diagonal from i matrix and assign the result again to i
>>j=outdiag(j); ↵    ← Removal of the diagonal from j matrix and assign the result again to j
>>C=outdiag(C); ↵    ← Removal of the diagonal from C matrix and assign the result again to C
>>sum(sum(C./(i-j).^2)) ↵← Computing the inverse element difference moment of order 2
```

ans =
            0.4429   ← This is the inverse element difference moment of order 2 of the dip.bmp

While applying the function jprobm, jprobn, or jprobmn to a practical image, the computation might take longer depending on the processor speed (for our computer it took 25 secs). Anyhow we close the chapter with the discussion of the statistical texture features.

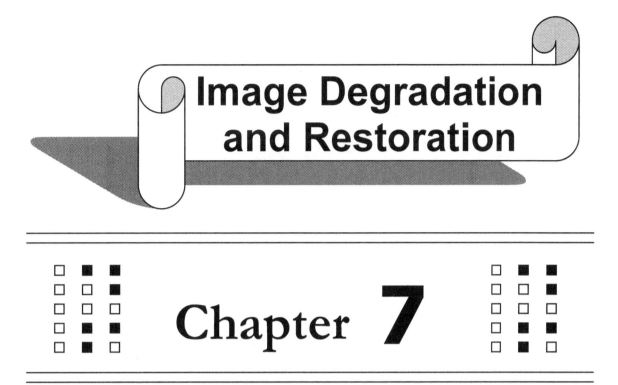

Chapter 7

When a digital image is transmitted for communication reason or processed, some unwanted distortion of the digital image may take place ñ that is degradation. The nature of practical degradation is completely unknown and to some extent follows defined randomness. A degraded digital image suffers some visional damage as regards to the pixel coordinates or their color level contents as far as the fixed number of pixels and the fixed number of color levels are concern. We attempt to simulate the noise or the digital degradation employing predefined random function and to find the theoretical remedy from the degradation so that the cause-effect study makes us understand practical image noise nature. Image restoration essentially instruments improvement of degraded image quality. In a nutshell our study highlights the following:

♣ ♣ Well-known two dimensional noise generation which is to be used for the degradation process
♣ ♣ Applying defined or randomly generated noises to the uncontaminated digital image
♣ ♣ Blurry image generation caused by the uniform linear motion
♣ ♣ Noise removal techniques and functions to acquire an undegraded digital image observing some objective criteria

7.1 Digital noise generation

Any unwanted signal or function is termed as a noise which is completely an unpredictable phenomenon. We assume that the noise may follow some defined pattern and find the way of removing the noise. Functional characteristics of the noise are just the characteristics of the defined pattern. We consider several noise patterns and study their comparative behavioral differences. Taking this as experience and applying the trial and error, we restore the noisy or corrupted image until the ideal or at least visibly acceptable one is achieved. A digital image function $f[m,n]$ is a two dimensional function and presumably the noise is so, which we say $\eta[m,n]$. The m and n are the pixel variables and the value of $f[m,n]$ or $\eta[m,n]$ is related with the gray/color or noise levels to the context of the digital image processing. The noise model which degrades an image can be additive or multiplicative that is $f[m,n] + \eta[m,n]$ or $f[m,n]\,\eta[m,n]$ respectively.

126

The noise generation means the generation of $\eta[m,n]$ in contrast the noisy image generation means the generation of $f[m,n]+\eta[m,n]$ or $f[m,n]\,\eta[m,n]$. In most noise types, the $\eta[m,n]$ is obtained from the random variable generations. Whatever be the noise additive or multiplicative happens to every pixel coordinate (m , n). Let us see the following noise types.

⌗ **Two dimensional uniformly distributed continuous random noise**

The term uniform means that any value of the noise $\eta[m,n]$ is equally likely. The $\eta[m,n]$ is a two dimensional discrete function thereby taking the shape of a rectangular matrix. The meaning of continuous is the generated values are fractional in general. We wish to generate uniformly distributed continous random noise in [0,1] with a mean 0.5. As far as digital image is concern, this is not enough and the image pixel size needs to be mentioned. Let us choose the image size as 4×5 and conduct the following:

MATLAB Command

```
>>eta=rand(4,5) ↵        ← workspace variable eta holds η[m,n]
```

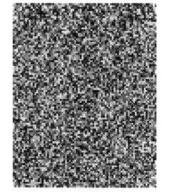

Figure 7.1(a)   *Uniformly distributed random noise*

```
eta =

    0.9501   0.8913   0.8214   0.9218   0.9355
    0.2311   0.7621   0.4447   0.7382   0.9169
    0.6068   0.4565   0.6154   0.1763   0.4103
    0.4860   0.0185   0.7919   0.4057   0.8936
```

The function **rand** intakes two input arguments, the first and second of which are the image pixelís row and column numbers respectively. By default it generates any decimal number between 0 and 1 with a mean 0.5. When you run the function, you may not see the same **eta** matrix due to the randomness. The next legitimate question is how the pure noise image looks like. Since we chose a small size 4×5, the noise image would be very tiny. Let us choose the noise image pixel size as 100×80 and implement the following:

```
>>eta=rand(100,80); ↵   ← eta holds η[m,n] of size 100×80
>>imshow(eta) ↵
```

Figure 7.1(b) *An impulsive noise image*

Figure 7.1(a) is the pure noise image display by dint of the function **imshow** (section 2.5). In MATLAB notation 0 and 1 refer to black and white respectively whereas the inbetween values indicate different shades of gray level ñ that is obvious from the image. Maximizing the figure window renders a better visual effect.

Above generation assumes that the image data is also in [0,1]. What if the range of image data falls in other than [0,1]. The MATLAB function **unifrnd** (abbreviation of the <u>unif</u>ormly <u>r</u>a<u>nd</u>om) generates uniformly distributed continuous random numbers from user supplied lower and upper limits. Let us say we intend to generate the uniformly distributed noise $\eta[m,n]$ from ñ5 to 6 of size 3×4 whose implementation is as follows:

```
>>eta=unifrnd(-5,6,3,4) ↵   ← variable eta holds η[m,n] in [−5,6]
```

Figure 7.2(a) *Digital image of the noise* $2\sin\left(\dfrac{2\pi}{10}m+\dfrac{2\pi}{7}n\right)$

```
eta =

    1.6753    3.3831    4.0355    3.7113
    0.3458    0.0211   -0.1083    5.1399
    4.8043   -4.7965    1.7698    3.1203
```

The **unifrnd** has four input arguments ñ the first and second of which are the supplied lower and upper limits of the generation respectively. The third and fourth input arguments are the required row and column numbers respectively. For a large size noise image like 100×80, the command is **eta=unifrnd(-5,6,100,80);** whose image outlook is similar to the figure 7.1(a) following the execution of **imshow(eta,[ ])**.

⌗ **Two dimensional uniformly distributed discrete random noise**

In other situation when the image gray or color levels are in [0,255] or [1,256] with integerwise variation, the noise is expected to be so. Let us say we wish to generate a uniformly distributed discrete noise $\eta[m,n]$ of size

4×5 in which the noise gray levels are integer and in [1,64]. The MATLAB function randint (abbreviation of the random integer) implements that as follows:

from 1 to 64 generation,
>>eta=randint(4,5,[1 64]) ↵

eta =

21	53	46	48	20
49	37	39	63	32
51	11	36	28	47
9	55	36	37	13

from ñ5 to 6 generation,
>>eta=randint(4,5,[-5 6]) ↵ ← eta⇔$\eta[m,n]$

eta =

-4	5	3	0	-4
-3	4	-2	2	1
5	2	1	-2	2
5	-1	5	1	2

The randint has three input arguments, the first and second of which intake the required row and column numbers respectively. The third input argument of the function as a two element row matrix conceives the range of the integers in $\eta[m,n]$. The range can be negative to positive as well for example ñ5 to 6. The $\eta[m,n]$ generation for the same size in [ñ5,6] is also presented above. A large size $\eta[m,n]$ with any discrete range (for example the size 100×80 and the gray level from ñ127 to 128) displays the image similar to the figure 7.1(a) for which the command we exercise is eta=randint(100,80,[-127 128]); imshow(eta,[ ]).

⊟ Two dimensional impulsive noise

An impulsive noise is a specific type of the uniformly distributed one. The impulse value depends on the image data class. Let us say the gray level values in a digital image are in [0,1]. In this case the impulse is 1, the maximum value of the image data. The $\eta[m,n]$ is composed of 0 or 1 (only two levels) with equal probability. We generate an impulsive noise $\eta[m,n]$ of size 4×5 on [0,1] as follows:

Figure 7.2(b) *Digital image of the noise* $2\sin\left(\frac{2\pi}{25}m-\frac{2\pi}{40}n\right)$

Impulse for [0,1] image,
>>eta=randsrc(4,5,[0 1]) ↵

eta =

1	1	0	0	0
0	1	0	1	1
1	1	0	0	1
0	0	1	1	1

Impulse for [0,255] image,
>>eta=randsrc(4,5,[0 255]) ↵ ←eta⇔$\eta[m,n]$

eta =

255	0	255	255	255
0	0	255	255	0
255	255	0	0	255
0	255	0	255	0

The MATLAB function randsrc (abbreviation of the random search) can generate different size matrices taking elements from a specific set in which the elements in the set have equal probability of coming in the generated matrix. The first and second input arguments of the function are the required row and column numbers for the noise $\eta[m,n]$ respectively. The third input argument of the function is the set of probable numbers as a row matrix. For instance, the two numbers 0 and 1 is put as [0 1]. If there were three numbers in the set for example ñ5, 78, and 2, the command would be randsrc(4,5,[-5 78 2]). In other circumstances when image data is in [0,255], the number 255 becomes the impulse. Similar implementation is also presented for the impulsive noise of the size 4×5 in [0,255] (above on the upper right). The last impulsive noise of size 100×80 outlooks as shown in the figure 7.1(b) by exercising the following:

>>eta=randsrc(100,80,[0 255]); ↵   ← eta ⇔ $\eta[m,n]$
>>imshow(eta,[ ]) ↵   ← For displaying the noise as an image

According to the display, the noise has only two levels either black or white corespondent 0 and 255 respectively. There is no inbetween gray level in the image like the figure 7.1(a).

⊟ Two dimensional additive white Gaussian noise (AWGN)

Additive white Gaussian noise is generated with the help of the MATLAB function randn. A Gaussian noise has two parameters – mean and variance. Theoretically the random values of $\eta[m,n]$ can be from minus infinity to plus infinity. The randn has the default mean 0 and variance 1. We generate the additive white Gaussian noise of mean 0 and variance 1 for the image size 4×5 as follows:

>>eta=randn(4,5) ↵   ← eta ⇔ $\eta[m,n]$

eta =

```
-0.8051  -2.1707   0.5077   0.3803   0.0000
 0.5287  -0.0592   1.6924  -1.0091  -0.3179
 0.2193  -1.0106   0.5913  -0.0195   1.0950
-0.9219   0.6145  -0.6436  -0.0482  -1.8740
```

The function has two input arguments ñ the first and second of which are the required row and column numbers of the noise image respectively. With the linear mapping, one can generate the Gaussian noise of other mean and variance. We intend to generate a Gaussian noise of mean μ and variance σ^2. The required generation is given by $\sigma X + \mu$ where X is equivalent to the Gaussian with 0 mean and 1 variance or the randn. To see the additive white Gaussian noise of mean 4 and variance 3 for the image size 4×5, we perform the following:

>>eta=4+sqrt(3)*randn(4,5) ↵   ← eta ⇔ $\eta[m,n]$

Figure 7.2(c) *Absolute value of the 2D DFT of* $2\sin\left(\dfrac{2\pi}{25}m - \dfrac{2\pi}{40}n\right)$ *displayed as a digital image*

eta =

```
7.2275   5.1786   4.4532   1.7994   3.0626
3.0949  -0.0956   6.1017   1.1185   1.6903
4.1791   5.7149   3.5243   2.7814   5.8579
2.6011   4.3791   3.7694   4.4865   2.7666
```

The function $\eta[m,n]$ should be $\sqrt{3}\,X + 4$ whose code is 4+sqrt(3)*randn(4,5). For the same noise we execute the command eta=4+sqrt(3)*randn(100,80); imshow(eta,[ ]) for a noise of size 100×80.

▭ Two dimensional sinusoidal noise

A two dimensional sinusoidal noise has the equation $\eta[m,n] = A\sin\left(\dfrac{2\pi}{T_m}m + \dfrac{2\pi}{T_n}n\right)$ where A is the amplitude of the noise, m and n are the pixel variables, T_m and T_n are the m and n directed pixel periods, and $f_m = \dfrac{1}{T_m}$ and $f_n = \dfrac{1}{T_n}$ are the m and n directed spatial frequencies respectively. We wish to view the sinusoidal noise for $A = 2$, $T_m = 10$, and $T_n = 7$ as a digital image of pixel size 100×80 and proceed as follows:

>>[m,n]=meshgrid(1:80,1:100); ↵
>>eta=2*sin(2*pi/10*m+2*pi/7*n); ↵ ← eta holds the two dimensional sinusoidal noise $\eta[m,n]$
>>imshow(eta,[ ]) ↵   ← The noise eta is first mapped in [0,1] and then displayed

With the required specification, the $\eta[m,n]$ becomes $2\sin\left(\dfrac{2\pi}{10}m + \dfrac{2\pi}{7}n\right)$. Section 10.11 addresses the detail discussion of the meshgrid for the functional computation in two dimension. In the first line of above command, the basis grid variables m and n, each of the size 100×80, hold $\begin{bmatrix} 1 & 2 & & 80 \\ 1 & 2 & \cdots & 80 \\ & & \vdots & \\ 1 & 2 & & 80 \end{bmatrix}$ and $\begin{bmatrix} 1 & 1 & & 1 \\ 2 & 2 & \cdots & 2 \\ \vdots & \vdots & & \vdots \\ 100 & 100 & & 100 \end{bmatrix}$ respectively. The scalar code (section 10.2) for $2\sin\left(\dfrac{2\pi}{10}m + \dfrac{2\pi}{7}n\right)$ is 2*sin(2*pi/10*M+2*pi/7*N). The figure 7.2(a) exhibits the digital image of the noise $\eta[m,n]$ which is periodic undoubtedly.

As another example, let us obtain the noise display of the same pixel size for another set of the spatial periods and sine representation which is $\eta[m,n] = 2\sin\left(\dfrac{2\pi}{25}m - \dfrac{2\pi}{40}n\right)$ and whose code in the second line of above implementation should be eta=2*sin(2*pi/25*m-2*pi/40*n);. Figure 7.2(b) shows the digital image of the noise from the execution of the third line command.

At this point the two dimensional discrete Fourier transform (section 4.1) of a two dimensional sine wave has one frequency component in the forward Fourier spectrum which corresponds to the resultant of f_m and f_n. Let us investigate that on the last example. The variable eta is holding the whole $\eta[m,n]$ function. We first take the two dimensional discrete Fourier transform of the image using the function fft2 and then display the transform as a digital image taking the absolute value as follows:

>>F=abs(fft2(eta)); ↵   ← Absolute value of the 2D DFT on eta is stored to F

>>imshow(F,[ ]) ↵   ← Displaying the F as a digital image by first mapping in [0,1]

Figure 7.2(c) shows the image of the transform in which we find two bright dots (at the lower left and upper right corners). Each of them corresponds to the resultant of the spatial frequencies $f_m = \frac{1}{25}$ and $f_n = \frac{1}{40}$ per pixel or section 4.1 discussed fundamental u and v respectively. Since the 2D DFT has half index symmetry, we find two dots.

7.2 Degraded digital image generation

We concentrated mainly on the generation of various noises in last section. Here and now we intend to degrade a digital image by applying some noise. Considering the dip.bmp of section 2.3 and making the image available in the working directory, we add the two dimensional noise function $\eta[m,n]$ with the digital image function $f[m,n]$ for the additive noise. The original image appearance of the dip.bmp is shown in figure 6.1(c). In terms of symbolism, the $\eta[m,n] + f[m,n]$ indicates the degraded image. The image pixel sizes for $\eta[m,n]$, $f[m,n]$, and $\eta[m,n] + f[m,n]$ are identical and the addition happens pixel by pixel. Our objective is to view the degraded image $\eta[m,n] + f[m,n]$ for which the following examples are rendered.

Figure 7.3(a) *Degraded dip.bmp in [0,255] with an impulsive noise 63*

Figure 7.3(b) *Degraded dip.bmp in [0,255] with an impulsive noise 127*

Figure 7.3(c) *Degraded dip.bmp in [0,255] with AWGN of mean 45 and variance 625*

Figure 7.3(d) *Degraded dip.bmp with uniformly distributed noise in [0,255]*

♦ ♦ **Example 1**

Add an impulsive noise to the gray dip.bmp. To this context, the information concerning the image data class, size, and range is very important. The reader can find the answer on the subject in subsection 6.1.2. The strength of the impulse completely depends on the user. Let us choose the impulse strength as 63 where the original image is in [0,255] so in the random generation we take the set as [0 63] in the third input argument of the randsrc as discussed in last section. However the adopted procedure is the following:

MATLAB Command

>>[f,m]=imread('dip.bmp'); ↵ ← reading and assigning intensity and colormap to f and m respectively
>>f=ind2gray(f,m); ↵   ← turning the indexed image [f,m] to gray image f in [0,1]
>>f=im2uint8(f); ↵   ← turning the gray image f in [0,1] to f in [0,255]

From the MATLAB workspace browser, the image size is 218×256 containing the unsigned 8-bit integer data class and the gray levels in [0,255] (table 2.B) and the last f holds the theory discussed $f[m,n]$.

>>eta=randsrc(218,256,[0 63]); ↵ ← eta holds the $\eta[m,n]$ corrupted by the impulse strength 63

>>D=double(f)+eta; ↵   ← D holds the degraded image $f[m,n] + \eta[m,n]$

>>imshow(D,[ ]) ↵   ← Displaying the degraded image first mapping the data in [0,1]

Figure 7.3(a) is the result from above statements. Since all computations must be carried out in double precision form, the conversion from the unsigned 8-bit integer to double class before addition is mandatory. What if we increase the impulse strength to 127. Depicted figure 7.3(b) is the outlook of the image dip.bmp with the impulse 127 for which the eta command should be eta=randsrc(218,256,[0 127]);. The other statements are the same as those of the last one. Less dense impulsive noise is sometimes termed as the salt and pepper noise.

130

♦♦ Example 2

This example adds the additive white Gaussian noise of mean 45 and variance 625 to the dip.bmp of the example 1 which has the size 218×256 and which is held in the workspace variable f. Concerning the noise generation of last section using randn, the σ^2 is 625 hence σ =25 and the procedure is as follows:

>>eta=45+25*randn(218,256); ↵   ← eta holds the $\eta[m,n]$ with the required mean and variance

>>D=double(f)+eta; ↵   ← D holds the degraded image $f[m,n]+\eta[m,n]$

>>imshow(D,[ ]) ↵   ← Displaying the degraded image first mapping the data in [0,1]

The image should look like figure 7.3(c) exercising the last line command. Since the image data is in [0,255], we have large number mean and variance. If the data were in [0,1], both mean and variance would be less in number.

♦♦ Example 3

Uniformly distributed discrete random noise in [0,255] (any level is equally probable) is to be added to the gray version dip.bmp. Employing the function randint of last section and drawing the f from the example 1, we generate the noisy image of the figure 7.3(d) as follows:

>>eta=randint(218,256,[0 255]); ↵← eta holds $\eta[m,n]$ with the given range of the noise level

>>D=double(f)+eta; ↵   ← D holds the degraded image $f[m,n]+\eta[m,n]$

>>imshow(D,[ ]) ↵   ← Displaying the degraded image first mapping the data in [0,1]

The first and second input arguments of the randint are now the row and column directed pixel numbers of the image dip.bmp.

♦♦ Example 4

In this example a sinusoidal noise of amplitude 25 and spatial periods T_m =10 and T_n =7 is to be added with the dip.bmp. So to say, the noise is expressed

by $\eta[m,n] = 25\sin\left(\dfrac{2\pi}{10}m+\dfrac{2\pi}{7}n\right)$.

Drawing the image stored in the workspace variable f from example 1 and functions of last section, we generate the noise and add with the gray dip.bmp as follows:

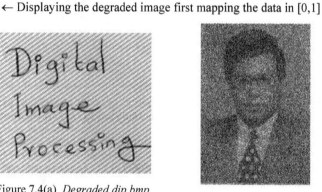

Figure 7.4(a) *Degraded dip.bmp image with the sinusoidal noise*

Figure 7.4(b) *Degraded man.jpg with the uniform noise in [0,255]*

>>[m,n]=meshgrid(1:256,1:218); ↵   ← Workspace browser says the image size 218×256

>>eta=25*sin(2*pi/10*m+2*pi/7*n); ↵   ← eta holds the two dimensional sinusoidal noise $\eta[m,n]$

>>D=double(f)+eta; ↵   ← D holds the degraded image $f[m,n]+\eta[m,n]$

>>imshow(D,[ ]) ↵   ← Displaying the degraded image first mapping the data in [0,1]

To be consistent with the image size, the workspace variables m and n hold the matrices $\begin{bmatrix} 1 & 2 & & 256 \\ 1 & 2 & \cdots & 256 \\ & & \vdots & \\ 1 & 2 & & 256 \end{bmatrix}$ and

$\begin{bmatrix} 1 & 1 & & 1 \\ 2 & 2 & \cdots & 2 \\ \vdots & \vdots & & \\ 218 & 218 & & 218 \end{bmatrix}$ respectively. Figure 7.4(a) presents the sinusoidally corrupted dip.bmp image. The noise

amplitude is very much connected with the gray levels. Here the image gray levels are in [0,255] that is why the amplitude 25 is large in number. If the image were in [0,1], the amplitude of sine would be closer to 1 for example 0.7.

♦♦ Example 5

Foregoing examples added various noises to the dip.bmp. As another image example, let us consider the man.jpg of subsection 6.1.1 and add uniformly distributed discrete random noise in [0,255] to the gray counterpart of the image in [0,255]. Assuming the image in the working directory, we conduct the following:

>>g=imread('man.jpg'); ↵   ← g holds the 3D array for the true color man.jpg

>>f=rgb2gray(g); ↵   ← f holds the gray counterpart (f⇔ $f[m,n]$) of man.jpg

Looking into workspace browser, the image size and data class are 361×253 and unsigned 8-bit integer (meaning in [0,255]) respectively. Consequently, the rest procedure by dint of aforementioned randint is as follows:

>>eta=randint(361,253,[0 255]); ↵   ← eta holds the uniformly distributed $\eta[m,n]$ in [0,255]

>>D=double(f)+eta; ↵   ← D holds the degraded image $f[m,n]+\eta[m,n]$

>>imshow(D,[ ]) ↵   ← Displaying the degraded image first mapping the data in [0,1]

Figure 7.4(b) presents the degraded image from the implementation. Formerly addressed noises can be added with this image as well in a similar fashion.

♦ ♦ Ready made tool of MATLAB

MATLAB function imnoise offers the provision for corrupting a digital image applying various types of noise. Referring to the example 1, we added an impulsive noise of strength 63 to the dip.bmp. The noise has the nickname **salt & pepper** associated with the function imnoise. When the noise is applied, the function imnoise can accept three input arguments ñ the first, second, and third of which are the digital image matrix $f[m,n]$, the noise type with exact MATLAB nickname as a string, and the percentage of the image pixels occupying the full impulse respectively. But one drawback of the function is

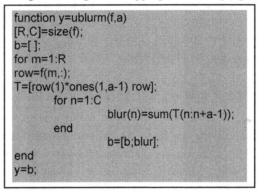

```
function y=ublurm(f,a)
[R,C]=size(f);
b=[ ];
for m=1:R
row=f(m,:);
T=[row(1)*ones(1,a-1) row];
    for n=1:C
            blur(n)=sum(T(n:n+a-1));
    end
        b=[b;blur];
end
y=b;
```

Figure 7.5(a) *The M-file codes for uniform blurring in the m direction only*

we can not apply an impulse other than the full gray value using the imnoise. We know that the image has the pixel size 218×256. If we select 7% of the total pixels to be corrupted, then 0.07×218×256 pixels are selected randomly by the imnoise. Since we changed the f for the last example, we redo the first two linesí implementation from the example 1 for a continual procedure and the noise addition takes place as follows:

>>D=imnoise(f,'salt & pepper',0.07); ↵ ← D holds the degraded image $f[m,n]+\eta[m,n]$

>>imshow(D) ↵   ← Displaying the degraded image, D return by default in [0,1]

For space reason, we excluded the degraded image display from the last execution. One thing becomes certain from the display that all pixels in the image are not affected. There is one space gap before and after the symbol & in the second input argument of the function. If we had the additive white Gaussian noise, the command would be D= imnoise(f,'gaussian',0,.02);. In the case of additive white Gaussian noise, the imnoise can accept four input arguments ñ the digital image matrix, noise type, mean of the Gaussian, and variance of the Gaussian respectively. In a similar fashion, the imnoise can be utilized for the other types of noise. One can learn the noise type and argument options affiliated with the function by executing help imnoise at the command prompt of MATLAB.

7.3 Blurry image generation due to uniform linear motion

On the circumstance that a digital image matrix $f[m,n]$ undergoes to a planar motion in m, n, or both m and n directions, the image suffers from the blurs. The m directed motion of the image gives us the perception as if the whole $f[m,n]$ is moving towards m. If the motion is linear, we call that the blur is generated by uniform linear motion.

To start with a simple case of uniform linear motion, assume that the motion is restricted only in the m direction. The amount of blur in the m direction is computed by the expression $b[m,n]=\frac{1}{a}\sum_{k=0}^{a-1}f[m-k,n]$ ([20] for derivation) where a is user defined positive integer (indicating pixel number for blur) and depends on how much blur is needed. The $b[m,n]$ is the noisy or blurry image we are after. The variables n and $\frac{1}{a}$ do not play any role in the summation and can be frozen but n changes from 0 to $N-1$ where N is the number of the n directed pixels in the given image. It means the summation takes place for a single row of the image for a fixed n. We also make sure that the size of the blurry image is identical with that of the original image. At

Figure 7.5(b) *The image dip.bmp is uniformly blurred in the m direction for a =15*

the beginning point when m =0, we see $f[m,n]$ needs the information from the negative value of m but that is not present. Without the loss of generosity we take repetitive first element before m =0 (assuming the origin at m =0 and n =0) and the number of the repetitions happens according to $a-1$.

Let the blurry computation be explained with the help of the modular matrix $f[m,n] =$

$$\begin{bmatrix} 4 & 4 & 6 & 5 & 7 \\ 8 & 2 & 1 & 0 & 3 \\ 9 & 2 & 2 & 21 & 3 \\ 3 & 23 & 7 & 6 & 5 \end{bmatrix}$$ and $a = 5$. The first row in the image is [4 4 6 5 7]. Repeating the first element $a - 1$

times, we have [4 4 4 4 4 4 6 5 7]. The $b[m,n]$ should be of order 4×5
(same as that of $f[m,n]$). We add every a elements at any pixel hence $b[0,0] = 4+4$
$+4+4+4=20$, $b[1,0] = 4+4+4+4+4=20$, $b[2,0] = 4+4+4+4+6=22$, $b[3,0] = 4+4+4+6+5=$
23, and $b[4,0] = 4+4+6+5+7=26$. Similar computation follows for the other rows of

$b[m,n]$ thereby providing complete $b[m,n]$ as $\begin{bmatrix} 20 & 20 & 22 & 23 & 26 \\ 40 & 34 & 27 & 19 & 14 \\ 45 & 38 & 31 & 43 & 37 \\ 15 & 35 & 39 & 42 & 44 \end{bmatrix}$. Finally

to map the gray levels for the image display, we divide every element in the $b[m,n]$
by the maximum in the $b[m,n]$ which is here 45. That is how the uniform linear
blurring in the m direction is accomplished. Figure 7.5(a) shows our written
function file codes for uniform blurring in the m direction only. The function
ublurm has two input arguments, the first and second of which are the image matrix
$f[m,n]$ and the positive integer constant a respectively. Type the program
statements of the figure 7.5(a) in the M-file editor of MATLAB and save the file by
the name ublurm in your working path of MATLAB. Let us verify our computation
with the said function ublurm as follows:

Figure 7.5(c) *The gray man.jpg is uniformly blurred in the m direction for a = 25*

MATLAB Command

>>f=[4 4 6 5 7;8 2 1 0 3;9 2 2 21 3;3 23 7 6 5]; ↵   ← Entering modular $f[m,n]$ matrix to f

>>b=ublurm(f,5) ↵   ← Calling the function ublurm for $a = 5$

```
b =
        20   20   22   23   26
        40   34   27   19   14
        45   38   31   43   37
        15   35   39   42   44
```

The 0 to 1 mapping can easily be carried out by the
mat2gray once $b[m,n]$ is available (table 2.C). Let us see
the following practical image examples on the uniform
linear blurring.

```
function y=ublurm(f,a)
[R,C]=size(f);
b=[ ];
for m=1:C
column=f(:,m);
T=[column(1)*ones(a-1,1);column];
    for n=1:R
                blur(n)=sum(T(n:n+a-1));
        end
                b=[b blur'];
end
y=b;
```

Figure 7.6(a) *The M-file codes for the uniform blurring in the n direction*

⬥ ⬥ Example 1

We intend to blur the gray version dip.bmp of
subsection 6.1.2 caused by the uniform linear motion only
in the m direction with $a = 15$. Since the blurring is
caused by the summational effect, the data class is
immaterial. Assuming the image and the ublurm in the
working directory, the step by step procedure is implemented as follows:

>>[f,m]=imread('dip.bmp'); ↵ ← reading and assigning intensity and colormap to f and m respectively

>>f=ind2gray(f,m); ↵   ← turning the indexed image [f,m] to gray image f in [0,1], f⇔ $f[m,n]$

>>b=ublurm(f,15); ↵   ← Calling the function ublurm with $a = 15$ where b⇔ $b[m,n]$

>>imshow(b,[ ]) ↵   ← Displaying the blurry image b after mapping in [0,1]

Figure 7.5(b) presents the blurry image so implemented in which the blur is conspicuously in the horizontal
direction.

⬥ ⬥ Example 2

In this example the gray version man.jpg of subsection 6.1.1 is blurred on account of the m directed
uniform linear motion for $a = 25$ for which the necessary commands are as follows:

>>f=imread('man.jpg'); ↵   ← The RGB man.jpg is read and assigned to f as 3D array

>>f=rgb2gray(f); ↵   ← The RGB image is converted to the gray image and assigned to f

>>f=double(f); ↵   ← Turning elements of f to double class for computation and assigned to f

>>b=ublurm(f,25); ↵   ← Calling the function ublurm with $a =25$ where b⇔$b[m,n]$
>>imshow(b,[ ]) ↵   ← Displaying the blurry image b after mapping in [0,1]

The blurry outcome from the implementation is seen in the figure 7.5(c).

♣ ♦ Example 3

What if an image is blurred causing only from the n directed motion whose equation is given by $b[m,n]=\dfrac{1}{a}\sum\limits_{k=0}^{a-1}f[m,n-k]$. Figure 7.6(a) shows the modified MATLAB functional statements for the n directed motion blurring, and we call the M-file function ublurn. Its input argument insertion happens like previously mentioned ublurm. Let us apply the function on the dip.bmp with $a =15$. Type the codes of the ublurn in the M-file editor and save the file by the name ublurn in the working directory. The implementation is identical to that of the example 1 except the ublurm replaced by ublurn. Figure 7.6(b) presents the n directed blurriness caused by the motion.

Figure 7.6(b) *The image dip.bmp is uniformly blurred in the n direction with $a =15$*

♣ ♦ Ready made tool of MATLAB for the motion blurring

The last three examples highlight the theoretical brief of the blurry image generation due to the uniform linear motion. In the examples 1 and 2 the motion is in the horizontally rightward (indicated by the m direction of the figure 7.6(c)). In the third example the motion is in the vertically downward (indicated by the $-n$ direction of the figure 7.6(c)). But the motion can also possess both the m and n directed components. Under this kind of situation, the a is not a scalar instead a vector which has the magnitude as well as the angle θ (shown in the figure 7.6(c)). The angle indicates the motion direction. Referring to section 5.7, the fspecial generates a mask from the required a and θ . In the example 1 we chose $a =15$ in the rightward m direction hence $\theta =0$ according to the figure 7.6(c). In the example 3 the θ should be 270^0 for the vertically downward direction. Of coarse the a and θ are user defined. Let us generate a mask for the example 1 as follows:

>>mask=fspecial('motion',15,0); ↵

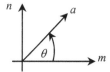

Figure 7.6(c) *The motion geometry for the blur generation of the image $f[m,n]$*

The function fspecial has three input arguments. The first one is the MATLAB indicatory statement that must be placed as the string 'motion'. The second and third of which are just discussed a (positive integer indicating the number of pixels for the uniform motion) and θ (in degrees) respectively. The workspace variable mask holds the mask generated from the required a and θ . Once the mask is ready, the next is to apply the mask to the image using two dimensional convolution (sections 3.10 and 5.8) with the help of the MATLAB function imfilter (the first input argument of which is the digital image matrix and the second one is the mask). Let us reimplement the example 1 by virtue of the imfilter as follows:

Figure 7.6(d) *The image dip.bmp is uniformly blurred in the m direction for $a =15$ using the built-in MATLAB functions fspecial and imfilter*

>>[f,m]=imread('dip.bmp'); ↵   ← reading and assigning intensity and colormap to f and m respectively
>>f=ind2gray(f,m); ↵   ← turning the indexed image [f,m] to gray image f in [0,1]
>>b=imfilter(f,mask); ↵   ← The f and b hold theory discussed $f[m,n]$ and $b[m,n]$ respectively

>>imshow(b,[ ]) ↵   ← Displaying the blurry image b after mapping in [0,1] as in the figure 7.6(d)

Comparing the figure 7.6(d) to the one in the figure 7.5(b) (carried out by our written function), extra narrow black bar appears at the edge. MATLAB functions pad the edges by zeroes (0 corresponds to black) but we did with the edge pixelís gray level that is why it is different from ours. Similarly, the directive blurring other than m or n directed can be generated by first generating the mask for it. As an example, the mask generation command should be mask=fspecial('motion',10,30); when $a =10$ and $\theta =30^0$ in accordance wth the figure 7.6(c).

134

7.4 Removal of noise from a degraded image

Given a degraded image, we try to restore the image to its original form by different image processing techniques. The restoration can happen in spatial or its frequency domain. Clearly defined noise pattern may not exist in a practical image. But the knowledge of knowns can assist us in detecting the probable noise or at least partially. Sometimes interactive or trial-and-error approach is required to identify the subtle noise types present in an image. In this section we try to restore some degraded image employing the functions demonstrated so far. Which method should be applied completely depends on the noise or interference pattern. The removal methods of the interference are obvious from the following subtitles.

Figure 7.7(a) *Degraded dip.bmp when 7% pixels are corrupted by impulsive noise*

Figure 7.7(b) *Restoring the image in 7.7(a) using 3×3 median filtering*

Figure 7.7(c) *Error image e[m,n] of dip.bmp following the median filtering*

Figure 7.7(d) *Degraded man.jpg when 7% pixels are corrupted by the impulsive noise*

Figure 7.7(e) *Restoring the degraded image in 7.7(d) using 3×3 median filtering*

Figure 7.7(f) *Error image e[m,n] of man.jpg following the median filtering*

7.4.1 Removal of impulsive noise using median filtering

Two key concepts are associated here ñ how an image becomes degraded with impulsive noise and how one can apply the median filtering. The reader is referred to sections 5.4 and 7.2 for the two concepts. Considering the gray version dip.bmp, we first add the impulsive noise to 7% image pixels and then apply the median filtering to remove the noise by taking a 3×3 mask size ñ this is our problem statement. Having drawn the functions from said sections, we implement the following:

MATLAB Command

```
>>[f,m]=imread('dip.bmp');      ← reading and assigning intensity and colormap to f and m respectively
>>f=ind2gray(f,m);              ← turning the indexed image [f,m] to gray image f in [0,1], f⇔ f[m,n]
>>D=imnoise(f,'salt & pepper',0.07);   ← D holds the degraded image  f[m,n]+η[m,n] in [0,1]
>>imshow(D)                     ← Displaying the degraded image stored in D
>>R=medfilt2(D,[3 3]);          ← R holds median filtered D image taking 3×3 mask
>>figure,imshow(R,[ ])          ← Displaying the restored image stored in R first mapping in [0,1]
>>e=f-R;                        ← e holds the error image i.e. e[m,n]
```

>>figure,imshow(e,[ ]) ↲   ← Displaying the error image stored in **e** first mapping in [0,1]

The figures 7.7(a), 7.7(b), and 7.7(c) are the outputs from the execution of the fourth, sixth, and eighth lines of above commands and they show the degraded, median filtered, and error images experimented on the dip.bmp respectively. If we call $r[m,n]$ is the reconstructed image in the spatial domain following the filtering (variable R contains $r[m,n]$), the error image is given by $e[m,n] = f[m,n] - r[m,n]$. The subtraction happens for every pixel in the image. For a perfect reconstruction, the error image should be entirely black indicating all values in $e[m,n]$ are zero. It is not possible to have 100% recovery of the corrupted image but at least visual acceptability must be upheld like the figure 7.7(b).

By fits and starts the mean square error (mse) is desired to check the performance on different

experimentation following the restoration, which is defined as mse= $\dfrac{\sum\limits_{n=1}^{N}\sum\limits_{m=1}^{M} |e[m,n]|^2}{MN}$ where $M \times N$ is the image

pixel size. The variable **e** is holding the error image $e[m,n]$ following the restoration. With the help of the function **mean2**, we calculate the mean square error on the error image first by squaring every pixel error by **e.^2** as follows:

>>mean2(e.^2) ↲

ans =
6.7397e-004

The **mean2** finds the mean of all elements in a rectangular matrix when it is the input argument of the function. Referring to the execution, the mean square error from the restoration is 6.7397×10^{-4} (e-004⇔10^{-4} in MATLAB). Due to the randomness, your computed error and ours may not be the same. Also the images in [0,255] result large number mse.

Figure 7.8(a) *Degrading gray man.jpg in [0,255] by adding discrete uniform noise in [0,31]*

Figure 7.8(b) *Restoration of the image in figure 7.8(a) using Wiener filter*

As another image example, let us choose the gray version man.jpg from subsection 6.1.1. The degradation is to be conducted by adding 7% impulsive noise and be median filtered with the 3×3 mask. The mean square error on the recovery is also required. Following is the prescription as steps:

>>f=imread('man.jpg'); ↲ ← f holds the three dimensional array for the RGB image
>>f=rgb2gray(f); ↲   ← turning RGB form to gray image and again assigned to f, f⇔$f[m,n]$

The rest commands are identical with those (third through sixth lines) of the dip.bmp. After executing the sixth line, we look at the workspace browser and find that the returns to the f and R are the unsigned 8-bit integer. For computation reason, they should be in double class hence we conduct the following for the error computation:

>>e=double(f)-double(R); ↲   ← e holds the error image i.e. $e[m,n]$
>>figure,imshow(e,[ ]) ↲   ← Displaying the error image stored in **e** first mapping in [0,1]

Figures 7.7(d), 7.7(e), and 7.7(f) show the degraded, restored, and error images from the median filter processing respectively. Also the mean square error is 17.4104 on execution of the **mean2(e.^2)**.

7.4.2 Removal of uniform or Gaussian noise using Wiener filtering

Section 7.2 illustrates how one can add uniform noise to a digital image for the degradation purpose. Wiener filtering theory is presented in section 5.6. Choosing the gray version man.jpg in [0,255] (subsection 6.1.1), the degradation applying a discrete uniform noise in [0,31] takes place through the intermediacy of section 7.2 mentioned function as follows:

MATLAB Command for the degradation:

>>f=imread('man.jpg'); ↲   ← Reading the RGB image and assigned to f, f is 3D array
>>f=rgb2gray(f); ↲ ← Converting the RGB image in f to gray form and assigned to f, where f⇔$f[m,n]$
and the image size is 361×253 looking into the workspace browser
>>eta=randint(361,253,[0 31]); ↲ ← Generating the discrete uniform noise in [0,31] of the image size
361×253, where eta⇔$\eta[m,n]$
>>D=double(f)+eta; ↲← Adding noise $\eta[m,n]$ to image f and D holds the degraded $f[m,n] + \eta[m,n]$
>>imshow(D,[ ]) ↲   ← Displaying the degraded image first mapping in [0,1]

Figure 7.8(a) presents the degraded man.jpg (which is stored in D) upon the addition of the uniform noise. We know from section 5.6 that the Wiener filter needs a user-defined variance to start with. As a common practice in Wiener filtering, the variance of the given degraded image is considered during commencing. The filtering is performed and the image quality is noticed whether it is visually acceptable. If it is not, we choose another variance and perform the same filtering. The trial and check approach is continued until the best picture is achieved. MATLAB function var (subsection 6.1.4) calculates the variance of gray levels in degraded image D as follows:

>>v=var(D(:)) ↵   ← D(:) turns the D as column matrix and the variance is assigned to v

v =
898.5367

Due to the randomness of the generation, your implemented variance might be different slightly from ours. Let us choose a 5×5 mask size for the filtering. With the chosen mask size and variance, the restored image $r[m,n]$ is obtained as follows:

Command for the restoration:

>>r=wiener2(D,[5 5],v); ↵ ← r holds the restored $r[m,n]$

>>figure,imshow(r,[ ]) ↵   ← Displaying the restored $r[m,n]$ first mapping in [0,1] as presented
in the figure 7.8(b)

If you think the image is not properly restored, choose another variance or mask size, execute the last two lines, and check the acceptability of the image until the best one is obtained. For example, choosing another mask size 6×6 and variance 905 needs to execute r=wiener2(D,[6 6],905);. Yet the degree of the noise presence may not allow us to have the perfect image like the original one but at least the image acceptability becomes improved due to noise removal.

Sometimes our eyes can not differentiate the restored images that are slightly different. If we hold the original image matrix $f[m,n]$, we can compute the mean square error (subsection 7.4.1) from the restored image $r[m,n]$. The pixel by pixel computation must be carried out on the same basis of the gray level. Following the filtering, the restored image data may not be in [0,255] or [0,1] scale. The restored image data held in r can be mapped to [0,1] by mat2gray and then to [0,255] by the im2uint8. From workspace browser, the original image matrix f is in the unsigned 8-bit integer form. Therefore we execute the following to find the mean square error from the restoration:

>>r=im2uint8(mat2gray(r)); ↵ ← r holds the restored $r[m,n]$ in unsigned 8-bit integer form in [0,255]

>>e=double(f)-double(r); ↵   ← e holds the error in restoration, $e[m,n] = f[m,n] - r[m,n]$

>>mse(e) ↵

ans =
2.3659e+003

The MATLAB function mse computes the mean square error taking the error matrix or $e[m,n]$ as the input argument. Even though we found the mean square error before using mean2, implementation of the mse is presented so that the reader has more option. Therefore in the restoration of the degraded man.jpg, we have the mean square error 2.3659×10^3 (e+003⇔10^3). As another trial, we choose different mask size and variance and compute the mean square error. The less is the mean square error, the better is the restoration. Nevertheless the mse computation is possible so far as the original image matrix is available.

Figure 7.8(c) *Restoration of the image dip.bmp using the Wiener filtering*

Additive white Gaussian noise removal

The Wiener filtering removes the additive white Gaussian noise from a degraded image too. Selecting the degraded image of example 2 from section 7.2 (degradation commands and corrupted display are in the section), we intend to practice the filtering. As far as the randomness of the noise is concern, when you run those commands and obtain the degraded image, you may not see identical degraded image as in the figure 7.3(c). Certainly the degraded image is stored in the workspace variable D and our Wiener filtering starts from the availability of D. Since we commence with the variance of the degraded image, let us find that as follows:

>>v=var(D(:)) ↵

v =
1.0178e+003

Also we need the mask size (say 5×5), and exercise the Wiener filtering on the D with the variance and mask size as follows:

```
>>r=wiener2(D,[5 5],v); ↵        ← r holds the restored r[m,n]
>>imshow(r,[ ]) ↵                ← Displaying the restored r[m,n] first mapping in [0,1]
```

For space reason we avoided its display. But we are not sure that this is the best-restored one until we try with several mask size and variance. Since the original image is available in the workspace variable f, apply the mse as the acceptability criterion as follows:

```
>>r=im2uint8(mat2gray(r)); ↵     ← r holds the restored r[m,n] in unsigned 8-bit integer form in [0,255]
>>e=double(f)-double(r); ↵       ← e holds the error in restoration, e[m,n] = f[m,n] − r[m,n]
>>mse(e) ↵

ans =
       6.7275e+003               ← the mean square error is 6.7275×10³ with the starting variance
```

We repeated the trial for the variance starting from 100 to 1200 with a step 100 from which the best visual turnout happened at the variance 900. However the figure 7.8(c) presents the restored image at the variance 900. Since for every variance we have to execute the last five line commands, it is better to execute them using a for-loop (for-loop counter controls the variance) written in an M-file (subsection 10.3.3).

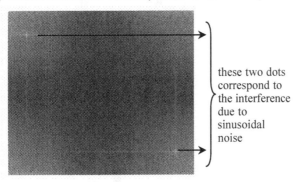

these two dots correspond to the interference due to sinusoidal noise

Figure 7.9(a) *Log-magnitude Fourier spectrum of the degraded image*

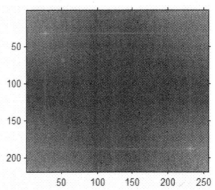

Figure 7.9(b) *Log-magnitude Fourier spectrum with axis on*

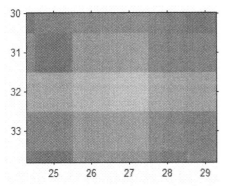

Figure 7.9(c) *Zooming the upper bright dot*

Figure 7.9(d) *Restoring the degraded image of the figure 7.4(a)*

7.4.3 Removal of sinusoidal noise

Concerning the section 7.2 implemented example 4, sinusoidally degraded dip.bmp image is held in the workspace variable D whose image display is shown in the figure 7.4(a). This is our test image and we intend to restore the degraded image. Section 7.1 outlines that the two dimensional discrete Fourier transform (symbolized by $F[u,v]$) of a pure two dimensional sinusoidal gives the perception of two bright dots in the magnitude Fourier spectrum (figure 7.2(c)). Since most of the image gray level energy is concentrated on the lower frequency portion of the spectrum, we use logarithmic scale to see the bright dots clearly. That is we need to display $\log(1+|F[u,v]|)$ as a digital image. In doing so we plan to identify the exact location of the bright dots. Having the D available in MATLAB workspace from the section 7.2, let us accomplish the following:

MATLAB Command
```
>>F=fft2(D); ↵     ← 2D DFT of degraded D is taken and the result is assigned to F, F⇔ F[u,v]
```

>>L=log(1+abs(F)); ↵   ← operation log(1+| F[u,v] |) is conducted and the result is assigned to L

>>figure,imshow(L,[ ]) ↵   ← Displaying L as a digital image by first mapping to [0,1]

Figure 7.9(a) presents the image display of the log-magnitude Fourier spectrum. In order to identify the bright dot coordinates, we take the help of the following command:

>>axis on ↵

Above command enables the image axis in terms of the image pixel size (218×256, the size of D from workspace browser). Now we click the zoom in icon in the figure 7.9(b) window menu bar (section 1.3) and select a target area keeping one dot of the figure 7.9(b) in the middle of the target area with the help of the mouse. With the release of the target area for sure we see the zoomed area. The reader needs several zoomings to see the bright dot distinctly (which becomes block because of the zooming). We carried out the zooming three times for the upper dot and whose result is the figure 7.9(c). From the figure, one can easily read off the location of the sinusoidal interference at the coordinates (32,27). Doubleclick the mouse at any point in the image area to go back to the previous image. In a similar way, the other bright dot coordinates found are at (188,231). Of coarse, these are the coordinates for the spatial frequency variables u and v as regards to the 2D DFT in MATLAB notation respectively.

At the moment we know the location of the strongest sinusoidal interference. The simplest approach for removing the interference is to turn the corresponding spatial frequency component to zero. The logarithmic display is only for finding the frequency location visually. Once found, we go back to the 2D DFT which is stored in F and set the frequency lines corresponding to the $u=32$, $v=27$, $u=188$, and $v=231$ to zero with the help of the command **zeros** (section 10.4) as follows:

>>F(32,:)=zeros(1,256); ↵   ← Setting the horizontal frequency line $u=32$ to zero

>>F(:,27)=zeros(218,1); ↵   ← Setting the vertical frequency line $v=27$ to zero

>>F(188,:)=zeros(1,256); ↵   ← Setting the horizontal frequency line $u=188$ to zero

>>F(:,231)=zeros(218,1); ↵   ← Setting the vertical frequency line $v=231$ to zero

The image transform size (size of F from workspace browser) also manifests that there are 256 and 218 elements in the horizontal and vertical directions respectively. The next rational step is to go back to the spatial or pixel domain with the help of the function ifft2 (section 4.1). But the spectrum has been altered because of the frequency removal and we obtain imaginary part on the inversion. It is important to take the absolute value to have all elements in the inversion matrix as the real (because the gray levels are real). Again the image data is changed from [0,1] or [0,255] resulting from the manipulation. Anyhow we conduct the following to restore the degraded image:

>>r=ifft2(F); ↵   ← r holds the restored image followed by the inverse 2D DFT

>>imshow(abs(r),[ ]) ↵   ← abs(r) for absolute value and [ ] for [0,1] mapping

Figure 7.9(d) depicts the restored image. Compared to the degraded version as in the figure 7.4(a), the image quality is better. Nevertheless compared to the original image as presented in the figure 6.1(c), still something needs to be done. The solution is to design a Butterworth band stop filter at the found frequency location. We keep that as an exercise for the reader (section 5.3).

A degraded digital image may or may not be perfectly restored but our effort can have them perceived better at least visually. That is the job of an image processing engineer or personnel. For further restoration reference, the reader can go through [20]. We intend to close the image degradation and restoration chapter along with this implementation.

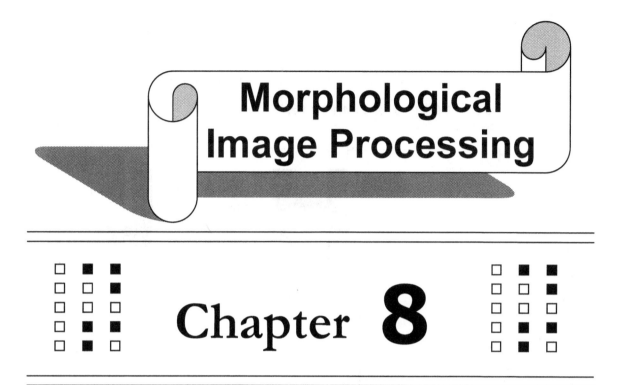

Morphological Image Processing

Chapter 8

Linguistically the meaning of the morphology concerns the biology or the shape of the image object. Morphological image processing describes or analyzes the form and structure of a digital image taking the arrangements and interrelationship among various parts of the digital image into account. Morphological processing techniques are different for the bilevel, gray, and color digital images. Because of the introductory nature of the text, we concentrate mostly on the bilevel or binary image morphologies. The morphology, as a mathematical tool, extracts corporeal digital image features that are employed for the subsequent image analysis. Our prototype based illustration outlines the following in this chapter:

- ❖ ❖ User defined binary image generation and simplistic set operations on the binary images
- ❖ ❖ Means of turning the softcopy images to the binary one needed for the morphologic operation
- ❖ ❖ Two momentous morphological operators – erosion and dilation applied to the binary images
- ❖ ❖ Compound morphological operations such as closing, opening, or hit and miss transform
- ❖ ❖ Acquiring the thin shape or skeleton and distance transform from a binary image
- ❖ ❖ Accessing to the built-in structuring elements and their application in a binary image

8.1 Binary image generation

For many digital image processing analyses, a binary image can be taken as the test image. The binary image has only two gray levels – 0 or 1. If the 0 represents the white background in the image, the 1 becomes black foreground or vice versa. In this section we generate some binary images from user definition. The image information is contained in a rectangular matrix in which the position indexes of the matrix elements represent the pixel positions and the value of the matrix element represents binary level either 0 or 1. In a simplistic way we intend to generate the letter H in MATLAB. Let us say we have the matrix $\begin{bmatrix} 1 & 0 & 0 & 1 \\ 1 & 0 & 0 & 1 \\ 1 & 1 & 1 & 1 \\ 1 & 0 & 0 & 1 \\ 1 & 0 & 0 & 1 \end{bmatrix}$. Connecting all 1 elements

in the matrix, we get the binary image H – that is what we require and carry out in the following:

MATLAB Command

```
>>M=[1 0 0 1;1 0 0 1;1 1 1 1;1 0 0 1;1 0 0 1]; ↵
>>imshow(M) ↵
```

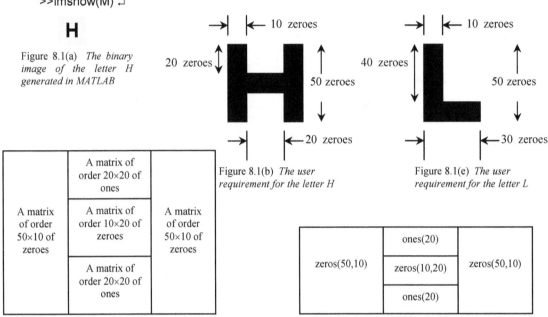

Figure 8.1(a) *The binary image of the letter H generated in MATLAB*

Figure 8.1(b) *The user requirement for the letter H*

Figure 8.1(e) *The user requirement for the letter L*

Figure 8.1(c) *The ones and zeroes placement for the letter H*

Figure 8.1(d) *The MATLAB commands for the generation of ones and zeroes in the figure 8.1(c)*

The first line in above implementation is the assignment of the binary image matrix to the workspace variable **M**. The second line just displays the image matrix **M** with the aid of the MATLAB function **imshow** (section 2.5). Upon the execution, you see a small H letter in the middle of the MATLAB figure window. You can maximize the figure window to see a larger shape of the H. The displayed letter has the white foreground and the black

background since MATLABís **imshow** function corresponds to $\begin{Bmatrix} 1 \text{ for white} \\ 0 \text{ for black} \end{Bmatrix}$. It does not provide a better look

because our paper is white. The image would have been better displayed if the foreground were black and the background were white. It means we need to invert the ones to zeroes and zeroes to ones in the matrix **M**. The inversion operator (subsection 10.3.1) in MATLAB is ~ hence we execute the following to display the image of the letter H at the maximized window as shown in the figure 8.1(a).

```
>>imshow(~M) ↵
```

We employed just one 1 for the generation of the letter body. To see a thick H body, employment of multiple ones is obvious. Let us say the letter body is composed of ten zeroes (to be consistent with MATLABís 0 for black foreground). Next legitimate query is what the height and middle width of the letter should be. Figure 8.1(b) shows the user required width and height of the letter H in terms of the zeroes. It should be pointed out that the rectangular matrix **M** must be formed with proper order while placing different ones and zeroes in the foreground and background of the image. The reader is referred to chapter 10 for hasty generation of matrices of ones and zeroes and forming larger matrices from the smaller ones. We can organize various ones and zeroes associated with the letter as shown in the figure 8.1(c) whose generation commands in MATLAB are shown in the figure 8.1(d). However, let us form the complete image matrix **M** for the letter H by the following:

```
>>M=[zeros(50,10) [ones(20);zeros(10,20);ones(20)] zeros(50,10)]; ↵
```

Now is the time for displaying our designed image letter and we do so as follows:

```
>>imshow(M) ↵
```

On execution we see the expected letter H in the MATLAB figure window (at the maximized window) like the one in the figure 8.1(b). In the following we present two more examples on the binary image generation.

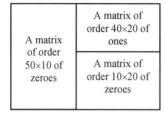

Figure 8.1(f) *The ones and zeroes placement for the letter L*

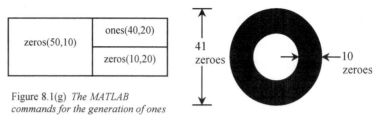

Figure 8.1(g) *The MATLAB commands for the generation of ones and zeroes of the figure 8.1(f)*

Figure 8.1(h) *The letter O with a width of ten zeroes*

♦ ♦ Example A

Let us generate the binary image of the letter L with the specifications given in the figure 8.1(e). The associated placement of the ones and zeroes and their MATLAB commands are shown in the figures 8.1(f) and 8.1(g) respectively. The complete command for the L image generation is as follows:

MATLAB Command

```
>>L=[zeros(50,10) [ones(40,20);zeros(10,20)]]; ↵
>>imshow(L) ↵
```

After running the command, we see the letter L at the maximized MATLAB figure window.

♦ ♦ Example B

Not all character images are having plane or straight sides. Most of the character images possess curvy sides like the letter O as shown in the figure 8.1(h). The letter is formed from two concentric circles. The inner and outer circles have the radii equivalent to 10 zeroes and 20 zeroes respectively.

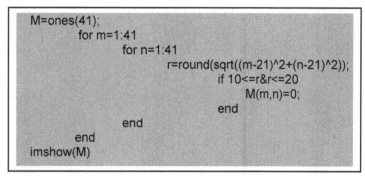

Figure 8.1(i) *M file contents for the generation of the image of the letter O*

The image generation needs little programming because we can not place so many zeroes in the matrix by typing.

Let us concentrate on the algorithm of the problem. First of all we generate a matrix of ones of order 41×41 and assign that to **M**. The central element (figure 3.7(b)) in the matrix has the position indexes (21,21). Any element in the matrix has the variable position indices (m , n). The radial distance of the variable point (m , n) to the central element at (21,21) is $r = \sqrt{(m-21)^2 + (n-21)^2}$. We use two for-loops that generate m and n each from 1 to 41 and calculate the radial distance r for every position in the matrix. If the r satisfies the condition $10 \le r \le 20$ for any (m , n) in the matrix **M**, we assign one 0 at that (m , n). But the problem is we end up with the fractional numbers during the computation of r . The position index must be an integer number not a fractional one so we employ literally some approximation $\begin{cases} \text{if the fractional element is more than 0.5,} \\ \text{we consider that as 1 else the fractional} \\ \text{part is zero} \end{cases}$ on the radial distance r so computed. For example, if the distance r is 2.5001 or 2.4999, we assume that as 3 or 2 respectively. MATLAB function round can perform the integer approximation towards the nearest integer. The MATLAB code for the distance $\sqrt{(m-21)^2 + (n-21)^2}$ is sqrt((m-21)^2+(n-21)^2). The logical condition $10 \le r \le 20$ is split in two parts as $10 \le r$ and $r \le 20$ for the if-programming reason. We compare each of the conditions separately and combine them by the AND operator (chapter 10) whose MATLAB counterpart is &. Anyhow we write the statements of the figure 8.1(i) in the M-file editor and run the file to see the image of the letter O same as the figure 8.1(h).

Thus and so the reader can devise any other binary image object paying attention to $\begin{cases} \text{the size of the image matrix} \\ \text{the position index in the matrix where to place 1} \\ \text{the position index in the matrix where to place 0} \end{cases}$ during the design. Just to mention one practical example, suppose you have drawn your country map in a graph paper. You can have the map boundary as a binary image by placing the map in an appropriate matrix dimension and 0 for the boundary.

8.2 Set operations on binary images

The most common set operations are the intersection of two sets, union of two sets, complement of a set, and difference of two sets. Here the set is the digital image matrix $f[m,n]$ whose elements are either the gray level 0 or 1. Any set operation to be conducted on the digital images must happen pixelwise. We explain various set operations to the context of the binary image in the following.

✦ ✦ Intersection of two binary images

Intersection of two binary images $f[m,n]$ and $g[m,n]$ emerges from the logical AND operation of the like positional elements which is symbolized by $f[m,n] \cap g[m,n]$. Let us say the two identical size modular images are $f[m,n] = \begin{bmatrix} 1 & 0 & 1 \\ 1 & 1 & 0 \end{bmatrix}$ and $g[m,n] = \begin{bmatrix} 0 & 1 & 1 \\ 1 & 1 & 0 \end{bmatrix}$. The logical AND operation returns 1 if both pixel values are 1 hence we have $f[m,n] \cap g[m,n] = \begin{bmatrix} 0 & 0 & 1 \\ 1 & 1 & 0 \end{bmatrix}$. Let us see how MATLAB performs the intersection with the aid of the logical AND operator (&) as follows:

```
>>f=[1 0 1;1 1 0]; ↵        ← f[m,n] is assigned to f
>>g=[0 1 1;1 1 0]; ↵        ← g[m,n] is assigned to g
>>h=f&g ↵                    ← workspace variable h holds f[m,n] ∩ g[m,n] result

h =
     0   0   1
     1   1   0
```

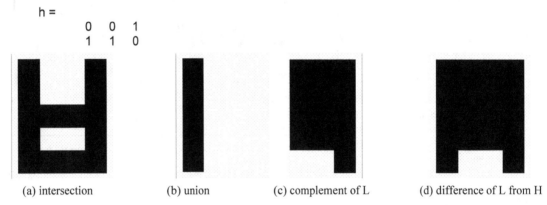

| (a) intersection | (b) union | (c) complement of L | (d) difference of L from H |

Figure 8.2(a)-(d) *Different set operations on the binary images of H and L*

✦ ✦ Union of two binary images

Union of the two binary images is symbolized by $f[m,n] \cup g[m,n]$ and defined in terms of the logical OR operations on every like positional pixels in the images. If any pixel (m , n) of the two images has 1, the return of the logical OR is 1 otherwise is 0. Performing the union operation on aforementioned modular binary images, we have $f[m,n] \cup g[m,n] = \begin{bmatrix} 1 & 1 & 1 \\ 1 & 1 & 0 \end{bmatrix}$ for which following is the implementation:

```
>>h=f|g ↵                    ← workspace variable h holds f[m,n] ∪ g[m,n] result

h =
     1   1   1
     1   1   0
```

The logical OR operator | can find the union of two binary images.

✦ ✦ Complement of a binary image

The complement of a binary image $f[m,n]$ is defined as the inversion of binary element that is 1 to 0 or 0 to 1. The operation is symbolized by $f[m,n]^c$ therefore $f[m,n]^c = \begin{bmatrix} 0 & 1 & 0 \\ 0 & 0 & 1 \end{bmatrix}$ and the implementation is as follows:

```
>>h=~f ↵          ← workspace variable h holds f[m,n]ᶜ result
```

```
h =
     0   1   0
     0   0   1
```

The inversion operator ~ can find the complement image.

♦ ♦ Difference between two binary images – $g[m,n]$ from $f[m,n]$

The difference of the two binary images is symbolized by $f[m,n] - g[m,n]$ which is equivalent to the set operation $f[m,n] \cap g[m,n]^c$ or in terms of the MATLAB operator f&(~g). For the prototype images, we should have $f[m,n] - g[m,n] = \begin{bmatrix} 1 & 0 & 0 \\ 0 & 0 & 0 \end{bmatrix}$ which can easily be verified by executing f&(~g).

♦ ♦ Set operations on practical images

Figure 8.3 *Difference of the text.tif from H*

To apply various set operations discussed so far, first we need two binary images. Let us consider the binary images of the letters H and L from the last section and generate them as follows:

```
>>H=[zeros(50,10) [ones(20);zeros(10,20);ones(20)] zeros(50,10)]; ↵      ← H⇔ f[m,n]
>>L=[zeros(50,10) [ones(40,20);zeros(10,20)]]; ↵                          ← L⇔ g[m,n]
```

Important point is any set operation on two binary images requires that their size be identical. Looking into the workspace browser, we find that the sizes for the H and L are 50×40 and 50×30 respectively. To have them of the same size 50×40, let us append 50×10 ones (appending white coincides with paper) to the rightside of L as follows:

```
>>L=[L ones(50,10)]; ↵   ← L again holds the appended L              ← L⇔ g[m,n]
```

Now we apply previously mentioned set operations on the identical size binary H and L images as follows:

```
>>h=H&L; ↵          ← Intersection of H and L is assigned to h, h⇔ f[m,n] ∩ g[m,n]
>>imshow(h) ↵       ← h is displayed as shown in the figure 8.2(a)
>>h=H|L; ↵          ← Union of H and L is assigned to h, h⇔ f[m,n] ∪ g[m,n]
>>imshow(h) ↵       ← h is displayed as shown in the figure 8.2(b)
>>h=~L; ↵           ← Complement of L is assigned to h, h⇔ g[m,n]ᶜ
>>imshow(h) ↵       ← h is displayed as shown in the figure 8.2(c)
>>h=H&~L; ↵         ← Difference of L from H is assigned to h, h⇔ f[m,n] ∩ g[m,n]ᶜ
>>imshow(h) ↵       ← h is displayed as shown in the figure 8.2(d)
```

As another example, we wish to take the difference of the MATLAB supplied image text.tif (execute imshow('text.tif') for display) from the letter H stored in the workspace and perform the following:

```
>>f=imread('text.tif'); ↵        ← f⇔ g[m,n]
```

The workspace variable f holds the text.tif image matrix. From workspace browser, we find the size of the f being 256×256. For identical size reason, the H is resized to pixel size 256×256 using imresize (section 3.7) as follows:

```
>>H=imresize(H,[256 256]); ↵     ← H⇔ f[m,n]
```

Now the variable H holds the resized 256×256 H image matrix. On having that, we carry out the following:

```
>>h=H&(~f); ↵   ← h holds the difference of text.tif from H, h⇔ f[m,n] ∩ g[m,n]ᶜ
>>imshow(h) ↵   ← Displaying the contents of h as a digital image
```

Figure 8.3 is the intended difference image. Any other composite set operation can be derived from the mentioned four operators. Moreover this is all about the binary images. Sometimes set operations on integer gray level such as in [0,255] scale might be required. We have some other set functions unique, ismember, Ö etc. To learn about these functions, execute help unique or help ismember.

8.3 How to obtain a binary image from a digital softcopy image?

Most morphological image processing starts with test binary images. Given a softcopy digital image file, one can convert the image to a binary image using the MATLAB built-in functions. Practical images are mostly colored and stored in terms of the indexed or RGB form (section 2.4). The MATLAB function im2bw (abbreviation of image to (2) black and white) converts an intensity, indexed, or RGB image to binary image. Let us consider the dip.bmp image of subsection 6.1.2 which is an indexed one. Our objective is to turn this image to a binary one. Obtain the image, place it in your working directory, and carry out the following:

MATLAB Command

```
>>[f,m]=imread('dip.bmp'); ↵
>>B=im2bw(f,m,0.6); ↵
```

To know about the image information, the reader can execute the function imfinfo of subsection 6.1.1. The first line of above command is to read the dip.bmp with the help of the MATLAB image reader imread and to store the intensity and colormap matrices to the workspace variables f and m respectively. In the second line, the function

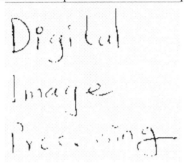

Figure 8.4(a) *The binary image from dip.bmp after applying a threshold 0.6*

Figure 8.4(b) *The binary image from dip.bmp after applying a threshold 0.8*

im2bw converts the indexed image components f and m to the binary image considering a threshold 0.6. The function im2bw has three input arguments ñ the first, second, and third of which are the intensity image matrix, colormap matrix, and threshold value respectively. The choice of the threshold is userís and must be within 0 and 1. The binary image from the dip.bmp is assigned to the workspace variable B and is displayed by the following:

```
>>imshow(B) ↵
```

Referring to the workspace browser, the data class of B is logical pointing out gray level 0 or 1. If T is the threshold and it is to be applied in the intensity image matrix $f[m,n]$, we set $f[m,n]=0$ for $f[m,n]>T$ and $f[m,n]=1$ for $f[m,n]<T$. The reverse operation is also acceptable that is $f[m,n]=1$ for $f[m,n]>T$ and $f[m,n]=0$ for $f[m,n]<T$. If $f[m,n]$ is scaled in [0,1], so is T which is what the im2bw does. For example, the intensity image matrix $f[m,n]=\begin{bmatrix} 0.1 & 0.25 & 0.4 \\ 0.3 & .8 & 0.2 \end{bmatrix}$ becomes the binary

Figure 8.4(c) *The man.jpg image after applying a threshold 0.6*

$\begin{bmatrix} 0 & 0 & 0 \\ 0 & 1 & 0 \end{bmatrix}$ at a choice of threshold 0.4. The choice of threshold 0.6 in the figure 8.4(a) is not enough to highlight the handwritten text. Let us choose the threshold as 0.8 and execute the B=im2bw(f,m,0.8); imshow(B) to see the handwritten text like the figure 8.4(b). The B is for sure a matrix of 1 and 0 holding the same size as that of the pixel size of dip.bmp. To verify our statement, doubleclick the B located in the workspace browser to see the binary image pixel values in the array editor.

A true color image like man.jpg of subsection 6.1.1 needs only two input arguments in the im2bw – the first and second of which are the RGB image as a three dimensional array and the threshold between 0 and 1 respectively. Let us implement the thresholding at 0.6 on making the man.jpg available in the working directory as follows:

```
>>f=imread('man.jpg'); ↵   ← Reading the man.jpg and f holds the 3D array
>>B=im2bw(f,0.6); ↵        ← B holds the binary image matrix after applying the threshold 0.6 on f
>>imshow(B) ↵              ← Displaying the binary image B
```

Figure 8.4(c) presents the binary image from above execution. If the image is intensity one, the command is similar to that of the RGB one.

8.4 Dilation of binary images

Dilation is the important kind of morphological transformation that combines two sets of data using the vector addition. The two sets of data are termed as the object and the structuring element respectively. For our implementation the object is a binary image and the structuring element is a user defined data set. Let us say I is the binary image matrix data set and S is the structuring element data set. Particularly the data sets are linked to the two dimensional Euclidean space. The Euclidean space is the binary image pixel coordinates or the structuring element coordinates.

The dilation of I by S is defined as the set of all points which lie in $I + S$. The operation has the symbolic representation $I \oplus S$ and is also called the Minkowski addition. Computationally we first add every data in S to every data in I and then discard the repetitive data to obtain $I \oplus S$.

Numerical example is the best way to have the concept focused. Let us say the Euclidean space data is given by the sets I =(0,0), (0,2), (1,1), (1,2), (2,2), and (3,1) and S =(0,0) and (0,1) on which the computation is shown below:

the first element coordinates (0,0) in S is added to those of every element in I to have: (0,0), (0,2), (1,1), (1,2), (2,2), and (3,1)

the second element coordinates (0,1) in S is added to those of every element in I to have: (0,1), (0,3), (1,2), (1,3), (2,3), and (3,2)

excluding the repetitive data but taking all data from both additions, we have $I \oplus S$ =(0,0), (0,2), (1,1), (1,2), (2,2), (3,1), (0,1), (0,3), (1,3), (2,3), and (3,2)

Figure 8.5(a) *Contents of the binary text.jpg*

Figure 8.5(b) *Dilated text.jpg*

The next question is how we relate the I with the binary image. The pixel variables m and n are assumed as vertically downward and horizontally rightward respectively that is $\downarrow \begin{smallmatrix} \rightarrow n \\ \\ m \end{smallmatrix}$. Looking into the given I data set, the ranges of m and n are 0-3 and 0-2 respectively therefore the size of I being 4×3. We put 1 in the coordinates of I and the rest are set to 0 thus $I[m,n] = \begin{bmatrix} 1 & 0 & 1 \\ 0 & 1 & 1 \\ 0 & 0 & 1 \\ 0 & 1 & 0 \end{bmatrix}$. The first element in the upper left of the binary image matrix has the coordinates (0,0). The third element in the second row of the binary image has the coordinates (1,2) which is in aforementioned I. Similarly the structuring element matrix becomes $S[m,n] = [1 \quad 1]$. The dilation of I by the structuring element S can also be written in the binary image matrix form as $I \oplus S = \begin{bmatrix} 1 & 1 & 1 & 1 \\ 0 & 1 & 1 & 1 \\ 0 & 0 & 1 & 1 \\ 0 & 1 & 1 & 0 \end{bmatrix}$.

Let us concise our expectation from MATLAB. We provide the image matrix $I[m,n]$ and structuring element matrix $S[m,n]$ and MATLAB should return the dilated matrix $I \oplus S$ for which we conduct the following:

MATLAB Command

```
>>I=[1 0 1;0 1 1;0 0 1;0 1 0];  ⏎   ← I⟺ I[m,n]
>>S=[1 1];  ⏎                    ← S⟺ S[m,n]
>>D=imdilate(I,S,'full')  ⏎
```

```
>>S=[0 1 1;0 1 1];  ⏎
>>D=imdilate(I,S,'full')  ⏎

D =
```

146

```
D =
          1  1  1  1                          1  1  1  1
          0  1  1  1                          1  1  1  1
          0  0  1  1                          0  1  1  1
          0  1  1  0                          0  1  1  1
                                              0  1  1  0
```

In the first and second lines of above command are to assign the $I[m,n]$ and $S[m,n]$ matrices to the variables I and S respectively. The MATLAB function imdilate (abbreviation of the <u>image dilate</u>) dilates a binary image which has three input arguments, the first and second of which are the binary image and the structuring element matrices respectively. The coordinate manipulation is hidden inside the function imdilate. The third input argument 'full' is a MATLAB indicatory statement which says that we need the full dilated matrix. The return of imdilate is assigned to the workspace variable D which is our expected $I \oplus S$.

If we exclude the input argument 'full', the return size of D is the same as that of the I. Not necessarily the structuring elements will be in one line, they can appear in two or more adjacent lines as well. For example, the $S[m,n]$ can be $\begin{bmatrix} 0 & 1 & 1 \\ 0 & 1 & 1 \end{bmatrix}$ indicating the coordinates set (0,0), (0,1), (0,2), (1,0), (1,1), and (1,2). Dilating the $I[m,n]$ with this structuring element $S[m,n]$ is also presented above in the right side. There are lot more options hidden in the function imdilate. One can learn more about the function executing help imdilate.

So long we mentioned only about the theoretical concept behind the image dilation. Now we wish to include one practical binary image example on text.jpg of section 2.3. Obtain the image and place it in your working directory. We intend to dilate the binary version of text.jpg employing the structuring element matrix $S[m,n] = \begin{bmatrix} 0 & 1 & 1 & 1 \\ 0 & 1 & 1 & 1 \end{bmatrix}$. Using the imfinfo of section 6.1.1, the image is an RGB or true color saved one. To obtain a binary image from the text.jpg, a threshold 0.6 is applied. Let us carry out the following:

MATLAB Command

```
>>f=imread('text.jpg'); ↵   ← Reading text.jpg and assigned to f where f is a 3D array
>>B=im2bw(f,0.6); ↵         ← Turning the f to a binary image B by applying the threshold 0.6 as
                              done in the last section, where B is the theory discussed I[m,n]
>>imshow(B) ↵               ← Displaying the binary version of the text.jpg
>>S=[0 1 1 1;0 1 1 1]; ↵    ← Entering the S[m,n] matrix for dilation, S⇔S[m,n]
>>D=imdilate(B,S); ↵        ← Dilated matrix is stored in D, D⇔I⊕S
>>figure,imshow(D) ↵        ← Displaying the dilated image D
```

The execution of the third line in above command shows the actual binary image in the figure 8.5(a) whose dilated counterpart is followed by the figure 8.5(b) upon the execution of the last line. Comparing the two figures, one can infer that the binary image becomes swollen on account of the dilation. We guess the reader is now in a position to experiment with various structuring elements and binary images. The swollen effect of the image dilation helps to identify the defects in the industrial applications.

Figure 8.5(c) *Eroded text.jpg image*

8.5 Erosion of binary images

Erosion is another important class of the morphological transformation that combines two sets of data but utilizing the vector subtraction. The symbolism and notation we discussed in last section is equally applicable here.

The erosion of I by S is defined as the set of all points which come from the vector subtraction of the set elements, also called the Minkowski subtraction and symbolized by $I \ominus S$. To proceed with the set computation, we first subtract every data in S from each data in I and then pick up the common data in the subtraction set. Let us choose the sets as I =(0,1), (0,2), (0,3), (1,1), (1,2), (1,3), (2,1), (2,2), (3,0), (3,1) and S =(0,0), (0,1) thereupon the set subtraction is as follows:

the first element coordinates (0,0) in S are subtracted from those of every element in I to have: (0,1), (0,2), (0,3), (1,1), (1,2), (1,3), (2,1), (2,2), (3,0), and (3,1)

the second element coordinates (0,1) in S are subtracted from those of every element in I to have: (0,0), (0,1), (0,2), (1,0), (1,1), (1,2), (2,0), (2,1), (3,−1), and (3,0) in the two subtraction sets, the common coordinate set is (0,1), (1,1), (0,2), (1,2), (2,1), and (3,0) which is the result of the erosion of I by S or $I \ominus S$

Following the convention of the m and n from the last section, we have the corresponding matrices $I[m,n] = \begin{bmatrix} 0 & 1 & 1 & 1 \\ 0 & 1 & 1 & 1 \\ 0 & 1 & 1 & 0 \\ 1 & 1 & 0 & 0 \end{bmatrix}$, $S[m.n] = \begin{bmatrix} 1 & 1 \end{bmatrix}$, and $I[m,n] \ominus S[m.n] = \begin{bmatrix} 0 & 1 & 1 \\ 0 & 1 & 1 \\ 0 & 1 & 0 \\ 1 & 0 & 0 \end{bmatrix}$. The MATLAB counterpart for the erosion

operation is imerode (abbreviation of the <u>image</u> <u>erode</u>) but the function returns the same size as that of the original

binary matrix hence we are supposed to have $\begin{bmatrix} 0 & 1 & 1 & 1 \\ 0 & 1 & 1 & 1 \\ 0 & 1 & 0 & 0 \\ 1 & 0 & 0 & 0 \end{bmatrix}$ as the $I[m,n] \ominus S[m.n]$ from MATLAB (repetition of

the last column). Let us conduct the implementation for erosion on the modular binary image as follows:

MATLAB Command

```
>>I=[0 1 1 1;0 1 1 1;0 1 1 0;1 1 0 0]; ↵      ← Entering I[m,n] matrix to I
>>S=[1 1]; ↵                                  ← Entering structuring element matrix S[m.n] to S
>>E=imerode(I,S) ↵                            ← Applying the function imerode

E =
        0   1   1   1
        0   1   1   1
        0   1   0   0
        1   0   0   0
```

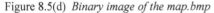

Figure 8.5(d) *Binary image of the map.bmp*

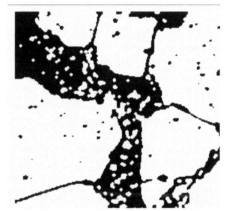

Figure 8.5(e) *Opening of the binary image map.bmp*

The function imerode has two input arguments, the first and second of which are the binary image and the structuring element matrices respectively. The function has many other option built-in (execute help imerode). The erosion result $I[m,n] \ominus S[m.n]$ is assigned to the workspace variable E.

With the introduced idea of the erosion, now is the time to visualize the effect of erosion on practical images. Let us consider the text.jpg image from the last section. We intend to see the effect of erosion on this 0.6

thresholded binary image using the structuring element $S[m.n] = \begin{bmatrix} 0 & 1 & 1 & 1 & 1 \\ 0 & 1 & 1 & 1 & 1 \end{bmatrix}$. The complete code of the erosion

process is as follows:

MATLAB Command

```
>>f=imread('text.jpg'); ↵     ← Reading text.jpg and assigned to f where f is a 3D array
>>B=im2bw(f,0.6); ↵           ← Turning f to a binary image B applying threshold 0.6, B⇔I[m,n]
>>S=[0 1 1 1 1;0 1 1 1 1]; ↵  ← Entering the S[m,n] matrix to S for erosion
>>E=imerode(B,S); ↵           ← Eroded image I[m,n] ⊖ S[m.n] is stored in E
>>imshow(E) ↵                 ← Displaying the eroded image
```

Figure 8.5(c) presents the erosion of the text.jpg image caused by the structuring element. Comparing to the original binary image of the text.jpg as shown in the figure 8.5(a), the erosion produces shrinking effect on the foreground image object.

8.6 Opening and closing of binary images

The opening or closing of a binary image means that we combine the effect of formerly discoursed dilation as well as erosion.

✦ ✦ Opening of a binary image

The opening of a binary image is defined as the application of an erosion immediately followed by a dilation employing the same structuring element. Since we discussed about the two operations in last two sections, we implement here only the MATLAB solutions. The MATLAB function imopen (abbreviation of the <u>im</u>age <u>open</u>) finds the opening of a binary image. Let us consider the map.bmp from section 2.3, collect the image, and place it in the working directory. Choosing a threshold 0.7 and a structuring element $S[m,n] = \begin{bmatrix} 0 & 1 & 1 & 0 \\ 1 & 1 & 1 & 1 \\ 1 & 1 & 1 & 1 \\ 0 & 1 & 1 & 0 \end{bmatrix}$, we perform the following:

MATLAB Command

```
>>f=imread('map.bmp');  ↵          ← Reading map.bmp and assigned to f, where f is a 3D array
>>B=im2bw(f,0.7);  ↵               ← Turning f to a binary image B by applying the threshold 0.7
>>imshow(B)  ↵                     ← Displaying the binary image
>>S=[0 1 1 0;1 1 1 1;1 1 1 1;0 1 1 0];  ↵  ← Entering the S[m,n] matrix to S
>>O=imopen(B,S);  ↵                ← Opened B by S is assigned to O
>>figure,imshow(O)  ↵              ← Displaying the opened image O
```

Figures 8.5(d) and 8.5(e) present the original binary image of the map.bmp and its opened version respectively. The function imopen has two input arguments, the first and second of which are the binary image and the structuring element matrices respectively. Small gaps and touching curves are removed or opened by virtue of the opening operation. It comes over visible looking into the upper left portion of just mentioned figures.

✦ ✦ Closing of a binary image

The closing of a binary image differs from the opening one in the sequence that first the dilation is carried out and then the erosion is performed. We have the MATLAB function imclose (abbreviation of the <u>im</u>age <u>close</u>) which computes the closing of a binary image. The function has two input arguments similar to those of the imopen. Considering the same binary image, threshold, and structuring element (it means the first four line commands of the opening implementation are identical), the function imclose can perform the closing of the map.bmp as follows:

Figure 8.5(f) *Closing of the binary image map.bmp*

```
>>C=imclose(B,S);  ↵               ← Closed B by S is assigned to C
>>figure,imshow(C)  ↵              ← Displaying the closed image C
```

Presented figure 8.5(f) is the result from the closing on the binary map.bmp. The operation is called closing in the sense that if the opening creates a small gap, the closing can fill that gap.

Whether it is imopen or imclose, the image size returned by both of them is the same as that of the binary image. The elements in the returned matrices are all logical. The reader can learn more other options on these two functions by executing help imopen or help imclose.

8.7 Hit and miss transform of binary images

The hit and miss transform of the binary image $I[m,n]$ by the structuring element $S[m,n]$ is denoted by $I[m,n] \otimes S[m,n]$ but the $S[m,n]$ is now a pair of structuring elements (call them as $S_1[m,n]$ and $S_2[m,n]$) rather than a single structuring element. Of coarse the structuring element is user-defined. The transform

$I[m,n] \otimes S[m,n]$ is defined as the set operation ($I[m,n] \ominus S_1[m,n]$) $\cap$ ($I[m,n]^c \ominus S_2[m,n]$) where $I[m,n]^c$, $\ominus$, and $\cap$ are the complement of the set $I[m,n]$, the erosion operator, and the set intersection operator respectively (sections 8.2 and 8.5). In order to see the transform's performing, let us consider the prototype binary image

$$I[m,n] = \begin{bmatrix} 1 & 0 & 0 & 1 & 1 & 1 \\ 0 & 1 & 1 & 1 & 1 & 0 \\ 0 & 0 & 0 & 1 & 1 & 1 \\ 1 & 1 & 1 & 1 & 1 & 1 \\ 0 & 0 & 0 & 1 & 0 & 0 \\ 1 & 1 & 1 & 1 & 1 & 1 \end{bmatrix}$$, the first structuring element $S_1[m,n] = \begin{bmatrix} 0 & 1 & 0 \\ 1 & 1 & 1 \\ 0 & 1 & 0 \end{bmatrix}$, and the second structuring

element $S_2[m,n] = \begin{bmatrix} 1 & 0 & 1 \\ 0 & 0 & 0 \\ 1 & 0 & 1 \end{bmatrix}$. Applying the said definition, one obtains the hit and miss transform of $I[m,n]$ as

$$I[m,n] \otimes S[m,n] = \begin{bmatrix} 0 & 0 & 0 & 0 & 0 & 0 \\ 0 & 0 & 0 & 0 & 0 & 0 \\ 0 & 0 & 0 & 0 & 0 & 0 \\ 0 & 0 & 0 & 0 & 0 & 0 \\ 0 & 0 & 0 & 0 & 0 & 0 \\ 0 & 0 & 0 & 1 & 0 & 0 \end{bmatrix}$$. Our objective is to obtain the $I[m,n] \otimes S[m,n]$ taking the inputs $I[m,n]$,

$S_1[m,n]$, and $S_2[m,n]$ for which we exercise the following:

MATLAB Command

\>>I=[1 0 0 1 1 1;0 1 1 1 1 0;0 0 0 1 1 1;1 1 1 1 1 1;0 0 0 1 0 0;1 1 1 1 1 1]; ↵ ← $I[m,n]$ is assigned to I

\>>S1=[0 1 0;1 1 1;0 1 0]; ↵   ← $S_1[m,n]$ is assigned to the workspace variable S1

\>>S2=[1 0 1;0 0 0;1 0 1]; ↵   ← $S_2[m,n]$ is assigned to the workspace variable S2

\>>T=bwhitmiss(I,S1,S2) ↵   ← Workspace variable T holds the $I[m,n] \otimes S[m,n]$

T =
```
        0    0    0    0    0    0
        0    0    0    0    0    0
        0    0    0    0    0    0
        0    0    0    0    0    0
        0    0    0    0    0    0
        0    0    0    1    0    0
```

The MATLAB function **bwhitmiss** (abbreviation of the <u>b</u>lack and <u>w</u>hite <u>hit</u> and <u>miss</u>) computes the hit and miss transform for the binary images. The function has three input arguments, the first, second, and third of which are the binary image matrix $I[m,n]$, the first structuring element $S_1[m,n]$, and second structuring element $S_2[m,n]$ respectively.

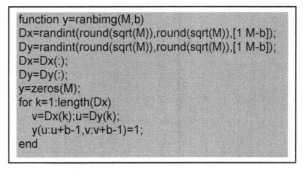

```
function y=ranbimg(M,b)
Dx=randint(round(sqrt(M)),round(sqrt(M)),[1 M-b]);
Dy=randint(round(sqrt(M)),round(sqrt(M)),[1 M-b]);
Dx=Dx(:);
Dy=Dy(:);
y=zeros(M);
for k=1:length(Dx)
    v=Dx(k);u=Dy(k);
    y(u:u+b-1,v:v+b-1)=1;
end
```

Figure 8.6(a) *Function file for the generation of a binary image filled by random squares*

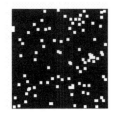

Figure 8.6(b) *A binary image of random squares*

Figure 8.6(c) *The binary image followed by the hit and miss transform*

Figure 8.7(a) *An empty rectangular box*

Figure 8.7(b) *Thin shape of the empty rectangular box*

✦ ✦ **Application of the hit and miss transform**

The morphological transform can locate simple shapes present in a binary image. To see the morphological implication, we need to have a binary image. Our written function file ranbimg as shown in the figure 8.6(a) can generate a binary image of the pixel size $M \times M$ which we fill by the random squares of the pixel size $b \times b$. The function has two input arguments M and b respectively. Write the source codes of figure 8.6(a) in a new M-file editor and save the file by the name ranbimg in your working directory. We wish to generate a binary image of size 100×100 which is to be filled by the random squares of the size 3×3. Let us carry out the following:

>>I=ranbimg(100,3); ↵

>>imshow(I) ↵

The function ranbimg generates the binary image and the variable I holds the image (which is our theory discussed $I[m,n]$). Figure 8.6(b) is the display followed by the last line command.

Referring to the figure 8.6(b), the tiny square boxes are isolated in nature. One can imagine the black color as the background and the white boxes as foreground. The hit and miss transform can pinpoint the foreground tiny boxes subject to some user defined pixel condition or in other words structuring element. A square of the pixel size 3×3 takes the shape

$$\begin{matrix} \bullet & \bullet & \bullet \\ \bullet & \bullet & \bullet \\ \bullet & \bullet & \bullet \end{matrix}$$

in which any pixel's directive notation is $west \leftarrow \bullet \rightarrow east$ with $north \uparrow$ and $south \downarrow$. Let us say we wish to locate the upper left corner of every 3×3 foreground square box such that the pixel in the square box has only east and south neighbors which is equivalent to the structuring element $\begin{bmatrix} 0 & 0 & 0 \\ 0 & 1 & 1 \\ 0 & 1 & 0 \end{bmatrix}$ (this is the theory discussed $S_1[m,n]$ and the operation is also called the hit operation) and that the pixel has no neighbors in the southwest, west, northwest, north, and northeast directions. The matrix $\begin{bmatrix} 0 & 0 & 0 \\ 0 & x & x \\ 0 & x & x \end{bmatrix}$ describes the directive requirement for the last situation where x means *donot care* condition (regardless of 0 or 1). But to be applicable in the hit and miss transform, we use the complement of the last matrix hence the second structuring element becomes $\begin{bmatrix} 1 & 1 & 1 \\ 1 & 0 & 0 \\ 1 & 0 & 0 \end{bmatrix}$ (taking the *donot care* as zeroes). The last matrix essentially is our theory discussed $S_2[m,n]$ and the related operation is termed as the miss operation. Now is the high time to see the application of the hit and miss transform as follows:

>>S1=[0 0 0;0 1 1;0 1 0]; ↵   ← $S_1[m,n]$ is assigned to the workspace variable S1

>>S2=[1 1 1;1 0 0;1 0 0]; ↵   ← $S_2[m,n]$ is assigned to the workspace variable S2

>>T=bwhitmiss(I,S1,S2); ↵   ← T holds the $I[m,n] \otimes S[m,n]$

>>imshow(T) ↵   ← Displaying the T as a digital image

Figure 8.6(c) shows the result of the transform conducted on the generated binary image. The tiny dots in the transform images correspond to the position we expected. The boxes we presented do not have to be square nonetheless it can be any other foreground objects. If the reader is interested to find the position indexes of such points, the function find of section 10.7 can be exercised.

8.8 Thinning or skeletonizing a binary image

The objectivity of the thinning attributes the fact that the thinned or skeletonized representations of images can make the shape or pattern analysis easier. The thinning belongs to the morphological operation whose basic idea is to obtain the medial or mean shape of any image objects considering horizontal as well as vertical directions of the image.

Referring to the figure 8.7(a), we have an empty rectangular box. The empty box sides can represent the boundary of a digital image. Let us say a binary digital image is filled by all ones which correspond to the whiteness in the digital image. In order to generate this image of pixel size 40×40, we execute the following:

>>f=ones(40); ↵

The workspace variable f holds the image. The execution of the command imshow(f) displays the image which is just a white square block. Since the paper is white, the whiteness of the paper and that of the image coincide. The thinned shape of a digital image is very much related to the image objects boundary. Taking the midpoint both from the horizontal and from the vertical sides of the box boundary results the cross shape of the figure 8.7(b). This cross shape is termed as the thinned shape of the white square box image (held in the variable f) ñ this is what we want from MATLAB. We conduct the following to do so:

>>g=bwmorph(f,'skel','inf'); ↵

>>imshow(g) ↵

The MATLAB function bwmorph (abbreviation of the black and white morphology) performs a lot of morphological operations on the binary images. Of those, the thinning or skeletonizing is one which has the reserve word 'skel' and appears as the second input argument in the function bwmorph. It is evident that the first input argument of the function is the binary image matrix. There are more than a dozen algorithms to find the thin shape of an image (reference [78]). Most of the thinning algorithms

Figure 8.7(c) *Thin shape of a white square rectangular box returned by MATLAB*

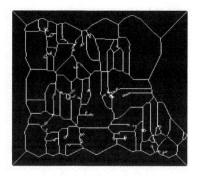

Figure 8.7(d) *Thin shape of the binary version of the dip.bmp*

operate on iterative basis. The third input argument of the function indicates the number of iteration required (user defined). Let us say we intended to find the thinned shape using 3 iterations in that case the command would have been g=bwmorph(f,'skel',3);. The string 'inf' (appears as the third input argument in the function and the abbreviation for the infinity) indicates the continuation of the iteration until stability. However the variable g holds the thinned shape following the computation whose image display is the figure 8.7(c) and whose expected shape is that of the one in the figure 8.7(b).

Let us see the thinned shape for a practical image considering the gray version dip.bmp. We turned the image to a binary one in section 8.3 using the following two line commands:

>>[f,m]=imread('dip.bmp'); ↵

>>B=im2bw(f,m,0.6); ↵

The variable B has the binary image which is derived from the dip.bmp (display in figure 8.4(a)). We find the thin shape of the binary dip.bmp until the stable point as shown in the figure 8.7(d) utilizing the following commands:

>>g=bwmorph(B,'skel','inf'); ↵

>>imshow(g) ↵

By default the return image g is a binary one as well. The thinned shape or skeleton pixels are all 1 assigned which correspond to white.

8.9 Distance transform of a binary image

The distance transform of a binary image is defined as the Euclidean distance (for every pixel) to the nearest nonzero value pixel in the image with the exception that 1 valued pixel has the 0 distance. Let us consider

the modular binary image $f[m,n] = \begin{bmatrix} 1 & 0 & 1 & 0 \\ 0 & 1 & 1 & 0 \\ 1 & 0 & 0 & 1 \\ 0 & 0 & 0 & 1 \\ 0 & 0 & 0 & 1 \end{bmatrix}$. The transform matrix has the same size as that of the original one.

The first element in the first row of $f[m,n]$ has the coordinates (1,1) and the nonzero elements

$\begin{Bmatrix} \text{the element coordinated by (1,3) in the first row} \\ \text{the element coordinated by (3,1) in the first column} \\ \text{the element coordinated by (2,2) in the diagonal} \end{Bmatrix}$ whose defined distance values are $\begin{Bmatrix} 2 \\ 2 \\ 0 \end{Bmatrix}$ respectively therefore

the transform value is 0 for the element (1,1). The second element in the fourth row of $f[m,n]$ whose coordinates are (4,2) has the nearest 1 element coordinated by (3,1) therefore the distance transform value for the pixel (4,2) is

$\sqrt{(4-3)^2 + (2-1)^2} = 1.4142$. Continuing this way, one ends up with the complete distance transform matrix for the

example binary image as $D = \begin{bmatrix} 0 & 1 & 0 & 1 \\ 1 & 0 & 0 & 1 \\ 0 & 1 & 1 & 0 \\ 1 & 1.4142 & 1 & 0 \\ 2 & 2 & 1 & 0 \end{bmatrix}$. Our objective is to obtain D from $f[m,n]$ for which one can

utilize the MATLAB function bwdist (abbreviation of the black and white distance) as follows:

MATLAB Command

>>f=[1 0 1 0;0 1 1 0;1 0 0 1;0 0 0 1;0 0 0 1]; ↵   ← Entering $f[m,n]$ to f

>>D=bwdist(f) ↵   ← D holds the distance transform of $f[m,n]$

152

D =

0	1.0000	0	1.0000
1.0000	0	0	1.0000
0	1.0000	1.0000	0
1.0000	1.4142	1.0000	0
2.0000	2.0000	1.0000	0

The input argument of the bwdist is the binary image matrix $f[m,n]$. To see the application in a practical image, let us consider the binary version of the dip.bmp from section 8.3 but with a threshold 0.8 whose straightforward implementation is as follows:

```
>>[f,m]=imread('dip.bmp'); ↵ ← f is intensity and m is colormap
>>B=im2bw(f,m,0.8); ↵         ← B holds the binary image
>>D=bwdist(B); ↵          ← D holds the distance transform
>>imshow(D,[ ]) ↵         ← Displaying the transform as a digital
                            image first mapping in [0,1]
```

Presented figure 8.7(e) is the distance transform image display from above implementation.

Figure 8.7(e) *Distance transform image of the binary counterpart of dip.bmp*

8.10 Finding perimeter of binary images

The perimeter or boundary line of smaller binary regions located in a binary image can be determined with the help of the MATLAB function bwperim (abbreviation of the <u>b</u>lack and <u>w</u>hite <u>perim</u>eter). The input argument of the bwperim is the binary image matrix. From the last section, the workspace variable B holds the binary image matrix for the image dip.bmp. We apply the function bwperim on B as follows:

MATLAB Command

```
>>P=bwperim(B); ↵
>>imshow(P) ↵
```

Figure 8.8(a) *Detected perimeters of the binary image regions in the dip.bmp*

The workspace variable P holds the image after the perimeter taking which is a logical array or another binary image by default. Figure 8.8(a) presents the result from the execution. We also found the perimeter image of the man.jpg (section 8.3) as shown in the figure 8.8(b) by exercising the following:

```
>>f=imread('man.jpg'); ↵  ← Reading man.jpg and assigned to f where
                             f is a 3D array
>>B=im2bw(f,0.6); ↵        ← Turning the f to a binary image B by
                             applying the threshold 0.6
>>P=bwperim(B); ↵          ← Finding the permeter image P from B
>>imshow(P) ↵
```

Looking into the workspace browser, one can learn about the size of the perimeter image matrix which is the same as that of the original binary image. For example, the sizes of B and P are 361×253. Since the perimeter matrix P is holding only 0 and 1, in some context one might be interested to find the pixel coordinates of 1s and 0s. We can apply the MATLAB function find (section 10.7) to detect these coordinates in the last perimeter image matrix P. For instance, let us find the coordinates of the pixels which have the 1s in the P as follows:

```
>>[R,C]=find(P==1); ↵
```

Figure 8.8(b) *Perimeters of the binary image regions in the man.jpg*

The workspace variables R and C, as column matrix individually, hold the row and column indices of the required pixels respectively. In a similar fashion the command [R,C]=find(P==0); returns the indices for the 0s in the P.

8.11 Built-in structural elements

We know from previous sections that the structural elements which are used in various morphological operations are completely user defined. MATLAB offers some easiness by providing a number of built-in structural elements. The function strel (abbreviation of the <u>str</u>uctural <u>el</u>ements) is the mother of all these built-in structural elements. The built-in structural elements are application dependent. Let us say we intend to generate a diamond shape ◊ structuring element whose horizontal and vertical axes lines must contain three 1-valued pixels from the center one. We do so by the following:

MATLAB Command
>>S=strel('diamond',3) ↵

S =

Flat STREL object containing 25 neighbors.
Decomposition: 3 STREL objects containing a total of 13 neighbors

Neighborhood:
```
0   0   0   1   0   0   0
0   0   1   1   1   0   0
0   1   1   1   1   1   0
1   1   1   1   1   1   1
0   1   1   1   1   1   0
0   0   1   1   1   0   0
0   0   0   1   0   0   0
```

The workspace variable S contains the structuring element. The function strel has two input arguments, the first and second of which are the reserve word 'diamond' for the diamond structuring element and the number of the horizontal or vertical pixel width in terms of the 1-valued pixel respectively. If the second input argument number is N, the size of the S will be $2N+1 \times 2N+1$. The return of the function strel is an object rather than a structuring element matrix. Above execution also says the object containing 25 neighbors it means that there are twenty five 1-valued pixels in the structuring element S. Again the execution is also displaying three strel objects can be found in decomposed form. The decomposed forms are basically the modular or prototype structuring element derived from the S. In order to see them, we seek help from the MATLAB function getsequence as follows:

Figure 8.8(c) *A binary image of three square blocks connected by a line*

Figure 8.8(d) *Dilation removes the connecting line of the figure 8.8(c) with the aid of the diamond structuring element*

>>D=getsequence(S); ↵

The workspace variable D holds all the modular structuring elements returned from the getsequence. Looking into the workspace browser, the class of the D is strel object rather than so used double or other data type. According to the execution, there are three strel objects and we have them from the D by writing D(1), D(2), and D(3) respectively as follows:

for the first strel object:
>>D(1) ↵

ans =

Flat STREL object containing 5 neighbors.

Neighborhood:
```
0   1   0
1   1   1
0   1   0
```

for the third strel object:
>>D(3) ↵

ans =

Flat STREL object containing 4 neighbors.

Neighborhood:
```
0   1   0
```

for the second strel object:
>>D(2) ↵

ans =

Flat STREL object containing 4 neighbors.

Neighborhood:
```
0   1   0
1   0   1
0   1   0
```

```
1   0   1
0   1   0
```

The diamond shape structuring elements are not the ones included in the strel family. There are a number of members whose brief descriptions are as follows:

Syntax of the structuring element	Brief descriptions
S=strel('disk',r)	disk shaped structuring element of the radius r for example strel('disk',3)
S=strel('line',Ln,Deg)	linear structuring element where Ln is the line length and Deg is the counterclockwise line angle from the horizontal axis for example strel('line',4,45)
S=strel('octagon',r)	octagonal structuring element where r is the distance from the structuring element origin to the sides of the octagon and r is nonnegative multiple of 3 for example strel('octagon',6)
S=strel('pair',offset)	two member structuring element, one member located at the origin, offset is a two element row matrix, and the second member in the offset indicates the distance from the center for example strel('pair',[1 3])
S=strel('periodicline',A,B)	structuring element of 2A+1 members, B is a two element row matrix indicating row and column offsets, for example strel('periodicline',2,[1 4])
S=strel('rectangle',B)	rectangle shape structuring element, B is a two element row matrix indicating rectangle size for example strel('rectangle',[3 4])
S=strel('square',B)	square shape structuring element of width B for example strel('square',4)
S=strel(M)	user defined structuring element of arbitrary shape where M is a matrix of 1s and 0s for example strel([1 0 1;0 0 0;1 1 1])

More workspace assistance is available following the execution of help strel.

❖ ❖ Application of the built-in structuring elements to a digital image

In order to apply the built-in structuring element, let us generate the binary image (section 8.1) of the figure 8.8(c) by executing the following codes in the command window:

```
>>Z=zeros(30); O=ones(30); ↵
>>B=[Z O Z O Z]; ↵
>>B(15,:)=0; ↵
>>imshow(B) ↵
```

The workspace variable B holds the binary image. At this point we intend to conduct the image dilation (section 8.4) on the workspace B employing a diamond structuring element of pixel width 2 so that the connecting lines of the three square blocks in the figure 8.8(c) is removed. Let us proceed with the following:

```
>>S=strel('diamond',2); ↵      ← S holds the required structuring element
>>G=imdilate(B,S); ↵           ← G holds the dilated image following the image dilation
>>imshow(G) ↵                  ← Displaying the contents of G
```

Figure 8.8(d) presents the dilated image in which the connecting line of the three square blocks is removed.

We have tried to render a flavor of the morphological operations on the binary digital images. The scope and application of the morphological processing is extensive. Since the text is introductory, we do not wish to include all associated materials of the heading. We bring an end to the chapter with the elementary discussion of the digital morphology.

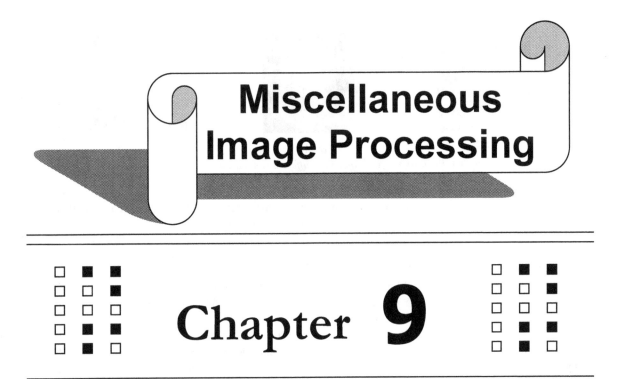

Miscellaneous Image Processing

Chapter 9

The preceding chapters addressed specific class of digital image processing problems according to the chapter titles. The scope and applications of the digital image processing are so huge that paying even attention to all relevant topics is an enormous task. To the degree that the text is introductory in nature, we wish to be concise in the subject matter presentation. Here in this chapter miscellaneous image processing topics outline the following:

♦ ♦ Point spread function generation and power spectral density of a digital image
♦ ♦ Programming the histogram equalization of a digital image and its built-in tool
♦ ♦ Seven invariant moments and correlation of digital images with applications
♦ ♦ Digital image basis, circulant matrix implication, and image encoding
♦ ♦ Warping, pseudocoloring, forming eigenimages, and region processing of digital images

9.1 Point spread function generation

In digital image processing the point spread function is defined in terms of the radially symmetric two dimensional Gaussian function. In section 5.7 we discussed this function by the heading normalized and rotationally symmetric Gaussian mask. The mask is basically the point spread function (also called PSF). Now the PSF function is to be displayed as a digital image. We presented a 4×5 mask or point spread function in the section. If one displays this mask as an image, the image will be a very small block. Drawing the same function, let us generate a mask of the size 100×100 and of standard deviation 5 as follows:

MATLAB Command

```
>>h=fspecial('gaussian',[100 100],5);  ↵ ← the PSF or h[m,n] is assigned to h
```

The content of h is displayed as a digital image further mapping the $h[m,n]$ values between 0 and 1 by the following:

>>imshow(h,[ ]) ↵

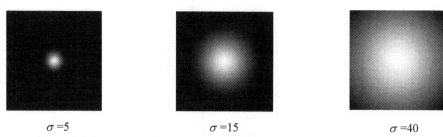

$\sigma = 5$ $\sigma = 15$ $\sigma = 40$

Figure 9.1 *Point spread function under different standard deviations*

The result is the leftmost part of the figure 9.1. Let us choose two more standard deviations ñ 15 and 40 and display their images in a similar fashion. Their execution results are also presented in the same figure. As the standard deviation increases, the intensity in the image spreads out that is why the function is called point spread function.

The PSF just mentioned is MATLAB built-in and generated in discrete sense. Some reader might be interested in continuous sense and spatially defined PSF for instance $h(x,y) = e^{-\frac{x^2+y^2}{2\sigma^2}}$ where x and y are not necessarily integers and considering the variations $-5 \le x \le 5$ with x step 0.5 and $-4 \le y \le 4$ with y step 0.4. In this regard the function meshgrid is very effective (section 10.11). Generations of x and y grids are as follows:

>>[x,y]=meshgrid([-5:0.5:5],[-4:0.4:4]); ↵
>>h=exp(-(x.^2+y.^2)/25); ↵   ← Choosing $2\sigma^2 = 25$

In the last line implementation the workspace variable h holds the computed $h(x,y)$ for different x and y values. If you display this h as a digital image using imshow(h,[ ]), you see the image of the point spread function.

9.2 Power spectrum of a digital image

Referring to section 4.1, power spectrum or spectral density $P[u,v]$ of a digital image $f[m,n]$ is defined as the squared magnitude of the two dimensional discrete Fourier transform $F[u,v]$ or symbolically $P[u,v] = |F[u,v]|^2$. For an image of pixel size $M \times N$, the size of $F[u,v]$ or $P[u,v]$ is also the same. The MATLAB function fft2 computes $F[u,v]$ hence the computation of $P[u,v]$ is just the squared magnitude conducted on the return from the fft2. As an example, let us find the power spectrum of binary H concerning section 8.1 as follows:

MATLAB Command

>>H=[zeros(50,10) [ones(20);zeros(10,20);ones(20)] zeros(50,10)]; ↵ ←Forming H image, H⇔ $f[m,n]$
>>F=fft2(H); ↵   ← 2D DFT of $f[m,n]$ is assigned to F, F⇔ $F[u,v]$
>>P=abs(F).^2; ↵   ← $P[u,v] = |F[u,v]|^2$ is computed and assigned to P

Now you can display the power spectrum stored in P as an image with the help of the imshow. Due to squaring of $F[u,v]$, the spatial frequency components become more concentrated and most energy becomes confined in the low frequency components. Under this circumstance, you find just a single dot as the spectrum. Logarithmic scale is applied for spreading the frequency components in the power spectrum display and we perform that by the operation $\log_{10}(1 + P[u,v])$ as follows:

>>L=log10(1+P); ↵ ← $\log_{10}(1 + P[u,v])$ is conducted and the result is assigned to L

>>imshow(L,[ ]) ↵ ← Displays the power spectrum in logarithmic scale by first mapping in [0,1]

Since the power spectrum also has the half index symmetry, one can use the command imshow(fftshift(L),[ ]) for the half indexedly flipped version of the spectrum. The image is very similar to that of the figure 4.1(i).

The total spectral power in a digital image is defined as the $\sum_{v=0}^{N-1} \sum_{u=0}^{M-1} P[u,v]$ which is equivalent to the sum of all elements in the $P[u,v]$ matrix. For the H example at hand we compute that as follows (section 10.9 for sum):

>>T=sum(sum(P)) ↵   ← $\sum_{v=0}^{N-1} \sum_{u=0}^{M-1} P[u,v]$ is conducted and the result is assigned to T

T =

       1.6000e+006   ← e+006 means 10^6

Therefore the total image spectral power for the said letter H is 1.6×10^6.

Sometimes $P[u,v]$ power spectral concentration for different u and v is needed as a function of the radial distance r in the half indexedly flipped power spectrum. In this regard first the half indexedly flipped power spectrum is found by the function **fftshift** (section 4.1) on **P** and then we compute the radial distance from the center point of the flipped transform as follows:

>>S=fftshift(P); ↵ ← S holds the half indexedly flipped power spectrum of $P[u,v]$

For the radial distance from the center of **S**, it is important to know the image or its spectrum size which is here 50×40 (workspace browser). The central point in the power spectrum is $\left(\dfrac{M+1}{2},\dfrac{N+1}{2}\right)$. For the even number pixel size, the central point becomes virtual whereas for the odd number pixel size, it is real because the pixel coordinates (u, v) are always positive integer. However for every (u, v) coordinates in $P[u,v]$, the radial distance $r=\sqrt{\left(u-\dfrac{M+1}{2}\right)^2+\left(v-\dfrac{N+1}{2}\right)^2}$ from the central point in the flipped spectrum **S** is computed (we use **meshgrid**, section 10.11) as follows:

>>[u,v]=meshgrid(1:40,1:50); ↵

>>r=sqrt((u-25.5).^2+(v-20.5).^2); ↵   ← Because M =50 and N =40 for the H image

The second line in above command is the MATLAB code for the radial distance. The r held in the workspace variable **r** is a matrix of the same size as that of the $P[u,v]$ which bears only the radial distance from the center point to different (u, v). The **r** has no relation with the image spectra except the pixel size but the elements in **r** are fractional due to the computation. We can round the values in **r** to the nearest integer by the function **round** and again keep those to **r** as follows:

>>r=round(r); ↵

It is required that we find the image spectral power as a percentage of the total spectral power stored in **T** within some specific radius ñ this is the problem statement. Let us say we want to find

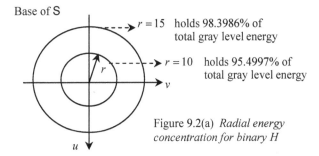

Base of S

$r =15$ holds 98.3986% of total gray level energy

$r =10$ holds 95.4997% of total gray level energy

Figure 9.2(a) *Radial energy concentration for binary H*

the total spectral power in the flipped spectrum within the radius 10 (can be stated by $r \le 10$). Using the MATLAB function **find** (section 10.7) returns the position indexes of those frequency components in **r** as follows:

>>[R,C]=find(r<=10); ↵

The **R** and **C** each as column matrix hold the (u, v) coordinates of the $r \le 10$ frequency components respectively. The commands R(1) and C(1) mean the first u and v coordinates in the $r \le 10$ respectively. Whatever be the length of the column matrix **R** or **C** (they have the same length), one can find that by writing **length(R)**. We pick up all $r \le 10$ frequency components one by one from the **S** using the following command (sections 10.3.3 and 10.6 for the data accumulation):

>>W=[ ];for k=1:length(R) W=[W S(R(k),C(k))]; end ↵

All $r \le 10$ frequency components are held in the workspace variable **W** as a row matrix. To see the percentage image spectral energy compared to the total spectral energy in $r \le 10$, we carry out the following:

>>100*sum(W)/T ↵

ans =
       95.4997

Therefore 95.4997% of the image energy is in the $r \le 10$ frequencies in the flipped spectrum. Similarly the command [R,C]=find(r<=15); finds the position indices of the frequencies $r \le 15$ and which hold 98.3986% of the total gray level energy (can be verified by the last two lines command). Presented figure 9.2(a) is the radial energy concentration portrayal in the flipped spectrum for the binary H.

What if we have a practical digital image. Considering the gray version man.jpg from subsection 6.1.1, we intend to find the image spectral energy concentration within $r \le 80$ in the flipped spectrum of the image. Making the image available in the working directory, we conduct the following:

>>f=imread('man.jpg'); ↵ ← Image is read and assigned to f, f is 3D array

>>f=rgb2gray(f); ↵   ← Turning the f to gray image and again assigned to f

>>F=fft2(f); ↵   ← F holds the 2D DFT of the image, F⇔ $F[u,v]$

>>P=abs(F).^2; ↵   ← $P[u,v]$ is computed and assigned to P

>>T=sum(sum(P)); ↵   ← Total image spectral power is assigned to T

```
>>S=fftshift(P); ↵          ← S holds the half indexedly flipped spectrum
>>[M,N]=size(f); ↵          ← Knowing the image size M×N
>>[u,v]=meshgrid(1:N,1:M); ↵   ← Generating the meshgrid according to M and N
>>r=sqrt((u-(M+1)/2).^2+(v-(N+1)/2).^2); ↵  ← Writing the code of r in terms of M and N
>>r=round(r); ↵             ← Rounded r assigned to r again
>>[R,C]=find(r<=80); ↵      ← Finding the position indexes in r ≤ 80
>>W=[ ];for k=1:length(R) W=[W S(R(k),C(k))]; end ↵  ← Accumulation of r ≤ 80 frequencies in W
>>100*sum(W)/T ↵            ← % computation
```

ans =
99.5714

Therefore $r \leq 80$ frequencies in the flipped power spectrum of man.jpg concentrate 99.5714% of image energy.

9.3 Histogram equalization of a digital image

Histogram equalization of a digital image $f[m,n]$ is basically the redistribution of the image gray levels (the values of $f[m,n]$) in the sense that all levels of $f[m,n]$ are equally likely. The histogram of a digital image and its gray levelís probability are addressed in chapter 6. However, the following procedure is observed during the histogram equalization of a digital image:

step 1: we compute the frequency of occurrence for each gray level in the image $f[m,n]$,

step 2: we compute the probability of each gray level in the image,

step 3: we compute the cumulative probability density function (CDF) for the image gray levels,

step 4: we compute the cumulative probability density function (CDF) for the given number of gray levels considering equal probability,

step 5: the CDF found in step 3 is checked for the closest one found in step 4 to obtain the modified CDF for the histogram equalized image, and

step 6: the gray level of the $f[m,n]$ is replaced according to the closest gray level found in the step 5.

We consider the modular digital image $f[m,n] = \begin{bmatrix} 4 & 4 & 5 & 5 & 7 \\ 1 & 2 & 5 & 5 & 2 \\ 3 & 3 & 1 & 1 & 4 \\ 0 & 3 & 3 & 2 & 4 \\ 2 & 4 & 5 & 1 & 3 \end{bmatrix}$ of 8 gray levels (marked from 0 to 7) for

the illustration of the histogram equalization. Our objective is to obtain the histogram equalized image of the same size as that of $f[m,n]$ observing the six step procedure as follows:

Step 1: The image consists of 8 gray levels ranging from 0 to 7. The occurrence of each gray level is to be found. For instance the level 4 appears in the first, third, fourth, and fifth rows of the $f[m,n]$ and the total

number of occurrence is 5. Counting this way, one ends up with the table
$\begin{Bmatrix} gray & number\ of \\ level & occurrence \\ 0 & 1 \\ 1 & 4 \\ 2 & 4 \\ 3 & 5 \\ 4 & 5 \\ 5 & 5 \\ 6 & 0 \\ 7 & 1 \end{Bmatrix}$.

Step 2: The size of the image $f[m,n]$ is 5×5 hence containing 25 pixels. The probability for each gray level in

the $f[m,n]$ is computed by $\dfrac{number\ of\ occurrence}{total\ number\ of\ pixels}$. Therefore we obtain the table
$\begin{Bmatrix} gray & probability \\ level & \\ 0 & 0.04 \\ 1 & 0.16 \\ 2 & 0.16 \\ 3 & 0.20 \\ 4 & 0.20 \\ 5 & 0.20 \\ 6 & 0 \\ 7 & 0.04 \end{Bmatrix}$

(dividing the second column of the last table by 25). Of coarse the sum of all probabilities must be 1.

Step 3: The cumulative probability density function is defined as the successive addition of the probabilities

that is given by the table
$\begin{bmatrix} gray & CDF \\ level & \\ 0 & 0.04 \\ 1 & 0.20 \\ 2 & 0.36 \\ 3 & 0.56 \\ 4 & 0.76 \\ 5 & 0.96 \\ 6 & 0.96 \\ 7 & 1.00 \end{bmatrix}$
and derived from the

```
function r=hgram(f,L)
R=tabulate(1+f(:));
CDFi=cumsum(R(:,3))/100;
P=1/L*ones(L,1);
CDFn=cumsum(P);
s=[ ];
for k=1:L
    A=abs(CDFi(k)-CDFn);
    m=min(A);
    l=find(A==m);
    if l~=k
        s=[s;[k l]];
    end
end
r=f;
for k=1:length(s)
    [row,col]=find(f==s(k,1)-1);
    if ~isempty(row)
        for n=1:length(row)
            r(row(n),col(n))=s(k,2)-1;
        end
    end
end
```

last table. For instance, the gray levels 1 and 3 in the last table have the CDFs as $0.20=0.04+0.16$ and $0.56=0.04+0.16+0.16+0.20$ respectively and so on.

Step 4: There are 8 gray levels in the $f[m,n]$. As the definition of the histogram equalization says, each level must be of equal probability hence the probability of each level is $\frac{1}{8}$ or 0.125. If we had 256 levels as it happens in the practical images, the probability of each level would be $\frac{1}{256}$. With the equal probability and for the

modular image, the CDF should be
$\begin{bmatrix} gray & CDF \\ level & \\ 0 & 0.125 \\ 1 & 0.250 \\ 2 & 0.375 \\ 3 & 0.500 \\ 4 & 0.625 \\ 5 & 0.750 \\ 6 & 0.875 \\ 7 & 1.00 \end{bmatrix}$
(for

Figure 9.2(b) *Function file for finding the histogram equalized image matrix*

instance, the gray levels 2 and 4 CDFs are computed as $0.375=0.125+0.125+0.125$ and $0.625=0.125+0.125+0.125+0.125+0.125$ respectively).

Step 5: Now we have two CDFs –
$\begin{bmatrix} gray & CDF \\ level & \\ 0 & 0.04 \\ 1 & 0.20 \\ 2 & 0.36 \\ 3 & 0.56 \\ 4 & 0.76 \\ 5 & 0.96 \\ 6 & 0.96 \\ 7 & 1.00 \end{bmatrix}$
from the image and
$\begin{bmatrix} gray & CDF \\ level & \\ 0 & 0.125 \\ 1 & 0.250 \\ 2 & 0.375 \\ 3 & 0.500 \\ 4 & 0.625 \\ 5 & 0.750 \\ 6 & 0.875 \\ 7 & 1.00 \end{bmatrix}$
from the

equally likely gray level. Every gray level's CDF (not the gray level) in the former is checked for the closest one in that of the latter. Referring to the gray levels 0, 3, and 6, the 0.04, 0.56, and 0.96 in the former are the closest to the 0.125, 0.500, and 1.00 in those of the latter respectively. But the closest CDFs correspond to the gray levels 0, 3, and 7 in the latter respectively. That means there is no change in the gray levels 0 and 3 but the 6 must be replaced by the 7 in $f[m,n]$. Checking for the other gray levels, we find that
$\begin{cases} gray\ level\ in\ original\ image & 0\ \ 1\ \ 2\ \ 3\ \ 4\ \ 5\ \ 6\ \ 7 \\ gray\ level\ in\ equalized\ image & 0\ \ 1\ \ 2\ \ 3\ \ 5\ \ 7\ \ 7\ \ 7 \end{cases}$. So to say, any gray level in $f[m,n]$ from 0 to 3 and 7 will not undergo any change but 4 turns to 5 and 5 and 6 turn to 7 respectively.

step 6: Taking the change into account, we finally obtain the histogram equalized image of $f[m,n]$ as $r[m,n]=$

$\begin{bmatrix} 5 & 5 & 7 & 7 & 7 \\ 1 & 2 & 7 & 7 & 2 \\ 3 & 3 & 1 & 1 & 5 \\ 0 & 3 & 3 & 2 & 5 \\ 2 & 5 & 7 & 1 & 3 \end{bmatrix}$ – that is what we expect from the histogram equalization or programming.

✦✦ Programming the histogram equalization

Our written MATLAB function file hgram as presented in the figure 9.2(b) can find the histogram equalized image matrix $r[m,n]$. Write the codes of the hgram in the M-file editor, save the file by the name hgram, and execute the following:

```
>>f=[4 4 5 5 7;1 2 5 5 2;3 3 1 1 4;0 3 3 2 4;2 4 5 1 3];  ↵     ← Entering f[m,n] to variable f
>>r=hgram(f,8) ↵                    ← r holds the histogram equalized image matrix r[m,n]
```

```
r =
        5   5   7   7   7
        1   2   7   7   2
        3   3   1   1   5
        0   3   3   2   5
        2   5   7   1   3
```

The function hgram has two input arguments, the first and second of which are the image matrix (elements must be positive integer including 0 and assuming that the maximum gray level exists in the image) and the number of gray levels (positive integer) respectively.

The next justifiable question is how we apply the histogram equalization to a practical image. Let us consider the gray version dip.bmp from subsection 6.1.2, obtain the image, place it in the working directory, and conduct the following:

Figure 9.2(c) *Histogram equalized gray version of dip.bmp*

```
>>[f,m]=imread('dip.bmp');  ↵     ← Reading the image, where f is intensity and m is colormap
>>f=ind2gray(f,m);  ↵       ← turning the indexed image to gray one in [0,1] and assigned to f
>>f=im2uint8(f);  ↵         ← turning the [0,1] image values to [0,255] and assigned to f
>>f=double(f);  ↵           ← turning the data in f to double class and assigned to f for computation
```

For the hgram limitation, it is necessary to know the maximum gray level present in the image for which the following is conducted:

```
>>max(max(f))  ↵
```

```
ans =
        255
```

Fortunately the image possesses the maximum gray level 255 hence we apply the hgram as follows:

```
>>r=hgram(f,256);  ↵    ← r holds the histogram equalized image
```

There are 256 levels in [0,255] which is the second input argument in above function. For display reason, the double class data in r needs to be in unsigned 8-bit integer form as follows:

```
>>r=uint8(r);  ↵ ← converted unsigned 8-bit integer again assigned to r
>>imshow(r)  ↵ ← figure 9.2(c) shows the histogram equalized image
```

The foreground ƎDigital Image Processingí in the displayed image shows better contrast (original display in figure 6.1(c)), so does the background noise causing from the scanning. If an image possesses noise, we apply the noise removal techniques. One aspect is very obvious that the histogram equalization increases image contrast irrespective of the foreground or background.

Figure 9.2(d) *Histogram equalized man.jpg*

✦✦ Ready made tool of MATLAB for the histogram equalization

So far we discussed the image processing textbook related histogram equalization technique and its implementation. The MATLAB function histeq (abbreviation of the histogram equalization) performs all these computations or programming in a single line command. Making the image available in the working directory, let us equalize the histogram of the gray version man.jpg (subsection 6.1.1) as follows:

```
>>f=imread('man.jpg');  ↵       ← reading the RGB image, f is a 3D array
>>f=rgb2gray(f);  ↵             ← turning the f to a gray image and assigned to f again, f⇔ f[m,n]
>>r=histeq(f);  ↵               ← r holds the histogram equalized image, r⇔r[m,n]
>>imshow(r)  ↵                  ← displaying the histogram equalized image stored in r
```

Figure 9.2(d) shows the histogram equalized man.jpg. We can compare the contrast of the equalized one to that of the original image in figure 6.1(a) ñ for sure the contrast is improved. The input argument of the histeq is the digital image matrix $f[m,n]$ either in [0,1] for double class or [0,255] for unsigned 8-bit integer data. By default the return to r is the unsigned 8-bit integer. A lot more options are included in the function histeq (execute help histeq).

9.4 Seven invariant moments of a digital image

Given a digital image function $f[m,n]$ of the pixel size $M \times N$, a set of seven invariant moments $\{m_1, m_2, m_3, m_4, m_5, m_6, m_7\}$ (symbolically different from the pixel variable m) which are invariant to the translation, scaling, and rotation is given by the following relationships ([81]):

$$m_{00} = \sum_{n=0}^{N-1} \sum_{m=0}^{M-1} f[m,n], \qquad m_{10} = \sum_{n=0}^{N-1} \sum_{m=0}^{M-1} mf[m,n], \qquad m_{01} = \sum_{n=0}^{N-1} \sum_{m=0}^{M-1} nf[m,n],$$

$$\overline{m} = \frac{m_{10}}{m_{00}}, \qquad \overline{n} = \frac{m_{01}}{m_{00}}, \qquad \mu_{pq} = \sum_{n=0}^{N-1} \sum_{m=0}^{M-1} (m-\overline{m})^p (n-\overline{n})^q f[m,n],$$

$$\eta_{pq} = \frac{\mu_{pq}}{m_{00}^{\frac{p+q+2}{2}}},$$

$$\begin{cases}
m_1 = \eta_{20} + \eta_{02}, \\[2pt]
m_2 = (\eta_{20} - \eta_{02})^2 + 4\eta_{11}^2, \\[2pt]
m_3 = (\eta_{30} - 3\eta_{12})^2 + (3\eta_{21} - \eta_{03})^2, \\[2pt]
m_4 = (\eta_{30} + \eta_{12})^2 + (\eta_{21} + \eta_{03})^2, \\[2pt]
m_5 = (\eta_{30} - 3\eta_{12})(\eta_{30} + \eta_{12})[(\eta_{30} + \eta_{12})^2 - 3(\eta_{21} + \eta_{03})^2] + (3\eta_{21} - \eta_{03})(\eta_{21} + \eta_{03})[3(\eta_{30} + \eta_{12})^2 - (\eta_{21} + \eta_{03})^2], \\[2pt]
m_6 = (\eta_{20} - \eta_{02})[(\eta_{30} + \eta_{12})^2 - (\eta_{21} + \eta_{03})^2] + 4\eta_{11}(\eta_{30} + \eta_{12})(\eta_{21} + \eta_{03}), \text{ and} \\[2pt]
m_7 = (3\eta_{21} - \eta_{30})(\eta_{30} + \eta_{12})[(\eta_{30} + \eta_{12})^2 - 3(\eta_{21} + \eta_{03})^2] + (3\eta_{12} - \eta_{30})(\eta_{21} + \eta_{03})[3(\eta_{30} + \eta_{12})^2 - (\eta_{21} + \eta_{03})^2].
\end{cases}$$

```
function y=e(p,q,f)
m00=sum(sum(f));
[M,N]=size(f);
m=[0:M-1]'; m10=sum(sum(repmat(m,1,N).*f));
n=0:N-1;m01=sum(sum(repmat(n,M,1).*f));
m_=m10/m00; n_=m01/m00;
mu_pq=sum(sum((repmat(m,1,N)-m_).^p.*(repmat(n,M,1)-n_).^q.*f));
y=mu_pq/m00^((p+q+2)/2);
```

Figure 9.3(a) *M-file codes of the file* **e** *which computes* η_{pq}

```
function y=mominv(f)
m1=e(2,0,f)+e(0,2,f);
m2=(e(2,0,f)-e(0,2,f))^2+4*e(1,1,f)^2;
m3=(e(3,0,f)-3*e(1,2,f))^2+(3*e(2,1,f)-e(0,3,f))^2;
m4=(e(3,0,f)+e(1,2,f))^2+(e(2,1,f)+e(0,3,f))^2;
m5=(e(3,0,f)-3*e(1,2,f))*(e(3,0,f)+e(1,2,f))*((e(3,0,f)+e(1,2,f))^2-3*(e(2,1,f)+e(0,3,f))^2)+ ...
   (3*e(2,1,f)-e(0,3,f))*(e(2,1,f)+e(0,3,f))*(3*(e(3,0,f)+e(1,2,f))^2-(e(2,1,f)+e(0,3,f))^2);
m6=(e(2,0,f)-e(0,2,f))*(((e(3,0,f)+e(1,2,f))^2-(e(2,1,f)+e(0,3,f))^2))+ ...
   4*e(1,1,f)*(e(3,0,f)+e(1,2,f))*(e(2,1,f)+e(0,3,f));
m7=(3*e(2,1,f)-e(3,0,f))*(e(3,0,f)+e(1,2,f))*((e(3,0,f)+e(1,2,f))^2-3*(e(2,1,f)+e(0,3,f))^2)+ ...
   (3*e(1,2,f)-e(3,0,f))*(e(2,1,f)+e(0,3,f))*(3*(e(3,0,f)+e(1,2,f))^2-(e(2,1,f)+e(0,3,f))^2);
y=[m1 m2 m3 m4 m5 m6 m7]';
```

Figure 9.3(b) *M-file codes of the file* **mominv** *which computes the seven moments*

The m and n are the image pixel variables. The programming just needs the straightforward expressional code writing of the moments. Any double sum $\sum\sum$ is equivalent to the use of two **sum** functions of MATLAB. We write two function files – one for the computation of η_{pq} (presented in the figure 9.3(a) by the name e(p,q,f)) and the other for the computation of the seven moments $\{m_1, m_2, m_3, m_4, m_5, m_6, m_7\}$ (presented in the figure 9.3(b) by the name mominv(f)). The reader is referred to section 2.3 for the softcopy of these files. As a procedural step, type the codes of the figures 9.3(a) and 9.3(b) exactly as they appear in two different M-file editors of MATLAB and save them by the names e and mominv respectively. The input argument of the mominv is the digital image matrix $f[m,n]$ and both softcopy function files must be present in the same folder or directory. Our expectation is we provide the digital image matrix $f[m,n]$ (for example, $f[m,n] = \begin{bmatrix} 0 & 3 & 34 \\ 8 & 45 & 32 \\ 4 & 21 & 42 \end{bmatrix}$) and obtain the set of moments

$\{m_1, m_2, m_3, m_4, m_5, m_6, m_7\}$. But one problem is associated with the moment values, which are typically very less than 1. Taking logarithm with common base can overcome the problem. Additionally any negative value of the moment turns the logarithm to be complex and the logarithm of a number less than 1 is negative. On whose account we take first the absolute values of the seven moments and then the logarithm and at the end again take absolute values followed by the logarithm, which should provide us $\begin{bmatrix} 2.3213 \\ 5.9955 \\ 7.2992 \\ 8.7817 \\ 16.9049 \\ 11.9493 \\ 17.1914 \end{bmatrix}$ for the modular image matrix

$f[m,n]$. These all computations can happen by the following:

MATLAB Command

```
>>f=[0 3 34;8 45 32;4 21 42]; ↵    ← f[m,n] is assigned to workspace variable f
>>I=mominv(f); ↵                    ← I holds the {m₁,m₂,m₃,m₄,m₅,m₆,m₇} as a column matrix
>>L=abs(log10(abs(I))) ↵            ← L holds the | log₁₀ |{m₁,m₂,m₃,m₄,m₅,m₆,m₇}||
```

$\leftarrow$ $f[m,n]$ is assigned to workspace variable f

$\leftarrow$ I holds the $\{m_1, m_2, m_3, m_4, m_5, m_6, m_7\}$ as a column matrix

$\leftarrow$ L holds the $|\log_{10}|\{m_1, m_2, m_3, m_4, m_5, m_6, m_7\}||$

```
L =
        2.3213
        5.9955
        7.2992
        8.7817
       16.9049
       11.9493
       17.1914
```

Figure 9.4(a) *Image man.jpg scaled to 0.8 of its full scale*

Figure 9.4(b) *Image man.jpg scaled to 0.5 of its full scale*

✦ ✦ Numerical proof of the scale invariance for the seven moments

Here we would like to prove numerically the scale invariance of the seven moments considering the gray version man.jpg. Scale invariance means if we resize the digital image on the same pixel size and data class, we find the same seven moment values regardless of the scaling. Let us say we wish to compare the seven invariant moments for three different sizes for example full size, reduced to 0.8 of its size, and reduced to 0.5 of its size. The step by step implementation is described as follows:

```
>>f1=imread('man.jpg'); ↵        ← Reading the RGB image as 3D array and assigned to f1
>>f1=rgb2gray(f1); ↵             ← Turning the f1 to gray image and assigned to f1, f1⇔ f[m,n]
>>imshow(f1) ↵                   ← Figure 6.1(a) shows the image display of the f1
>>I1=mominv(double(f1)); ↵       ← I1 holds {m₁,m₂,m₃,m₄,m₅,m₆,m₇} for f1
>>L1=abs(log10(abs(I1))); ↵      ← L1 holds moments of f1 following logarithm and absolute value
```

At this point the full scale image of man.jpg is stored in f1 and we perform the scaling (section 3.7) as follows:

```
>>f2=imresize(f1,0.8); ↵         ← 0.8 scaled size of f1 is stored in f2
```

Incidentally, the f2 does not possess the same pixel size as that of the f1. From the MATLAB workspace browser, we find that the pixel sizes of f1 and f2 are 361×253 and 288×202 respectively. But for the moment comparison reason, their sizes must be identical. We pad f2 by zeroes (corresponding to black) until its size becomes the full scale size 361×253 with the help of the MATLAB function **padarray** as follows:

>>f2=padarray(f2,[361-288,253-202],'post'); ↵ ← Padded f2 is assigned again to f2

The function **padarray** can conceive three input arguments, the first, second, and third of which are the matrix to be padded, two element row matrix indicating the row and column numbers to be padded, and the MATLAB reserve word 'post' respectively. The 'post' means that the zeroes are added after the right side and bottom of the image matrix. The full scale row number is 361 and the 0.8 scaled row number is 288 therefore 361-288 rows are needed to have the same row size from f2. Similar interpretation also follows for the column numbers. Let us proceed with the following:

>>imshow(f2) ↵ ← Figure 9.4(a) shows 0.8 scaled and padded image stored in f2
>>l2=mominv(double(f2)); ↵ ← l2 holds { $m_1, m_2, m_3, m_4, m_5, m_6, m_7$ } for f2
>>L2=abs(log10(abs(l2))); ↵ ← L2 holds moments of f2 following logarithm and absolute value
>>f3=imresize(f1,0.5); ↵ ← 0.5 scaled size of f1 is stored in f3

Knowing the pixel size of f3 from the workspace browser (which is 180×126), we conduct the **padarray** as we did for the f2 as follows:

>>f3=padarray(f3,[361-180,253-126],'post'); ↵ ← Padded f3 is assigned again to f3
>>imshow(f3) ↵ ← Figure 9.4(b) shows 0.5 scaled and padded image stored in f3
>>l3=mominv(double(f3)); ↵ ← l3 holds { $m_1, m_2, m_3, m_4, m_5, m_6, m_7$ } for f3
>>L3=abs(log10(abs(l3))); ↵ ← L3 holds moments of f3 following logarithm and absolute value
>>[L1 L2 L3] ↵ ← Displaying the moments together for the three images

ans =

2.9739	2.9742	2.9738	← corresponding to m_1
6.9305	6.9330	6.9292	← corresponding to m_2
11.8284	11.8297	11.8297	← corresponding to m_3
12.7882	12.7842	12.7566	← corresponding to m_4
25.5420	25.5380	25.4172	← corresponding to m_5
16.5858	16.5821	16.5158	← corresponding to m_6
25.1280	25.1223	25.0879	← corresponding to m_7
↑	↑	↑	
full	0.8	0.5	← scales of man.jpg

The command **[L1 L2 L3]** (section 10.6) displays the seven moments side by side for the three images respectively. Since a digital image possesses fixed number of pixels and fixed number of color levels, the interpolation, an essential process for the scaling, causes to lose some image information. This sort of interpolation takes place literally for thousands of pixels. Nevertheless the discrepancy in the moment numerics is after the first decimal or

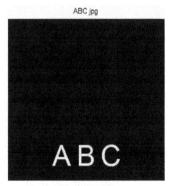

Figure 9.5(a) *Display of the image ABC.jpg*

Figure 9.5(c) *Display of the image A.jpg*

Figure 9.5(b) *Correlation image of the images ABC.jpg and A.jpg*

even thereafter. Ignoring the slight discrepancies, one can say that the seven moments are scale invariant. For sure two different images result two different moment sets which the reader can easily verify now by taking another image of the same data class and size. One important application of the moment invariance is the image objectís recognition by a robot. Suppose a robot has to recognize different parts of a car during the manufacturing process. The moment sets for different parts are stored in the memory of the robot. Each time the robot finds an object, calculates the seven moments, compares them with the stored values, and identifies the object. However the reader can verify the translational and rotational invariances in a similar fashion.

9.5 Correlation of two digital images

Let us say we have two digital images – $f[m,n]$ of pixel size $M \times N$ and $g[m,n]$ of pixel size $R \times S$. Their correlation image is given by the relationship $R[m,n] = \sum_q \sum_p f[p,q]g[p-m,q-n]$ assuming the pixel size of $f[m,n]$ is larger than that of $g[m,n]$ (that is $M > R$ and $N > S$). Considering the $g[m,n]$ as a mask, we first slide the mask over the mask of $f[m,n]$ until all pixels are covered thereby resulting the size of $R[m,n]$ as $(M+R-1) \times (N+S-1)$. The correlation image $R[m,n]$ is then mapped to [0,1] or [0,255] for the display reason.

However, let us consider the modular images $f[m,n] = \begin{bmatrix} 7 & 5 & 5 \\ 8 & 4 & 4 \\ 0 & 3 & 6 \end{bmatrix}$ and $g[m,n] = \begin{bmatrix} 4 & 4 \\ 3 & 6 \end{bmatrix}$ for the correlation

computation. Employing the expression for $R[m,n]$, one obtains $R[m,n] = \begin{bmatrix} 42 & 51 & 45 & 15 \\ 76 & 96 & 76 & 32 \\ 32 & 66 & 77 & 34 \\ 0 & 12 & 36 & 24 \end{bmatrix}$. The minimum

and maximum elements in $R[m,n]$ are 0 and 96 respectively which can be mapped to [0,1] by dividing each element by 96. The orders of the $f[m,n]$, $g[m,n]$, and $R[m,n]$ are 3×3, 2×2, and 4×4 (since 3+2–1=4 both for the row and column) respectively. Our objective is to obtain $R[m,n]$ starting from $f[m,n]$ and $g[m,n]$ for which the MATLAB function xcorr2 (abbreviation of cross (x) correlation in two (2) dimensions) can be useful as follows:

MATLAB Command

```
>>f=[7 5 5;8 4 4;0 3 6]; ↵        ← f[m,n] is assigned to f
>>g=[4 4;3 6]; ↵                  ← g[m,n] is assigned to g
>>R=xcorr2(f,g) ↵                 ← computed R[m,n] is assigned to R


R =
      42    51    45    15
      76    96    76    32
      32    66    77    34
       0    12    36    24
```

The function xcorr2 has two input arguments, the first and second of which are the image matrices $f[m,n]$ and $g[m,n]$ respectively. Elements stored in R can now be turned to [0,1] by writing the command mat2gray(R) if it is necessary.

⬧ ⬧ Application of the image correlation

The correlation of two images can be used to investigate the region similarity between the two images. Within the image $f[m,n]$, the image to be matched is $g[m,n]$. If any image region of $f[m,n]$ is similar to that of $g[m,n]$, brighter intensity is noticed in the correlated image $R[m,n]$ indicating the best match. We exercise the concept taking the gray version of the images ABC.jpg and A.jpg from section 2.3 as $f[m,n]$ and $g[m,n]$ respectively. Obtain the images and place them in your working directory. The commands imshow('ABC.jpg') and imshow('A.jpg') display the images like the figures 9.5(a) and 9.5(c) respectively. Let us carry out the following:

```
>>f=imread('ABC.jpg'); ↵       ← ABC.jpg is read and assigned to f, which is an RGB image
>>f=rgb2gray(f); ↵    ← turning the RGB image f to gray image and assigned to f again, f⟺ f[m,n]
>>g=imread('A.jpg'); ↵       ← A.jpg is read and assigned to g, which is an RGB image
>>g=rgb2gray(g); ↵        ← turning the RGB g to gray image and assigned to g again, g⟺ g[m,n]
```

Looking into the MATLAB workspace browser, we find that the f and g are of unsigned 8-bit integer data class but for the computation reason we need the double class:

```
>>f=double(f); g=double(g); ↵   ← turning the unsigned 8-bit integer to the double class and assigned
```

>>R=xcorr2(f,g); ↵   ← computed $R[m,n]$ is assigned to R

>>imshow(R,[ ]) ↵   ← displaying $R[m,n]$ as a gray image first mapping in [0,1]

Figure 9.5(b) depicts the resulting correlation image from the images ABC.jpg and A.jpg in which strong intensity (lower left region) indicates a matching of A.jpg in ABC.jpg. The matching measure is qualititative rather than quantitative. Workspace browser indicates that the pixel sizes of the ABC.jpg, A.jpg, and correlation images are 300×300, 50×115, and 349×414 respectively. The row pixel number comes from 349=300+50−1, so does the column pixel number.

✦✦ Correlation coefficient between two identical size images

The correlation coefficient of two identical size images tells us how much similar two digital images $f[m,n]$ and $g[m,n]$ is. The correlation coefficient of the two images is defined as $r =$

$$\frac{\sum_n\sum_m (f[m,n]-\overline{f}[m,n])(g[m,n]-\overline{g}[m,n])}{\sqrt{\sum_n\sum_m (f[m,n]-\overline{f}[m,n])^2 \sum_n\sum_m (g[m,n]-\overline{g}[m,n])^2}}$$ where $\overline{f}[m,n]$ and $\overline{g}[m,n]$ are the mean intensity or gray level in

the whole $f[m,n]$ and $g[m,n]$ respectively. If the value of r is close to 1, the two images are very similar. The MATLAB function corr2 (abbreviation of the <u>corr</u>elation coefficient in two (<u>2</u>) dimensions) computes the r. As an example, let us say $f[m,n] = \begin{bmatrix} 9 & 5 & 5 \\ 7 & 8 & 9 \\ 2 & 0 & 7 \end{bmatrix}$ and $g[m,n] = \begin{bmatrix} 4 & 5 & 5 \\ 7 & 8 & 9 \\ 2 & 0 & 7 \end{bmatrix}$. Using the expression for r, one computes the r

as 0.8489 and which is implemented as follows:

>>f=[9 5 5;7 8 9;2 0 7]; ↵   ← digital image $f[m,n]$ is assigned to f

>>g=[4 5 5;7 8 9;2 0 7]; ↵   ← digital image $g[m,n]$ is assigned to g

>>r=corr2(f,g) ↵   ← computed r is assigned to r

r =
      0.8489

The function corr2 has two input arguments, the $f[m,n]$ and $g[m,n]$ image matrices respectively. A perfect match should return $r=1$. Let us implement that for the image ABC.jpg:

>>f=imread('ABC.jpg'); ↵ ← ABC.jpg is read and assigned to f, which is an RGB image

>>f=rgb2gray(f); ↵   ← turning the RGB image f to gray image and assigned to f again

>>f=double(f); ↵ ← turning the unsigned 8-bit integer to the double class and assigned to f again

>>r=corr2(f,f) ↵   ← computed r is assigned to r

r =
      1

Figure 9.6(a) *Image basis for* $\begin{Bmatrix} u=3 \\ v=2 \end{Bmatrix}$ *in enlarged scale*

If the $g[m,n]$ is of small size which is to be matched within the region of $f[m,n]$, we compute the r at every pixel inside $f[m,n]$ using two for-loops (subsection 10.3.3)

```
[m,n]=meshgrid(1:8);
B=[ ];
for u=1:8
        R=[ ];
        for v=1:8
            I=cos(pi*(2*m-1)*(u-1)/16).*cos(pi*(2*n-1)*(v-1)/16);
            R=[R mat2gray(I) ones(8,2)];
        end
        [r,c]=size(R);
        B=[B;R;ones(2,c)];
end

imshow(B)
```

Figure 9.6(b) *M-file statements for the generation of 2D DCT image bases*

and check the value of r whether it is close to 1 thus finding the similarity of $g[m,n]$ in the region of the $f[m,n]$.

9.6 Digital image basis generation

Chapter 4 discusses the implementation of the digital image transforms. The common strategy in the image transform is to map a digital image to the transform domain through a well-defined kernel. For instance, the two dimensional discrete Fourier transform (section 4.1) $F[u,v]$ of the digital image $f[m,n]$ of size $M \times N$ is also of size $M \times N$. Or in other words the $f[m,n]$ is dissected in $M \times N$ sinusoids in the transform domain and every image gray level or intensity value in $f[m,n]$ can be expressed linearly in terms of these $M \times N$ sinusoids. The transform variables u and v also follow the same variation as the pixel variables m and n do which is $\begin{cases} for & m, & 0 \ to \ M-1 \\ for & n, & 0 \ to \ N-1 \end{cases}$. For each set of u and v, one obtains the image of the kernel for different m and n – this is one basis image. Since there are $M \times N$ sets of u and v, supposedly there exist $M \times N$ image bases. Our objective is to obtain these image bases for different image transforms.

Let us consider the two dimensional discrete cosine transform (section 4.3) for the image basis computation and rewrite the transform $F[u,v] = \sum\limits_{n=1}^{N} \sum\limits_{m=1}^{M} w[u,v] f[m,n] \cos\dfrac{\pi(2m-1)(u-1)}{2M} \cos\dfrac{\pi(2n-1)(v-1)}{2N}$. We drop the summation signs (because we are interested to see the whole m - n domain or image not a single pixel) and the

$f[m,n]$ (dropping $f[m,n]$ means giving equal importance to all pixels) from the expression to obtain the kernel $w[u,v]\cos\dfrac{\pi(2m-1)(u-1)}{2M} \cos\dfrac{\pi(2n-1)(v-1)}{2N}$. Multiplying by the constant $w[u,v]$ does not change the image basis property for any set of u and v hence it can be dropped as well. Next one needs to decide the image size and let us choose the image size as 8×8. It means each of the variables m, n, u, and v varies from 1 to 8 and $M = 8$ and $N = 8$ (following the MATLAB notation).

Let us find the image basis corresponding to $\begin{cases} u = 3 \\ v = 2 \end{cases}$ which becomes $\cos\dfrac{\pi(2m-1)}{8} \cos\dfrac{\pi(2n-1)}{16}$.

Inserting all m and n provides the image basis which is also of the pixel size 8×8. One way to compute the expression is to apply meshgrid (section 10.11) as follows:

```
>>[m,n]=meshgrid(1:8); ↵
>>I=cos(pi*(2*m-1)/8).*cos(pi*(2*n-1)/16); ↵
```

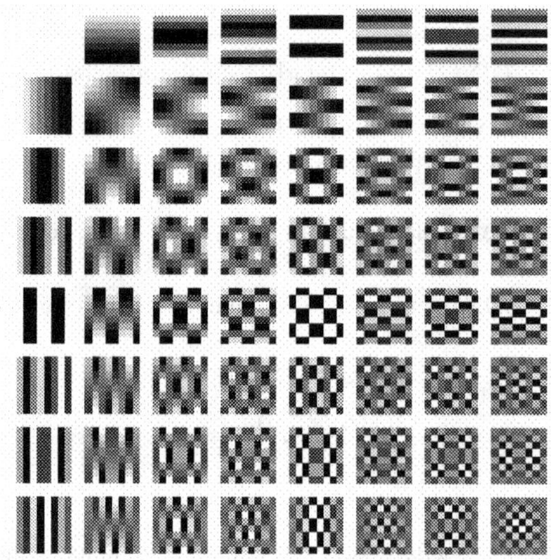

The first line in above command is the repetitive matricesí generation and the second line computes (section 10.2) the expression $\cos\dfrac{\pi(2m-1)}{8} \cos\dfrac{\pi(2n-1)}{16}$ from which the I

Figure 9.6(c) *Digital image bases of the 2D DCT for all u and v is*

holds the 8×8 image basis for $\begin{cases} u = 3 \\ v = 2 \end{cases}$. When I is to be viewed as a digital image, we map the values of I in [0,1] using mat2gray as follows:

```
>>I=mat2gray(I) ↵          ← mapped values again assigned to I
```

I =

1.0000	0.7071	0.2929	0.0000	0	0.2929	0.7071	1.0000
0.9239	0.6756	0.3244	0.0761	0.0761	0.3244	0.6756	0.9239
0.7832	0.6173	0.3827	0.2168	0.2168	0.3827	0.6173	0.7832
0.5995	0.5412	0.4588	0.4005	0.4005	0.4588	0.5412	0.5995
0.4005	0.4588	0.5412	0.5995	0.5995	0.5412	0.4588	0.4005
0.2168	0.3827	0.6173	0.7832	0.7832	0.6173	0.3827	0.2168
0.0761	0.3244	0.6756	0.9239	0.9239	0.6756	0.3244	0.0761
0.0000	0.2929	0.7071	1.0000	1.0000	0.7071	0.2929	0.0000

The image viewing of I as shown in the figure 9.6(a) can happen just by the following:

```
>>imshow(I) ↵
```

In order to view all image bases, little programming rather manual calculation is necessary. Control on all u and v can occur using two for-loops. Since there should be separation among the image bases, we intentionally insert some ones (which is equivalent to white) among various image bases. Let us put 8×2 ones in the row direction inbetween the image bases. We also intend to keep the rows separated by two ones width. Type all statements of the figure 9.6(b) in the M-file editor and run the file. You see all image bases for the two dimensional discrete cosine transform as shown in figure 9.6(c). There are 8×8 blocks or image bases in the last figure and each block possesses one set of u and v. For instance, the upper left and lower right in the figure correspond to $\begin{Bmatrix} u=1 \\ v=1 \end{Bmatrix}$ and $\begin{Bmatrix} u=8 \\ v=8 \end{Bmatrix}$ respectively. The modular basis seen from the intersection (where $\begin{Bmatrix} u=5 \\ v=1 \end{Bmatrix}$) of the first column and the fifth row of the figure 9.6(c) has alternate bars which means two gray levels. In fact any 8×8 image can be expressed as the linear combination of these 64 images of the figure 9.6(c) ñ that is the implication of the image bases. In image processing textbook notion, $\begin{Bmatrix} u=1 \\ v=1 \end{Bmatrix}$ turns to be $\begin{Bmatrix} u=0 \\ v=0 \end{Bmatrix}$ or the average component. From all u and v, subtract 1 to have them consistent with the image processing textbook notation. The upper left image basis appears to be white that means it is of constant intensity. If the image were of 32×32 size, the modifications we need in the statements of the figure 9.6(b) would be [m,n]=meshgrid(1:32);, for u=1:32, for v=1:32, I=cos(pi*(2*m-1)*(u-1)/64).*cos(pi*(2*n-1)*(v-1)/64);, and R=[R mat2gray(I) ones(32,2)]; in the first, third, fifth, sixth, and seventh lines respectively. In a similar fashion the reader can obtain the image bases for any other transform by first having the transform kernel. It should be noted that the computational time becomes augmented with the enlargement of the image size.

9.7 Coded digital image generation

Instead of intensity value or gray level, alphanumeric characters for each pixel can be used to represent a digital image. For espionage reason or image encryption, the coded images can be transmitted. Also the coded image can be a relief for a system which does not support image file transmission directly. The alphanumeric characters are completely user defined. Let us say an 8 level digital image in [0,7] is to be coded in terms of the capital letters A through H consecutively. Considering the modular digital image matrix $f[m,n] = \begin{bmatrix} 0 & 2 & 5 \\ 7 & 4 & 2 \\ 7 & 1 & 5 \end{bmatrix}$ and applying the coding, we are supposed to have the image as $\begin{bmatrix} A & C & F \\ H & E & C \\ H & B & F \end{bmatrix}$. Our computer keyboard has specific ASCII coding for example the character A has the code 65. The MATLAB function char can display the ASCII character coding. Let us perform the following:

MATLAB Command

for A,	for A through H,	for the modular image $f[m,n]$,
>>char(65) ↵	>>char(65:72) ↵	>>f=[0 2 5;7 4 2;7 1 5]; ↵
		>>f=char(f+65) ↵
ans =	ans =	
		f =
A	ABCDEFGH	
		ACF
		HEC
		HBF

As you see the code 65 is equivalent to the capital A. Similarly the 65 through 72 represent the capital A through H which is also shown in above middle implementation. But the fact is our gray level in the example image starts with 0. If we add 65 to every pixel value in the example $f[m,n]$, we can follow the keyboard ASCII character coding. This can happen just by writing the command f+65. In the upper right implementation, first we assigned the image matrix $f[m,n]$ to the workspace variable f and then the character coding is performed on the f+65 in the second line. The result is again assigned to f. Looking into the workspace browser, one can find that the last f is now a character array of size 3×3 this is what we are after. Instead of transmitting the image gray level, we can transmit the character array.

♦ ♦ **How can we character code a practical image?**

A good resolution digital image does not possess 8 gray levels but frequently 256, 512, Ö etc levels are seen. Considering one fourth scaled and gray version of man.jpg from section 2.3, the image is to be coded in [0,31] using the characters from 0 through 9 and from A through V. The problem statement requires 32 gray levels to represent the image. Obtaining the image in the working directory, let us exercise the following:

```
>>f=imread('man.jpg'); ↵  ← reading the image and assigned to f, which is 3D array
>>f=imresize(f,1/4); ↵  ← resizing the image in f to one fourth of its size and assigned to f (section 3.7)
>>f=rgb2gray(f); ↵  ← turning the RGB image to gray image and again assigned to f
```

```
>>imshow(f) ↵          ← displays the reduced image like the one as shown in the figure 6.1(a)
```
Looking into the MATLAB workspace browser, the data class of f is unsigned 8-bit integer. Table 2.B says that the image gray level ranges from 0 to 255 but we need scaling down of [0,255] to [0,31]. Provided formula for scaling down of the gray level in section 4.2 is $N = \dfrac{(N_{max} - N_{min})R + N_{min}R_{max} - N_{max}R_{min}}{R_{max} - R_{min}}$ and applying the formula, the

image stored in f in [0,255] becomes the image in [0,31] just by multiplying $\dfrac{31}{255}$:

```
>>f=double(f); ↵       ← conversion of the data to double class for the computation reason
>>f=31*f/255; ↵        ← the image in [0,31] is assigned to f again which is f[m,n]
```
Fractional gray level appears causing from the computation but coding needs integer value. We avoid the fractional values by rounding the gray levels to the nearest integer with the help of MATLAB function round as follows:
```
>>f=round(f); ↵        ← the rounded image is again assigned to f
```
To pick up any pixel from the last f, two for-loops are required (subsection 10.3.3). For the whole image, we can not find the coded image manually rather little programming is required. Workspace browser says the size of the f is 90×63. The integers 0 through 9 have the ASCII coding 48 though 57 and the capital letters A through V have the ASCII coding 65 through 86 respectively. We check every pixel value of $f[m,n]$ (MATLAB code f(m,n)) whether it is in $0 \le f[m,n] \le 9$. If it is, the coding is char(48+f(m,n)). The logical condition $0 \le f[m,n] \le 9$ is broken as $0 \le f[m,n]$ and $f[m,n] \le 9$ whose code is 0<=f(m,n)&f(m,n) <=9 (subsection 10.3.1). If it is not, the character coding becomes char(65+f(m,n)-10) because we are sure that the image is in [0,31]. Initially we form a character array g of the same size (which is 90×63) as that of the image $f[m,n]$ by writing the command

```
g=char(ones(90,63));
for m=1:90
        for n=1:63
                if 0<=f(m,n)&f(m,n)<=9
                        g(m,n)=char(48+f(m,n));
                else
                        g(m,n)=char(65+f(m,n)-10);
                end
        end
end
```

Figure 9.7(a) *The MATLAB statements for the generation of a coded image*

g=char(ones(90,63));. Following the checking and coding of every pixel, we assign the code in the corresponding position of the character array g. However, all programming statements are shown in the figure 9.7(a). Type the statements in the M-file editor and run the file. One can view the coded image just by calling the g from the command prompt as follows:
```
>>g ↵
```

g =

MMMMMMMMMMMMMMMMMMNNNONOOOOOOOOOOOOOOOOOOOOOOOOOOOOOOOOOOOOOOOOOOOOO

        ⋮

OOO ONOPP PPPP PPPPOO PPN MMRQ MNNRP MMNO PPPOO OOOOOP PPPPP PPO PPPQ QQP QQ P

For space reason, we just presented the first and last rows of the character array g. Looking at the codes of the image in the MATLAB workspace, there is no way of knowing how the image looks like until we decode it. Thus we can generate the coded image for any other practical image.

9.8 Circulant matrix implementation

In digital image restoration problems we create the degradation model to study the noise nature. The circulant matrices are used to analyze the image degradation model. Also the matrix can be used for the pattern recognition of images. We point out here how one generates the circulant matrices in MATLAB. If the elements in a row or column matrix are shifted by one element to the right/left or up/down but keeping the number of elements same (also termed as the cyclic shifting), we can have the circulant matrix H. Let us consider the row matrix $R = [0 \ \ 2 \ \ 3 \ \ 8 \ \ 1]$ and shift the elements in R one by one to the right as follows:

        [0 2 3 8 1] ← original
        [1 0 2 3 8] ← shift by one element
        [8 1 0 2 3] ← shift by two elements

[3 8 1 0 2] ← shift by three elements, and so on.

There are five elements in R hence four possible circular shifts are there (equal to the number of elements−1). In the fifth shift we return to the original row matrix. The MATLAB function circshift (abbreviation of the circular shift) can generate circularly shifted array as follows:

MATLAB Command

>>R=[0 2 3 8 1]; ↵   ← Assigning the row matrix R to the workspace variable R

>>circshift(R,[1 1]) ↵   ← shifting the elements in R by 1 element to the right

ans =

    1   0   2   3   8

>>circshift(R,[1 2]) ↵   ← shifting the elements in R by 2 elements to the right

ans =

    8   1   0   2   3

The function circshift has two input arguments, the first one accepts a rectangular matrix in general. The second input argument is a two element row matrix, the first element of which indicates the dimension ñ for the row directed shifting 1 and for the column directed shifting 2 and the second element of which indicates the number of elements to be shifted (+ for the rightward shifting and ñ for the leftward shifting). If we intend to form a matrix from all possible shifting, we first assign the circshift(R,[1 2]) to some variable v and then use the command v=[v;circshift(R,[1 2])] for each shifting (section 10.6). There is one function called circul (abbreviation of the circulant matrix) which generates the complete circulant matrix $H = \begin{bmatrix} 0 & 2 & 3 & 8 & 1 \\ 1 & 0 & 2 & 3 & 8 \\ 8 & 1 & 0 & 2 & 3 \\ 3 & 8 & 1 & 0 & 2 \\ 2 & 3 & 8 & 1 & 0 \end{bmatrix}$ (obtained by placing all

possible circularly shifted elements row after row) but its path is not defined in the default MATLAB path. Use Microsoft Windows Search or Find files facility to find the file location of circul. We found the file in the location C:\MATLAB6p5\toolbox\matlab\elmat\private. With the help of the Windows Explorer, copy the file in your working path or directory and then execute the following:

>>H=circul(R) ↵   ← the circulant matrix is assigned to the workspace variable H

H =

    0   2   3   8   1
    1   0   2   3   8
    8   1   0   2   3
    3   8   1   0   2
    2   3   8   1   0

The circulant matrix has some theoretical implications. Let us define the complex exponential column vector w_m

(complex roots of unity) as $w_m = [1 \quad e^{j\frac{2\pi}{M}} \quad e^{j\frac{2\pi}{M}2} \quad e^{j\frac{2\pi}{M}3} \quad .. e^{j\frac{2\pi}{M}m} \quad .. \quad e^{j\frac{2\pi}{M}(M-1)}]^T$, where T is the transposition operator for turning the row matrix to a column one just for the space reason and m can integerwise vary from 0 to $M-1$. The M is the number of the elements in the row matrix R we mentioned earlier. The theoretical implication concerning the circulant matrix is then expressed as $H w_m = \lambda_m w_m$ where $H w_m$ is the matrix multiplication of H and w_m and λ_m is the mth eigenvalue (which is a scalar) of H and w_m is one eigenvector corresponding to m (subsection 4.6.1). Numerically we intend to implement that the relationship functions for the example circulant matrix H. In order to verify, we first find the eigenvalues of the circulant matrix H and assigned those to the workspace variable E as follows:

>>E=eig(H) ↵   ← variable E holds eigenvalues λ_m for different m as a column matrix

E =

    14.0000
     0.9721 + 5.3431i
     0.9721 - 5.3431i
    -7.9721 + 1.9879i
    -7.9721 - 1.9879i

The first eigenvalue λ_0 from E can be picked up just by writing E(1) similarly the second one by writing E(2) and so on. In the row matrix R, there are five elements so m can vary from 0 to 4. The next point is to generate the eigenvector w_m from the complex exponential column matrix. It can happen as follows:

for m =0, w_0 is generated by the command exp(j*2*pi*[0:4]'*0/5),

for m =1, w_1 is generated by the command exp(j*2*pi*[0:4]'*1/5),

for m =2, w_2 is generated by the command exp(j*2*pi*[0:4]'*2/5), and so on.

Let us conduct the following:

>>w0=exp(j*2*pi*[0:4]'*0/5); ↵   ← w_0 is generated and assigned to the workspace variable w0

for the matrix multiplication of H and w_0,   **for the multiplication of λ_0 and w_0,**

>>H*w0 ↵   >>E(1)*w0 ↵

ans =   ans =
   14   14.0000
   14   14.0000
   14   14.0000
   14   14.0000
   14   14.0000

Therefore numerically we verified $H\,w_0 = \lambda_0\,w_0$ similarly one can verify the eigenvalues and eigenvectors relationship $H\,w_m = \lambda_m\,w_m$ for the other eigenvalues. The order of the eigenvector multiplication may not follow the order of eigenvalue stored in E but for sure one eigenvalue from E will satisfy the circulant matrix relationship.

The reader can ask what the use of this circulant matrix implementation is. We wish to explain how it becomes useful to the context of a digital image. It is evident that there are M eigenvalues and M eigenvectors for a circulant matrix H of order $M \times M$. Placing M eigenvectors side by side, one obtains the matrix W of order $M \times M$ and placing corresponding M eigenvalues as the diagonal, one obtains the diagonal matrix D of order $M \times M$. Any digital image is absolutely deterministic that is it has fixed number of pixels and fixed number of gray or color levels. We can turn the whole image matrix as a row matrix R as we mentioned earlier. With the notion of the circulant matrix and observing the matrix order, one can find a form $H\,W = D\,W$ or $D = W^{-1}\,H\,W$. For a particular digital image D is unique and different digital image has different D. So when a computer or machine recognizes an image, it just compares the diagonal elements of two D s obtained from the two images. Thus the D serves the purpose of pattern recognition or feature extraction. The next question is how we can have this D for a digital image. Let us consider the gray version man.jpg from section 2.3. Having the image available in the working directory, let us carry out the following:

>>f=imread('man.jpg'); ↵ ← the image is read and assigned to f where f is an RGB image or 3D array

>>f=rgb2gray(f); ↵   ← turning the RGB image to the gray one and again assigned to f

From the workspace browser, we find the size of the last f as 361×253. It means 361×253=91333 pixels are there and the size of the matrix R would be 91333 and the circulant matrix H would be of the size 91333×91333. The machine has some memory and speed constraints with this sort of large size matrix. What we play is we resize or reduce the image stored in f to one tenth of its original size by the following (section 3.7):

>>f=imresize(f,1/10); ↵ ← reducing the image to one tenth of its size and assigned to f again

Now the workspace browser says that the size of f is 36×25 ñ acceptable for the computation. The whole image is turned to a column one by placing column after column using the command f(:). Aforementioned R is then obtained applying the transposition as follows:

>>R=f(:)'; ↵   ← R is holding the whole image as a row matrix

>>H=circul(R); ↵   ← 900×900 (seen in the workspace browser) circulant matrix is assigned to H

>>[W D]=eig(H); ↵

Now the function eig has two output arguments ñ W and D which contain the theory discussed matrices W and D respectively and what we are after. For sure the size of the diagonal matrix D is 900×900 (comes from 36×25=900). All eigenvalues as a column matrix from the D can be picked up just by writing the command diag(D). The first, second, third, Ö etc eigenvalues can be seen by the command D(1,1), D(2,2), D(3,3), Ö etc respectively and so on. For the example image, the values are as follows:

>>D(1,1) ↵   >>D(2,2) ↵   >>D(3,3) ↵

ans =   ans =   ans =
   1.4954e+005   4.9110e+002 +4.5504e+003i   4.9110e+002 -4.5504e+003i

The 1.4954e+005 means 1.4954×10^5 however taking another image of the same size the reader can verify that these eigenvalues are different from those of the other image. Thus and thus the circulant matrix can be efficacious in the digital image feature extraction.

9.9 Warping a digital image

Warping is a process through which a digital image $f[m,n]$ is mapped to the coordinate system of another digital image. Usually the second image is a real world object or three dimensional (3D) surface. The coordinate systemís notation is very important for the digital image warping. A lot many computer generated movies utilize warping for the animation or special effect generation. Figures 9.7(b) and 9.7(c) show the three dimensional coordinate system geometries for found in textbook and in MATLAB respectively. To start with the image warping, we have to have two elements ñ the digital image matrix $f[m,n]$ and the user defined coordinates (x, y, z) lying on the surface on which the image $f[m,n]$ is to be mapped.

Figure 9.7(b) *Conventional or textbook notation for the 3D coordinate system*

Figure 9.7(c) *MATLAB notation for the 3D coordinate system*

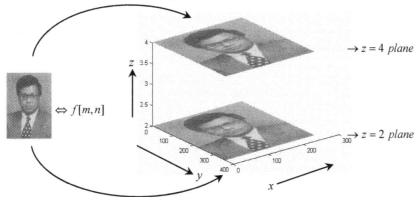

$\rightarrow z = 4$ *plane*

$\rightarrow z = 2$ *plane*

Figure 9.7(d) *Warping the image man.jpg in the planes $z = 2$ and $z = 4$*

$\Leftrightarrow f[m,n]$

Referring to the figure 9.7(d), the image man.jpg of section 2.3 is to be mapped on the planes $z = 2$ and $z = 4$ in accordance with the MATLAB coordinate system shown in the figure 9.7(c). This is the problem statement concerning the image warping.

Any plane like $z = 2$ or $z = 4$ is a special type of surface. In order to warp the image, the user must define some points on the plane or surface. But for every point on the plane we need to provide three coordinates (x, y, z) according to the coordinate system. Placing the image in working directory, we implement the following:

MATLAB Command

>>f=imread('man.jpg'); ↵ ← The image is read and assigned to the workspace variable f

Workspace browser provides the size information of f as 361×253×3. The third dimension is just for the three color planes and the pixel size of man.jpg (361×253) is quitely related with the coordinate variation in the mentioned plane complying the coordinate system. That is, the coordinates in the plane come from $1 \le x \le 361$, $1 \le y \le 253$, and $z = 2$ where x, y, and z are all integers due to the digital nature of the image. As another alternative, the command **size** in collaboration with three output arguments (m, n, and o) is used where m and n have the return for the row and column pixel numbers respectively and o will have 3 indicating the color plane numbers:

>>[m,n,o]=size(f); ↵   ← Provided that the f is an RGB image

At this point the MATLAB function **warp** performs the image warping which takes four input arguments, the first, second, and third of which correspond to the x, y, and z in the addressed plane respectively. But to maintain the pixel consistency of the given image, the x, y, and z are all two dimensional matrices of the same size. This is essential because every pixel in the man.jpg must be mapped in the plane $z = 2$ and the image pixel of man.jpg also has its coordinates. One can use the function **meshgrid** (section 10.11) for the pixel variation of the given image as follows:

>>[x,y]=meshgrid(1:n,1:m); ↵
>>z=2*ones(size(x)); ↵

172

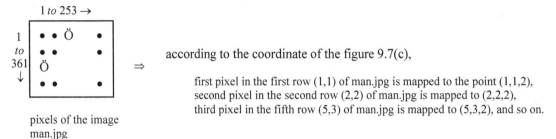

1 *to* 253 →

1
to
361
↓

pixels of the image
man.jpg

according to the coordinate of the figure 9.7(c),

⇒

first pixel in the first row (1,1) of man.jpg is mapped to the point (1,1,2),
second pixel in the second row (2,2) of man.jpg is mapped to (2,2,2),
third pixel in the fifth row (5,3) of man.jpg is mapped to (5,3,2), and so on.

Figure 9.8(a) *Illustration of the pixel mapping of the man.jpg in the plane* $z = 2$

In the last implementation, the command **size(x)** returns the pixel size of the image or the **x** matrix size. The command **ones(size(x))** generates a matrix of ones of the same size as that of **x**. Multiplying by 2, all elements in **z** (which is also of the same size as that of **x**) is 2 which indicates the value of z in the plane $z = 2$. Figure 9.8(a) illustrates how the pixels of the man.jpg are mapped in the plane $z = 2$ according to the coordinate of the figure 9.7(c). The first pixel in the first row (1,1) of man.jpg has the coordinates (1,1,2) in the required plane. We conduct the following to make sure that the pixel coordinates (1,1) in the image are truly mapped to (1,1,2) in the plane:

```
>>x(1,1) ↵          >>y(1,1) ↵          >>z(1,1) ↵

ans =              ans =              ans =
   1                 1                  2
```

Similarly you can find the mapped pointís coordinates for any other pixel in the image. Still and all, the straightforward implementation of the warping on the $z = 2$ plane is as follows:

```
>>warp(x,y,z,f) ↵
```

On execution of above command, the reader should see the image man.jpg mapped only on the $z = 2$ plane like the figure 9.7(d) (for space reason, its display is not shown). The fourth input argument of the function **warp** is the digital image matrix f. There is one more warping needed on the plane $z = 4$ as far as the beginning statement is concerned. We hold the displayed image on the existing figure window by writing the command **hold** as follows:

```
>>hold ↵
```

For the mapping on $z = 4$, the x and y coordinates are not changed only does the z from 2 to 4 hence we redo the **z** assignment and warping as follows:

```
>>z=4*ones(size(x)); ↵
>>warp(x,y,z,f) ↵
```

Now we see the image of the figure 9.7(d) and this is what we expect from MATLAB due to the warping. If the reader does not wish to see the axes in the figure, the command **axis off** can be exercised. We wish to include two more examples on the digital image warping in the following.

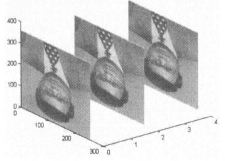

Figure 9.8(b) *Warping the image man.jpg on the planes* $x = 0$, $x = 2$, *and* $x = 4$

♦ ♦ Example 1

We intend to warp the image man.jpg on the planes $x = 0$, $x = 2$, and $x = 4$ according to the axes notation of the figure 9.7(c). The image pixelís variation is on the y-z plane (or parallel to it) therefore the grid generation takes place in the same plane as well. Similar implementation follows as shown below (assuming the f and [m,n,o] are in the workspace from the beginning example and you closed previous figure window):

```
>>[y,z]=meshgrid(1:n,1:m); ↵
>>x=0*ones(size(y)); ↵   ← x coordinatesí generation only for the plane x = 0
>>warp(x,y,z,f) ↵         ← warping only on the plane x = 0
>>hold ↵                  ← holding the drawn image for the successive warping
>>x=2*ones(size(y)); ↵   ← x coordinatesí generation only for the plane x = 2
>>warp(x,y,z,f) ↵         ← warping only on the plane x = 2
>>x=4*ones(size(y)); ↵   ← x coordinatesí generation only for the plane x = 4
>>warp(x,y,z,f) ↵         ← warping only on the plane x = 4
```

Figure 9.8(b) presents the warped images on different x planes. Looking into the figure, the reader might ask why the warped images are upside down. Well, the warping is a function of the grid generation and the image pixels organization. In the first line of this example if we exercised [y,z]=meshgrid(n:-1:1,m:-1:1); instead of [y,z]=meshgrid(1:n,1:m); keeping the other commands unchanged, we would see the properly warped images. Actually, the command n:-1:1 means decreasing grid from 253 to 1 (integerwise).

✦ ✦ Example 2

Ongoing two examples only illustrated warping on the planes. Frequently special effect in computer generated movies needs warping on the curved surface. Let us say the example surface function is defined as

$z = xe^{-x^2-y^2}$ where $0 \leq x \leq 2$ and $0 \leq y \leq 3$. Our objective is to map the image man.jpg on the surface of z.

First of all we need to generate the surface of z numerically but again with the aid of **meshgrid** function. This time the surface domain variable x or y does not change integerwise. For the sake of the numerical generation, we must decide the step size of x or y (let us say 0.01 in each direction). Hence, we obtain the **meshgrid** as follows:

>>[x,y]=meshgrid(0:.01:2,0:.01:3); ↵

The next step is to compute the z values for different x or y according to the given function $z = xe^{-x^2-y^2}$ whose MATLAB code is x.*exp(-x.^2-y.^2); (section 10.2). Let us carry out that:

>>z=x.*exp(-x.^2-y.^2); ↵

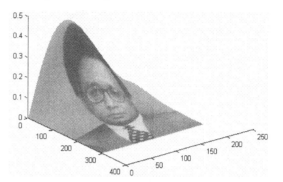

Figure 9.8(c) *Warping the image man.jpg on the surface* $z = xe^{-x^2-y^2}$

We assume that the variable f is not deleted from the workspace and the image stored in f is mapped on the surface $z = xe^{-x^2-y^2}$ by the following:

>>figure,warp(z,f) ↵   ← The command figure opens a new window for graphing

Figure 9.8(c) depicts the warping on the surface. We did not apply four input arguments in the function warp instead two ñ the numerical surface z and the image matrix f, this is another option from the function warp. The use of warp(x,y,z,f) would provide the warping in the absolute x and y grid values instead of the pixel numbers. This kind of thousand warpings is hidden in space related science fiction movies.

9.10 Pseudocoloring or false coloring a gray image

A color image is more distinctive and better perceived than a gray or monochrome image which is popularly known as the black and white image. Pseudocoloring means that we turn a black and white or gray image to the color form. We know from chapter 2 that a digital color image usually possesses two forms – RGB and indexed. Given a gray digital image $f[m,n]$, we attempt to find an RGB or indexed form in the pseudocoloring. Or in other words we seek for the triplet $\begin{Bmatrix} r[m,n] \\ g[m,n] \\ b[m,n] \end{Bmatrix}$ from $f[m,n]$ (section 2.4). The finding is of coarse user defined because the characteristic selection of the basic color (red, green, or blue) is completely userís choice. For the same gray image $f[m,n]$, we may have different color image for different color characteristic selection. There are two approaches seen for the pseudocoloring ñ spatial and its frequency domain based. As an introductory text, we concentrate on the spatial domain one.

Since we proceed with an example, let us consider the modular 4×4 gray image $f[m,n] = \begin{bmatrix} 6 & 5 & 3 & 1 \\ 6 & 7 & 2 & 0 \\ 3 & 4 & 1 & 0 \\ 4 & 5 & 1 & 3 \end{bmatrix}$ in

[0,7] scale. There are 8 levels in the scale [0,7] indicating 0 for black and 7 for white. If we wish to set the black as red, less numbered gray levels in the image such as 0 or 1 should be red. But in the digital image, the red color has also fixed number of levels (user defined). Let us say each of the basic colors has three levels in [0,2]. It means ñ 0 for complete absence, 1 for 50% presence, and 2 for complete presence. There should be a defined gray level slicing according to userís choice for example $\begin{Bmatrix} 0 \leq f[m,n] \leq 1 & for\ red \\ 2 \leq f[m,n] \leq 5 & for\ green \\ 6 \leq f[m,n] \leq 7 & for\ blue \end{Bmatrix}$ in the scale [0,7]. For the red, green,

and blue components, we have 2, 4, and 2 levels respectively. Since each of them is to be mapped in three levels, the red or blue color level assignment in [0,2] takes place as follows: $\begin{cases} f[m,n]=0 \Rightarrow r[m,n]=0 \\ f[m,n]=1 \Rightarrow r[m,n]=2 \\ f[m,n]=6 \Rightarrow b[m,n]=0 \\ f[m,n]=7 \Rightarrow b[m,n]=2 \end{cases}$. But the green

slice has 4 levels in [2,5] and it is to be mapped in [0,2] in 3 levels. We use the formula $\dfrac{(N_{max}-N_{min})R+N_{min}R_{max}-N_{max}R_{min}}{R_{max}-R_{min}}$ of section 4.2 which turns out to be $\dfrac{2R-4}{3}$ where R indicates any $f[m,n]$ in

[2,5]. Due to the computation, fractional values appear but we round the computed values to the nearest integer. The formula could have been used for the other two color levels. In that case we had had $2R$ and $2R-12$ for the red and blue components respectively, where R indicates $f[m,n]$ within the given slice. Anyhow the green slice

mapping becomes $\begin{cases} f[m,n]=2 \Rightarrow g[m,n]=0 \\ f[m,n]=3 \Rightarrow g[m,n]=1 \\ f[m,n]=4 \Rightarrow g[m,n]=1 \\ f[m,n]=5 \Rightarrow g[m,n]=2 \end{cases}$. Now we are in a position to find the RGB matrices from the

modular image $f[m,n]$ and in dong so $r[m,n]=\begin{bmatrix} 0 & 0 & 0 & 2 \\ 0 & 0 & 0 & 0 \\ 0 & 0 & 2 & 0 \\ 0 & 0 & 2 & 0 \end{bmatrix}$, $g[m,n]=\begin{bmatrix} 0 & 2 & 1 & 0 \\ 0 & 0 & 0 & 0 \\ 1 & 1 & 0 & 0 \\ 1 & 2 & 0 & 1 \end{bmatrix}$, and $b[m,n]=\begin{bmatrix} 0 & 0 & 0 & 0 \\ 0 & 2 & 0 & 0 \\ 0 & 0 & 0 & 0 \\ 0 & 0 & 0 & 0 \end{bmatrix}$.

The main requirement here is to obtain the matrices $r[m,n]$, $g[m,n]$, and $b[m,n]$ from $f[m,n]$ for which we conduct the following:

MATLAB Command

```
>>f=[6 5 3 1;6 7 2 0;3 4 1 0;4 5 1 3];  ↵
```
← Assigning the gray image matrix $f[m,n]$ to f

for the red image matrix $r[m,n]$ **:**

```
>>t=f;  ↵
```
← Assigning the f to the intermediate variable t
```
>>z=~(t>1);  ↵
```
← Finding a logical matrix z where $0 \le f[m,n] \le 1$ is satisfied for $r[m,n]$
```
>>r=z.*(2*t)  ↵
```
← r holds the scalar multiplication of z and 2*t where 2*t $\Leftrightarrow 2R$ mapping

```
r =

     0    0    0    2
     0    0    0    0
     0    0    2    0
     0    0    2    0
```

for the green image matrix $g[m,n]$ **:**

```
>>t=f;  ↵
```
← Assigning the f to the intermediate variable t
```
>>z=~((t<2)|(t>5));  ↵
```
← Finding a logical matrix z where $2 \le f[m,n] \le 5$ is satisfied for $g[m,n]$
```
>>g=z.*round((2*t-4)/3)  ↵
```
← g holds the scalar multiplication of z and round((2*t-4)/3) where

$$\text{round}((2\text{*}t\text{-}4)/3) \Leftrightarrow \frac{2R-4}{3} \text{ mapping}$$

```
g =

     0    2    1    0
     0    0    0    0
     1    1    0    0
     1    2    0    1
```

Figure 9.8(d) *The display of the modular gray image $f[m,n]$*

for the blue image matrix $b[m,n]$ **:**

```
>>t=f;  ↵
```
← Assigning the f to the intermediate variable t
```
>>z=~(t<6);  ↵
```
← Finding a logical matrix z where $6 \le f[m,n] \le 7$ is satisfied for $b[m,n]$
```
>>b=z.*(2*t-12)  ↵
```
← b holds the scalar multiplication of z and (2*t-12) where (2*t-12) $\Leftrightarrow$ $2R-12$ mapping

```
b =

     0    0    0    0
     0    2    0    0
     0    0    0    0
     0    0    0    0
```

for the black and white image display:
```
>>imshow(f,[ ])  ↵
```

for the pseudocolor image display:
```
>>I(:,:,1)=r; I(:,:,2)=g; I(:,:,3)=b;  ↵
```

>>imshow(mat2gray(I)) ⏎

Since we need the gray image matrix $f[m,n]$ for each of the three color matrices, we assign that to some intermediate variable t for the processing so that the f is not altered. We find some matrix z whose elements are either 0 or 1. The element in the z is 1 if the value of $f[m,n]$ satisfies $0 \leq f[m,n] \leq 1$ otherwise the element in the z is 0 for the red image. For the programming reason, we apply the method of inversion (subsection 10.3.1). The command t>1 returns a logical matrix in which every element in the matrix is 1 if any value in the $f[m,n]$ is

greater than 1 thereby returning $\begin{bmatrix} 1 & 1 & 1 & 0 \\ 1 & 1 & 1 & 0 \\ 1 & 1 & 0 & 0 \\ 1 & 1 & 0 & 1 \end{bmatrix}$ for the $r[m,n]$. When the command ~(t>1) is used, the return to the z

is $\begin{bmatrix} 0 & 0 & 0 & 1 \\ 0 & 0 & 0 & 1 \\ 0 & 0 & 1 & 1 \\ 0 & 0 & 1 & 0 \end{bmatrix}$. The red color mapping is done by $2R$ where R is the $f[m,n]$ or t whose MATLAB code is 2*t

thereby obtaining $\begin{bmatrix} 12 & 10 & 6 & 2 \\ 12 & 14 & 4 & 0 \\ 6 & 8 & 2 & 0 \\ 8 & 10 & 2 & 6 \end{bmatrix}$. The scalar multiplication operator .* (section 10.2) or the element by element

multiplication of z and 2*t just returns $r[m,n] = \begin{bmatrix} 0 & 0 & 0 & 2 \\ 0 & 0 & 0 & 0 \\ 0 & 0 & 2 & 0 \\ 0 & 0 & 2 & 0 \end{bmatrix}$ what we are after. Similar explanation follows for

the other two color components. The rational or division form gives the fractional numbers that is why we rounded the computed or mapped values only for the green component using the MATLAB function round. For the gray image display of $f[m,n]$, we use the command imshow(f,[ ]) and which is presented in the figure 9.8(d) at maximized window view. The second input argument [ ] of imshow turns the f data to [0,1] scale. Section 2.4 says that the RGB color version of the figure 9.8(d) can be displayed if the triplet $\begin{Bmatrix} r[m,n] \\ g[m,n] \\ b[m,n] \end{Bmatrix}$ is fed as a three

dimensional array (subsection 10.12.1), which is I in above implementation. The first page of the array I is designated as I(:,:,1) and $r[m,n]$ is assigned to that by the command I(:,:,1)=r;. Similar assignment follows for the other two color components to the second and third pages of I respectively. Since the data for the I is double class (workspace browser), we need to map the data in [0,1] to be applicable for the imshow. The mat2gray turns all three page data of I in [0,1]. However the command imshow(mat2gray(I)) displays the color version of the figure 9.8(d) but we are unable to show you the color modular image because the text is written in black and white form. For sure MATLAB will not disappoint you and you need to maximize the figure window for a better view. We attach an example on pseudocoloring for a practical image in the following.

♦ ♦ A practical image example

Let us consider the image dip.bmp from section 2.3. Nowadays most of the images are in color form. The gray or monochrome images are phasing out slowly yet they are important to understand the digital image basics. Referring to the section 2.7 when an indexed image is read with two output arguments, the returns are the intensity and the colormap matrices respectively. We ignore the colormap matrix and the intensity matrix can serve the purpose of having a gray image. Making the image available in the working directory, let us conduct the following:

>>[f,m]=imread('dip.bmp'); ⏎ ← The image is read, f and m are the intensity and colormap respectively
The workspace variable f holds gray image whose outlook can be seen by exercising imshow(f) like the figure 6.1(c). Our objective is to turn this gray image to color form from user-defined color selection. Looking into the figure 6.1(c), the background is white and let us turn it as blue. Color selection is not the only factor in pseudocoloring, the knowledge of the gray level needs to be known prior to the color selection. Workspace browser displays that the data class of f is uint8 hence possessing 256 levels in [0,255] according to the table 2.B. Let us conduct the following:

>>min(min(f)) ⏎   >>max(max(f)) ⏎

ans =   ans =
    132   255

Actually we found the minimum and maximum gray levels present in the image (section 10.10). Despite any gray level from 0 to 255 is equally likely in the image, only the gray levels ranging from 132 to 255 occupy the image. The whiteness in the image is related with the gray values which are closer to 255. With the found information, let us define the gray slicing as $\begin{Bmatrix} 0 \le f[m,n] \le 180 & for\ green \\ 181 \le f[m,n] \le 228 & for\ red \\ 229 \le f[m,n] \le 255 & for\ blue \end{Bmatrix}$ and each color level is to be represented by 32 levels in [0,31]. The next step is to find the gray level to color component mapping expression using the formula

$\dfrac{(N_{max} - N_{min})R + N_{min}R_{max} - N_{max}R_{min}}{R_{max} - R_{min}}$ from which the summarized requirement is $\begin{Bmatrix} [0,180] & for\ green \\ [181,228] & for\ red \\ [229,255] & for\ blue \end{Bmatrix} \to [0,31]$.

Therefore we have the mapping expression $\dfrac{31R - 5611}{47}$, $\dfrac{31R}{180}$, and $\dfrac{31R - 7099}{26}$ for the red, green, and blue components respectively (given components are not in the RGB order). Drawing the notations, conceptions, and functions from the beginning example we perform the pseudocoloring as follows:

for the red component matrix $r[m,n]$ **:**

```
>>t=double(f); ↵
```
← Assigning the double class f to the intermediate variable t
```
>>z=~((t<181)|(t>228)); ↵
```
← Finding a logical matrix z where $181 \le f[m,n] \le 228$ is satisfied for $r[m,n]$
```
>>r=z.*round((31*t-5611)/47); ↵
```
← r holds the scalar multiplication of z and round((31*t-5611)/47) where (31*t-5611)/47 $\Leftrightarrow \dfrac{31R - 5611}{47}$ mapping

for the green component matrix $g[m,n]$ **:**

```
>>t=double(f); ↵
```
← Assigning the double class f to the intermediate variable t
```
>>z=~(t>180); ↵
```
← Finding a logical matrix z where $0 \le f[m,n] \le 180$ is satisfied for $g[m,n]$
```
>>g=z.*round(31*t/180); ↵
```
← g holds the scalar multiplication of z and round(31*t/180) where 31*t/180 $\Leftrightarrow \dfrac{31R}{180}$ mapping

for the blue component matrix $b[m,n]$ **:**

```
>>t=double(f); ↵
```
← Assigning the double class f to the intermediate variable t
```
>>z=~(t<229); ↵
```
← Finding a logical matrix z where $229 \le f[m,n] \le 255$ is satisfied for $b[m,n]$
```
>>b=z.*round((31*t-7099)/26); ↵
```
← b holds the scalar multiplication of z and round((31*t-7099)/26) where (31*t-7099)/26 $\Leftrightarrow \dfrac{31R - 7099}{26}$ mapping

for the pseudocolor image display:

```
>>I(:,:,1)=r; I(:,:,2)=g; I(:,:,3)=b; ↵
```
← Delete previous I by executing clear I to receive no warning
```
>>imshow(mat2gray(I)) ↵
```

Successful implementation of above for sure will be reflected looking into figure window of MATLAB which is what we intended for. Computation always takes place on the double data class that is why the command t=double(f); is used instead of t=f; unlike previous example. Thus you can apply different gray slice according to your choice and view multicolored image from the same gray image.

♦ ♦ Ready made tool of MATLAB

The last two examples focused the spatial domain theory implementation on the pseudocoloring of a gray image. MATLAB has its own tool of pseudocoloring through which the gray image is turned to an indexed one not an RGB one (section 2.4). The function grayslice turns a gray image to a pseudocolor one based on the user-defined level number and colormap. Let us see the functioning of the grayslice on the dip.bmp gray image stored in f as follows:

```
>>g=grayslice(f,16); ↵
>>imshow(g,jet(16)) ↵
```

The first line of above command says that the grayslice has two input arguments, the first and second of which are the gray image matrix and decided level number in the intensity matrix of the indexed image respectively (we chose 16 levels in the intensity part of the required indexed image). The resulting intensity image matrix is assigned to the workspace variable g in which the gray levels are in [0,15] in spite of the data class of g being unsigned 8-bit integer (doubleclick the g on the workspace browser). The intensity levels 16 through 255 remain off. In the second line we used MATLAB built-in colormap jet for 16 levels indicated by jet(16). If the number of intensity levels in the first line were 128, the second line command would be imshow(g,jet(128)). However we see the expected color form of the dip.bmp in the figure window. Apart from the jet, there are a number of built-in colormaps supplied in the workspace namely autumn, bone, colorcube, cool, copper, flag, gray, hot, hsv, lines, pink, prism, spring, summer, white, and winter. Each of them functions similarly so the reader can have various colorful images from the same black and white image. One use of the pseudocoloring is to archive the old image data banks because they are in black and white form.

9.11 Obtaining an eigenimage from a digital image

The concept of eigenimage is derived from the singular value decomposition of a rectangular matrix which utilizes the vector outer products of column and row matrices. The eigenvalue and eigenvector notions are only applicable for the square matrix whose discussions can be seen in section 4.6. Given a digital image matrix $f[m,n]$ of order $M \times N$, it can be expressed by the summation formula as follows: $f[m,n] = \sum_{j=1}^{J}\sqrt{\lambda_j}\,u_j v_j$ where u_j and v_j are the eigenvectors of the matrices $g_1[m,n]$ and $g_2[m,n]$ ($g_1[m,n] = f[m,n] \times f[m,n]^T$ and $g_2[m,n] = f[m,n]^T \times f[m,n]$) respectively. The $g_1[m,n]$ and $g_2[m,n]$ are square matrix with the orders $M \times M$ and $N \times N$ and the u_j and v_j are the column and row matrices respectively. The J is the minimum between M and N and T is the matrix transposition operator. The λ_j is the j-th eigenvalue of the minimum order matrix between $g_1[m,n]$ and $g_2[m,n]$. The $\sqrt{\lambda_j}$ is called the j-th singular value of the decomposition. Expanding the summation, one can write the given image as the J term series like $f[m,n]$ $= \sqrt{\lambda_1}u_1 v_1 + \sqrt{\lambda_2}u_2 v_2 + \sqrt{\lambda_3}u_3 v_3 + \ddot{O}\, .. \quad + \sqrt{\lambda_J}u_J v_J$, each of which is an eigenimage and there are J eigenimages. The u_j is a column matrix of length M but the v_j is a row matrix of length N on that account the order of any eigenimage $\sqrt{\lambda_j}\,u_j v_j$ is $M \times N$. Both the $g_1[m,n]$ and $g_2[m,n]$ are symmetric matrices and share identical eigenvalues. The larger dimension of the two inherits 0 eigenvalues (apart from the identical ones) as well as corresponding eigenvectors but we ignore them for the decomposition.

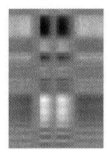

Figure 9.9(a) *The second eigenimage of the gray version man.jpg*

Figure 9.9(b) *The man.jpg from the first 45 eigenimages out of 253*

The eigenimage decomposition is clarified by the prototype image $f[m,n] = \begin{bmatrix} 4 & 1 & 0 & 9 \\ 5 & 7 & -1 & 0 \\ 6 & 9 & 4 & 2 \end{bmatrix}$ for which few intermediate computations are as follows: $f[m,n]^T = \begin{bmatrix} 4 & 5 & 6 \\ 1 & 7 & 9 \\ 0 & -1 & 4 \\ 9 & 0 & 2 \end{bmatrix}$, $M = 3$, $N = 4$, $J = 3$, $g_1[m,n] = f[m,n] \times$

$f[m,n]^T = \begin{bmatrix} 98 & 27 & 51 \\ 27 & 75 & 89 \\ 51 & 89 & 137 \end{bmatrix}$, $g_2[m,n] = f[m,n]^T \times f[m,n] = \begin{bmatrix} 77 & 93 & 19 & 48 \\ 93 & 131 & 29 & 27 \\ 19 & 29 & 17 & 8 \\ 48 & 27 & 8 & 85 \end{bmatrix}$, the eigenvalues of $g_1[m,n]$

are $\begin{bmatrix} \lambda_1 \\ \lambda_2 \\ \lambda_3 \end{bmatrix} = \begin{bmatrix} 10.9423 \\ 73.1662 \\ 225.8915 \end{bmatrix}$, the eigenvectors of $g_1[m,n]$ are $u_1 = \begin{bmatrix} 0.1073 \\ 0.7912 \\ -0.6020 \end{bmatrix}$, $u_2 = \begin{bmatrix} 0.9062 \\ -0.3269 \\ -0.2682 \end{bmatrix}$, and $u_3 = \begin{bmatrix} 0.4090 \\ 0.5168 \\ 0.7521 \end{bmatrix}$ for

$\lambda_1 = 10.9423$, $\lambda_2 = 73.1662$, and $\lambda_3 = 225.8915$ respectively, the eigenvalues of $g_2[m,n]$ are 0, 10.9423, 73.1662, and 225.8915, and the eigenvectors of $g_2[m,n]$ are $v_0 = [0.7783 \quad -0.5314 \quad 0.1717 \quad -0.2869]$, $v_1 = [0.2337$ $0.0688 \quad -0.9672 \quad -0.0721]$, $v_2 = [-0.0445 \quad 0.4438 \quad 0.0872 \quad -0.8908]$, and $v_3 = [0.5810 \quad 0.7183 \quad 0.1658$ $0.3450]$ respectively.

There are three eigenimages in $f[m,n]$, first of which is computed as $\sqrt{\lambda_1}u_1v_1 = \sqrt{10.9423}\begin{bmatrix} 0.1073 \\ 0.7912 \\ -0.6020 \end{bmatrix} \times$

$[0.2337 \quad 0.0688 \quad -0.9672 \quad -0.0721] = \begin{bmatrix} 0.0829 & 0.0244 & -0.3433 & -0.3433 \\ 0.6117 & 0.1801 & -2.5314 & -0.1887 \\ -0.4654 & -0.1370 & 1.9261 & 0.1435 \end{bmatrix}$ similarly the other two become

$\sqrt{\lambda_2}u_2v_2 = \begin{bmatrix} 0.3453 & -3.4399 & -0.6758 & 6.9047 \\ -0.1246 & 1.2410 & 0.2438 & -2.4911 \\ -0.1022 & 1.0180 & 0.2000 & -2.0434 \end{bmatrix}$ and $\sqrt{\lambda_3}u_3v_3 = \begin{bmatrix} 3.5717 & 4.4155 & 1.0191 & 2.1209 \\ 4.5129 & 5.5789 & 1.2876 & 2.6797 \\ 6.5676 & 8.1190 & 1.8739 & 3.8998 \end{bmatrix}$. If we add

the last three eigenimages, we end up with the given modular image matrix of $f[m,n]$. To the context of the digital image processing, the problem statement is to obtain the three eigenimages from $f[m,n]$.

⊟⊟ How to obtain the modular eigenimages from MATLAB?

There is a function called svd (abbreviation of the singular value decomposition) in MATLAB which takes the modular image matrix as the input argument and returns three matrices say U, D, and V. The U is composed of placing the eigenvectors of $g_1[m,n]$ as side by side columns that is U=$[u_1 \quad u_2 \quad u_3 \quad ..]$. Again V is composed of placing the eigenvectors of $g_2[m,n]$ as side by side columns that is V=$[v_1 \quad v_2 \quad v_3 \quad Ö]^T$. The D is a diagonal matrix whose diagonal elements are the singular values but placed in descending order. The placement of the eigenvectors and singular values are in order. However let us see the decomposition as follows:

```
>>f=[4 1 0 9;5 7 -1 0;6 9 4 2]; ↵   ← Entering the modular image matrix f[m,n] to f
>>[U D V]=svd(f) ↵                   ← Applying the function on the modular image f
```

U =

-0.4090	0.9062	-0.1073	← u_1 is the third column of U⇔U(:,3)
-0.5168	-0.3269	-0.7912	u_2 is the second column of U⇔U(:,2)
-0.7521	-0.2682	0.6020	u_3 is the first column of U⇔U(:,1)

D =

15.0297	0	0	0	← $\sqrt{\lambda_3}$ =15.0297=D(1,1)
0	8.5537	0	0	$\sqrt{\lambda_2}$ =8.5537=D(2,2)
0	0	3.3079	0	$\sqrt{\lambda_1}$ =3.3079=D(3,3)

V =

-0.5810	0.0445	-0.2337	-0.7783	← v_1 is transpose of the third column⇔V(:,3)'
-0.7183	-0.4438	-0.0688	0.5314	v_2 is transpose of the second column⇔V(:,2)'
-0.1658	-0.0872	0.9672	-0.1717	v_3 is transpose of the first column⇔V(:,1)'
-0.3450	0.8908	0.0721	0.2869	fourth column corresponding to 0 is not used

The eigenvalues are unique but not the eigenvectors so you may see the eigenvectors with a multiplication of ñ1. The first diagonal element D(1,1) corresponds to the first columns of U and V, and so does the others. Our computed first eigenimage is obtained by $\sqrt{\lambda_1}u_1v_1$ whose code is D(3,3)*U(:,3)*V(:,3)' and the return is as follows:

```
>>I1=D(3,3)*U(:,3)*V(:,3)' ↵   ← The first eigenimage of f[m,n] is assigned to I1 or I1⇔ √λ₁u₁v₁
```

I1 =

```
        0.0829   0.0244   -0.3433   -0.0256
        0.6117   0.1801   -2.5314   -0.1887
       -0.4654  -0.1370    1.9261    0.1435
```

Similarly the other two eigenimages can be computed by the commands I2=D(2,2)*U(:,2)*V(:,2)' and I3=D(1,1)*U(:,1)*V(:,1)' respectively. We intend to see whether these eigenimages sum to retrieve $f[m,n]$ as follows:

```
>>I=I1+I2+I3 ↵   ← The sum of all eigenimages is assigned to the workspace variable I
```

I =

```
        4.0000   1.0000   -0.0000   9.0000
```

5.0000　7.0000　-1.0000　-0.0000　　　← Exactly the given modular image $f[m,n]$
6.0000　9.0000　4.0000　2.0000

Finding the eigenimage one at a time for three times can easily be implemented through a for-loop (subsection 10.3.3) whose code is for k=1:3 D(k,k)*U(:,k)*V(:,k)'; end. For the summation of the component eigenimages, the programming artifice is needed. Initially before the for-loop we assign 0 to matrix I. Each time we get one eigenimage handled by the for-loop counter and adds that to the I successively until all three or the last index of the for-loop is finished. However the retrieval of the $f[m,n]$ using for-loop takes place as follows:

>>I=0; ↵
>>for k=1:3 I=I+D(k,k)*U(:,k)*V(:,k)'; end ↵
>>I ↵　　　　　　　　　　　　　　　← after calling you should see the retrieved $f[m,n]$

⊟⊟ What is the implication of the theory in a practical image?

So long we discussed the theory behind the eigenimage and its MATLAB style of implementation. A natural query is what the implication of the eigenimage is. In the last prototype example, each eigenimage is having matrix size 3×4 means 12 elements but it is constructed from the outer product of the column and row matrices whose sizes are 3 and 4 respectively. The seven elements of coarse require less computer memory space than 12 elements. For image recognition purpose, these eigenvalues and column-row eigenvectors are used as the matching criteria for different images.

Now we intend to see some eigenimage of the gray version man.jpg of section 2.3 (figure 6.1(a)). By making the image available in the working directory, we conduct the following:

>>f=imread('man.jpg'); ↵　　　　← Reading the image and put to f, f is a 3D array and RGB image
>>f=rgb2gray(f); ↵　　　← Turning the RGB image f to gray image f in [0,255] (workspace browser)
>>f=double(f); ↵　　　　← Turning the data class to double for computation reason and assigned to f
>>[U D V]=svd(f); ↵　　　← Applying the singular value decomposition on the image f

From workspace browser, the theory-discussed variables are f= $f[m,n]$, M =361, N =253, the size of $g_1[m,n]$ = 361×361, and the size of $g_2[m,n]$ =253×253. Therefore we must have 253 eigenvalues, 253 sets of column-row eigenvectors, and 253 eigenimages. For instance let us see the appearance of the second eigenimage as follows:

>>I2=D(2,2)*U(:,2)*V(:,2)'; ↵　　← I2 holds the second eigenimage of the gray man.jpg
>>imshow(mat2gray(I2)) ↵　　　← Displaying I2 as an intensity image but first mapping in [0,1]

Figure 9.9(a) shows the second eigenimage of the gray man.jpg. Out of 253 eigenimages, let us discard the 46-th through 253-rd ones and construct the man.jpg from the first 45 eigenimages as follows:

>>I=0; for k=1:45 I=I+D(k,k)*U(:,k)*V(:,k)'; end ↵ ← I holds the approximated image
>>imshow(mat2gray(I)) ↵　← Displaying the I as an intensity image but first mapping in [0,1]

Figure 9.9(b) is the result from the last line execution, which is visually acceptable compared to the original one in the figure 6.1(a).

9.12 Encoding a digital image

A softcopy digital image file size is dependent on the pixel numbers and color levels necessary to represent it. Let us say the modular gray image $f[m,n]$ has the representation $\begin{bmatrix} 1 & 2 & 255 & 2 \\ 1 & 3 & 254 & 3 \\ 2 & 3 & 255 & 1 \end{bmatrix}$ in [0,255]. In order to represent these 256 levels, we need 8 bits (because 2^8=256). Concerning the modular image, there are only five levels out of the 256 levels (which are 1, 2, 3, 254, and 255). The next power of 2 for the number five is 3 hence 3 bits are enough to represent the modular $f[m,n]$. The rest five bits out of eight are redundant. If we can code these five gray levels with suitable scheme, we remove the redundancy without losing any image information. This redundancy removal idea is termed as the image encoding. According to the information theory, image encoding is termed as the source coding. Image gray levels are assumed to be the source symbol. There are many image encoding schemes available whose reference can be [20], [79], and [80]. However briefly we introduce three image encoding schemes namely run length encoding, natural encoding, and Huffman encoding in the following.

♦ ♦ Run length encoding

The basic procedure in the run length encoding is to scan the digital image gray levels along the horizontal or vertical direction of the image and map the row or column gray levels to the j-th gray level g_j and the j-th run length l_j respectively. Along a particular scan line, pixels having the same gray level is the g_j and the number of repetitions of g_j in the line segment is the l_j. As usual we proceed with the modular image

$$f[m,n] = \begin{bmatrix} 1 & 2 & 2 & 2 \\ 3 & 3 & 254 & 254 \\ 1 & 1 & 3 & 3 \end{bmatrix}$$ in [0,255]. In the first row of $f[m,n]$,

the gray levels 1 and 2 occur 1 and 3 times respectively hence $\begin{Bmatrix} g_1 = 1 \\ l_1 = 1 \end{Bmatrix}$ and $\begin{Bmatrix} g_2 = 2 \\ l_2 = 3 \end{Bmatrix}$. Again in the second row, the gray levels 3 and 254 each appear two times so the coding for the second row is $\begin{Bmatrix} g_1 = 3 \\ l_1 = 2 \end{Bmatrix}$ and $\begin{Bmatrix} g_2 = 254 \\ l_2 = 2 \end{Bmatrix}$ similarly the third row coding is $\begin{Bmatrix} g_1 = 1 \\ l_1 = 2 \end{Bmatrix}$ and $\begin{Bmatrix} g_2 = 3 \\ l_2 = 2 \end{Bmatrix}$. For the sake of programming, we place g_j and l_j as the row of another matrix therefore for the whole $f[m,n]$ we are

supposed to have $\overset{g_j \quad l_j}{\begin{bmatrix} 1 & 1 \\ 2 & 3 \end{bmatrix}}$, $\overset{g_j \quad l_j}{\begin{bmatrix} 3 & 2 \\ 254 & 2 \end{bmatrix}}$, and $\overset{g_j \quad l_j}{\begin{bmatrix} 1 & 2 \\ 3 & 2 \end{bmatrix}}$ for the first,

second, and third rows respectively. That is our expectation from MATLAB implementation.

To the context of MATLAB, the storing of the run length codes can best happen using the cell array whose discussion is seen in subsection 10.12.3. Our written function (figure 9.9(c)) rle can return the run length codes as a rectangular matrix by taking the row matrix of the digital image as the input. Type the codes of the figure 9.9(c) in the M-file editor (section 1.3) and save the file by the name rle in your working path of MATLAB. Let us verify the run length codes of the first row for the modular image as follows:

```
function code=rle(row)
%Input must be a row matrix
row=[row NaN];
code=[];
n=1;
while n~=length(row)
    if row(n)~=row(n+1)
        code=[code;[row(n) 1]];
    else
        k=n;
        cc=0;
        while ~(row(n)~=row(k))
            k=k+1;
            cc=cc+1;
            if k==length(row)
                break;
            end
        end
        code=[code;[row(n) cc]];
        n=k-1;
    end
    n=n+1;
end
```

Figure 9.9(c) *Function rle for the run length encoding of a row matrix*

>>row1=[1 2 2 2]; ↵   ← Assigning the first row of $f[m,n]$ to the workspace variable row1
>>C=rle(row1) ↵   ← Calling the function rle and assigning the return to the variable C

C =
         1   1   ← Exactly the code of the first row of $f[m,n]$
         2   3

Now we pick up every row of $f[m,n]$, find its code C, and assign the C to one cell (the order is maintained as the first row of $f[m,n]$ in the first cell of **code**, the second row is in the second cell of **code**, and so on) of the cell array **code** as follows:

>>f=[1 2 2 2;3 3 254 254;1 1 3 3]; ↵   ← Assigning the $f[m,n]$ to the workspace variable f
>>[M,N]=size(f); ↵   ← Finding the row and column sizes M and N of f respectively
>>for m=1:M row=f(m,:); C=rle(row); code{m,1}=C; end ↵   ← C holds the code of each row
>>code ↵   ← Calling the variable
code =
         [2x2 double]   ← Corresponds to the first row codes
         [2x2 double]   ← Corresponds to the second row codes
         [2x2 double]   ← Corresponds to the third row codes
>>code{3,1}(:,:) ↵   ← To view the third row run length codes

ans =
         1   2
         3   2

In above implementation, the for-loop counter index m selects the mth row from the image matrix f using the command f(m,:). The mth row is assigned to the workspace variable row. The chosen cell array is a column one that is why the second input index of the cell array **code** is 1. Above execution also includes how the third row run length codes can be reached from the cell array **code**.

The run length coding applied to a practical image:

From the implemented modular image, we intend to extend the implementation for the gray version man.jpg of subsection 6.1.1. Assuming the image in the working directory, we conduct the following:

>>f=imread('man.jpg'); ↵ ← Reading and assigning the image to f, f is a 3D array (subsection 10.12.1)
>>f=rgb2gray(f); ↵ ← Turning the RGB image f to the gray image f, where f in [0,255]
>>f=double(f); ↵ ← Turning the data class to double and assigned to f for the computation reason, f⇔theory-discussed $f[m,n]$

>>[M,N]=size(f); ↵ ← Finding the row and column sizes M and N of f respectively
>>for m=1:M row=f(m,:); C=rle(row); code{m,1}=C; end ↵

The workspace variable **code** now holds the run length codes for the whole image. Referring to the workspace browser, the size of the image is 361×253. Just to see the code of last row in the image, we perform the following:

>>code{361,1}(:,:) ↵ ← Calling the last line pixelsí code from the cell array **code**

ans =

234	1
233	1	← For space reason, only the first two are shown out of 86 codes (browser)

⋮

↑ ↑

g_j l_j ← The theory-discussed symbology

♦ ♦ Natural code

The natural code means the binary code of the image gray levels. If we say there are 256 gray levels in the image $f[m,n]$ in [0,255], the number of binary digits required is $\log_2 256 = 8$. We know that the number 5 has the binary representation 101. MATLAB function **dec2bin** (abbreviation of the <u>dec</u>imal to (2) <u>bin</u>ary) converts an integer to its equivalent binary number as a string or character array as follows:

>>dec2bin(5) ↵   >>dec2bin(5,8) ↵

ans =   ans =

101   00000101

If we intend to convert the integer number out of 8 bits, five zeroes are placed before the number equivalent of 5 and for which the second input argument of the function is 8. Its implementation is also shown above on the right. For a set of numbers for example R=[5 7], the **dec2bin** returns a rectangular character matrix in which the first and second rows are the binary equivalents 101 and 111 respectively. The reverse conversion that is binary-to-decimal takes place using the **bin2dec** (abbreviation of the <u>bin</u>ary to (2) <u>dec</u>imal). Just to verify the binary 101, we perform the following:

>>bin2dec('101') ↵

ans =
          5

For a set of numbers, the binary equivalent can be placed as row by row in a rectangular matrix as follows:

>>bin2dec(num2str([101;111])) ↵

ans =
          5
          7

For a set of binary numbers like the codes of 5 and 7, the function **num2str** (abbreviation of the <u>num</u>ber to (2) <u>str</u>ing) is required because the data entering takes place as decimal.

```
function code=huff(p)
if sum(p)~=1
    disp('Please check the probability vector')
    break;
end
p=flipud(sort(p));
code=[];
for k=1:length(p)
    code=[code;blanks(length(p)-1)];
end
h=0;
for k=length(p):-1:2
    h=h+1;
    code(k,h)='1';
    code(k-1,h)='0';
end
for k=1:length(p)-2
    pind{k}=1:k;
end
pind=fliplr(pind);
q=p;
for k=1:length(q)-1
    C{k}=q;
    m=length(q);
    q(m-1)=q(m-1)+q(m);
    q=q(1:m-1);
    q=flipud(sort(q));
end
for k=length(pind):-1:1
    m=pind{k};
    prev=C{k};
    aft=C{k+1};
    for n=1:length(m)
        r=find(aft==prev(n));
        code(n,k)=code(r(end),k+1);
    end
end
code=flipud(code);
```

Figure 9.9(d) *Function file for the Huffman coding*

✦ ✦ Huffman encoding

The Huffman coding starts with the probability of the gray levels of a digital image. The sum of all probabilities of the gray levels in an image is 1. To start the coding, we sort the probabilities in descending order and assign 1 to the last element and 0 to the element before the last element or vice versa. The last two probabilities are added and the new probability set is descendingly sorted again. This operation is continued until we end up with two probabilities and the assignment takes place in all intermediate probability vectors. For any unassigned probability in the vector, we check where it is occurring in the next set and bring the code for it in the current position. That is from the last sorted two, we go back to the sorted three and from the last sorted three to the last four and so on until we reach to the original probability vector we started with. The appearance of equal probability does not allow us to have the unique codes but the codes are optimum.

Let us consider the modular image matrix $f[m,n] = \begin{bmatrix} 1 & 2 & 255 & 2 \\ 1 & 3 & 254 & 3 \\ 2 & 3 & 255 & 1 \end{bmatrix}$ which holds five gray levels and

whose probabilities are $\begin{Bmatrix} gray & its \\ level & probability \\ 1 & 0.25 \\ 2 & 0.25 \\ 3 & 0.25 \\ 254 & 0.0833 \\ 255 & 0.1667 \end{Bmatrix}$ (subsection 6.1.5). Following the procedure of the Huffman code,

we obtain one code set (because of the nonuniqueness) as $\begin{Bmatrix} gray & its\ Huffman \\ level & code \\ 1 & 1 \\ 2 & 01 \\ 3 & 101 \\ 254 & 1101 \\ 255 & 1110 \end{Bmatrix}$. Our written function file huff

can take the probability vector (must be a column one) as its input argument and returns the Huffman codes as a character array. Type the statements of the figure 9.9(d) in the M-file editor (section 1.3), save the file by the name huff in the working directory, and execute the following:

>>p=[.25 .25 .25 .0833 .1667]'; ↵ ← Assigning the probability vector to p as a column vector
>>code=huff(p) ↵   ← Calling the function file huff and assigning the code to code

```
code =
      1
      01
      101
      1101
      1110
```

From the workspace browser, the size of the character array code is 5×4. In order to pick up the third one, we exercise the command code(3,:) but the size of the picked up is 1×4 indicating one blank character on the right.

If we intend to find the probability vector using MATLAB, the command tabulate of subsection 6.1.5 is exercised as follows:

>>f=[1 2 255 2;1 3 254 3;2 3 255 1]; ↵ ← Assigning the modular image $f[m,n]$ to f
>>T=tabulate(1+f(:)); ↵   ← T holds the frequency and probability percentage table
>>[M,N]=size(T); ↵   ← Knowing the matrix size M×N of the T

From the subsection 6.1.5, the second column of T holds the frequency of the gray levels in $f[m,n]$. We check every frequency in the second column using a for-loop and if it is zero, that is unnecessary for code finding. Those unnecessary 0 frequency indexes are accumulated (subsection 10.3.3) in the workspace variable ind as follows:

>>ind=[ ]; for k=1:M if T(k,2)==0,ind=[ind;k];end, end ↵

We remove those unwanted rows from T as follows:

>>T(ind,:)=[ ] ↵

```
T =
      2.0000    3.0000    25.0000      ← For gray level 1
      3.0000    3.0000    25.0000      ← For gray level 2
      4.0000    3.0000    25.0000      ← For gray level 3
```

255.0000	1.0000	8.3333	← For gray level 254
256.0000	2.0000	16.6667	← For gray level 255
↑	↑	↑	
gray level	frequency	probability percentage	

All we need is the third column of T but after division by 100 to make the sum of probability as 1 as follows:

>>p=T(:,3)/100; ↵   ← p holds the probability vector we found earlier

Now the command huff(p) can be executed to see the Huffman codes.

The Huffman coding applied to a practical image:

Now we intend to find the Huffman codes for the gray version dip.bmp image of subsection 6.1.2. The gray levels we consider are in [0,255]. Placing the image in the working directory, we conduct the following:

>>[f,Mp]=imread('dip.bmp'); ↵ ← Reading the indexed image, f is intensity matrix and Mp is colormap
>>f=ind2gray(f,Mp); ↵ ← Turning the indexed image to gray image and assigned to f, where f in [0,1]
>>f=im2uint8(f); ↵   ← Turning the image data in [0,1] to data in [0,255] and assigned to f
>>f=double(f); ↵   ← Turning the image data to double data class for computation reason
>>T=tabulate(1+f(:)); ↵ ← Finding the frequency table T of the gray levels
>>[M,N]=size(T); ↵   ← Knowing the matrix size M×N of the T
>>ind=[ ]; for k=1:M if T(k,2)==0,ind=[ind;k];end, end ↵ ← Index finding of unwanted 0 frequency
gray levels
>>T(ind,:)=[ ]; ↵   ← Removal of the unwanted 0 frequency gray levels from the T
>>p=T(:,3)/100; ↵   ← p holds the probability vector needed for the Huffman code
>>code=huff(p) ↵   ← Calling the function file huff and assigning the codes of dip.bmp to code

code =

1
01
001
⋮

If the gray levels corresponding to these codes are required, the command T(:,1)-1 can return those as a column matrix. Workspace browser displays that the sizes of T and code are 124×3 and 124×123 respectively indicating the presence of 124 gray levels out of 256.

Left eye of man.jpg is to be taken out of the image

Figure 9.10(a) *User requirement for the region based processing of digital image man.jpg*

Figure 9.10(b) *The binary image* P *for left eyeglass frame region processing*

Figure 9.10(c) *The figure 9.10(a) taking the left eyeglass frame region off*

9.13 Image region based processing

Given a digital image, we may select a polygonal zone within the image and manipulate the polygonal zone from user specifications. Considering the image man.jpg of section 2.3, the left eye with glass is to be taken out from the image (shown in the figure 9.10(a)) ñ this is one problem statement regarding the region based image processing. Making the image available in the working directory, we carry out the following:

```
>>f=imread('man.jpg'); ↵          ← Reading the image, where f is a 3D array
>>imshow(f) ↵                     ← Displaying the image
```

We use the mouse pointer to select the eyeglass frame of the image in figure 9.10(a) as a polygon. In order to do so, we execute the following:

```
>>P=roipoly; ↵
```

The function roipoly (abbreviation of the <u>r</u>egion <u>o</u>f <u>i</u>nterest as a <u>polygon</u>) enables the mouse pointer. Move on to the image area of the figure window and find the cross hair + active on it. We scan the left eyeglass frame of figure 9.10(a) using the cross of the crosshair. Start by bringing the cross at any point on the eyeglass frame, click the leftbutton of the mouse, move to the adjacent point on the eyeglass frame, click the leftbutton of the mouse, again move to the next point, and so finish the scanning on the whole eyeglass frame. At the end we are supposed to return to the point where we started at and rightclick the mouse at the end. In doing so, we generated a binary image of the same pixel size as that of the original image but the zones inside and outside the left eyeglass frame are white (means gray level 1) and black (means gray level 0) respectively. Obviously so generated image is stored in the workspace variable P. We can view the image as shown in the figure 9.10(b) using the following:

```
>>figure,imshow(P) ↵
```

Referring to the workspace browser, the sizes of f and P are identical which is 361×253 and the data class of P is logical. If we take complement (section 8.2) image of the P using ~P, the white region turns to black and vice versa. Multiplication by 1 does not change the gray level of an image but does by the 0. This fact is utilized here to take the eye with the glass frame off from the image. The pixel by pixel multiplication of f and P best happens by the scalar multiplication (section 10.2). Another problem is there, we can not multiply a three dimensional array f (because it is a true color image) by a two dimensional array P whence the scalar multiplication happens in each color image. We need to pick them up from the workspace f as follows:

```
>>r=f(:,:,1); ↵                   ← Picking up the red image from f and assigned to r
>>g=f(:,:,2); ↵                   ← Picking up the green image from f and assigned to g
>>b=f(:,:,3); ↵                   ← Picking up the blue image from f and assigned to b
```

Now we perform the scalar multiplication of the inverted P with each of the color component images as follows but keeping in mind that the all computation happens for the double class data:

```
>>r_new=double(~P).*double(r); ↵  ← Scalar multiplication of inverted P and r is assigned to r_new
>>g_new=double(~P).*double(g); ↵  ← Scalar multiplication of inverted P and g is assigned to g_new
>>b_new=double(~P).*double(b); ↵  ← Scalar multiplication of inverted P and b is assigned to b_new
```

The new RGB image which must be a three dimensional array (subsection 10.12.1) is formed as follows:

```
>>new_f(:,:,1)=r_new; ↵  ← Assigning the red component r_new to the first page of new_f
>>new_f(:,:,2)=g_new; ↵  ← Assigning the green component g_new to the second page of new_f
>>new_f(:,:,3)=b_new; ↵  ← Assigning the blue component b_new to the third page of new_f
```

We named the newly formed RGB image as new_f. Workspace browser says that the data class of the f is unsigned 8-bit integer which is in [0,255]. Multiplying by 0 or 1 still keeps the data in [0,255] but as double format so we turn the double class data of new_f to unsigned 8-bit using uint8(new_f) therefore the expected image like the figure 9.10(c) is obtained by the following:

```
>>figure,imshow(uint8(new_f)) ↵
```

You find both images in color form in MATLAB figure window but the text display is in the black and white form. We present two more examples for the region based processing of the same image.

Figure 9.10(d) *The binary image P for the example 1*

Figure 9.10(e) *The foreground of gray version man.jpg*

Figure 9.10(f) *The background of gray version man.jpg*

♦♦ Example 1

In image segmentation problems, we separate the image foreground from the background. The method we just illustrated can easily be applied to the separation. Now the problem statement is to separate the foreground from the background in the gray version man.jpg for which the following is exercised:

```
>>f=imread('man.jpg');  ↵    ← Reading the image, where f is a 3D array
>>f=rgb2gray(f);  ↵          ← Turning the RGB image f to gray image and assigned to f again
>>imshow(f)  ↵               ← Displaying the gray image f
>>P=roipoly;  ↵              ← Giving control to the mouse pointer for tracing the foreground
```

Now we trace the image foreground boundary as we did around the eyeglass frame of the beginning problem. Figure 9.10(d) shows the binary image P due to the tracing on execution of figure,imshow(P). The scalar multiplications of P and inverted P with the f provides the foreground and background of the gray version man.jpg respectively, following is the implementation.

```
>>F=double(P).*double(f);  ↵     ← F holds the scalar multiplication of P and f
>>B=double(~P).*double(f);  ↵    ← B holds the scalar multiplication of inverted P and f
>>figure,imshow(uint8(F))  ↵     ← Displays the foreground F as shown in the figure 9.10(e)
>>figure,imshow(uint8(B))  ↵     ← Displays the background B as shown in the figure 9.10(f)
```

♦♦ Example 2

Apart from the mouse pointer selection, user defined polygonal area selection option is also associated in the function roipoly. In this example we intend to turn the right portion of the coat to black in the gray version man.jpg. The pixval function of the subsection 6.1.3 provides the pixel coordinates on the image area. From the example 1, the variable f is holding the gray version man.jpg image. Execute first figure,imshow(f) and then pixval at the command prompt. Now moving the crosshair of the mouse on the image area, we find the approximate quadrilateral coordinates for the right part of the coat are (131,361), (180,197), (253,226), and (253,361). Let us perform the following:

```
>>m=[131 180 253 253];  ↵    ← Assigning all m coordinates as
                               row matrix to the variable m
>>n=[361 197 226 361];  ↵    ← Assigning all n coordinates as
                               row matrix to the variable n
>>P=roipoly(f,m,n);  ↵       ← Finding the binary image matrix
                               P from the entered m and n
```

Figure 9.10(g) The right coat part of man.jpg is turned to black

Unlike previous example, the input arguments of the function roipoly are the digital image matrix, all *m* coordinates as row matrix, and all *n* coordinates as row matrix respectively. Having found the binary P, the expected image matrix new_f is obtained as follows:

```
>>new_f=double(~P).*double(f);  ↵   ← new_f holds the scalar multiplication of inverted P and f
>>figure,imshow(uint8(new_f))  ↵    ← Displays the figure 9.10(g) with aforementioned change
```

With the implemented function, the reader can explore the functions roifill and roifilt2 which work in a similar fashion for the region based processing (execute help roifill or help roifilt2).

9.14 Extraction of color information and its manipulation

Color information of a color image is mainly associated with the indexed and the RGB image types whose discussions are presented in sections 2.4 and 2.8. Given a color digital image, we may need to extract its various color information. In subsection 6.1.6, we addressed the histogram finding of the RGB image. The problem with the RGB image representation is its pixel color values are fixed. It is not feasible to manipulate every pixel color value while there are thousands in an image. The indexed type possesses a colormap which can be manipulated in accordance with the user requirement.

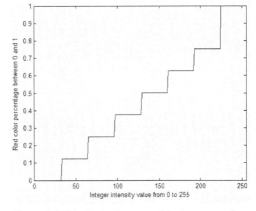

Figure 9.11(a) Red colormap of the image test.bmp

186

Now the problem statement is to find the color information of the test.bmp of section 2.3. The function imfinfo of subsection 6.1.1 tells us that the image is an indexed one indicating the availability of intensity and colormap matrices. Let us obtain them through the image reader but first making the image available in the working directory as follows:

>>[f,Mp]=imread('test.bmp'); ↵

The workspace variables f and Mp hold the intensity and colormap matrices respectively. The workspace browser says the data class of f is unsigned 8-bit integer hence the intensity values are in [0,255]. The Mp is of double class and its obvious size is 256×3. The first, second, and third columns of Mp are red, green, and blue component maps respectively each for the 256 levels. If we wish to extract the red colormap only, we pick up the first column of Mp as follows:

>>r_map=Mp(:,1); ↵ ← Picking up the first column of Mp and assigned to the variable r_map

In order to see the red colormap plot, we execute the following:

>>plot(r_map) ↵

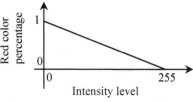

Figure 9.11(a) depicts the red colormap of the image test.bmp. From the figure window, we added the x and y labels by going through the Insert menu and set the x axis limits to [0,255] by going through the Edit menu. The red color values lie in between 0 and 1 in terms of the percentage. The other two colormaps are picked up by the commands g_map=Mp(:,2); and b_map=Mp(:,3); for green and blue respectively. In a similar fashion, the two can also be graphed.

Figure 9.11(b) *User defined red colormap characteristics*

The reader might say I want to design my own colormap. This example illustrates that. If you execute imshow('test.bmp'), you see the color image. Figure 9.11(a) says that the red colormap is a staircase one. Why do not we turn it to the one in the figure 9.11(b)? Let us not forget that the color value of the colormap must be between 0 and 1 and for 256 levels. One way of forming the colormap is to generate a vector of integers from 255 to 0 with decrement 1 and divide each element in the vector by 255 to turn the vector in [0,1] as follows:

>>r_new=[255:-1:0]'/255; ↵ ← The generated column vector is assigned to workspace variable r_new

We do not wish to change the other two colormaps (for green and blue). The r_new must be column one as far as the size of three colormaps is concern. Now we need to devise the new colormap with the modification as follows:

>>Mp(:,1)=r_new; ↵

We replaced the first column of Mp by the new red colormap r_new using above command. The image is seen with the modified colormap by the following:

>>figure,imshow(f,Mp) ↵

Comparing the two images in the MATLAB figure window, you must perceive some changes in the color display for example white background turns to cyan (table 2.D), red turns to black, and so on. The reader can design any colormap for any of the three components. Let us see the following examples regarding the colormap manipulation.

✦ ✦ Example 1

Modify only the green colormap of the test.bmp according to the equation $g[n] = \cos\frac{\pi n}{512}$ where n is the intensity level and vary integerwise from 0 to 255. Since we modified the red component previously, the image needs to be read again:

>>[f,Mp]=imread('test.bmp'); ↵

Now we generate the column vector for the n as [0:255]' and the functional calculation for the $g[n]$ takes place as follows:

>>n=[0:255]'; g=cos(pi*n/512); ↵

The workspace variable g holds the new green colormap. The green colormap in the Mp occupies the third column hence we execute the replacement of only the green colormap as follows:

>>Mp(:,3)=g; ↵

The image with the modified colormap can be viewed using figure,imshow(f,Mp) in which the background appears as yellow.

✦ ✦ Example 2

Starting with an indexed or RGB image, we can display the image in another color space like hue-saturation-value or intensity space (section 2.8), abbreviatedly known as HSV. We wish to display the test.bmp indexed image in the HSV space. There is no direct conversion function from the indexed type to HSV space. But through the intermediacy of RGB space, the conversion is easily achieveable:

```
>>[f,Mp]=imread('test.bmp'); ↵
>>R=ind2rgb(f,Mp); ↵
>>H=rgb2hsv(R); ↵
```

In the second line of above implementation we turned the indexed image from the intensity (f) and colormap (Mp) matrices to RGB image and assigned that to the workspace variable R. Workspace browser says that the R is a three dimensional array indicating a true color image (every pixel has its own color). In the last line we turned the image R from RGB space to HSV space and assigned that to the workspace H. The H is also a three dimensional array whose image content is seen by executing figure,imshow(H). The background of test.bmp changes from white to blue due to color space conversion. Note that data class of H or R is double in [0,1] (can be verified using the datastats of subsection 6.1.4). If you want to store them as unsigned 8-bit integer, im2uint8 can be exercised.

✦ ✦ Example 3

As another color space, we choose the NTSC format (section 2.8). We intend to see the test.bmp image in this color space therefore the implementation we conduct is the following:

```
>>[f,Mp]=imread('test.bmp'); ↵
>>R=ind2rgb(f,Mp); ↵
>>H=rgb2ntsc(R); ↵
```

There is also no direct conversion function for the indexed type to the NTSC space that is why we turned the indexed image in the RGB one (which is R) in the second line. The rgb2ntsc turned the RGB image R to the NTSC image H in the last line. The NTSC image H is a three dimensional array and double class as well. To be acceptable for display by the imshow, the data range for each page of the three dimensional array must be in [0,1] but unfortunately the data range is not in [0,1] due to the color space conversion (use datastats(H(:)) for verification). Any rectangular matrix data is turned to [0,1] using mat2gray but it happens page by page basis in the 3D H. We carry out the following in order to do so:

```
>>H(:,:,1)=mat2gray(H(:,:,1)); ↵ ← Turning the 1st page of H in [0,1] and again assigned to the 1st page
>>H(:,:,2)=mat2gray(H(:,:,2)); ↵ ← Turning the 2nd page of H in [0,1] and again assigned to the 2nd page
>>H(:,:,3)=mat2gray(H(:,:,3)); ↵ ← Turning the 3rd page of H in [0,1] and again assigned to the 3rd page
>>imshow(H) ↵                    ← Displays the image H in the NTSC color space
```

One can use the command colorbar to view the color scale in the image.

✦ ✦ Example 4

Find the hue-saturation-intensity characteristic for the HSV image of the example 2. The characteristic is basically the histogram for each of the three components whose elaborate discussion is seen in subsections 6.1.5 and 6.1.6. The histogram is best found in discrete gray level form not in fractional form as far as the digital image is concern. From the example 2, the workspace variable H is holding the HSV image whose data class is double. The three pages of the three dimensional array H are the hue, saturation, and color value respectively. We turn each of them to unsigned 8-bit integer (assuming 256 levels) from [0,1] using im2uint8 as follows:

```
>>H=im2uint8(H); ↵
```

Let us say we are interested to view the saturation characteristics (related to second page of H). In order to do so:

```
>>S=H(:,:,2); ↵     ← S holds the saturation page of the array H
```

Now the reader can execute the imhist or our mentioned method to find the histogram of the saturation page for the image test.bmp, which is the saturation characteristic of digital image as well.

9.15 Links for further topics

Online assistance of MATLAB guides the reader to get into more functions that are accessible from the command prompt. Few links are provided in the following so that one can reach to more image processing implementations:

>>dctdemo ↵	Displays a dialog window in which the reader can view how discrete cosine transform coefficients can compress a digital image. Slider bar allows the reader to select the transform coefficients. This is the idea behind the lossy compression of a digital image.
>>edgedemo ↵	Displays a dialog window in which the reader can view the effect of the edge detection for various images using different methods. Both the automatic and manual threshold selection options are in the window.
>>qtdemo ↵	Considering blocks, quadtree decomposition subdivides an image region that contain similar pixels. The decomposition can be useful for the image compression. The decomposition is mainly conducted on the range of

	thresholds. Displayed window provides the option for selecting thresholds and for viewing the quadtree decomposition for a number of images.
>>firdemo ↵	Displays a dialog window in which the reader can view the two dimensional digital filtering effect on various images. Different design method and different filter type options are there to see filter characteristics as well as the filtered images.
>>roidemo ↵	Demonstrates region of interest processing for the digital images. The reader can select any polygonal region in a digital image using the mouse pointer and can perform image processing operation only to the selected polygon. A lot of image processing techniques are there such as histogram equalization, contrast manipulation, filtering, etc.
>>imadjdemo ↵	Demonstrates the intensity characteristics such as contrast, brightness, gamma correction, etc on various images. Histograms before and after the image intensity adjustment as well as the input-output image characteristics are displayed.
>>landsatdemo ↵	Demonstrates the satellite imagery change subject to different color bands taken over some cities and rivers from the satellite.
>>nrfiltdemo ↵	Demonstrates the noise addition and its removal on various images. Filtering type and its mask size selection options are also there.

Latter in this chapter we addressed the region based processing of images. An image region possesses a lot of properties such as convex hull, Euler number, centroid, area, Ö etc. The MATLAB function **regionprops** gives the provision for measurement of these properties. In order to learn more about the function, execute the following:

>>help regionprops ↵

MATLAB is also equipped with the extended examples. But most of them is for the advanced users not for the beginners although the term advanced or beginner is relative. When we execute **help images** at the command prompt, we find a summary of the image processing toolbox functions. In the last paragraph you find the functional names of the extended examples. For instance, a mapping like the warping of the section 9.9 is the conformal mapping which has the help file function name **ipexconformal**. Execution of **ipexconformal** at the command prompt opens a navigatory window. Thus other functions can be explored.

However we close the chapter with the discussion of the links for the advanced topics.

Programming Issues

Chapter 10

In most former chapters, concentrations have been given to the MATLAB built-in image processing functions. Many practical image processing applications require that an M-file be written alongside the built-in functions. The M-file contents are basically the language codes of MATLAB. This chapter highlights the commonly used syntaxes of the M-file programming and some built-in functions relevant to the image processing applications whose captions are the following:

- ❖ ❖ M-file and MATLAB coding of mathematical functions
- ❖ ❖ Control statements of the M-file for the source code writing such as operators, for-loops, Ö etc
- ❖ ❖ User-defined matrix generation, matrix coloning, and matrix manipulation to the context of the digital image processing
- ❖ ❖ Pixel based computations such as maximum, sorting, and summing of the image elements
- ❖ ❖ Finding the pixel positions in an image subject to logical conditions
- ❖ ❖ Repetitive and reshaped matrices generation and vectorization of the for-loops
- ❖ ❖ Three momentous data arrangement namely three dimensional, structure, and cell arrays
- ❖ ❖ Writing image matrix data to softcopy and softcopy conversion from one form to other
- ❖ ❖ Function file generation subject to one/multiple inputs and one/multiple outputs

10.1 What is an M-file?

An M-file is a script or text file that contains a sequence of executable MATLAB statements. If the MATLAB commands are just two or three lines, they can be executed in the command window. But if we have many executable commands, a file is required where we place all commands sequentially so that any modification or editing can be performed according to the user's convenience. Thus the M-files are written externally by the users. Almost all image processing toolbox functions are written in an M-file. The next consequential query is how one can write and execute an M-file whose answer is provided in chapter 1.

10.2 MATLAB coding of functions

MATLAB codes a function or expression in terms of a string, which is the set of characters placed consecutively. One distinguishing feature of MATLAB is that the variable itself is a matrix. The strings adopted for computation can be divided into two classes – scalar and vector. The scalar computation results the order of the output matrix same as that of the variable matrix. On the contrary, the order for the vector computation is determined in accordance with the matrix algebra rules. A list of symbolic functions and their MATLAB counterparts is presented in table 10.A. The operators for the arithmetic computations are as follows:

addition	+
subtraction	−
multiplication	*
division	/
power	^

The operation sequence of different operators in a scalar or vector string observes the following order:

enclosing braces	( )	first,
power operator	^	then,
division operator	/	next,
multiplication operator	*	after that,
addition operator	+	then, and
subtraction operator	−	finally.

The syntax of the scalar computation urges to use .*, ./, and .^ in lieu of *, /, and ^ respectively. The operators *, /, or ^ are never preceded by . for the vector computation. The vector string is the MATLAB code of any symbolic expression or function often found in mathematics. Starting from the simplest one, we present some examples for writing the long expressions in MATLAB for the scalar form and for the vector form as well.

♦ ♦ Write the MATLAB code in scalar and vector forms for the following functions

A . $\sin^3 x \cos^5 x$ B . $2 + \ln x$ C . $x^4 + 3x - 5$ D . $\dfrac{x^3 - 5}{x^2 - 7x - 7}$ E . $\sqrt{|x^3| + \sec^{-1} x}$

F . $(1 + e^{\sin x})^{x^2 + 3}$ G . $\dfrac{\cosh x + 3}{\sqrt{\dfrac{x+4}{\log_{10}(x^3 - 6)}}}$ H . $\dfrac{1}{(x-3)(x+4)(x-2)}$ I . $\dfrac{u^2 v^3 w^9}{x^4 y^7 z^6}$

J . $\dfrac{a}{x+a} + \dfrac{b}{y+b} + \dfrac{c}{z+c}$ K . $\dfrac{1}{1 + \dfrac{1}{1 + \dfrac{1}{x}}}$

In tabular form, they are coded as follows:

Example	String for scalar computation	String for vector computation
A	sin(x).^3.*cos(x).^5	sin(x)^3*cos(x)^5
B	2+log(x)	2+log(x)
C	x.^4+3*x-5	x^4+3*x-5
D	(x.^3-5)./(x.^2-7*x-7)	(x^3-5)/(x^2-7*x-7)
E	sqrt(abs(x.^3)+asec(x))	sqrt(abs(x^3)+asec(x))
F	(1+exp(sin(x))).^(x.^2+3)	(1+exp(sin(x)))^(x^2+3)
G	(cosh(x)+3)./sqrt((x+4)./log10(x.^3-6))	(cosh(x)+3)/sqrt((x+4)/log10(x^3-6))
H	1./(x-3)./(x+4)./(x-2)	1/(x-3)/(x+4)/(x-2)
I	u.^2.*v.^3.*w.^9./x.^4./y.^7./z.^6	u^2*v^3*w^9/x^4/y^7/z^6
J	a./(x+a)+b./(y+b)+c./(z+c)	a/(x+a)+b/(y+b)+c/(z+c)
K	1./(1+1./(1+1./x))	1/(1+1/(1+1/x))

We present one numerical example to quote the difference between the scalar and the vector computations. Let us say we have the matrices $A = \begin{bmatrix} 3 & 5 \\ 7 & 8 \end{bmatrix}$, $B = \begin{bmatrix} 5 & 2 & 1 \\ 0 & 1 & 7 \end{bmatrix}$, and $C = \begin{bmatrix} 3 & 2 & 9 \\ 4 & 0 & 2 \end{bmatrix}$. The scalar computation is not possible between the matrices A and B because of their unequal order nor is between the matrices A and C for the same reason. On the contrary the scalar multiplication can be conducted between B and C for having the same order and which is $B .* C = \begin{bmatrix} 15 & 4 & 9 \\ 0 & 0 & 14 \end{bmatrix}$ (element by element multiplication). Matrix algebra rule says that any matrix A

of order $M \times N$ can only be multiplied with another matrix B of order $N \times P$ so that the resulting matrix has the order $M \times P$. For the numerical example of A and B, we have $M = 2$, $N = 2$, and $P = 3$. We obtain the vector-multiplied matrix as $A \times B = \begin{bmatrix} 3 \times 5 + 5 \times 0 & 3 \times 2 + 5 \times 1 & 3 \times 1 + 5 \times 7 \\ 7 \times 5 + 8 \times 0 & 7 \times 2 + 1 \times 8 & 7 \times 1 + 8 \times 7 \end{bmatrix} = \begin{bmatrix} 15 & 11 & 38 \\ 35 & 22 & 63 \end{bmatrix}$, and which has the MATLAB code A*B not A.*B. Similar interpretation follows for the operators * and /.

Table 10.A Some mathematical functions and their MATLAB counterparts

Mathematical notation	MATLAB notation	Mathematical notation	MATLAB notation	Mathematical notation	MATLAB notation
$\sin x$	sin(x)	$\sin^{-1} x$	asin(x)	π	pi
$\cos x$	cos(x)	$\cos^{-1} x$	acos(x)	A+B	A+B
$\tan x$	tan(x)	$\tan^{-1} x$	atan(x)	A−B	A−B
$\cot x$	cot(x)	$\cot^{-1} x$	acot(x)	A×B	A*B
$\operatorname{cosec} x$	csc(x)	$\sec^{-1} x$	asec(x)	e^x	exp(x)
$\sec x$	sec(x)	$\operatorname{cosec}^{-1} x$	acsc(x)	A^B	A^B
$\sinh x$	sinh(x)	$\sinh^{-1} x$	asinh(x)	$\ln x$	log(x)
$\cosh x$	cosh(x)	$\cosh^{-1} x$	acosh(x)	$\log_{10} x$	log10(x)
$\operatorname{sec} hx$	sech(x)	$\sec h^{-1} x$	asech(x)	$\sqrt{x}$	sqrt(x)
$\operatorname{cosec} hx$	csch(x)	$\operatorname{cosec} h^{-1} x$	acsch(x)	$\sum$	sum
$\tanh x$	tanh(x)	$\tanh^{-1} x$	atanh(x)	$\prod$	prod
$\coth x$	coth(x)	$\coth^{-1} x$	acoth(x)	$\mid x \mid$	abs(x)

10.3 Control statements of M-file programming

Most of MATLAB commands utilized in various chapters invoked so far some built-in M-file functions related to the digital image processing. These built-in functions are inherently composed of program statements, logical verifications, looping operations, conditional execution of the group statementsÖ etc. There are a number of control statements in MATLAB. The control statements followed by the specific syntax observe the sequence of operations, the limit of repetitive computation, and the selection of multiple objective tasks. Understanding of these statements would divulge the insight or the hidden algorithms of the MATLAB image processing functions.

10.3.1 Comparative and logical operators

The comparative operators are mainly used for the comparison of two elements or image matrix elements. In MATLAB we have six comparative operators as presented follows:

	Mathematical Notation	MATLAB Notation
equal to	=	==
not equal to	≠	~=
greater than	>	>
greater than or equal to	≥	>=
less than	<	<
less than or equal to	≤	<=

The output of the expression pertaining to the comparative operators is logical – either true (indicated by 1) or false (indicated by 0). For example, when A=3 and B=4, the comparisons A=B, A ≠ B, A>B, A ≥ B, A<B, and A ≤ B should be false (0), true(1), false(0), false(0), true(1), and true(1) respectively. We can implement these comparative operators as follows:

MATLAB Command

```
>>A=3; ↵              >>A>B ↵                  >>A<B ↵
>>B=4; ↵
>>A==B ↵              ans =                    ans =
                             0                        1
ans =                 >>A>=B ↵                 >>A<=B ↵
```

```
                        0
        >>A~=B ↵                        ans =                        ans =
                                          0                            1
        ans =
          1
```

There are two operands A and B in above implementation. Each of the operands can be a matrix in general. In that case the logical decision takes place element by element basis on all elements in the matrix. For instance, if A=$\begin{bmatrix} 5 & 8 \\ 5 & 7 \end{bmatrix}$ and B=$\begin{bmatrix} 2 & 1 \\ -2 & 9 \end{bmatrix}$, A>B should be $\begin{bmatrix} 5>2 & 8>1 \\ 5>-2 & 7>9 \end{bmatrix} = \begin{bmatrix} 1 & 1 \\ 1 & 0 \end{bmatrix}$. Again if A happens to be a scalar (say A=4), the single scalar is compared to all elements in the B therefore A≤B should be $\begin{bmatrix} 4\leq2 & 4\leq1 \\ 4\leq-2 & 4\leq9 \end{bmatrix} = \begin{bmatrix} 0 & 0 \\ 0 & 1 \end{bmatrix}$. In a similar fashion B also operates on A however we implement them as follows:

when A and B are matrices,   **when A is scalar and B is matrix,**

```
        >>A=[5 8;5 7]; ↵                        >>A=4; ↵
        >>B=[2 1;-2 9]; ↵                       >>B=[2 1;-2 9]; ↵
        >>A>B ↵                                 >>A<=B ↵


        ans =                                   ans =
          1   1                                   0   0
          1   0                                   0   1
```

The basic logical operations performed are NOT, OR, and AND. The characters ~, |, and & of the keyboard are adopted for the logical NOT, OR, and AND respectively. In all logical outputs the 1 and 0 stand for true and false respectively. All logical operators apply to the matrices in general. Let us see some examples in the following:

For the matrix A=$\begin{bmatrix} 0 & 0 \\ 0 & 1 \end{bmatrix}$, NOT(A) operation provides $\begin{bmatrix} 1 & 1 \\ 1 & 0 \end{bmatrix}$ as follows:

```
        >>A=[0 0;0 1]; ↵
        >>~A ↵


        ans =
          1   1
          1   0
```

The logical OR and AND operations on the like positional elements of the two matrices A=$\begin{bmatrix} 1 & 1 \\ 0 & 1 \end{bmatrix}$ and B=$\begin{bmatrix} 0 & 1 \\ 1 & 1 \end{bmatrix}$

must return $\begin{bmatrix} 1 & 1 \\ 1 & 1 \end{bmatrix}$ and $\begin{bmatrix} 0 & 1 \\ 0 & 1 \end{bmatrix}$ respectively as follows:

Command for A OR B,   **for A AND B,**   **for A XOR B,**

```
        >>A=[1 1;0 1]; ↵             >>A&B ↵                 >>xor(A,B) ↵
        >>B=[0 1;1 1]; ↵
        >>A|B ↵                      ans =                   ans =
                                       0   1                   1   0
        ans =                         0   1                   1   0
          1   1
          1   1
```

If A or B is a single 1 or 0, it operates on all elements of the other. Sometimes we need to check the interval of the spatial domain of an image for instance $-6 \leq x \leq 8$. The interval is split in two parts $-6 \leq x$ and $x \leq 8$. In terms of the logical statement one can express $-6 \leq x \leq 8$ as (−6<=x)&(x<=8). There is no operator for the XOR logical operation instead the MATLAB function xor syntaxed by xor(A,B) implements the operation as indicated above.

There are two more logical functions by the name **any** and **all** found in MATLAB. Both functions in general conceive a rectangular matrix but operate on columns. If any element in the columns of the rectangular matrix is 1, the output returned by **any** is 1 otherwise 0. If all elements in the columns of the rectangular matrix are 1, the output returned by **all** is 1 otherwise 0. Let us implement that on previously mentioned A:

Command for any on the matrix A,   **for all on the matrix A,**

```
        >>any(A) ↵                              >>all(A) ↵


        ans =                                   ans =
          1   1                                   0   1   ← Both functions work on columns of A
```

If we want to perform the operation on the whole rectangular matrix A, two **any** or **all** functions are required as follows (one for the columns and the other for the resulting row):

>>any(any(A)) ↵   >>all(all(A)) ↵

ans =   ans =
             1   0   ← For the whole matrix A

There is another option. First we turn the rectangular matrix A to a column one by writing the command A(:) and then use the function **any** or **all** as follows:

>>any(A(:)) ↵   >>all(A(:)) ↵

ans =   ans =
             1   0   ← For the whole matrix A

This sort of operation becomes useful especially in the binary images in which we have only 2 levels ñ 0 and 1.

10.3.2 Suppressing any execution

Let us assign the row matrix [2 3 4 8 3 8] to A by the following:
>>A=[2 3 4 8 3 8] ↵

A =
        2   3   4   8   3   8

MATLAB displays the assignment. Now use the up arrow key from the keyboard to see the last command and type one semicolon at the end of the statement as follows:

>>A=[2 3 4 8 3 8]; ↵
>>   ← Assignment is not displayed

Any MATLAB command ending with a semicolon stops displaying the assignment or contents of the variable. If the user is sure about the command, displaying steps in the command window during execution can be suppressed by appending one semicolon at the end of each MATLAB statement for longer image matrix or other execution. It is applicable for the statements written in an M-file too.

10.3.3 For-loop structure

A for-loop performs similar operations for a specific number of times and must be started by the **for** and terminated by an **end** statements. Following the **for** there must be a counter. The counter of the for-loop can be any variable that counts integer or fractional values depending on the increment or decrement. If the MATLAB command statements between the **for** and **end** of a for-loop are few words lengthy, one can even write the whole for-loop in one line. The programming syntax and some examples on the for-loop are as follows:

♦ ♦ Program syntax

for *counter* = starting value : increment or decrement of the counter value : final value
   Executable MATLAB command(s)
end

♦ ♦ Example 1

Our problem statement is to compute $y = \cos x$ for $x = 10^0$ to 70^0 with the increment 10^0 . Let us assign the output value to some variable y, where y should be [$\cos 10^0$ $\cos 20^0$ $\cos 30^0$ $\cos 40^0$ $\cos 50^0$ $\cos 60^0$ $\cos 70^0$]=[0.9848   0.9397   0.866   0.766   0.6428   0.5   0.342]. In the programming, y(1) means the first element in the row matrix y, and so do others. The MATLAB code for the $\cos x$ is **cos(x)** where x is in radians. The for-loop counter expression should be k=1:1:7 to have a control on the position index in the matrix y. Since the computation needs 10 to 70, one can generate that by k*10 and the degree to radian conversion can take place by writing 10*k*pi/180 or k*pi/18.

Executable M–file:
```
for k=1:1:7
        y(k)=cos(k*pi/18);
end
```

Or, as a one line:
```
for k=1:1:7 y(k)=cos(k*pi/18); end
```

Steps we need:
Open the MATLAB editor (section 1.3), type the executable statements, and save the editor contents as a file (which is an M-file) by the name **test** in your working path.
Interactive sessions with the command window:
>>test ↵
>>y ↵

y =
    0.9848   0.9397   0.8660   0.7660   0.6428   0.5000   0.3420

♦ ♦ Example 2

For-loop sometimes helps us accumulate data consecutively controlled by the loop index. The reader is referred to section 10.6 more about the data accumulation. In this example we accumulate some data rowwise according to the for-loop counter index. Let us say for k =1 to 3, we intend to accumulate the k^2 side by side. At the end we should have [1 4 9] assigned to some variable f - this is our problem statement. Let us see the for-loop for the accumulation as follows (see the right shifting):

for the right shifting,   **for the left shifting,**
>>f=[ ]; for k=1:3 f=[f k^2]; end ↵   >>f=[ ]; for k=1:3 f=[k^2 f]; end ↵
>>f ↵   >>f ↵

f =   f =
    1   4   9   9   4   1

The code for k^2 is k^2. The statement f=[ ]; means that an empty matrix is assigned to f outside the loop but at the beginning. This is necessary for the initialization. An empty matrix does not have any size and completely empty, it follows the null symbol $\varnothing$ of the matrix algebra. The k variation in our problem is put as the for-loop index. Let us see how the for-loop accumulates:

When k=1	f=[f k^2];	returns	f=[[ ] 1^2];	⇒	f=1;
When k=2	f=[f k^2];	returns	f=[1 2^2];	⇒	f=[1 4];
When k=3	f=[f k^2];	returns	f=[1 4 3^2];	⇒	f=[1 4 9];

The accumulation is happening from the left to the right. A single change can provide us the shifting from the right to the left which is f=[k^2 f];. The complete code and its execution result are also shown above.

Another accumulation could be columnwise that is we wish to see the output like $\begin{bmatrix} 1 \\ 4 \\ 9 \end{bmatrix}$. We just insert the row separator of the rectangular matrix (done by the operator ;) in the command f=[f k^2]; as follows:

for the down shifting,   **for the up shifting,**
>>f=[ ]; for k=1:3 f=[f;k^2]; end ↵   >>f=[ ]; for k=1:3 f=[k^2;f]; end ↵
>>f ↵   >>f ↵

f =   f =
     1   9
     4   4
     9   1

Again the shifting can happen either from the up to down or from the down to up. Both implementations are shown above.

♦ ♦ Example 3

Many image processing problems need writing multiple for-loops. Access to every pixel in a digital image happens to practicing two for-loops. Suppose the modular digital image is $f[m,n] = \begin{bmatrix} 4 & 3 & 5 \\ 9 & 0 & 3 \end{bmatrix}$ which has the numbers of rows and columns as 2 and 3 respectively. The range selection of the for-loop counter must come from the row and column numbers. We intend to pick up every element from the image matrix f and display it in the MATLAB workspace.

Executable M–file:
```
f=[4 3 5;9 0 3];
for m=1:2
    for n=1:3
```

$$f(m,n)$$
$$\text{end}$$
$$\text{end}$$

Steps we need:

Open the MATLAB editor, type above command statements in the M-file, and save the file by the name **test**. Execute **test** from the command prompt and you see the elements assigned to the default **ans** are displayed rowwise. The first line in the command is to enter the matrix $f[m,n]$ to f. The outer for-loop gives control on the rows whereas the inner one does on the columns. If you exchange the second and the third lines, the element selection happens columnwise instead of rowwise.

What if we want to access every pixel on a practical digital image for instance intensity part of dip.bmp from subsection 6.1.2. The solution is as follows:

```
[f,Mp]=imread('dip.bmp');
[M,N]=size(f);
for m=1:M
        for n=1:N
                f(m,n);
        end
end
```

The image is read by the function **imread** and whose intensity and colormap matrices are assigned to f and Mp respectively. The function **size** has two output arguments (**M** and **N**) which assume the row and column directed pixel numbers of the image respectively.

✦ ✦ Example 4

Sometimes employing two for-loops, the image processing data is accumulated first columnwise and then rowwise. Actually row and column oriented accumulations mentioned in the example 2 are combined here for the two dimensional function. Let us compute the image intensity function $f(x, y) = x + y$ for $-1 \leq x \leq 0$ and $0 \leq y \leq 1$ with the step 0.5 for x or y. The two dimensional computation should be

$$\begin{bmatrix} f(-1, 0) & f(-1, 0.5) & f(-1, 1) \\ f(-0.5, 0) & f(-0.5, 0.5) & f(-0.5, 1) \\ f(0, 0) & f(0, 0.5) & f(0, 1) \end{bmatrix}$$

$$= \begin{bmatrix} -1 & -0.5 & 0 \\ -0.5 & 0 & 0.5 \\ 0 & 0.5 & 1 \end{bmatrix}$$, and we expect the last matrix from MATLAB. There are two independent variables hence

the use of two for-loop variables is compulsory. The complete program is as follows:

Executable M–file:

```
r=[ ];
f=[ ];
for x=-1:0.5:0
        for y=0:0.5:1
                r=[r x+y];
        end
                f=[f;r];
                r=[ ];
end
```

Sessions with the command window:

Type above statements in the M-file by the name **test** and execute the following:

```
>>test ↵
>>f ↵

f =
                -1.0000   -0.5000          0
                -0.5000          0     0.5000
                     0     0.5000     1.0000
```

Referring to the M-file program, the r and f refer to the row and column of the rectangular matrix respectively. The initializations r=[ ]; and f=[ ]; mean that r and f are empty matrices. The term r=[r x+y]; places the computed data of x+y on the right side of the last r depending on the for-loop counter until one row placement is finished. The other term f=[f;r]; places the row stored in r down the last f. Before the end of the second loop's **end**, the command r=[ ];

196

is inserted. This is necessary otherwise r would contain all computations in a row matrix. In doing so, a mark of distinction for the consecutive rows of the rectangular matrix is accomplished. However note that the matrix only contains the functional values of $x+y$ and there is no information regarding the x or y. The reader has to keep a mark what these matrix values correspond to.

10.3.4 Simple if/if-else/nested if structure

The conditional commands are performed by the if-else statements. Also comparisons and checkings need if-else statements. We can have different if-else structures namely simple-if, if-else, or nested-if depending on the programming circumstances which are discussed in the following.

Simple if

The program syntax of simple-if is as follows:

if *logical expression*
    Executable MATLAB command(s)
end

Example: If $x \geq 1$, we compute $y = \sin x$. When $x = 2$, we should see $y = \sin 2 = 0.9093$.

Executable M–file:
```
x=2;
if x>=1
    y=sin(x);
end
```
Steps: Save the statements in an M-file by the name **test** and execute the following.
Check from the command window after running the M–file:
```
>>y ↵

y =
    0.9093
```

If-else

The general program syntax for the if-else structure is as follows:

if *logical expression*
    Executable MATLAB command(s)
else
    Executable MATLAB command(s)
end

Example: When $x = 1$, we compute $y = \sin\dfrac{x\pi}{2} = 1$ otherwise $y = \cos\dfrac{x\pi}{2}$.

Executable M–file:
```
x=1;
if x==1
    y=sin(x*pi/2);
else
    y=cos(x*pi/2);
end
```
Steps: Same as before.
Check from the command window after running the M–file:
```
>>y ↵

y =
    1
```
If we had x=2; in the first line of the M-file, we would see y= $\cos \pi = -1$.

Nested-if

The third type of the if structure is the nested-if whose program syntax is as follows:

if *logical expression*
    Executable MATLAB command(s)
elseif *logical expression*
    Executable MATLAB command(s)

$$\vdots$$

elseif *logical expression*

   Executable MATLAB command(s)

else

   Executable MATLAB command(s)

end

Example: The best example can be taking the decision of grades out of 100 based on the achieved number of a student. The grading policy is stated as if the achieved number of a student is greater than or equal 90, greater than or equal to 80 but less than 90, greater than or equal to 70 but less than 80, greater than or equal to 60 but less than 70, greater than or equal to 50 but less than 60, and less than 50, then the grade is decided as A, B, C, D, E, and F respectively.

In the following program, the **N** and **g** refer to the number achieved and the grade respectively. If the number **N** is 77, the grade **g** should be **C**. Any character is argumented under the single inverted comma.

Executable M–file:

```
        N=77;
    if N>=90
        g='A';
    elseif (N<90)&(N>=80)
        g='B';
    elseif (N<80)&(N>=70)
        g='C';
    elseif (N<70)&(N>=60)
        g='D';
    elseif (N<60)&(N>=50)
        g='E';
    else
        g='F';
    end
```

Check from the command window after running the M–file:

```
    >>g ↵

    g =

    C
```

10.3.5 User input during the run time of an M-file

Sometimes it is necessary to have some input or functional argument from the user when an M-file program is being run. It can be accomplished by the command input. Assume that we need any integer from 1 to 10 from the user whose implementation can be conducted without opening an M-file as follows:

```
    >>A=input('Enter any integer from 1 to 10: '); ↵
    >>Enter any integer from 1 to 10: 5 ↵        ← Suppose, 5 is typed at the cursor
    >>A ↵                                         ← To make sure, what there is in A

    A =
        5
```

The input argument of the function input can be any string placed by the single inverted comma. Whatever input receives the MATLAB prompt is assigned to the variable **A**. Integers are not the only inputs that the function accepts, as another example a column matrix of three decimal numbers (considering $\begin{bmatrix} 2.1 \\ 3.2 \\ 1.5 \end{bmatrix}$) is to be asked from the user:

```
    >>A=input('Enter the decimal column matrix of 3 elements: '); ↵
    >>Enter the decimal column matrix of 3 elements: [2.1 3.2 1.5]' ↵
                                                (Type the above at the blinking cursor)
    >>A ↵                         ← To see the contents of A

    A =
        2.1000
```

```
        3.2000
        1.5000
```
Next example shows a string input say the name of a student is needed:
```
    >>A=input('What is the name of the student:  ');  ↵
    >>What is the name of the student:  'Rebeca' ↵      ← Type 'Rebeca' at the blinking cursor
    >>A ↵                                               ← Display the contents of A

    A =

    Rebeca
```
The string can even be a file name with relevant file extension. For easy understanding we executed the input at the command prompt but it can appear in any M-file if some data, string, or file name is required during the execution of the M-file.

10.3.6 Switch-case-otherwise structure

The switch-case-otherwise structure provides the programming technique to choose a particular set of executable commands from several sets. The switch requires a key to make the structure operational and the key is compared to each available case. The structure executes the set of commands only the case that matches with the key. The basic form for the switch-case-otherwise structure is as follows:

```
switch    key for opening the switch
case  I
            Executable MATLAB command(s)
case  II
            Executable MATLAB command(s)
                    ⋮
                    ⋮

otherwise
            Executable MATLAB command(s)
end
```

Example: Suppose, a university library has the policy that the teachers, the researchers, and the students can borrow 10, 8, and 5 books respectively. Other people of the university can not borrow a book. The teachers, researchers, and students have the codes T, R, and S respectively. Other than the university staff or student nobody is allowed to issue a book. To check how many books one can borrow, we can run the following M-file.

Executable M-file:
```
    I=input('Enter your code : ');
    switch I
            case 'T', disp('You can borrow 10 books');
            case 'R', disp('You can borrow 8 books');
            case 'S', disp('You can borrow 5 books');
            otherwise, disp('You are not supposed to borrow any books')
    end
```

Steps: Save the statements in a new M-file by the name test and run the file from the command prompt.

Interactive sessions with the command window:
```
        >>test ↵
        Enter your code : 'R' ↵
        You can borrow 8 books
        >>test ↵
        Enter your code : 'D' ↵
        You are not supposed to borrow any books
```

The input given by the user is assigned to I which serves the key to the switch. Since the code is a character from the user, that must be entered under the single inverted comma. Whichever is entered to I is checked with all possible cases. The example key is a character one and it can be a numeric as well. Let us see the next example where a numeric key is used.

Example: The binary numbers either 0 or 1 can represent a digital signal. We set the −1 and 1 for the 0 and 1 of the digital signal respectively. But we are also interested in detecting a 0 value in the digital signal. Therefore the possible digital signal values are −1, 0, and 1. If the signal has the value other than the specified three, it is termed as a noise. A practical digital signal is composed of thousands of zeroes and ones. For simplicity, we enter the signal values from the command window to see the implementation of the structure.

Executable M-file:

```
I=input('Enter the signal value : ');
switch I
        case -1, disp('The is a negative digital signal');
        case 0, disp('The signal value is 0');
        case 1, disp('This is a positive digital signal');
        otherwise, disp('This is a noise')
end
```

Steps: Save the statements in a new M-file by the name test.

Interactive sessions with the command window:

```
>>test ↵
Enter the signal value : 7 ↵
This is a noise
>>test ↵
Enter the signal value : 1 ↵
This is a positive digital signal
```

Now the input from the user is not a character therefore we do not need to use the single inverted comma while entering any input. The case directives are also numerical.

10.3.7 While-end structure

The while-end structure also performs the looping operations similar to the for-loop but subject to the logical condition. Inside the while-end structure a set of similar commands is carried out until the logical expression beside the while is satisfied. The general form of the structure is as follows:

Program syntax: while *logical expression*

Executable MATLAB command(s)

```
        end
```

Example: A positive integer greater than 1 will be asked from the user. The sum of the squares from 1 to that integer is required to compute.

Executable M-file:

```
I=input('Enter any integer greater than 1: ');
k=0;
s=0;
while ~(k>I)
    s=s+k^2;
    k=k+1;
end
```

Explanations: The I is not known beforehand and that is the user's choice taken form the command prompt via the command input. We preset 0 to each of k and s. The counter index k inside the while-end loop is increased by 1 for each looping operation using the command k=k+1;. The variable s adds consecutively the sum of squares for all integers less than I, which is achieved by s=s+k^2;. Just to have a check, if we input 7 at the command prompt, the output should be $1^2 + 2^2 + 3^2 + 4^2 + 5^2 + 6^2 + 7^2 = 140$ that is what is required from the programming.

Steps: Save the statements in a new M-file by the name test.

Interactive sessions with the command window:

```
>>test ↵
Enter any integer greater than 1: 7 ↵
>>s ↵

s =
        140
```

The expression 'k is not greater than I' is written as ~(k>I) in the place of the logical expression of while (subsection 10.3.1 for operator reference).

10.3.8 Comment on executable statements

There is no hard and fast rule for naming the assignees. You can choose any variable to assign the output of an executable statement. This creates a problem of understanding for an M-file accessible to multiple users. If an

M-file programmer writes some comment beside each executable statement, that can help the others to go through the program. This is accomplished by the character % which appears at the beginning of each sentence. The commentary sentence can appear at any column of an M-file. For example, we could have explained the contents of I in the last M-file as follows:

I=input('Enter any integer greater than 1: '); % I is the user input

The line followed by % does not affect the programming.

10.3.9 Break statement

The break statement is practiced to terminate the loop or iterative operations such as for-loop or while-end loop subject to certain condition.

Example: Let us compute the sum of all integer squares from 1 to 20. But as soon as the sum is greater than 400, we terminate the computation and display the sum. The sums of the squares up to 10 and up to 11 are 385 and 506 respectively.

Executable M-file:

```
            s=0;
       for k=1:20
            s=s+k^2;
            if s>400
                break;
            end
       end
       disp(s)
```

Steps: Save the statements in a new M-file by the name test:

Interactive sessions with the command window:

```
    >>test ↵
        506
```

The for-loop generates the integer counter index from 1 to 20. We compute the successive sum by the command s=s+k^2;, where s=0 at the beginning. For every k, we check the sum whether s>400 by using the if-end. As soon as s>400, the for-loop is broken and s returns the last value. The command disp just displays the contents of the variable s. For the multiple or nested loop, the break statement terminates the innermost loop.

10.3.10 String and its related functions

The string is a set of characters that are placed consecutively. Each character often found in the keyboard has the unique numeric code stored in MATLAB depending on the character set encoding of a given font. Usually we do not access these values. The characters can appear from the first 127 codes of ASCII. We work on the characters as they are displayed on the screen. Typical examples of strings include naming a variable or an array, arguments of an M-file, MATLAB codes of a symbolic expression, etc. The strings can be evaluated, compared, or split as if they are numbers and they can be static or dynamic. The static strings are the preassigned set of characters on the other hand the dynamic strings are created when an M-file or some executable command is being run. The reader is referred to section 10.2 for the string that is used for mathematical computation. Let us execute the following:

>>s='MATLAB'; ↵

Above command says that we assigned the word or string MATLAB to the variable s. Another explanation of the string can be that the string is a character array. For example the s is a character array which has 6 letters or characters. If you know the code of an ASCII character, it can be converted to the character by the MATLAB function char. For example, the characters #, $, %, &, ', (,), *, and + have the numeric codes 35, 36, 37, 38, 39, 40, 41, 42, and 43 respectively. We have them as follows:

>>char([35:43]) ↵

ans =

#$%&'()*+

A lot of string related functions are included in MATLAB. To learn about these functions, execute the following:

>>help strfun ↵

10.4 Formation of matrix of ones, zeroes, and constants

When we generate a binary image, the matrices of ones and zeroes can be helpful. The MATLAB commands ones and zeros implement the user-defined matrix of ones and zeroes. Each function can conceive two input arguments, the first and second of which are the required numbers of rows and columns respectively. Let us

say we intend to form the matrices $A = \begin{bmatrix} 1 & 1 & 1 \\ 1 & 1 & 1 \\ 1 & 1 & 1 \\ 1 & 1 & 1 \end{bmatrix}$, $B = \begin{bmatrix} 1 & 1 & 1 \\ 1 & 1 & 1 \\ 1 & 1 & 1 \end{bmatrix}$, and $C = \begin{bmatrix} 1 & 1 & 1 & 1 \\ 1 & 1 & 1 & 1 \end{bmatrix}$. Their orders are 4×3, 3×3, and

2×4 respectively and the implementations are as follows:

MATLAB Command

for A,   **for B,**   **for C,**

   >>A=ones(4,3) ↵   >>B=ones(3) ↵   >>C=ones(2,4) ↵

A =   B =   C =

```
   1  1  1                1  1  1                1  1  1  1
   1  1  1                1  1  1                1  1  1  1
   1  1  1                1  1  1
   1  1  1
```

Either the number of rows or columns will do if the matrix is a square. For the row and column matrices of ones for example of length 6, the commands would be ones(1,6) and ones(6,1) respectively.

     Formation of the matrix of zeroes is quite similar to that of the matrix of ones. Replacing the function

ones by **zeros** does the formation. Matrix of zeroes like $A = \begin{bmatrix} 0 & 0 & 0 \\ 0 & 0 & 0 \\ 0 & 0 & 0 \\ 0 & 0 & 0 \end{bmatrix}$, $B = \begin{bmatrix} 0 & 0 & 0 \\ 0 & 0 & 0 \\ 0 & 0 & 0 \end{bmatrix}$, and $C = \begin{bmatrix} 0 & 0 & 0 & 0 \\ 0 & 0 & 0 & 0 \end{bmatrix}$ whose

orders are 4×3, 3×3, and 2×4 respectively are formed as follows:

Command for A,   **for B,**   **for C,**

   >>A=zeros(4,3) ↵   >>B=zeros(3) ↵   >>C=zeros(2,4) ↵

A =   B =   C =

```
   0  0  0                0  0  0                0  0  0  0
   0  0  0                0  0  0                0  0  0  0
   0  0  0                0  0  0
   0  0  0
```

A matrix of constants can be obtained first by creating a matrix of ones of the required size and then multiplying by

the constant number. For example, the matrix $\begin{bmatrix} 0.2 & 0.2 & 0.2 \\ 0.2 & 0.2 & 0.2 \\ 0.2 & 0.2 & 0.2 \\ 0.2 & 0.2 & 0.2 \end{bmatrix}$ can be generated by the command 0.2*ones(4,3).

10.5 Coloning of matrices

     Coloning of matrices becomes important when we manipulate the digital images in the pixel or spatial domain. Digital images are in other words giant size matrices. New matrices or images can be built from the matrix or image we have in the workspace of MATLAB. We can pick up a portion of the digital image using the coloning. All you need is the proper manipulation of the colon operator :.

     Let us see some coloning by assigning the row matrix $A = [2 \quad 4 \quad 3 \quad -10 \quad 0 \quad 9 \quad 73 \quad 29 \quad -31 \quad 50]$ to the workspace variable A:

MATLAB Command

   >>A=[2 4 3 -10 0 9 73 29 -31 50]; ↵

Suppose, we want to form a matrix B, where B will be the second, third, and ninth element of A i.e. $B = [4 \quad 3 \quad -31]$:

   >>B=A([2 3 9]) ↵   ← The input argument of A is a row matrix indicating position indices

   B =

         4   3 -31   ← B holds the required matrix

A matrix C is to be formed from the third through the eighth elements of A i.e. $C = [3 \quad -10 \quad 0 \quad 9 \quad 73 \quad 29]$. We do the following:

   >>C=A(3:8) ↵   ← The input argument 3:8 indicates the third through eighth

   C =

$$3 \quad -10 \quad 0 \quad 9 \quad 73 \quad 29 \qquad \leftarrow \text{C holds the required matrix}$$

What if we have a column matrix like $D = \begin{bmatrix} 2 \\ 4 \\ 5 \\ -10 \\ 0 \\ 6 \\ 73 \\ 7 \\ -31 \\ 50 \end{bmatrix}$, we enter the matrix into the MATLAB workspace as follows:

>>D=[2 4 5 -10 0 6 73 7 -31 50]'; ↵   ← D holds the D

We form a matrix E from the tenth and the seventh elements of D i.e. $E = \begin{bmatrix} 50 \\ 73 \end{bmatrix}$ and F from the first five

elements of D i.e. $F = \begin{bmatrix} 2 \\ 4 \\ 5 \\ -10 \\ 0 \end{bmatrix}$:

formation of the matrix E,   **formation of the matrix F,**

>>E=D([10 7]) ↵   >>F=D(1:5) ↵

E =   F =

    50   2
    73   4
                                             5
                                            -10
                                             0

Now we present how the coloning of a rectangular matrix can be accomplished. Let us input the $G =$

$$\begin{bmatrix} 8 & 64 & 27 & 56 & 98 & 43 & 4 \\ -64 & 216 & 729 & 40 & 12 & 23 & 568 \\ 678 & -90 & 70 & 61 & 67 & 445 & 3 \\ 1 & 47 & 45 & 72 & 34 & -5 & -7 \\ 3 & 87 & 82 & 29 & 10 & -16 & -59 \end{bmatrix}$$ to G by the following:

>>G=[8 64 27 56 98 43 4;-64 216 729 40 12 23 568;678 ... ↵
    -90 70 61 67 445 3;1 47 45 72 34 -5 -7;3 87 82 29 10 -16 -59] ↵

G =   ← G holds the G

```
    8   64   27   56   98   43    4
  -64  216  729   40   12   23  568
  678  -90   70   61   67  445    3
    1   47   45   72   34   -5   -7
    3   87   82   29   10  -16  -59
```

In above MATLAB Command, the last word of the first line is 678. After typing 678, we leave one space by pressing spacebar, and then type three dots from the keyboard. These three dots mean continuation of the MATLAB Command. Press Enter key and type the other matrix elements of the row which were interrupted. The three dots (Ö) are called the ellipsis.

Anyhow the required matrix elements from the G are shown by the elements inside the dotted box in the following.

Matrix H is to be formed from the second and the fourth columns of G :

$$\begin{bmatrix} 8 & \boxed{64} & 27 & \boxed{56} & 98 & 43 & 4 \\ -64 & \boxed{216} & 729 & \boxed{40} & 12 & 23 & 568 \\ 678 & \boxed{-90} & 70 & \boxed{61} & 67 & 445 & 3 \\ 1 & \boxed{47} & 45 & \boxed{72} & 34 & -5 & -7 \\ 3 & \boxed{87} & 82 & \boxed{29} & 10 & -16 & -59 \end{bmatrix}$$

Matrix K is to be formed from the third and the fifth rows of G :

$$\begin{bmatrix} 8 & 64 & 27 & 56 & 98 & 43 & 4 \\ -64 & 216 & 729 & 40 & 12 & 23 & 568 \\ 678 & -90 & 70 & 61 & 67 & 445 & 3 \\ 1 & 47 & 45 & 72 & 34 & -5 & -7 \\ 3 & 87 & 82 & 29 & 10 & -16 & -59 \end{bmatrix}$$

Matrix L is to be formed from the fourth through seventh columns of G :

$$\begin{bmatrix} 8 & 64 & 27 & 56 & 98 & 43 & 4 \\ -64 & 216 & 729 & 40 & 12 & 23 & 568 \\ 678 & -90 & 70 & 61 & 67 & 445 & 3 \\ 1 & 47 & 45 & 72 & 34 & -5 & -7 \\ 3 & 87 & 82 & 29 & 10 & -16 & -59 \end{bmatrix}$$

Matrix M is to be formed from the third through fifth rows of G :

$$\begin{bmatrix} 8 & 64 & 27 & 56 & 98 & 43 & 4 \\ -64 & 216 & 729 & 40 & 12 & 23 & 568 \\ 678 & -90 & 70 & 61 & 67 & 445 & 3 \\ 1 & 47 & 45 & 72 & 34 & -5 & -7 \\ 3 & 87 & 82 & 29 & 10 & -16 & -59 \end{bmatrix}$$

Finally, matrix N is to be formed from the intersection of the third through fifth rows and the fourth through seventh columns of G :

$$\begin{bmatrix} 8 & 64 & 27 & 56 & 98 & 43 & 4 \\ -64 & 216 & 729 & 40 & 12 & 23 & 568 \\ 678 & -90 & 70 & 61 & 67 & 445 & 3 \\ 1 & 47 & 45 & 72 & 34 & -5 & -7 \\ 3 & 87 & 82 & 29 & 10 & -16 & -59 \end{bmatrix}$$

Formations of the required H, K, L, M, and N assigned to the respective workspace variables are presented as follows:

for the formation of H,
```
>>H=G(:,[2 4]) ↵
```

H =
```
    64   56
   216   40
   -90   61
    47   72
    87   29
```

for the formation of N,
```
>>N=G(3:5,4:7) ↵
```

N =
```
   61   67  445    3
   72   34   -5   -7
   29   10  -16  -59
```

for the formation of M,
```
>>M=G(3:5,:) ↵
```

M =
```
  678  -90   70   61   67  445    3
    1   47   45   72   34   -5   -7
    3   87   82   29   10  -16  -59
```

for the formation of K,
```
>>K=G([3 5],:) ↵
```

K =
```
  678  -90   70   61   67  445    3
    3   87   82   29   10  -16  -59
```

for the formation of L,
```
>>L=G(:,4:7) ↵
```

L =
```
   56   98   43    4
   40   12   23  568
   61   67  445    3
   72   34   -5   -7
   29   10  -16  -59
```

Any data class (table 2.B) can be the matrix elements. Summarizing all, we use the commands matrix name(desired row/rows,:), matrix name(:,desired column/columns), and matrix name(desired row/rows, desired column/columns) for selecting the row, column, and submatrices from the existing matrix respectively.

♦ ♦ Deleting rows/columns from a matrix

Given a rectangular matrix G (present in the workspace), we intend to delete its fifth row so that we have

the matrix $\begin{bmatrix} 8 & 64 & 27 & 56 & 98 & 43 & 4 \\ -64 & 216 & 729 & 40 & 12 & 23 & 568 \\ 678 & -90 & 70 & 61 & 67 & 445 & 3 \\ 1 & 47 & 45 & 72 & 34 & -5 & -7 \end{bmatrix}$ following the deletion and do so by the following:

```
>>G(5,:)=[ ] ↵
```

G =

$$
\begin{array}{rrrrrrr}
8 & 64 & 27 & 56 & 98 & 43 & 4 \\
-64 & 216 & 729 & 40 & 12 & 23 & 568 \\
678 & -90 & 70 & 61 & 67 & 445 & 3 \\
1 & 47 & 45 & 72 & 34 & -5 & -7
\end{array}
$$

So to delete a row from a matrix, we use the command matrix name(row number,:)=[ ]. A range of row deletion is also possible for example the command G(4:5,:)=[ ] is applicable for the deletion of the fourth and the fifth rows from the G. The instant you delete the row or rows, the size of the resulting matrix becomes different from the original one. Again let us say we intend to delete the third and the seventh columns from the resulting

$$
\begin{bmatrix}
8 & 64 & 27 & 56 & 98 & 43 & 4 \\
-64 & 216 & 729 & 40 & 12 & 23 & 568 \\
678 & -90 & 70 & 61 & 67 & 445 & 3 \\
1 & 47 & 45 & 72 & 34 & -5 & -7
\end{bmatrix}
$$ (held in last G) so that we get the matrix $\begin{bmatrix} 8 & 64 & 56 & 98 & 43 \\ -64 & 216 & 40 & 12 & 23 \\ 678 & -90 & 61 & 67 & 445 \\ 1 & 47 & 72 & 34 & -5 \end{bmatrix}$

from the deletion:

>>G(:,[3 7])=[ ] ↵

G =

$$
\begin{array}{rrrrr}
8 & 64 & 56 & 98 & 43 \\
-64 & 216 & 40 & 12 & 23 \\
678 & -90 & 61 & 67 & 445 \\
1 & 47 & 72 & 34 & -5
\end{array}
$$

For above implementation, we used the command matrix name(:,column number (s) as a row matrix)=[ ]). Thus the reader can delete any selected rows or columns from a rectangular matrix.

10.6 Forming a large matrix from smaller ones

A practical digital image is noting but a large size matrix. Forming a large matrix from smaller ones means in a sense forming a composite image from subimages. Prior to the formation, it is necessary that we are familiar about the appending of a row or column with an existing matrix in MATLAB workspace. Let us go through the following in this regard.

♣ ♣ **Appending rows**

Assume that the matrix $A = \begin{bmatrix} 1 & 3 & 5 \\ 2 & 6 & 8 \\ 9 & 5 & 0 \\ 4 & 7 & 8 \end{bmatrix}$ is formed by appending two row matrices [9 5   0] and [4   7

8] with the matrix $B = \begin{bmatrix} 1 & 3 & 5 \\ 2 & 6 & 8 \end{bmatrix}$. Let us enter the matrix B into MATLAB and append one row after another by

the command shown below:

MATLAB Command

for entering B,	for appending the first row,	for appending the second row,
>>B=[1 3 5;2 6 8] ↵	>>B=[B;[9 5 0]] ↵	>>A =[B;[4 7 8]] ↵

B =

$$
\begin{array}{rrr}
1 & 3 & 5 \\
2 & 6 & 8
\end{array}
$$

B =

$$
\begin{array}{rrr}
1 & 3 & 5 \\
2 & 6 & 8 \\
9 & 5 & 0
\end{array}
$$

A =

$$
\begin{array}{rrr}
1 & 3 & 5 \\
2 & 6 & 8 \\
9 & 5 & 0 \\
4 & 7 & 8
\end{array}
$$

In the command B=[B;[9 5 0]], the row [9 5 0] is appended with the existing B (must be inside the third bracket) and the result is again assigned to B. The semicolon places the [9 5 0] downward. You can add as many rows as you want but the important point is the number of elements in each row that is to be appended must be equal to the number of columns of the existing B.

♣ ♣ **Appending columns**

Considering $C = \begin{bmatrix} 1 & 3 & 5 & 9 & 3 \\ 2 & 6 & 8 & 0 & 1 \\ 9 & 5 & 0 & 1 & 9 \end{bmatrix}$ in which C is formed by appending two column matrices $\begin{bmatrix} 9 \\ 0 \\ 1 \end{bmatrix}$ and

$\begin{bmatrix} 3 \\ 1 \\ 9 \end{bmatrix}$ from $D = \begin{bmatrix} 1 & 3 & 5 \\ 2 & 6 & 8 \\ 9 & 5 & 0 \end{bmatrix}$. Let us get the D into MATLAB and append one column after another as follows:

for entering D,	**for appending the first column,**	**for appending the second column,**
>>D=[1 3 5;2 6 8;9 5 0] ↵	>>D=[D [9 0 1]'] ↵	>>C =[D [3 1 9]'] ↵

D =	D =	C =
1 3 5	1 3 5 9	1 3 5 9 3
2 6 8	2 6 8 0	2 6 8 0 1
9 5 0	9 5 0 1	9 5 0 1 9

The command [D [9 0 1]'] has one space gap between the existing D and the column to be added. We must make sure that the number of the elements in each column that is to be appended is exactly equal to the number of rows of the existing matrix.

♦ ♦ Appending with the empty matrix

Computed data accumulation can happen with the use of the empty matrix which has the MATLAB code [ ]. Let us execute the following:

>>D=[ ]; ↵   ← We assigned an empty matrix to D
>>D=[D 3] ↵   ← We accumulated 3 to the existing D on the right

D =
          3
>>D=[D 7] ↵   ← We accumulated 7 to the existing D on the right
D =
          3   7

The accumulation we presented places the data on the right. The left accumulation can happen by writing the command D=[3 D]. For understanding we presented 3 and 7 but the elements can come from any other function or computation for instance one can write D=[sin(x) D] where x may be controlled by some for-loop. In a similar fashion one can accumulate the data column orientedly by writing D=[D;3] or D=[D;7].

♦ ♦ Building a large matrix from smaller matrices

With the added notion of the matrix appending now we are in a position to build a composite matrix from smaller ones. Let us build a composite matrix $E = \begin{bmatrix} A & B \\ C & D \end{bmatrix}$ by taking four submatrices $A = \begin{bmatrix} 0 & -5 & 6 \\ 7 & 6 & 9 \end{bmatrix}$,

$B = \begin{bmatrix} 1 & 7 \\ 9 & 1 \end{bmatrix}$, $C = \begin{bmatrix} 1 \\ 1 \end{bmatrix}$, and $D = \begin{bmatrix} -1 & 0 & 10 & 11 \\ 9 & 7 & 13 & 14 \end{bmatrix}$ so that we have $E = \begin{bmatrix} 0 & -5 & 6 & 1 & 7 \\ 7 & 6 & 9 & 9 & 1 \\ 1 & -1 & 0 & 10 & 11 \\ 1 & 9 & 7 & 13 & 14 \end{bmatrix}$ as follows:

>>A=[0 -5 6;7 6 9]; ↵   ← We assign the matrix A to A
>>B=[1 7;9 1]; ↵   ← We assign the matrix B to B
>>C=[1;1]; ↵   ← We assign the matrix C to C
>>D=[-1 0 10 11;9 7 13 14]; ↵   ← We assign the matrix D to D
>>E=[A B;C D] ↵   ← The composite matrix E is formed

E =
          0   -5   6   1   7
          7   6   9   9   1
          1   -1   0   10   11
          1   9   7   13   14

As regards to fifth line E=[A B;C D] of above command, the command A B gives us $\begin{bmatrix} 0 & -5 & 6 & 1 & 7 \\ 7 & 6 & 9 & 9 & 1 \end{bmatrix}$.

To merge the A and B, we should keep in mind that the numbers of rows of A and B have to be the same (here it is 2). Similarly using the command C D merges the C and D and provides $\begin{bmatrix} 1 & -1 & 0 & 10 & 11 \\ 1 & 9 & 7 & 13 & 14 \end{bmatrix}$. The matrix formed by the command A B will be placed on the top of the matrix formed by C D if the command [A B;C D] is used. The number of columns formed by the A B (here it is 5) and the number of columns formed by the C D (it is also 5) must have to be identical. Matrix E stored in E can again be merged with some other matrices to form another larger dimension matrix. However the reader can assume that the matrices A, B, C, and D are subimages as far as the digital nature of an image is concern.

10.7 Position indexes of image elements with conditions

The image matrix elements contain different class of data. Sometimes we intend to know the gray or color level based on specific condition. The section addresses the finding of the position indexes (or in other words the pixel coordinates) of the gray or color levels from the digital image matrix for which the MATLAB function find is useful. The general format of the command is [R C]=find(condition), where the indexes R and C for the row and column directed pixels respectively.

To proceed with, let us consider the modular digital image $f[m,n] = \begin{bmatrix} 11 & 10 & 11 & 10 \\ 12 & 10 & -2 & 0 \\ -7 & 17 & 1 & -1 \end{bmatrix}$. We would

like to know what the position indexes of the elements are where the elements are greater than 10. The elements of $f[m,n]$ being greater than 10 have the position indexes (1,1), (2,1), (3,2), and (1,3). As it happens, MATLAB finds the required index in accordance with columns. Placing the row and column

indexes vertically we have $\begin{bmatrix} 1 \\ 2 \\ 3 \\ 1 \end{bmatrix}$ and $\begin{bmatrix} 1 \\ 1 \\ 2 \\ 3 \end{bmatrix}$ respectively. Hence the output arguments R and C of the find must

hold these two column matrices. The input argument of the find must be a logical statement, any element in $f[m,n]$ greater than 10 is written as $f[m,n] > 10$. However the position indexes are found as follows:

MATLAB Command

where elements of $f[m,n]$ >10,

```
>>f=[11 10 11 10;12 10 -2 0;-7 17 1 -1]; ↵
>>[R C]=find(f>10) ↵

R =
    1
    2
    3
    1
C =
    1
    1
    2
    3
```

for the row matrix D,

```
>>D=[-10 34 1 2 8 4]; ↵
>>R=find(D>=8) ↵

R =
    2    5
```

for the column matrix E,

```
>>E=[-2 8 -2 7]'; ↵
>>C=find(E~=-2) ↵

C =
    2
    4
```

where elements of $f[m,n]$ =10,

```
>>[R C]=find(f==10) ↵

R =
    1
    2
    1
C =
    2
    2
    4
```

where elements of $f[m,n]$ ≤0,

```
>>[R C]=find(f<=0) ↵

R =
    3
    2
    2
    3
C =
    1
    3
    4
    4
```

To work with other conditions, what are the position indexes in the matrix $f[m,n]$ where the elements are equal to 10? The answer is (1,2), (2,2), and (1,4). Again, the position indexes where the elements are less than or equal to zero are (3,1), (2,3), (2,4), and (3,4). Both implementations are presented above. It should be pointed out that the operator = = is used for the logical comparison and that the operator = is used for the assignment (subsection 10.3.1). We considered a rectangular matrix in above implementation, let us see how find works for a row or column matrix. As an example, let us take $D = [-10 \quad 34 \quad 1 \quad 2 \quad 8 \quad 4]$ from which we find the position indexes of the elements where they are greater than or equal to 8. Obviously, they are the 2nd and 5th elements. Here, we do not need two output arguments of the find. Again let us find the position indexes of the elements of the column

matrix $E = \begin{bmatrix} -2 \\ 8 \\ -2 \\ 7 \end{bmatrix}$ where the elements are not equal to ñ2. The 2nd and 4th elements are not equal to ñ2. The

executions for the last two examples are also presented along with previous implementation. The output of the function find is a row one for the row matrix and a column one for the column matrix.

10.8 Reshaping and repetitive matrices

A digital image matrix needs a variety of manipulations during its processing. A long row or column matrix can be converted to a rectangular matrix by the function reshape. Following examples are presented for the formations of the reshaped and repetitive matrices.

⌗ Reshaping matrices

Let us consider the row matrix $R = [3 \quad 14 \quad -9 \quad 0 \quad 12 \quad 11 \quad 56 \quad 78 \quad 9 \quad 34 \quad 91 \quad 30]$. There are 12 elements in R. Whatever be the order of the reshaped matrix, the product of the order of the reshaped matrix must be 12. From the elements of R, we may have 3×4, 4×3, 6×2, or 2×6 matrices. When the elements are placed consecutively, they can come either in column by column or in row by row.

From R, let us form a matrix N of order 3×4 in which the first column will be the first three elements of R, the second column will be the second three elements of R, and so will be the others i.e. R is reshaped as

$N = \begin{bmatrix} 3 & 0 & 56 & 34 \\ 14 & 12 & 78 & 91 \\ -9 & 11 & 9 & 30 \end{bmatrix}$. Again a matrix M of order 3×4 can be formed from R like $M = \begin{bmatrix} 3 & 14 & -9 & 0 \\ 12 & 11 & 56 & 78 \\ 9 & 34 & 91 & 30 \end{bmatrix}$

placing the elements in rows. Their formations are as follows:

MATLAB Command

for the formation of N,
```
>>R=[3 14 -9 0 12 11 56 78 9 34 91 30]; ↵
>>N=reshape(R,3,4) ↵

N =
        3    0   56   34
       14   12   78   91
       -9   11    9   30
```

for the formation of M,
```
>>M=reshape(R,4,3)' ↵

M =
        3   14   -9    0
       12   11   56    7
        9   34   91   30
```

The reshape intakes three input arguments ñ the first, second, and third of which are the input row or column matrix, the wanted row number, and the wanted column number respectively. The function always works on columns that is why we first turn the number of rows to the number of columns and vice versa and then apply the

matrix transposition with the operator ' to obtain M. What if we have the test column matrix $C = \begin{bmatrix} 5 \\ 7 \\ -9 \\ 7 \\ 23 \\ 11 \\ 9 \\ 10 \end{bmatrix}$. We wish

to form $O = \begin{bmatrix} 5 & -9 & 23 & 9 \\ 7 & 7 & 11 & 10 \end{bmatrix}$ of order 2×4 placing the elements columnwise and also $P = \begin{bmatrix} 5 & 7 & -9 & 7 \\ 23 & 11 & 9 & 10 \end{bmatrix}$

placing the elements rowwise from the C. They are reshaped as follows:

for the formation of O,
```
>>C=[5 7 -9 7 23 11 9 10]'; ↵
>>O=reshape(C,2,4) ↵

O =
        5   -9   23    9
        7    7   11   10
```

for the formation of P,
```
>>P=reshape(C,4,2)' ↵

P =
        5    7   -9    7
       23   11    9   10
```

⊟ **Repetitive matrices**

If a row, column, or rectangular matrix is given, another rectangular matrix might be required to form by placing the given matrix repetitively. The repetition is obviously user defined for which the function **repmat** (abbreviation of the <u>rep</u>etition of <u>mat</u>rices) is advantageous. The common syntax of the function is **repmat**(given row/column/ rectangular matrix, the number of repetitions along the row, the number of repetitions along the column). Let us say the matrix $D = \begin{bmatrix} 3 & -1 & 0 \\ 3 & -1 & 0 \\ 3 & -1 & 0 \end{bmatrix}$ is to be formed from $R = [3 \ -1 \ \ 0]$ by placing three R s one over the other. Again let us form $E = \begin{bmatrix} 4 & 4 & 4 & 4 \\ 10 & 10 & 10 & 10 \\ -7 & -7 & -7 & -7 \end{bmatrix}$ placing four column matrices $C = \begin{bmatrix} 4 \\ 10 \\ -7 \end{bmatrix}$ side by side. Letting the rectangular matrix $A = \begin{bmatrix} 4 & 10 \\ 7 & 0 \end{bmatrix}$, the matrix F is to be formed from six A s by placing 3 A up and 3 A down i.e. $F = \begin{bmatrix} A & A & A \\ A & A & A \end{bmatrix} = \begin{bmatrix} 4 & 10 & 4 & 10 & 4 & 10 \\ 7 & 0 & 7 & 0 & 7 & 0 \\ 4 & 10 & 4 & 10 & 4 & 10 \\ 7 & 0 & 7 & 0 & 7 & 0 \end{bmatrix}$. All examples are implemented as follows:

from the same row matrix R ,
```
>>R=[3 -1 0]; ↵
>>D=repmat(R,3,1) ↵

      D =
             3  -1   0
             3  -1   0
             3  -1   0
```
from the same column matrix C ,
```
>>C=[4 10 -7]'; ↵
>>E=repmat(C,1,4) ↵


E =
           4    4    4    4
          10   10   10   10
          -7   -7   -7   -7
```

from the same rectangular matrix A ,
```
>>A=[4 10;7 0]; ↵
>>F=repmat(A,2,3) ↵

      F =
            4   10    4   10    4   10
            7    0    7    0    7    0
            4   10    4   10    4   10
            7    0    7    0    7    0
```

10.9 Summing or producting all elements in a matrix

In many image computations we need to perform the operation $\sum_{n}\sum_{m} f[m,n]$ for which the MATLAB function **sum** is very effective. The **sum** can add all elements when its input argument is a row, column, or rectangular matrix. Our example matrices are $R = [1 \ ñ2 \ 3 \ 9]$, $C = \begin{bmatrix} 23 \\ -20 \\ 30 \\ 8 \end{bmatrix}$, and $A = \begin{bmatrix} 2 & 4 & 7 \\ -2 & 7 & 9 \\ 3 & 8 & -8 \end{bmatrix}$. The sums of all elements are 11, 41, and 30 for R , C , and A respectively. For the rectangular matrix, the function operates on columns and results a row matrix and then another **sum** is required to add the elements from the resulting row matrix. See the summations of all types of the matrices below:

MATLAB Command

for the row matrix R ,	for the column matrix C ,	for the rectangular matrix A ,
`>>R=[1 -2 3 9]; ↵` `>>sum(R) ↵`	`>>C=[23 -20 30 8]'; ↵` `>>sum(C) ↵`	`>>A=[2 4 7;-2 7 9;3 8 -8]; ↵` `>>sum(sum(A)) ↵`
`ans =` 　　11	`ans =` 　　41	`ans =` 　　30

Actually **sum**(f) is equivalent to $\sum_{m} f[m]$ when $f[m]$ is a row or column vector on the other hand **sum**(**sum**(f)) is to $\sum_{n}\sum_{m} f[m,n]$.

Like the summation the multiplication of all elements in a matrix can happen through the use of the function prod (abbreviation of the <u>product</u>). For the example matrices, the products of all elements in the matrices are ñ54, ñ110400, and 1354752 for the R, C, and A respectively and we can find them as follows:

>>prod(R) ↵   >>prod(C) ↵   >>prod(prod(A)) ↵

ans =   ans =   ans =
     -54   -110400   1354752

The function prod also operates on columns for a rectangular matrix. One can say that the prod(f) and prod(prod(f)) are equivalent to the mathematical notations $\prod_m f[m]$ and $\prod_n \prod_m f[m,n]$ respectively.

10.10 Maximum/minimum and sorting from a matrix

The MATLAB function max (abbreviation of the <u>maximum</u>) can find the maximum element from a row or column matrix when the matrix is its input argument. If the argument of the max is a rectangular matrix, the function operates on columns. The row matrix $R = [1 \quad ñ2 \quad 3 \quad 9 \quad 78 \quad 90 \quad -90]$, column matrix $C = \begin{bmatrix} 23 \\ -20 \\ 30 \\ 8 \end{bmatrix}$, and

rectangular matrix $A = \begin{bmatrix} 2 & 4 & 7 \\ -2 & 7 & 9 \\ 3 & 8 & -8 \end{bmatrix}$ have the maximum values 90, 30, and 9 respectively. How the maximum

for different matrices are found is shown below:

MATLAB Command

for the row matrix,   **for the column matrix,**   **for the rectangular matrix,**

 >>R=[1 -2 3 9 78 90 -90]; ↵   >>C=[23 -20 30 8]'; ↵ >>A=[2 4 7;-2 7 9;3 8 -8]; ↵

 >>max(R) ↵   >>max(C) ↵   >>max(max(A)) ↵

ans =   ans =   ans =
     90   30   9

For the rectangular matrix, the output of the inner max is a row matrix on finding the maximum of each column and the maximum for the whole rectangular matrix is found by the outer max.

Just mentioned row, column, and rectangular matrices have the minimum values ñ90, ñ20, and ñ8 for the R, C, and A respectively. MATLAB has the function min for finding the minimum from a matrix. Findings of all minimums from those matrices are shown in the following:

for the R,   **for the C,**   **for the A,**

 >>min(R) ↵   >>min(C) ↵   >>min(min(A)) ↵

ans =   ans =   ans =
     -90   -20   -8

The functions are equally applicable for the floating-point or decimal numbers.

Using the MATLAB function sort can sort the elements of a row or column matrix in ascending order. In the case of a rectangular matrix, sorting operation will be over each column. In ascending order, the sorting of the

row matrix $R = [1 \quad ñ2 \quad 3 \quad 9 \quad 0 \quad -5]$, column matrix $C = \begin{bmatrix} 23 \\ -20 \\ 30 \\ 8 \\ -10 \end{bmatrix}$, and rectangular matrix $A = \begin{bmatrix} 2 & 4 & 7 \\ -2 & 7 & 9 \\ 3 & 8 & -8 \\ 0 & -3 & -1 \end{bmatrix}$

over columns should return us $A = [-5 \quad -2 \quad 0 \quad 1 \quad 3 \quad 9]$, $B = \begin{bmatrix} -20 \\ -10 \\ 8 \\ 23 \\ 30 \end{bmatrix}$, and $D = \begin{bmatrix} -2 & -3 & -8 \\ 0 & 4 & -1 \\ 2 & 7 & 7 \\ 3 & 8 & 9 \end{bmatrix}$ respectively. We

conduct their implementations as follows:

MATLAB Command

for the row matrix,
```
>>R=[1 -2 3 9 0 -5]; ↵
>>A=sort(R) ↵
```

A =
```
    -5  -2   0   1   3   9
```

for the rectangular matrix,
```
>>A=[2 4 7;-2 7 9;3 8 -8;0 -3 -1]; ↵
>>D=sort(A) ↵
```

D =
```
    -2  -3  -8
     0   4  -1
     2   7   7
     3   8   9
```

for the column matrix,
```
>>C=[23 -20 30 8 -10]'; ↵
>>B=sort(C) ↵
```

B =
```
   -20
   -10
     8
    23
    30
```

If all elements in a rectangular matrix are required to be sorted in ascending order, the command **sort(A(:))** can be exercised where A(:) turns the rectangular A to a column one. The elements of the matrices can be the decimal numbers too. Another query would be about the sorting in descending order. One can take the help of the functions **fliplr** (flip from the left to right) and **flipud** (flip from the up to down) to have the descendingly ordered elements if their arguments are row and column respectively. For example, the ascendingly ordered elements of R are stored in A. We execute the following to have the descendingly ordered elements:
```
>>fliplr(A) ↵
```

ans =
```
     9   3   1   0  -2  -5
```

If it is necessary, you can assign the output of the execution to some variable of your choice. What if we intend to have the sorting with index. For example, the column matrix $C = \begin{bmatrix} 23 \\ -20 \\ 30 \\ 8 \\ -10 \end{bmatrix}$ has the ascendingly sorted form

$B = \begin{bmatrix} -20 \\ -10 \\ 8 \\ 23 \\ 30 \end{bmatrix}$ but the elements in B had the position indices $\begin{bmatrix} 2 \\ 5 \\ 4 \\ 1 \\ 3 \end{bmatrix}$ in C. Our objective is to have these indices as well

and we execute the following for that:
```
>>[B,I]=sort(C) ↵
```
Upon execution, the reader should see the sorted elements as well as their indices assigned to the workspace variables B and I respectively. We avoided their display for the space reason. Now the function **sort** has two output arguments. They must be placed inside the third brace and separated by a comma, the first and second of which hold the return for the ascendingly ordered elements and their previous indices respectively.

10.11 Vectorizing the for-loops

In digital image processing problems literally we have thousands of pixels in one picture frame. To have control on every pixel in the digital image, we need two **for**-loops (subsection 10.3.3). If some checking operation is to be carried out inside the **for**-loop, this may take lengthy execution time. To avoid the time consuming situation, one can vectorize the **for**-loops employing the technique mentioned in this section.

◆ ◆ Vectorizing a single for-loop

A single **for**-loop is associated with the computation of one dimensional function. Let us say we intend to compute the function $f[m] = m^2 + 2m$ for $-2 \leq m \leq 3$ where the m is an integer. One should have $f[m]$ as $[0 \quad -1 \quad 0 \quad 3 \quad 8 \quad 15]$ following the computation. In the subsection 10.3.3 the single **for**-loop is discussed here just the code of the computation is provided:

Computation of $f[m]$ using for-loop:
```
>>f=[ ]; ↵
```

Computation of $f[m]$ using vector:
```
>>m=-2:3; ↵
```

```
>>for m=-2:3 f=[f m^2+2*m]; end ↵
>>f ↵
```

```
>>f=m.^2+2*m ↵
```

f =

       0   -1   0   3   8   15

f =

       0   -1   0   3   8   15

In for-loop, the computation happens one at a time ñ one for one counter index m. But in the vectorized computation we generate the whole range of m first by writing m=-2:3; that is m=[-2 -1 0 1 2 3]. The functional code of m^2+2m for the vectorized notion is completely different from the for-loop one. In the for-loop we use the vector string of the function whereas the scalar code in the vectorized computation (section 10.2). The vectorized computation follows the type of m i.e. if m is a row or column matrix, so is f. In either case the independent variable m information is lost we have to remember it.

Let us compute the expression m^2+2m again but for different m instead of consecutive one for example $m =[-9\ \ 7\ \ 5\ \ 2]$. After the computation we must have $f[m]=[63\ \ 63\ \ 35\ \ 8]$ for different m.

Computation of $f[m]$ using for-loop:

```
>>M=[-9 7 5 2]; f=[ ]; ↵
>>for m=1:length(M) f=[f M(m)^2+2*M(m)]; end ↵
>>f ↵
```

f =

    63 63 35 8

Computation of $f[m]$ using vector:

```
>>m=[-9 7 5 2]; ↵
>>f=m.^2+2*m ↵
```

f =

    63 63 35 8

Referring to above implementations, M holds all values of m as a row matrix in the for-loop. The command length(M) returns the number of elements in the matrix M. The M(1), M(2), Ö mean the first, secondÖ element in M respectively. The M(m) can be thought as the m of the expression m^2+2m. The command length is effective for long matrix and unknown number of elements. However, we assigned the four elements to the variable m for the vectorized counterpart.

♦ ♦ Vectorizing a double for-loop

Vectorizing a double for-loop computes two dimensional discrete function such as $f[m,n]$ which is closely related with the image processing calculation. Choosing example 4 of subsection 10.3.3 for which we exercised two for-loops in the computation of $f(x,y)=x+y$ for $-1\le x\le 0$ and $0\le y\le 1$ with a step 0.5 both for

x and y and found $f(x,y)=\begin{bmatrix} -1 & -0.5 & 0 \\ -0.5 & 0 & 0.5 \\ 0 & 0.5 & 1 \end{bmatrix}$ – this is what we expect from the vectorized computation.

Computation of $f(x,y)$ using vectorization:

```
>>x=[-1:0.5:0]'; ↵
>>y=0:0.5:1; ↵
>>X=repmat(x,1,length(y)); ↵
>>Y=repmat(y,length(x),1); ↵
>>f=X+Y ↵
```

f =

      -1.0000   -0.5000   0
      -0.5000   0   0.5000
          0   0.5000   1.0000

Concerning above implementation, the workspace variables x and y hold $-1\le x\le 0$ and $0\le y\le 1$ with a step 0.5 where $x=\begin{bmatrix} -1 \\ -0.5 \\ 0 \end{bmatrix}$ and y=[0 0.5 1] respectively. Note that the x and y must be column and row matrices respectively (simultaneously x and y can not be row or column). We call the workspace variables X and Y as the computational grid and they are produced from the repetitive matrices. The X is formed from the column by column repetition of x and the number of repetitions happens according to the number of elements of y. On the other hand Y is formed from the row by row repetitions of y and the number of repetitions happens according to the number of elements of x (section 10.8 for repmat) on that $X=\begin{bmatrix} -1 & -1 & -1 \\ -0.5 & -0.5 & -0.5 \\ 0 & 0 & 0 \end{bmatrix}$ and $Y=\begin{bmatrix} 0 & 0.5 & 1 \\ 0 & 0.5 & 1 \\ 0 & 0.5 & 1 \end{bmatrix}$. The scalar code (section 10.2) of $x+y$ should have been x+y. Instead of the variables x and y, we write the grid variables which are X and Y respectively that is why f=X+Y. It is important to mention that the X, Y, and f must be identical in size which is here 3×3. We chose the x and y vectors as the column and row matrices respectively. If you choose x as row and y as column, we end up with the transposed $f(x,y)$ but in that case the second and third input arguments of repmat become interchanged to maintain the consistent matrix order.

As another example, let us compute $f[m,n]=m^2-mn+n^2$ for $-1\le m\le 3$ and $1\le n\le 3$ where m and n are integers. Plugging different m and n values, one obtains $f[m,n]=\begin{bmatrix}3 & 7 & 13\\1 & 4 & 9\\1 & 3 & 7\\3 & 4 & 7\\7 & 7 & 9\end{bmatrix}$ – our objective is to have the computed $f[m,n]$ matrix. Using two for-loops like the example 4 of subsection 10.3.3 and vectorized concept just mentioned, we present the following:

M-file contents for the computation of $f[m,n]$ using for-loop:

```
r=[ ];
f=[ ];
for m=-1:3
        for n=1:3
                r=[r m^2-m*n+n^2];
        end
        f=[f;r];
        r=[ ];
end
>>f ↵

f =
        3    7    13
        1    4    9
        1    3    7
        3    4    7
        7    7    9
```

Computation of $f[m,n]$ using vectorized concept:

```
>>m=[-1:3]'; ↵
>>n=1:3; ↵
>>M=repmat(m,1,length(n)); ↵
>>N=repmat(n,length(m),1); ↵
>>f=M.^2-M.*N+N.^2 ↵

f =
        3    7    13
        1    4    9
        1    3    7
        3    4    7
        7    7    9
```

For the for-loop, the reader needs to write the codes in an M-file (chapter 1). After running the M-file, the f can be called from the workspace to see its contents. To make the vectorized concept easier, we attached various matrices flow as follows: $m=\begin{bmatrix}-1\\0\\1\\2\\3\end{bmatrix}$, $n=[1\ \ 2\ \ 3]$, $M=\begin{bmatrix}-1 & -1 & -1\\0 & 0 & 0\\1 & 1 & 1\\2 & 2 & 2\\3 & 3 & 3\end{bmatrix}$, and $N=\begin{bmatrix}1 & 2 & 3\\1 & 2 & 3\\1 & 2 & 3\\1 & 2 & 3\\1 & 2 & 3\end{bmatrix}$. The vector and scalar codes of the m^2-mn+n^2 are m^2-m*n+n^2 and m.^2-m.*n+n.^2 respectively. But as we mentioned, we place the grid variables in the scalar code not the base vectors m or n which is why f=M.^2-M.*N+N.^2.

♦ ♦ Vectorizing a double for-loop using meshgrid

The MATLAB function meshgrid can vectorize the double for-loop computations conveniently. Aforementioned repmat operation is hidden in the meshgrid. In this function we only input the independent variableís variations with steps. With the meshgrid, previously computed $f[m,n]=m^2-mn+n^2$ for $-1\le m\le 3$ and $1\le n\le 3$ is carried out as follows:

```
>>[M,N]=meshgrid(1:3,-1:3); ↵     ← generation of the grids M and N
>>f=M.^2-M.*N+N.^2 ↵              ← scalar code of m² – mn + n² assuming M⇔ m and N⇔ n

f =
        3    7    13
        1    4    9
        1    3    7
        3    4    7
        7    7    9
```

The function meshgrid has two input arguments, the n and m variations of $f[m,n]$ with steps as a row matrix. Note that the n variation is first, then is the m variation. The M and N have the same meanings as we mentioned earlier. The code writing of $f[m,n]$ follows the scalar one (section 10.2).

To work with another meshgrid example, let us compute $f(x,y) = x^2 y^3$ for $-1 \le x \le 0$ with 0.5 step along the x and for $0 \le y \le 1.2$ with 0.6 step along the y. The computation can happen by the following:

>>[X,Y]=meshgrid(0:0.6:1.2,-1:0.5:0); ↵   ← y variation with step first then for the x

>>f=X.^2.*Y.^3 ↵   ← scalar code of $x^2 y^3$ assuming X⇔x and Y⇔y

```
f =
        0   -0.3600   -1.4400
        0   -0.0450   -0.1800
        0         0         0
```

In image processing computations, the expression like $\sum\limits_{n=0}^{4} \sum\limits_{m=0}^{6} e^{j\frac{2\pi(m-1)(n-1)}{35}}$ is often seen which becomes a scalar following the computation. The function meshgrid can rescue us from the computation as shown below:

>>[M,N]=meshgrid(0:4,0:6); ↵   ← generation of the grids M and N

>>f=exp(j*2*(M-1).*(N-1)/35); ↵   ← scalar code of $e^{j\frac{2\pi(m-1)(n-1)}{35}}$ assuming M⇔m and N⇔n

>>sum(sum(f)) ↵   ← double summation (section 10.9) using two sums

```
ans =
        33.6709 + 3.7623i
```

The complex variable $j = \sqrt{-1}$ has the code either small case i or j in MATLAB. If both the m and n varied from 0 to 4, writing one variation like [M,N]=meshgrid(0:4); would be enough.

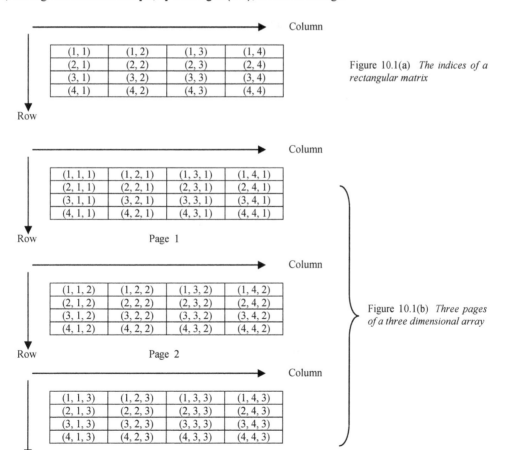

Figure 10.1(a) *The indices of a rectangular matrix*

Page 1

Page 2

Page 3

Figure 10.1(b) *Three pages of a three dimensional array*

10.12 Three dimensional, structure, and cell arrays

In most chapters we manipulated digital gray image data which is provided in a rectangular matrix and in essence is a two dimensional array. The matrix-oriented arrangement of data is not convenient for the true color image (section 2.4) in which the information demands multidimensional array. An amalgamate of numeric and character is obvious to store header or image information. There are three types of data arrangement apart from the rectangular matrix called three dimensional, structure, and cell arrays for which following discourse is rendered.

10.12.1 Three dimensional arrays

A rectangular matrix has two dimensions – one in the horizontal and the other in the vertical directions. Conformably any element position of the rectangular matrix needs two indexes to describe it – row and column. For example, a 4×4 rectangular matrix has the position indexes as shown in the figure 10.1(a). Suppose the 4×4 rectangular matrix fits in one page of a book. If we have two more pages each containing a 4×4 rectangular matrix, how can one accommodate the three pages in one variable? This necessitates the use of a three dimensional array. The position indexes of the rectangular matrices contained in the three pages can be labeled as shown in the figure 10.1(b). If one places the three pages sequentially, the three dimensional block of the figure 10.1(c) is formed. That is how a three dimensional array is created. One can assign any integer or floating-point values to the memory element corresponding to these position indexes. There are three position indexes of an element in the three dimensional array – dimension 1 (row), dimension 2 (column), and dimension 3 (page).

To see the procedure of the data entry, let us assume that the three page data of a three dimensional array

is given as follows: page 1: $\begin{bmatrix} 8 & 3 & 6 \\ 2 & 2 & 1 \end{bmatrix}$, page 2: $\begin{bmatrix} 0 & 4 & 4 \\ 5 & 3 & 8 \end{bmatrix}$, and page 3: $\begin{bmatrix} -1 & 2 & 7 \\ -5 & 5 & 6 \end{bmatrix}$ and name the three

dimensional array as A. Following is the implementation:

MATLAB Command

```
>>A(:,:,1)=[8 3 6;2 2 1]; ↵        ← Entering the elements of page 1
>>A(:,:,2)=[0 4 4;5 3 8]; ↵        ← Entering the elements of page 2
>>A(:,:,3)=[-1 2 7;-5 5 6]; ↵      ← Entering the elements of page 3
>>A ↵                              ← To see what in A is

ans(:,:,1) =                       ← Corresponds to page 1
        8   3   6
        2   2   1
ans(:,:,2) =                       ← Corresponds to page 2
        0   4   4
        5   3   8
ans(:,:,3) =                       ← Corresponds to page 3
       -1   2   7
       -5   5   6
```

The first, second, and third pages of the array are designated by A(:,:,1), A(:,:,2), and A(:,:,3) respectively. The two colons mean all elements along the row and column directions in the page respectively. Most manipulations of the rectangular matrix can be extended for the three dimensional array. Some manipulations pertaining to the three dimensional A are presented in the following. The third page element 7 has the index (1,3). It is called by

```
>>A(1,3,3) ↵

ans =
        7
```

You can change the value say by 10 and have carried out as follows:

```
>>A(1,3,3)=10; ↵
>>A(:,:,3) ↵                       ← To see only the third page

ans =
       -1   2   10
       -5   5   6
```

You can even assign the single page to some other variable. Suppose, you want to remove the third page from A. Let us carry out the following:

```
>>A(:,:,3)=[ ]; ↵
>>                                 ← It is done
```

A long row or column matrix can be converted to a three dimensional array by using the reshape (section 10.8). For example, let us choose R=[1   8   61   11   40   68   34   12   45   32   89   43] from which we wish

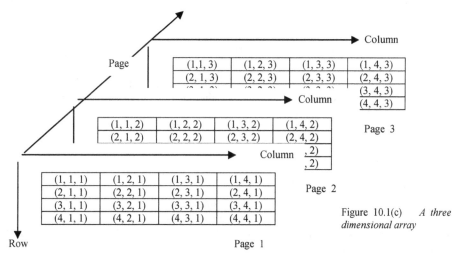

Figure 10.1(c)   *A three dimensional array*

to form a three dimensional array B concerning the two pages $\begin{bmatrix} 1 & 61 & 40 \\ 8 & 11 & 68 \end{bmatrix}$ and $\begin{bmatrix} 34 & 45 & 89 \\ 12 & 32 & 43 \end{bmatrix}$. There are twelve

elements in R and the product of row, column, and page numbers must be 12. The formation is shown below:

```
>>R=[1 8 61 11 40 68 34 12 45 32 89 43]; ↵        ← Entering all elements of R to R
>>B=reshape(R,2,3,2) ↵                            ← Applying the function and assigning the array to B

B(:,:,1) =                                        ← Displays the first page of B
        1   61   40
        8   11   68
B(:,:,2) =                                        ← Displays the second page of B
       34   45   89
       12   32   43
```

Needless to point out that the conversion is columnwise. The reverse conversion that is a three dimensional array A can be converted to the column matrix by using the command A(:). The last A of the workspace is containing the

first two pages. Squares to all elements of A are $\begin{bmatrix} 64 & 9 & 36 \\ 4 & 4 & 1 \end{bmatrix}$ (page 1) and $\begin{bmatrix} 0 & 16 & 16 \\ 25 & 9 & 64 \end{bmatrix}$ (page 2) respectively.

You can have that on execution of A.^2 as follows:
```
>>A.^2 ↵

ans(:,:,1) =
       64    9   36
        4    4    1
ans(:,:,2) =
        0   16   16
       25    9   64
```
One can add one more page by assigning a 2×3 matrix to

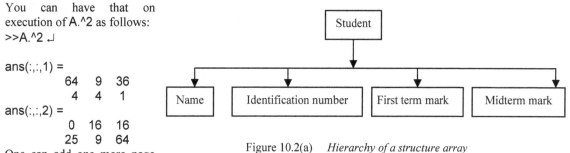

Figure 10.2(a)   *Hierarchy of a structure array*

A(:,:,3). Adding some scalar, say 5, to each element of A is accomplished by A+5. The multiplication of two three dimensional arrays is not defined. The pages of the array can be multiplied according to the rules of matrix algebra for example page 2 with page 3 by A(:,:,2)*A(:,:,3). For simplicity, we have shown all manipulations taking the integer array elements but the elements can be floating-points, characters, or even symbolic variables. In the digital image processing context, the pages 1, 2, and 3 represent the red, green, and blue color planes respectively.

10.12.2 Structure arrays

All elements of a two or three dimensional array are identical data. The data can be integers, floating-points, complex numbers, or symbolic variables. A structure array is another data arrangment which has the mixed type of arrays as individuals and the individuals are termed as members. Suppose a physics teacher teaches two classes. For each class, he wants to keep the examination records for all students applying the hierarchy of the figure 10.2(a). Let us assume that the names, the identification numbers, the first term marks out of 30, and the

midterm marks out of 30 for five students are $\begin{bmatrix} \text{Reza} \\ \text{Shameem} \\ \text{John} \\ \text{Rebeca} \\ \text{Richard} \end{bmatrix}$, $\begin{bmatrix} 91 \\ 92 \\ 89 \\ 96 \\ 95 \end{bmatrix}$, $\begin{bmatrix} 23.5 \\ 29.7 \\ 23 \\ 9 \\ 12 \end{bmatrix}$, and $\begin{bmatrix} 25.5 \\ 27.7 \\ 21 \\ 20 \\ 19 \end{bmatrix}$ respectively. The data we

have is of mixed type for instance the names and the identification numbers are characters and integers respectively. We enter various data as follows:

MATLAB Command

```
>>N=strvcat('Reza','Shameem','John','Rebeca','Richard'); ↵      ← We assign the names to N
>>I=[91 92 89 96 95]'; ↵                                        ← We assign the identification numbers to I
>>F=[23.5 29.7 23 9 12]'; ↵                                     ← We assign the first term grades to F
>>M=[25.5 27.7 21 20 19]'; ↵                                    ← We assign the midterm grades to M
```

The names are entered as a string placing under the single inverted comma. The MATLAB function **strvcat** (abbreviation of the <u>str</u>ing <u>v</u>ertically <u>cat</u>enated) places its input argument strings vertically. The maximum number of characters in the names is in Shameem, which is 7. Therefore the N is a character array of size 5×7. We entered all numerical values as column matrices. The identification numbers, the first term marks, and the midterm marks are assigned to the workspace variables I, F, and M respectively. The MATLAB function **struct** constructs a structure array from various members. In MATLAB terminology, the members are called the fields. We name various fields as Name, ID, Fgrade, and Mgrade respectively. Following is the structure formation:

```
>>S=struct('Name',N,'ID',I,'Fgrade',F,'Mgrade',M) ↵      ← We name the structure array as S

    S =

            Name:   [5x7 char    ]                        ←'Name' is a 2 dimensional array
              ID:   [5x1 double  ]
          Fgrade:   [5x1 double  ]
          Mgrade:   [5x1 double  ]
```

To invoke a particular member from the structure S, we execute the command S.member. For instance, the identification numbers and the names are invoked by the following:

for the identification numbers	**for the names**	**for specific element**
>>S.ID ↵	>>S.Name ↵	>>S.ID(2) ↵
ans =	ans =	ans =
91		92
92	Reza	>>S.Name(2,:) ↵
89	Shameem	
96	John	ans =
95	Rebeca	
	Richard	Shameem

You can even assign S.ID or S.Name to some other workspace variable. A specific element of the field ID (say second one, which is 92) can be accessed by S.ID(2). Since the field Name is a two dimensional character array, the second name Shameem is addressed by S.Name(2,:). Above execution also shows their implementations.

Suppose the final examination marks out of 40, which are $\begin{bmatrix} 35.5 \\ 37.7 \\ 24 \\ 30 \\ 23 \end{bmatrix}$ for the respective students, are available at the end of the semester. The new hierarchy is pictured in the figure 10.2(b). He wants to add the final marks with the existing structure. Let us name

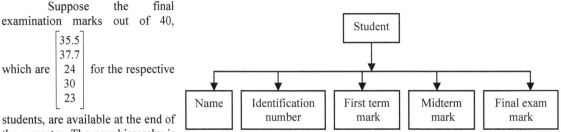

Figure 10.2(b) *Adding a field final exam mark to the existing hierarchy*

the field as Final. The function **setfield** can add a field to the existing structure S as follows:

>>FN=[35.5 37.7 24 30 23]'; ↵   ← We assign the final examination marks to **FN**
>>Physics1=setfield(S,'Final',FN) ↵   ← The new structure is named as **Physics1**

Physics1 =
                Name: [5x7 char   ]
                  ID: [5x1 double]
              Fgrade: [5x1 double]
              Mgrade: [5x1 double]
               Final: [5x1 double]   ← The field **Final** is added here

The function **setfield** has three input arguments ñ the first, second, and third of which are the existing structure name, the field name to be added, and the values to be assigned to the field respectively. Sometimes removal of a field may be required. One can implement that by the function **rmfield**. Let us remove the last field **Final** as follows:

>>rmfield(Physics1,'Final') ↵

ans =
                Name: [5x7 char   ]
                  ID: [5x1 double]
              Fgrade: [5x1 double]
              Mgrade: [5x1 double]

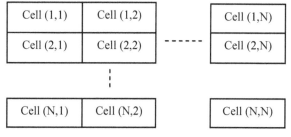

Figure 10.2(c)   *A two dimensional cell array of order N×N*

Referring to the implementation, the variable values are not necessary for the removal, only the field name is enough. The assignee **Physics1** is still having the first term, midterm, and final grades because we did not assign the output to any variable following the removal. Finally, let us aggregate all marks to have the total grades out of 100 and put them to another field **Total** as follows:

>>T=Physics1.Fgrade+Physics1.Mgrade+Physics1.Final; ↵ ← Sums of all marks are assigned to **T**
>>Physics1=setfield(Physics1,'Total',T); ↵   ← The total grade is put to field **Total**
>>Physics1.Total ↵   ← To see the total grades out of 100

ans =
        84.5000
        95.1000
        68.0000
        59.0000
        54.0000

10.12.3 Cell arrays

A cell array is composed of cells, where the cells can contain ordinary arrays (of real, integer, or complex numbers), structure arrays, three dimensional arrays, character arraysÖ etc. Figure 10.2(c) shows a two dimensional cell array of order N×N. To be specific, we intend to construct a cell array of order 2×3. The cells of a cell array are indexed like a rectangular matrix but using the second brace {..}. The position indexes of different cells are A{1,1}, A{1,2}, A{1,3}, A{2,1}, A{2,2}, and A{2,3} respectively (considering the name of the cell array as A). For example, let us assign the matrices

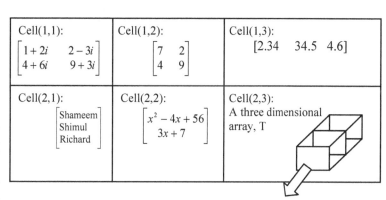

Three pages of the three dimensional array corresponding to cell(2, 3) are

$$\begin{bmatrix} 2 & 3 \\ 4 & 5 \end{bmatrix}, \quad \begin{bmatrix} 11.1 & 30.3 \\ 12.2 & 51.9 \end{bmatrix}, \quad \text{and}$$

$$\begin{bmatrix} 19 & 36 \\ 2.2 & 55 \end{bmatrix} \text{ respectively.}$$

Figure 10.3(a)   *Two dimensional cell array A of order 2×3*

$$\begin{bmatrix} 1+2i & 2-3i \\ 4+6i & 9+3i \end{bmatrix}, \begin{bmatrix} 7 & 2 \\ 4 & 9 \end{bmatrix}, [2.34 \quad 34.5 \quad 4.6], \begin{bmatrix} \text{Shameem} \\ \text{Shimul} \\ \text{Richard} \end{bmatrix}, \text{ and } \begin{bmatrix} x^2-4x+56 \\ 3x+7 \end{bmatrix} \text{ and a three dimensional array T}$$

with three pages $\begin{bmatrix} 2 & 3 \\ 4 & 5 \end{bmatrix}, \begin{bmatrix} 11.1 & 30.3 \\ 12.2 & 51.9 \end{bmatrix}$, and $\begin{bmatrix} 19 & 36 \\ 2.2 & 55 \end{bmatrix}$ respectively to different cells of A. The schematic representation of different cell content is shown in the figure 10.3(a) for which the implementation is presented as follows:

>>A{1,1}=[1+2i 2-3i;4+6i 9+3i]; ↵ ← Assigning the complex matrix $\begin{bmatrix} 1+2i & 2-3i \\ 4+6i & 9+3i \end{bmatrix}$ to cell(1,1)

>>A{1,2}=[7 2;4 9]; ↵ ← Assigning the integer matrix $\begin{bmatrix} 7 & 2 \\ 4 & 9 \end{bmatrix}$ to cell(1,2)

>>A{1,3}=[2.34 34.5 4.6]; ↵ ← Assigning floating-point matrix [2.34 34.5 4.6] to cell(1,3)

>>A{2,1}=strvcat('Shameem','Shimul','Richard'); ↵ ← Assigning the two dimensional character

array $\begin{bmatrix} \text{Shameem} \\ \text{Shimul} \\ \text{Richard} \end{bmatrix}$ to cell (2,1)

>>syms x ↵

>>A{2,2}=[x^2-4*x+56;3*x+7]; ↵ ← Assigning the symbolic matrix $\begin{bmatrix} x^2-4x+56 \\ 3x+7 \end{bmatrix}$ to cell(2,2)

>>T(:,:,1)=[2 3;4 5]; ↵ ← Assigning the first page of T
>>T(:,:,2)=[11.1 30.3;12.2 51.9]; ↵ ← Assigning the second page of T
>>T(:,:,3)=[19 36;2.2 55]; ↵ ← Assigning the third page of T
>>A{2,3}=T ↵ ← Assigning the three dimensional array T to cell(2,3)

A =
    [2x2 double]   [2x2 double]   [1x3   double]
    [3x7 char]   [2x1 sym]   [2x2x3   double]

Cell(1,1):A	Cell(1,2):[47 31]

Figure 10.3(b) *1×2 cell array B showing cell inside cell*

Instead of displaying the contents, A is showing the type of the component cells. Some maneuverings of the cell arrays are presented in the following. The cell(1,2) has the 2×2 integer matrix. The element having the position index (2,1) of this matrix is 4. Let us access the element as follows:

>>A{1,2}(2,1) ↵

ans =
    4

Placing cell inside cell is also possible. Suppose, another cell array B of order 1×2 is to be built, where the cell(1,1) and the cell(1,2) of B contain the previous mentioned 2×3 cell array A and a row matrix [47 31] respectively (figure 10.3(b)). It is just the matter of assignment as follows:

>>B{1,1}=A; ↵
>>B{1,2}=[47 31]; ↵
>>B ↵

Cell(1,2): $\begin{bmatrix} 7 & 2 \\ 4 & 9 \end{bmatrix}$
Cell(2,2): $\begin{bmatrix} x^2-4x+56 \\ 3x+7 \end{bmatrix}$

Figure 10.3(c) *Subset of cell array A*

B =
    {2x3 cell}   [1x2 double]

Cell indexing similar to an ordinary array can access to the subset of a cell. For instance the cells of the cell array A taken from the intersection of the first and second rows and the second column, which are shown in figure 10.3(c), are invoked as follows:

>>A(1:2,2) ↵

ans =
    [2x2   double]
    [2x1   sym]

Let us delete the cell(1,3) and the cell(2,3) from A as follows:

```
>>A{1,3}=[ ];  ↵
>>A{2,3}=[ ]  ↵
```

A =

[2x2 double]	[2x2 double]	[ ]
[3x7 char]	[2x1 sym]	[ ]

← 2 deleted cells

Reshaping, catenating, and forming three dimensional arrays of the cell arrays can be accomplished too. Some functions, which handle different types of arrays, are supplied in the table 10.B.

Table 10.B Some functions pertaining to multidimensional, structure, and cell arrays

Purpose	Function	Purpose	Function
To concatenate arrays	cat	To see structure field names	fieldnames
To know the number of array dimensions	ndims	To check whether a field is in a structure array	isfield
To permute array dimensions	permute	To display contents of a cell array	celldisp
To shift array dimensions	shiftdim	To convert a numeric array to cell array	num2cell
To remove singleton dimensions	squeeze	To convert a cell array to structure array	cell2struct
To check whether an array is a structure array	isstruct	To convert a structure array to cell array	struct2cell
To create a cell array	cell	To check whether an array is a cell array	iscell

10.13 Writing image matrix data to a softcopy file

Once some image analysis is performed, the reader may need to write the image matrix data to a supportable softcopy file such as JPEG or others. MATLAB offers the provision for writing the image matrix data and related information of a digital image to a portable softcopy file with the aid of the function imwrite (abbreviation of the image write). Referring to section 2.4, there are four types of digital image. Also the tables 2.A and 2.B present the supportable image formats and the data class for the softcopy respectively. Their knowledge is important prior to soft file writing. Let us implement following examples assuming the softcopy file name is **test**.

♦ ♦ Binary image

Let us say we have the binary digital image matrix $f[m,n] = \begin{bmatrix} 1 & 0 & 0 \\ 1 & 1 & 1 \\ 0 & 0 & 1 \end{bmatrix}$ and wish to write the image

matrix as a JPEG file. The procedure is as follows:

```
>>f=[1 0 0;1 1 1;0 0 1];  ↵        ← Assigning the image matrix f[m,n] to f
>>imwrite(logical(f),'test.jpg')  ↵  ← Writing the f data to the file by the name test.jpg
>>dir  ↵                            ← To see all files present in the working directory
```

You must find the file test.jpg in your working folder or path. A binary image can best be stored as a logical array but the data assigning happens in double class. That is why before writing the softcopy, logical(f) is conducted. The function imwrite has two input arguments ñ the first and second of which are the digital image matrix and the file name as a string with exact extension name (for example .jpg for JPEG image) respectively.

♦ ♦ Intensity or gray image

An intensity or gray image has the image data in [0,1] for fractional or in [0,255] for 256 integer gray levels. The image writing is similar to that of the binary one. If the f data is in [0,1] and fractional, the necessary command is imwrite(f,'test.jpg'). If the f data is not in [0,1], the command mat2gray on f can be applied hence the writing command should be imwrite(mat2gray(f),'test.jpg'). In the case of 256 integer gray levels in [0,255] when entered as double class, unsigned 8-bit integer format is the most appropriate one therefore the command is imwrite(uint8(f),'test.jpg'). If the digital image matrix possesses more gray levels than 256, the unsigned 16-bit or higher format can be used.

220

♣ ♣ Indexed color image

The color image possesses intensity and colormap matrices. Considering the 5 level image matrix $f[m,n]$

$$= \begin{bmatrix} 1 & 4 & 0 & 0 \\ 0 & 2 & 3 & 1 \\ 1 & 2 & 0 & 0 \end{bmatrix} \text{ and the colormap matrix } M = \begin{cases} level & R & G & B \\ 0 & 0 & 0 & 0 \\ 1 & 0.2555 & 0.7899 & 0.1111 \\ 2 & 0.5432 & 0.6789 & 0.6541 \\ 3 & 0.7921 & 0.7892 & 0.8543 \\ 4 & 1 & 1 & 1 \end{cases} \text{ from section 2.4, the writing for}$$

the indexed image as a JPEG file by the name test is as follows:

>>f=[1 4 0 0;0 2 3 1;1 2 0 0]; ↵   ← Assigning the intensity matrix to f
>>M=[0 0 0;0.2555 0.7899 0.1111;0.5432 0.6789 0.6541;0.721 0.7892 0.8543;1 1 1]; ↵
>>imwrite(uint8(f),M,'test.jpg') ↵
>>dir ↵   ← To see all files present in the working directory

Above implementation is syntactically correct but conceptually wrong. Most image data storage happens to be in unsigned-8 bit integer which requires 256 levels in f in [0,255] and 256×3 colormap matrix for M. For example reason it is not feasible that we type such a huge matrix. However, the function imwrite is now having three input arguments for the indexed type ñ the first, second, and third of which are the intensity image matrix $f[m,n]$, the colormap matrix M, and the given file name with proper file format respectively. For the double class data, the function imwrite converts the data to the unsigned 8-bit integer by first subtracting 1. Since we chose the five gray levels from 0 to 4, that causes negative number when subtracted from 0 thereby giving some error. To avoid that error, one can add 1 to every gray level of $f[m,n]$ for which the command would be imwrite(f+1,M,'test.jpg'). If the gray levels were labeled in [1,5], this addition would not be necessary. Again if the data class of f is originally unsigned 8 or 16-bit integers, no conversion takes place. The colormap matrix must have three columns, and its row number is exactly the number of intensity levels chosen for the $f[m,n]$ for example here it is 5×3. Elements of the colormap matrix M must be of double class ranging from 0 to 1 and fractional.

♣ ♣ True color image

The last image type we introduced in section 2.4 is the RGB or true color image for which one needs the primary color component matrices. Let us take the primary color component matrices as $r[m,n] = \begin{bmatrix} 1 & 4 & 0 & 0 \\ 0 & 2 & 3 & 1 \\ 1 & 2 & 0 & 0 \end{bmatrix}$

for the red, $g[m,n] = \begin{bmatrix} 2 & 3 & 0 & 0 \\ 0 & 2 & 3 & 1 \\ 1 & 1 & 2 & 2 \end{bmatrix}$ for the green, and $b[m,n] = \begin{bmatrix} 4 & 4 & 1 & 3 \\ 0 & 2 & 3 & 1 \\ 2 & 3 & 2 & 1 \end{bmatrix}$ for the blue – all in [0,4]. These

component matrices are entered as the three dimensional array pages (section 10.12.1) and let us enter them as follows:

>>f(:,:,1)=[1 4 0 0;0 2 3 1;1 2 0 0]; ↵ ← Assigning $r[m,n]$ as the first page of three dimensional f
>>f(:,:,2)=[2 3 0 0;0 2 3 1;1 1 2 2]; ↵ ← Assigning $g[m,n]$ as the second page of three dimensional f
>>f(:,:,3)=[4 4 1 3;0 2 3 1;2 3 2 1]; ↵ ← Assigning $b[m,n]$ as the third page of three dimensional f
>>imwrite(mat2gray(f),'test.jpg') ↵
>>dir ↵   ← To see all files present in the working directory

The fourth line in above implementation writes the three dimensional data stored in f to the softcopy file test.jpg. The function has two input arguments ñ three dimensional array name and softcopy file name. The data class of f must be in [0,1] for double class (that is why mat2gray is used) or in [0,255] for unsigned 8-bit integer. For the double class f in [0,255], we exercise the command imwrite(uint8(f),'test.jpg').

The function imwrite also has other options for intaking more arguments for the JPEG file format. There is an input argument called quality that measures the compression quality of an image ranging from 0 to 100. The more is the number, the better is quality. Let us say we want a quality of 75, then the implementation is as follows:

>>imwrite(f,'test.jpg','quality',75) ↵

The word quality input argumented as a string and as the third performs the image writing. The number 75 follows the fourth input argument of the function.

So far we presented the procedure for writing the image matrix data in a JPEG file format for the binary, intensity, indexed, and RGB images. Writing the image matrix data in the file format other than the JPEG takes place in a similar fashion. As presented in the table 2.A, let us say the windows bit map file format (which has the file extension bmp) is selected. For the last RGB type color image, the command would have been as follows:

>>imwrite(mat2gray(f),'test.bmp') ↵

The file types of the table 2.A have different options for taking their associated input arguments. A comprehensive help can immediately be seen by executing the following:

>>help imwrite ↵

It should be pointed out that the data class of the image matrix or colormap as well as the range must be checked before any image writing because the image file formats allow only specific data class and range.

10.14 Conversion of soft type images

A softcopy digital image file differs from the other in the method of data storage class, image compression involved, coding used, default pixel size, etc. Some imaging system may support one specific soft type but available image might be in other soft type. Needless to mention, softcopy image conversion is essential under those circumstances. MATLABís figure window or the image reader function plays a gateway role in the soft copy image conversion. Whatever is plotted and displayed in the figure window of MATLAB can be stored as a supportable soft image file like JPEG, BMP, or PNG.

Let us consider the function **ezplot** of MATLAB which plots any mathematical function of the type $f(x)$ within $-2\pi \le x \le 2\pi$. As an example let us say $f(x) = \sin x$ and plot it as follows:

>>ezplot('sin(x)') ↵

For sure the reader should see the plot of the figure 10.4(a). From this figure window, let us click the File then

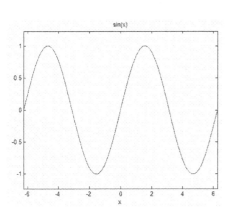

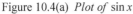

Figure 10.4(a) *Plot of* $\sin x$

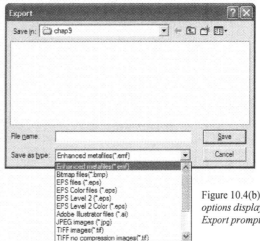

Figure 10.4(b) *Soft file type options displayed by the Export prompt window*

Export from the menu bar of the window. Figure 10.4(b) presents the Export prompt window in which you find different soft image types in the Save as type slot. Let us choose Bitmap files with the help of mouse from the popup menu of the figure 10.4(b) and write any file name (say **test**) in the slot of File name of the window. In doing so, we saved the contents of the figure window by the file name **test.bmp** in the working directory. After that the reader can check whether the file **test.bmp** exists by the following:

>>dir ↵

Next we display the captured image test.bmp with the help of **imshow** as follows:

>>imshow('test.bmp') ↵

The execution now shows you the figure 10.4(a) as an image not as a graph.

As another example, let us consider the true color image man.jpg from section 2.3. Obtain the image in your working directory and execute the following command to see the image:

>>imshow('man.jpg') ↵

Now by going through the Export of the File menu as we did before, one can save the image to any other type in the popup menu of the figure 10.4(b). But the problem is every format has some default setting which may turn to end up with a resized or distorted image.

Another option is the employment of the image reader function. For example we intend to convert the image man.jpg to man.tif without displaying the image. Following execution assists us attain that:

>>f=imread('man.jpg'); ↵   ← Reading the man.jpg image, f is 3D array

>>imwrite(f,'man.tif'); ↵   ← Writing the man.tif image from f

The details of the functions are mentioned in sections 2.7 and 10.13 respectively. This method permits us write the image data with exact pixel and color information without any distortion or resizing.

10.15 Creating a function file

A function file is a special type of M-file which has some user defined input and output arguments. Both arguments can be single or multiple. The first line in a function file always starts with the word function. The function file must be in your working path or its path must be defined in MATLAB. Depending on the problem, a function file is written by the user and can be called from the MATLAB command prompt or from another M-file. For convenience, long and clumsy programs are split into smaller modules and these modules are written in a function file. However the basic structure of a function file is as follows:

MATLAB Command Prompt $\qquad$ function file

$$>> g = \text{call } f \qquad \Longrightarrow \qquad g\underbrace{(y_1, y_2, ..., y_m)}_{\text{output arguments}} = f\underbrace{(x_1, x_2, x_3, ..., x_n)}_{\text{input arguments}}$$

We present the following examples for illustration of the function files keeping in mind that the arguments' order and types of the caller and the function files are identical.

⬚⬚ Example 1

Let us say $f(x) = x^2 - x - 8$ is to be implemented as a function file. When $x = -3$ and $x = 5$, we are supposed to have 4 and 12 respectively. The code for the function is x^2-x-8 assuming x is a scalar. We have one input (which is x) and one output (which is $f(x)$). Open a new M-file editor (chapter 1), type the codes of the figure 10.5(a) exactly as they appear in the M-file, and save the file by the name f. The assignee y and independent variable x can be any name of your choice and which are the output and input arguments of the function respectively. Again the file and function name f can be user-chosen any name only the point is the chosen function or file name should not exist in MATLAB. Let us call the function to verify the programming as follows:

for $x = -3$,   **for** $x = 5$,

    >>g=f(-3) ⏎   ← call $f(x)$ for $x = -3$ >>g=f(5) ⏎   ← call $f(x)$ for $x = 5$

    g =   g =
       4   12

You can write dozens of MATLAB executable statements in the file but whatever is assigned to the y last returns the function f(x) to g.

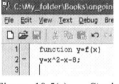

Figure 10.5(a)   *Single input ñ single output function file*

⬚⬚ Example 2

Example 1 presents one input-one output function how if we handle multiple inputs and one output. The input argument names are separated by commas. The three variable function $f(x_1, x_2, x_3) = x_1^2 - 2x_1 x_2 + x_3^2$

Figure 10.5(b) *Multiple inputs ñ single output function file*

is to be written in a function file. The input arguments (assuming all scalar) are x_1, x_2, and x_3 and the output argument is the functional value. The x_1 is written as x1, and so is the others. Follow the procedure of example 1 but the code should be as shown in the figure 10.5(b). Let us inspect the function (with $x_1 = 3$, $x_2 = 4$, and $x_3 = 5$, the output must be $f(3, 4, 5) = 3^2 - 2 \times 3 \times 4 + 5^2 = 10$) as follows:

    >>g=f(3,4,5) ⏎   ← calling $f(x_1, x_2, x_3)$ for $x_1 = 3$, $x_2 = 4$, and $x_3 = 5$

    g =
       10

The function not only works for the scalar inputs but also does for matrices in general for example a set of input

argument values are $x_1 = \begin{bmatrix} 2 \\ 3 \\ 4 \end{bmatrix}$, $x_2 = \begin{bmatrix} -2 \\ 2 \\ 5 \end{bmatrix}$, and $x_3 = \begin{bmatrix} 1 \\ 0 \\ 3 \end{bmatrix}$. The outputs should look like $\begin{bmatrix} 2^2 - 2 \times 2 \times (-2) + 1^2 \\ 3^2 - 2 \times 3 \times 2 + 0 \\ 4^2 - 2 \times 4 \times 5 + 3^2 \end{bmatrix} = \begin{bmatrix} 13 \\ -3 \\ -15 \end{bmatrix}$

which is the result of the scalar computation (section 10.2) of $f(x_1, x_2, x_3)$ from x_1, x_2, and x_3. The modified statement in the second line of the figure 10.5(b) now should be y=x1.^2-2*x1.*x2+x3.^2;. On making the modification and saving the file, let us carry out the following:

    >>x1=[2 3 4]'; ⏎   ← x_1 values are assigned to x1 as a column matrix

    >>x2=[-2 2 5]'; ⏎   ← x_2 values are assigned to x2 as a column matrix

>>x3=[1 0 3]'; ↵   ← x_3 values are assigned to x3 as a column matrix

>>f(x1,x2,x3) ↵   ← now calling $f(x_1, x_2, x_3)$ using column matrix input argument

ans =

    13

    -3

    -15

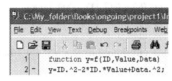

If it is necessary, the output can be assigned to some other workspace variable v writing v=f(x1,x2,x3) at the command prompt. The input arguments of

Figure 10.5(c)   *Function file of the figure 10.5(b) using different input variable names*

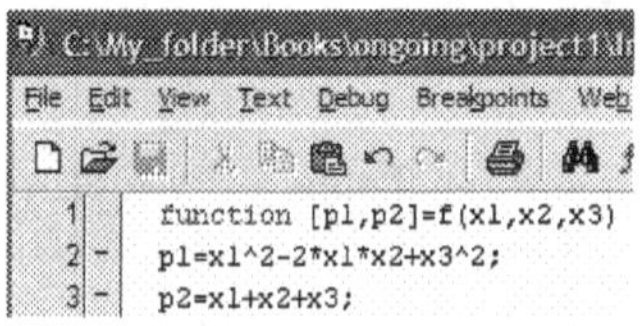

Figure 10.5(d)   *Function file for three input and two output arguments*

the function file do not have to be the mathematics symbol. Suppose x_1 =ID, x_2 =Value, and x_3 =Data, one could have written the function file as shown in the figure 10.5(c).

⊡⊡ Example 3

To illustrate the multi-input and multi-output function file, consider that p_1 and p_2 are to be found from three variables x_1, x_2, and x_3 (all are scalars) employing the expressions $p_1 = x_1^2 - 2x_1 x_2 + x_3^2$ and $p_2 = x_1 + x_2 + x_3$ whose function file (type the codes in the M-file editor and save the file by the name f) is presented in the figure 10.5(d). On choosing x_1 =4, x_2 =5, and x_3 =6, one should get p_1 =12 and p_2 =15 for which the following is conducted at the command prompt:

>>[p1,p2]=f(4,5,6) ↵   ← calling the function file f for p_1 and p_2 using x_1 =4, x_2 =5, and x_3 =6

p1 =

    12

p2 =

    15

More than one output arguments (which are here p_1 are p_2 and represented by p1 and p2 respectively) separated by commas and placed inside the third bracing following the word function of the figure 10.5(d). When we call the function from the command prompt, the output argument writing is similar to that of the function file one (that is why we write [p1,p2] at the command prompt as output arguments). The output argument variable names do not have to be p1 and p2 and can be any name of user choice. If there were three output arguments p_1, p_2, and p_3, the output arguments in the function file would be written as [p1,p2,p3] and their calling would happen in like manner.

As an open system, MATLAB has plentiful resources for programming every branches of the digital image processing. Application dependent digital image processing needs the graphical user interface and simulink modeling which are beyond the scope of the book. Our deliberation includes to the introductory programming for the digital image processing. Once preliminary computations are reasoned out, advanced programming can facilely be conducted. We hope our easy implementations and pertinent minute details would inspire the reader to work in MATLAB for his/her working platform. However we bring an end to the text with this.

Appendix A
List of MATLAB functions addressed in the text

Table A   MATLAB functions employed in the text for image processing applications

MATLAB function name	Function(s)
abs	It finds magnitude values of all elements from a complex matrix in general
all	It checks whether all elements in a binary vector are 1
angle	It finds phase angle values in radians of all elements from a complex matrix in general
any	It finds any element in a binary vector is 1 (at least 1 element)
axis on	It brings the axis in an image
blkproc	It performs block based computation on a digital image
bwdist	It computes the distance transform of binary images
bwhitmiss	It performs the Hit and Miss transform on a binary image from user defined structuring element
bwmorph	This is the mother function for a lot of morphological processings on the binary images
bwperim	It finds the perimeter of binary images
char	It takes ASCII code in double form as input and returns the corresponding character
circshift	It circularly shifts the elements of an array from user requirement
circul	It generates complete circulant matrix by considering all possible circular shifts of a row or column vector
class	It returns the information about the data class of a workspace variable
conj	It returns the conjugate of a complex number matrix in general
conv2	It computes two dimensional discrete convolution of two discrete functions
corr2	It computes the correlation coefficient of two identical size digital images
cov	It finds the covariance of the random variables entered as the columns of a rectangular matrix
datastats	It finds the statistics of data in a row or column vector
dct2	It computes two dimensional forward discrete cosine transform of a digital image matrix
dctmtx	It returns discrete cosine transform matrices of different order
dec2bin	It converts a double class integer number to its equivalent binary string
dftmtx	It returns discrete Fourier transform matrices of different order
diag	It picks up the diagonal elements from a rectangular matrix in general
diff	It takes the numerical difference between the successive elements in a row or column matrix
dir	It shows all files present in the current working directory
double	It converts any valid input data to double class for computation
dwt2	It computes two dimensional forward discrete wavelet transform of a digital image matrix
edge	It is the mother function name for many edge detection techniques on a digital image
eig	It computes the eigenvalues and eigenvectors of a square matrix
eps	It returns a very small quantity epsilon
eye	It generates identity matrices of various orders
ezplot	It graphs expression dependent y versus x type functions
factor	It factorizes an integer or some mathematical expression
fft2	It computes two dimensional forward discrete Fourier transform of a digital image matrix
fftshift	It flips a digital image matrix about the half indices along the horizontal and vertical directions
figure	It opens a new MATLAB figure window
find	It finds the positional indices in a rectangular matrix in general subject to various logical conditions
fliplr	It flips the elements in a vector from the left to the right
flipud	It flips the elements in a vector from the up to the down
for-end	Beginning and ending statements of a for-loop
fspecial	It is the mother function name for many image processing masks
function	Reserve word in MATLAB for generating multiple input and output function
getsequence	It decomposes the return by the strel to the component structural elements

Continuation of the table A

MATLAB function name	Function(s)
gray2ind	It converts an intensity or gray image to indexed form color image
grayslice	It performs false coloring by dividing the image gray levels in equal slices
grid	It draws grid lines in the last opened graph
hadamard	It returns Hadamard matrices of different orders
hgram	Author written M-file that finds the histogram equalized image matrix
histeq	Toolbox function that finds the histogram equalized image
hold	It holds the last figure window for superimposing the subsequent plots
hough	Author written M-file that returns the Hough transform of a digital image
hsv2rgb	It changes an image in HSV color space to the image in RGB color space
huff	Author written M-file that finds Huffman codes from the unity sum probability vector (only for the column vector)
idct2	It computes two dimensional inverse discrete cosine transform of a two dimensional discrete function in general
idwt2	It computes two dimensional inverse discrete wavelet transform from the forward counterpart
if-end	Beginning and ending statements of logical if syntax
ifft2	It computes two dimensional inverse discrete Fourier transform from the forward counterpart
im2bw	It turns a color image to binary image using user defined threshold
im2uint8	It converts its input in [0,1] double class to unsigned 8-bit integer in [0,255]
imabsdiff	It finds the absolute difference of two identical size images
imadd	It adds two identical pixel size images
imag	It finds the imaginary parts from all elements in a complex number matrix in general
imclose	It performs the closing of a binary image from user defined structuring element
imcomplement	It finds the complement image of a digital image
imcrop	It crops or discards some portion of the image from the user requirement
imdilate	It performs the dilation of a binary image from user defined structuring element
imdivide	It finds the division of two identical size images
imerode	It performs the erosion of a binary image from user defined structuring element
imfilter	It performs spatial domain filtering of a digital image from user defined mask
imfinfo	If describes the details of a softcopy digital image
imhist	It plots the histogram of a digital image but taking samples of actual histogram
imlincomb	It finds the linear combination of multiple images from the user requirement
immultiply	It finds the multiplication of two identical size images
imnoise	It adds noise to a given digital image from user requirements
imopen	It performs the opening of a binary image from user defined structuring element
imread	It reads differently stored digital image files
imresize	It scales up or down a digital image from user defined pixel size
imrotate	It rotates a digital image by user defined angle
imshow	It displays an image from the digital image matrix or from digitally stored softcopy files both in gray and color forms
imsubtract	It subtracts two identical pixel size images
imtransform	It can take the geometric transform of an image
imwrite	It writes the matrix data as an image soft copy file for exporting
ind2gray	It converts an indexed type color image to a gray or black and white image
ind2rgb	It converts an indexed type color image to RGB or true color image
input	It can take input from the user at the command prompt during the run time of an M-file
int16	It converts its input to signed 16-bit integer
int32	It converts its input to signed 32-bit integer
int8	It converts its input to signed 8-bit integer
isgray	It checks a workspace variable whether it is a gray image
isind	It checks a workspace variable whether it is an indexed image
isrgb	It checks a workspace variable whether it is an RGB image
jprobm	Author written M-file that returns the discrete joint probability density function of an image subject to some operator along the horizontal direction

Continuation of the table A

MATLAB function name	Function(s)
jprobmn	Author written M-file that returns the discrete joint probability density function of an image subject to some operator along the diagonal direction
jprobn	Author written M-file that returns the discrete joint probability density function of an image subject to some operator along the vertical direction
length	It finds the length or the number of elements in a row or column matrix
log	It takes the natural logarithm on all elements in a rectangular matrix
log10	It takes logarithm on base 10 on all elements in a matrix
log2	It takes logarithm on base 2 on all elements in a matrix
logical	It converts double class 0 and 1 to logical 0 and 1 respectively
maketform	It defines the transform operator needed for the geometric transform of an image
mat2gray	It linearly converts matrix elements in [0,1] range
max	It finds the maximum values along the columns of a rectangular matrix in general
mean	It finds the average values along the columns of a rectangular matrix in general
mean2	It finds the mean of all elements in a rectangular matrix
medfilt2	It performs median filtering taking the image matrix as its input
median	It finds the median value in a row or column vector
mesh	It graphs the surface plot of a two dimensional discrete function covered by a net or mesh
meshgrid	It generates two rectangular matrices for the computation of two dimensional function, one along the horizontal and the other along the vertical
min	It finds the minimum values along the columns of a rectangular matrix in general
mominv	Author written M-file that computes the seven invariant moments of an image in collaboration with the function file $e(p,q,f)$
mse	It computes the mean square error taking the error matrix as input
nextpow2	It returns a number which is the next power of 2
nlfilter	It performs pixel based computation on a digital image
ntsc2rgb	It changes an image in NTSC color space to the image in RGB color space
num2str	It converts a number to its string or characters set form
ones	It generates rectangular matrices of ones in general
outdiag	Author written M-file that removes the diagonal from a square matrix
padarray	It pads a two dimensional array from user definition
pixval	It provides mouse driven access to pixel value and location
plot	It graphs y versus x data
prod	It products all elements in a row or column matrix
ranbimg	Author written M-file that generates binary image filled with random squares
rand	It generates uniformly distributed random number in [0,1] in continuous sense
randint	It generates user defined random integers
randn	It generates normally distributed random numbers or Gaussian with 0 mean and 1 variance
randsrc	It generates random numbers from user defined set
range	It returns the range of data in a row or column vector
real	It finds the real parts from all elements in a complex number matrix in general
repmat	It generates repetitive matrices from the same rectangular matrix in general
reshape	It can turn a long row or column vector to user defined rectangular array
rgb2gray	It converts an RGB or true color image to gray or intensity image
rgb2hsv	It changes an image in RGB color space to the image in HSV color space
rgb2ind	It converts an RGB or true color image to indexed type color image
rgb2ntsc	It changes an image in RGB color space to the image in NTSC color space
rgb2ycbcr	It changes an image in RGB color space to the image in YCbCr color space
rle	Author written M-file that finds the run length encoding only for a row vector
rmfield	It can remove a member from an existing structure array
roipoly	It is used to find the polygon using a mouse which is used for the region processing
round	It rounds any fractional number towards its closest integer
setfield	It can add a member to an existing structure array
single	It converts its input to single precision number

Continuation of the table A

MATLAB function name	Function(s)
size	It returns the size of one, two, or three dimensional array
sort	It sorts the elements in an array in ascending order
sqrt	It takes the square root of all elements in a matrix
std	It computes the standard deviation of data in a row or column vector
strel	It is the mother function of many built-in structural elements
struct	It constructs a structure array from the user definition
strvcat	It places the strings on top of other to form a rectangular character array
subplot	It divides a MATLAB figure window in subwindows from user definition
sum	It sums all elements in a row or column matrix
surf	It graphs the surface plot of a two dimensional discrete function covered by surface
svd	It computes the singular value decomposition of a digital image to obtain the eigenimage
switch-end	They are the beginning and ending statements of the **switch-case-otherwise** programming
syms	It declares the independent variable in an expression for the symbolic computation
tabulate	It finds the frequency or probability of positive integer gray levels
ublurm	Author written M-file that generates blurry image due to linear motion only in the horizontal direction
ublurn	Author written M-file that generates blurry image due to linear motion only in the vertical direction
uint16	It converts its input to unsigned 16-bit integer
uint32	It converts its input to unsigned 32-bit integer
uint8	It converts its input to unsigned 8-bit integer
unifrnd	It generates uniformly distributed random numbers between user defined two intervals in continuous sense
var	It computes the variance of data in a row or column vector
warp	It maps images on user defined three dimensional surfaces
waveinfo	It describes the basic characteristics of an analyzing wavelet
wfilters	It returns analyzing wavelet filter coefficients for the discrete wavelet transform
while-end	Beginning and ending statements of the **while-end** control statement used in programming
whos	It displays the workspace variable size, occupied bytes, and data class
wiener2	It performs Wiener filtering of a digital image
xcorr2	It computes the two dimensional discrete correlation of two digital images
ycbcr2rgb	It changes an image in YCbCr color space to the image in RGB color space
zeros	It generates rectangular matrix of zeroes of user defined size

Appendix B
List of symbols presented in the text

$\Leftrightarrow$	which is equivalent to
$\lrcorner$	pressing the Enter key from the keyboard
$\rightarrow$	clicking sequence of mouse
$\Rightarrow$	clicking the mouse or provides
$\leftarrow$	short explanation of the MATLAB execution
$>>$	MATLABís command prompt
$2\downarrow$	downsampling by a factor of 2
$2\uparrow$	upsampling by a factor of 2
$[\,]$	empty matrix
$[0,1]$	the fractional value between 0 and 1 inclusive
$[0,255]$	any positive integer between 0 and 255
n	digital filter order
j	complex number
p	any pixel in the digital image
r	correlation coefficient of two identical size images
r_0	spatial cutoff frequency
α	contrast enhancement parameter
λ	eigenvalue of a square matrix
I	identity matrix
∇^2	Laplacian operator
f_m	m directed spatial cutoff frequency of 2D sinusoid
T_m	m directed spatial period of 2D sinusoid
f_n	n directed spatial cutoff frequency of 2D sinusoid
T_n	n directed spatial period of 2D sinusoid
σ	standard deviation of some data
σ^2	variance of some data
μ	mean of some data
φ	rotation of a pixel by an angle φ about the pixel coordinates origin
N	the number of the column pixels in the image $f[m,n]$
M	the number of the row pixels in the image $f[m,n]$
T	threshold or transform matrix
T	transposition operator
C_{ij}	the gray level cooccurrence matrix
$P[i,j]$	discrete joint probability density function
G_m	m directed discrete gradient of the digital image $f[m,n]$
G_n	n directed discrete gradient of the digital image $f[m,n]$
G	magnitude gradient $G = \sqrt{G_m^2 + G_n^2}$
T^{-1}	matrix inverse of T
T_1^*	complex conjugate of T_1
H_N	Hadamard matrix of order $N \times N$
$N_D(p)$	four diagonal neighbors of a pixel
$N_4(p)$	four neighbors of a pixel
$N_8(p)$	the eight neighbors of a pixel
(r,θ)	Hough space radius and angle

m , n	pixel variables in the horizontal and vertical directions of the image $f[m,n]$ respectively
$f[m,n]$	digital image matrix or discrete image intensity function
$b[m,n]$	blue component of the color image
$b[m,n]$	blurry image due to uniform linear motion
$R[m,n]$	correlation of two digital images
$g[m,n]$	green component of the color image or another intensity image
$i[m,n]$	illuminance component of an image
$h[m,n]$	intensity function for the mask used in the discrete filtering
$e[m,n]$	error image between original and reconstructed one
$r[m,n]$	red component of the color image or another intensity image
$r[m,n]$	reflectance component of an image
$r[m,n]$	the filtered image
$\eta[m,n]$	two dimensional random function acting for the noise
$S[m,n]$	structuring elements as an image
$\delta[m-n]$	unit sample located at n
$f_b[m,n]$	block chosen for the Wiener filtering
$f[m,n]^c$	complement image of the $f[m,n]$
$I \oplus S$	dilation of I by S
$I \ominus S$	erosion of I by S
$f[m,n] \cap g[m,n]$	intersection of identical size binary images $f[m,n]$ and $g[m,n]$
$f[m,n] \cup g[m,n]$	union of identical size binary images $f[m,n]$ and $g[m,n]$
$f[m,n] * g[m,n]$	discrete convolution between $f[m,n]$ and $g[m,n]$
$I[m,n] \otimes S[m,n]$	hit and miss transform of $I[m,n]$ by the structuring element image $S[m,n]$
u , v	spatial frequency variables which are integers also
$G[u,v]$	2D DFT on $f[m,n]$
$F[u,v]$	two dimensional discrete transform of a digital image $f[m,n]$
$\angle F[u,v]$	phase angle of the discrete complex transform function $F[u,v]$
$|F[u,v]|$	magnitude value of the discrete complex transform function $F[u,v]$
$\text{Im}\{F[u,v]\}$	imaginary part of the discrete complex transform function $F[u,v]$
$\text{Re}\{F[u,v]\}$	real part of the discrete complex transform function $F[u,v]$
$H[u,v]$	2D digital filter transfer function in spatial frequency domain
$\{A,H,V,D\}$	matrix quadruplet of the discrete wavelet transform
$\{m_1,m_2,...,m_7\}$	the set of seven invariant moments
2D	two dimensional
3D	three dimensional
LP	lowpass
HP	highpass
CDF	cumulative probability density function
DCT	discrete cosine transform
DFT	discrete Fourier transform
PSF	point spread function
RGB	short for the red, green, and blue
DWT	discrete wavelet transform
IDCT	inverse discrete cosine transform
IDFT	inverse discrete Fourier transform
IDWT	inverse discrete wavelet transform

230

References

[1] Marcus, Marvin, ì *Matrices and MATLAB − A Tutorial* î, 1993, Prentice Hall, Englewood Cliffs, New Jersey.

[2] Mohammad Nuruzzaman, ì *Tutorials on Mathematics to MATLAB*î, 2003, AuthorHouse, Bloomington, Indiana.

[3] Mohammad Nuruzzaman, ì *Modeling and Simulation In SIMULINK for Engineers and Scientists*î, 2005, AuthorHouse, Indiana.

[4] Ogata, Katsuhiko, ì *Solving Control Engineering Problems with MATLAB*î, 1994, Prentice Hall, Englewood Cliffs, New Jersey.

[5] Prentice Hall, Inc., ì *The Student Edition of MATLAB for MS-DOS Personal Computers*î, 1992, Prentice Hall, Englewood Cliffs, New Jersey.

[6] Gander, Walter. and Hrebicek, Jiri., ì *Solving Problems in Scientific Computing Using MAPLE and MATLAB*î, Third Edition, 1997, Springer–Verlag, New York.

[7] D. M. Etter, ì *Engineering Problem Solving with MATLAB*î, 1993, Prentice Hall, Englewood Cliffs, New Jersey.

[8] Jackson, Leland B., ì *Digital Filters and Signal Processing with MATLAB Exercises*î, Third Edition, 1996, Kluwer Academic Publishers, Boston.

[9] James B. Dabney and Thomas L. Harman, *"Mastering Simulink® 4"*, 2001, Prentice Hall, New Jersey.

[10] Duffy, Dean G., *"Advanced Engineering Mathematics with MATLAB"*, Second Edition, 2003, Chapman & Hall, CRC, Boca Raton.

[11] Alan V. Oppenheim and Ronald W. Schafer, *"Discrete-Time Signal Processing"*, 1989, Prentice Hall, New Jersey.

[12] Joyce Van de Vegte, *"Fundamentals of Digital Signal Processing"*, 2002, Prentice Hall, New Jersey.

[13] Ali S. Hadi, ì *Matrix Algebra − As A Tool*î, 1996, Duxbury Press, California.

[14] Part-Enander, Eva, *"The MATLAB Handbook"*, 1998, Addisson Wesley, Harlow.

[15] Biran, Adrian B and Breiner, Moshe, ì *MATLAB for Engineers*î, 1997, Addison Wesley, Harlow.

[16] Math Works Inc., ì *MATLAB Reference Guide*î, 1993, Natick, Massachusets.

[17] Cleve Moler and Peter J. Costa, ì *MATLAB Symbolic Math Toolbox*î, 1997, User's Guide, Version 2.0, Natick, Massachusetts.

[18] Hanselman, Duane C. and Littlefield, Bruce R., ì *Mastering MATLAB 5: A Comprehensive Tutorial*î, 1998, Prentice Hall, Upper Saddle River, New Jersey.

[19] Shampine, Lawrence F. and Reichelt, Mark W., *"The MATLAB ODE Suite"*, 1996, The Math-Works, Inc., Natick, MA.

[20] Rafael C. Gonzalez and Paul Wintz, *"Digital Image Processing"*, Second Edition, 1987, Addison-Wesley Publishing Company, Massachusetts.

[21] Sing Tze Bow, *"Pattern Recognition and Image Preprocessing"*, Second Edition, 2002, Marcel Dekker, Inc., New York.

[22] Milan Sonka, Vaclav Hlavac, and Roger Boyle, *"Image Processing, Analysis and Machine Vision"*, 1995, Chapman & Hall Computing, New York.

[23] Maria Petrou and Panagiota Bosdogianni, *"Image Processing - The Fundamentals"*, 2003, John Wiley & Sons, Ltd., New York.

[24] John C. Russ, *"The Image Processing Handbook"*, Third Edition, 1999, CRC Press, Florida.

[25] Weidong Kou, *"Digital Image Compression Algorithms and Standards"*, 1995, Kluwer Academic Publishers, Boston.

[26] John Goutsias, Luc Vincent, and Dan S. Bloomberg, *"Mathematical Morphology and Its Applications to Image and Signal Processing"*, 2000, Kluwer Academic Publishers, Boston.

[27] B. Girod, G. Greiner, and H. Niemann, *"Principles of 3D Image Analysis and Synthesis"*, 2000, Kluwer Academic Publishers, Boston.

[28] K. S. Fu, *"Digital Pattern Recognition"*, 1976, Springer-Verlag, New York.

[29] Zahid Hussain, *"Digital Image Processing - Practical Applications of Parallel Processing Techniques"*, 1991, Ellis Horwood, New York.

[30] Harley R. Myler and Arthur R. Weeks, *"Computer Imaging Recipes in C"*, 1993, P T R Prentice Hall, Englewood Cliffs, New Jersey.

[31] J. K. Aggarwal, R. O. Duda, and A. Rosenfeld, *"Computer Methods in Image Analysis"*, 1977, IEEE Press, New York.

[32] Kenneth R. Castleman, *"Digital Image Processsing"*, 1996, Prentice Hall, Englewood Cliffs, New Jersey.

[33] Ioannis Pitas, *"Digital Image Processing Algorithm Algorithms"*, 1993, Prentice Hall International, Hemel Hempstead, Hertfordshire, England.

[34] Robert J. Schalkoff, *"Digital Image Processing and Computer Vision"*, 1989, Wiley, New York.

[35] Leonard Bolc and Zenon Kulpa, *"Digital Image Processing Systems"*, 1981, Springer-Verlag, New York.

[36] Bernd Jahne, *"Digital Image Processing: Concepts, Algorithms, and Scientific Applications"*, 1991, Springer-Verlag, New York.

[37] Gregory A. Baxes, *"Digital Image Processing ñ A Practical Primer"*, 1984, Prentice Hall, Englewood Cliffs, New Jersey.

[38] Jan. Teuber, *"Digital Image Processing"*, 1993, Prentice Hall, New York.

[39] William K. Pratt, *"Digital Image Processing"*, 1978, Wiley, New York.

[40] Shi-Kuo Chang and Erland Jungert, *"Symbolic Projection for Image Information Retrieval and Spatial Reasoning"*, 1996, Academic Press, New York.

[41] Yuval Fisher, *"Fractal Image Compression: Theory and Application"*, 1995, Springer-Verlag, New York.

[42] Ferdinand van der Heijden, *"Image Based Measurement Systems: Object Recognition and Parameter Estimation"*, 1994, John Wiley & Sons, New York.

[43] V. A. Kovalevsky, *"Image Pattern Recognition"*, 1980, Springer-Verlag, New York.

[44] Luc Florack, *"Image Structure"*, 1997, Kluwer Academic Publishers, Norwell, Massachusetts.

[45] Gaurav Sharma, *"Digital Color Imaging Handbook"*, 2003, CRC Press, New York.

[46] Jorge L. C. Sanz, "*Image Technology*", 1996, Springer-Verlag, New York.

[47] Randy Crane, "*A Simplified Approach to Image Processing ñ Classical and Modern Techniques in C*", 1997, Prentice Hall PTR, Upper Saddle River, New Jersey.

[48] Niels Haering and Niels Da Vitoria Lobo, "*Visual Event Detection*", 2001, Kluwer Academic Publishers, Norwell, Massachusetts.

[49] Alireza Bab-Hadia Shar and David Suter, "*Data Segmentation and Model Selection for Computer Vision ñ A Statistical Approach*", 2000, Springer-Verlag, New York.

[50] Wolfgang Gerhartz, "*Imaging and Information Storage Technology*", 1992, VCH, New York.

[51] J. R. Parker, "*Algorithms for Image Processing and Computer Vision*", 1997, Wiley Computer Publishing, New York.

[52] L. Prasad and S. S. Iyengar, "*Wavelet Analysis with Applications to Image Processing*", 1997, CRC Press, New York.

[53] Jacques Blanc-Talon and Dan C. Popescu, "*Imaging and Vision Systems: Theory, Assessment, and Applications*", 2001, Nova Science Publishers, Inc., New York.

[54] Martial Hebert, Jean Ponce, Terry Boult, and Ari Gross, "*Object Representation in Computer Vision*", 1994, Springer-Verlag, New York.

[55] Rafael C. Gonzalez, Richard E. Woods, and Steven L. Eddins, "*Digital Image Processing Using MATLAB*", 2004, Pearson Prentice Hall, Upper Saddle River, New Jersey.

[56] The MathWorks, Inc., "*Image Processing Toolbox: Userís Guide*", Version 4, 2003, Natick, Massachusetts.

[57] E. O. Brigham, "*The Fast Fourier Transform and Its Applications*", 1988, Prentice Hall, Upper Saddle River, New Jersey.

[58] P. Soille, "*Morphological Image Analysis: Principles and Applications*", 2003, Second Edition, Springer-Verlag, New York.

[59] K. R. Castleman, "*Digital Image Processing*", 1979, Prentice Hall, Englewood Cliffs, New Jersey.

[60] Lora G. Weiss, "*Wavelets and Wideband Correlation Processing*", IEEE Signal Processing Magazine, January 1994, pp.13-32.

[61] Murk Bottema, Bill Moran, and Sofia Suvorova, "*An Application of Wavelets in Tomography*", Digital Signal Processing Magazine, 8, 1998, pp.244-254.

[62] Olivier Rioul and Martin Vetterli, "*Wavelets and Signal Processing*", IEEE Signal Processing Magazine, October 1991, pp.14-38.

[63] F. Hlawatsch and G. F. Boudreaux-Bartels, "*Linear and Quadratic Time-Frequency Signal Representations*", IEEE Signal Processing Magazine, April 1992, pp.21-67.

[64] A. Cohen, Ingrid Daubechies, and J.-C. Feauveau, "*Biorthogonal Bases of Compactly Supported Wavelets*", Communications on Pure and Applied Mathematics, June 1992, Vol. XLV, No. 5, pp.485-560.

[65] Stephane G. Mallat, "*A Theory for Multiresolution Signal Decomposition: The Wavelet Representation*", IEEE Transac. on Pattern Analysis and Machine Intelligence, Vol. 11, No. 7, July 1989, pp.674-693.

[66] Ingrid Daubechies, "*Orthonormal Bases of Compactly Supported Wavelets*", Communications on Pure and Applied Mathematics, October 1988, Vol. XLI, No. 7, pp.909-996.

[67] Ingrid Daubechies, "*The Wavelet Transform, Time-Frequency Localization and Signal Analysis*", IEEE Transactions on Information Theory, September 1990, Vol. 36, No. 5, pp.961-1005.

[68] Stephane G. Mallat, "*Multifrequency Channel Decompositions of Images and Wavelet Models*", IEEE Transactions on Acoustics, Speech, and signal Processing, Vol. 37, No. 12, December 1989, pp.2091-2110.

[69] Ingrid Daubechies, "*Where Do Wavelets Come From? – A Personal Point of View*", Proceedings of the IEEE, Vol. 84, No. 4, April 1996, pp. 510-513.

[70] Wen-Liang Hwang and Stephane Mallat, "*Singularities and Noise Discrimination with Wavelets*", ICASSP-92, March 23-26, Vol. 4, Digital Signal Processing 1, pp. 377-380.

[71] Nader Moayeri, Ingrid Daubechies, Qing Song, and Hong Shen Wang, "*Wavelet Transform Image Coding Using Trellis Coded Vector Quantization*", ICASSP-92, March 23-26, Vol. 4, Digital Signal Processing 1, pp. 405-408.

[72] M. Holschneider, "*Wavelets: An Analysis Tool*", Oxford University Press Inc., New York, 1995.

[73] Ingrid Daubechies, "*Different Perspectives on Wavelets*", American Mathematical Society, Proceedings of Symposia in Applied Mathematics, Vol. 47, 1993.

[74] S. Mallat, "*Wavelets for A Vision*", Proceedings of the IEEE, Vol. 84, No. 4, April 1996, pp. 604-614.

[75] Michael Unser and Akram Aldroubi, "*A Review of Wavelets in Biomedical Applications*", Proceedings of the IEEE, Vol. 84, No. 4, April 1996, pp. 626-638.

[76] Y. Meyer, "*Wavelets and Applications*", Springer-Verlag, France, 1992.

[77] I. Daubechies, "*Ten Lectures on Wavelets*", 1992, SIAM, Philadelphia. Okay

[78] Mohammad Nuruzzaman, "*An Algorithm for Thinning The Binary Images*", April 2002, The 9th Annual IEEE Technical Exchange Meeting, Dhahran, Saudi Arabia.

[79] Bernard Sklar, "*Digital Communications ñ Fundamentals and Applications*", 1988, Prentice-Hall International, Inc., Englewood Cliffs, New Jersey.

[80] Jr. George C. Clark and J. Bibb Cain, "*Error-Correction Coding for Digital Communications*", 1988, Plenum Press, New York.

[81] M. K. Hu, "*Visual Pattern Recognition by Moment Invariants*", 1962, IRE Transaction on Information Theory, vol. IT-8, pp. 179-187.

Subject Index